Developments in European Politics

Developments titles available from Palgrave Macmillan

Alistair Cole, Patrick Le Galès and Jonah Levy (eds)
DEVELOPMENTS IN FRENCH POLITICS 3

Maria Green Cowles and Desmond Dinan (eds)
DEVELOPMENTS IN THE EUROPEAN UNION 2

Patrick Dunleavy, Richard Heffernan, Philip Cowley and
Colin Hay (eds)
DEVELOPMENTS IN BRITISH POLITICS 8

Stephen Padgett, William E. Paterson and Gordon Smith (eds)
DEVELOPMENTS IN GERMAN POLITICS 3*

Gillian Peele, Christopher J. Bailey, Bruce Cain and B. Guy Peters (eds)
DEVELOPMENTS IN AMERICAN POLITICS 5

Stephen White, Judy Batt and Paul Lewis (eds)
DEVELOPMENTS IN CENTRAL AND EAST EUROPEAN
POLITICS 3*

Stephen White, Zvi Gitelman and Richard Sakwa (eds)
DEVELOPMENTS IN RUSSIAN POLITICS 6*

Of Related Interest

Ian Holliday, Andrew Gamble and Geraint Parry (eds)
FUNDAMENTALS IN BRITISH POLITICS

If you have any comments or suggestions regarding the above or
other possible *Developments* titles, please write to Steven Kennedy,
Palgrave Macmillan, Houndmills, Basingstoke RG21 6XS, UK
or e-mail s.kennedy@palgrave.com

* Rights world excluding North America

Developments in European Politics

edited by

Paul M. Heywood
Erik Jones
Martin Rhodes
and
Ulrich Sedelmeier

palgrave
macmillan

First published 2006 by
PALGRAVE MACMILLAN
Houndmills, Basingstoke, Hampshire RG21 6XS and
175 Fifth Avenue, New York, N.Y. 10010
Companies and representatives throughout the world

PALGRAVE MACMILLAN is the global academic imprint of the Palgrave Macmillan division of St. Martin's Press, LLC and of Palgrave Macmillan Ltd. Macmillan® is a registered trademark in the United States, United Kingdom and other countries. Palgrave is a registered trademark in the European Union and other countries.

ISBN-13: 978-0-230-00040-7   hardback
ISBN-10: 0-230-00040-1   hardback
ISBN-13: 978-0-230-00041-4   paperback
ISBN-10: 0-230-00041-X   paperback

This new book is a direct replacement for *Developments in West European Politics 2* edited by Paul Heywood, Erik Jones and Martin Rhodes (2002)

This book is printed on paper suitable for recycling and made from fully managed and sustained forest sources.

A catalogue record for this book is available from the British Library.

A catalog record for this book is available from the Library of Congress.

10 9 8 7 6 5 4 3 2 1
15 14 13 12 11 10 09 08 07 06

Printed and bound in China

Contents

List of Tables and Figures

Tables

Figures

Preface and Acknowledgements

In the Preface to the 2002 volume, *Developments in West European Politics 2* (*DWEP* 2), the editors noted that a lot had changed in West European politics since the 1997 publication of the original volume. That pace of change has continued unabated since 2002. In particular, the formal entry of 10 new member states to the European Union on 1 May 2004 fundamentally altered the parameters of what had remained until then a Europe clearly divided between West and East. That division no longer makes the same kind of sense. For that reason, rather than produce a *DWEP 3*, we recognized that a volume on contemporary European politics must now accommodate developments across a Europe conceived in far broader terms than had been the case in the earlier volumes.

The challenge for both editors and authors has been to provide coverage of major political developments across a much wider range of countries than before – a requirement that calls for wider expertise deployed within a more confined space. To help with the editorial task, the editors of *DWEP* 2 were delighted to welcome Uli Sedelmeier onto the editorial team in order to broaden our own expertise and help us focus on the core political issues which cut across both Western and Eastern Europe. All four editors are very grateful to our fellow authors, some of whom contributed chapters to *DWEP* or *DWEP* 2 but most of whom were new to the project, for rising to the challenge of focusing on this more broadly conceived understanding of Europe.

We were lucky in being able to bring most of the authors together in March 2005 at a two-day workshop, hosted by the SAIS Bologna Center of the Johns Hopkins University. The workshop provided an opportunity for authors to present preliminary chapters and for the editors to discuss in detail the overall shape of the volume. Erik Jones was instrumental in organizing the workshop which benefited from generous financial support provided by the Parachini Family Fund, without which it would not have been possible. He would also like to thank Kimberly de Liguori Carino and Sarah Bignami for excellent administrative, research and editorial assistance.

Martin Rhodes would like to thank Jacqueline Gordon at the EUI in Florence for assistance in the early phases of this project, and Ulrich Sedelmeier is grateful for funding from a Marie Curie Intra-European Fellowship (contract MEIF-CT-2005-514104) at the Robert Schuman

Centre of the European University Institute, Florence. Paul Heywood is grateful to Caroline Reffin for essential assistance towards the final stages of the project, and also – as ever – to Mary Vincent for every kind of support. The editors would also like particularly to thank Frederick Hood for preparing the index.

All four editors owe an enormous debt of gratitude to Steven Kennedy, at Palgrave Macmillan, who has been closely involved and constructively critical through every stage of the project. We still remain indebted above all to the late, and very much missed, Vincent Wright who was co-editor of *DWEP* with Martin Rhodes and Paul Heywood, and who remains the source of enduring intellectual inspiration.

PAUL M. HEYWOOD
ERIK JONES
MARTIN RHODES
ULRICH SEDELMEIER

Notes on the Contributors

Sabina Avdagić is a Post-Doctoral Fellow at the Max Planck Institute for the Study of Societies in Cologne.

Federica Bicchi is a Lecturer in International Relations of Europe in the Department of International Relations at the London School of Economics and Political Science.

Tanja A. Börzel is Professor of Political Science and holds the Chair in European Integration at the Free University of Berlin.

Colin Crouch is Professor of Governance and Public Management at the Warwick Business School.

Rachel A. Epstein is Assistant Professor at the Graduate School of International Studies at the University of Denver.

Cyrille Fijnaut is Professor of International and Comparative Criminal Law at the University of Tilburg, The Netherlands.

Alexandra Gheciu is a Research Associate in the Department of Politics and International Relations at Oxford University.

Klaus Goetz is Chair of German and European Government in the Faculty of Economics and Political Science at the University of Potsdam.

Virginie Guiraudon is Marie Curie Professor in Social and Political Sciences at the European University Institute.

Anton Hemerijck is Director of the Netherlands Council for Government Policy and Associate Professor in Public Administration at Leiden University.

Paul M. Heywood is Dean of the Graduate School and Sir Francis Hill Professor of European Politics at the University of Nottingham.

Elena Jileva is a Jean Monnet Research Fellow at the European University Institute.

Erik Jones is Resident Professor of European Studies at the SAIS Bologna Center of Johns Hopkins University and Research Associate in the international economics programme at Chatham House (the Royal Institute for International Affairs) in London.

Michael Keating is Professor of Regional Studies and Head of the Department of Political and Social Sciences at the European University Institute.

Maarten Keune is a Senior Researcher at the European Trade Union Institute in Brussels.

Ivan Krastev is Chairman of the Board of the Centre for Liberal Strategies in Sofia and the Director of the Open Century Center at the Central European University in Budapest.

Zdenek Kühn is Assistant Professor at the Charles University Law School in Prague, Czech Republic.

John Madeley is a Lecturer in Government at the London School of Economics and Political Science.

Peter Mair is Professor of Comparative Politics at the European University Institute in Florence and at Leiden University in The Netherlands.

Cas Mudde is Senior Lecturer in the Department of Political Science of the University of Antwerp in Belgium.

Letizia Paoli is a Senior Research Fellow at the Max Planck Institute for Foreign and International Criminal Law in Freiburg, Germany and Professor of General Criminology at the K. U. Leuven Faculty of Law in Belgium.

Martin Rhodes is a Professor in the Graduate School of International Studies at the University of Denver.

Ulrich Sedelmeier is a Senior Lecturer in International Relations at the London School of Economics and Political Science and a Marie Curie Fellow at the European University Institute.

Karen Smith is Reader in International Relations at the London School of Economics and Political Science.

Gábor Tóka is Associate Professor of Political Science and Head of the Department of Political Science at the Central European University in Budapest.

Ingrid van Biezen is a Senior Lecturer in the Department of Political Science and International Studies at the University of Birmingham.

Richard Whitman is Professor of Politics at the University of Bath and Senior Fellow, Europe at Chatham House (the Royal Institute of International Affairs) in London.

List of Abbreviations

ACP	African, Caribbean and Pacific Countries
ALF	Animal Liberation Front
ALTHEA	Military operation in Bosnia and Herzegovina
ATCSA	Anti-Terrorism, Crime and Security Act
ATTAC	Association for the Taxation of Financial Transactions for the Aid of Citizens
B&H	Blood & Honour
BZÖ	Alliance for Austria's Future
CCC	Czech Constitutional Court
CDPC	European Committee on Crime Problems
CEC	Conference of European Churches
CEE	Central and Eastern European
CEECs	Central and Eastern European Countries
CEEP	Centre Européen des Entreprises à participation Publique et des entreprises d'intérèt économique générale
CEO	Chief Executive Officer
CFSP	Common Foreign and Security Policy
Co.Co.Co.	Italian new flexible labour contract
CoR	Committee of the Regions
CPI	Corruption Perceptions Index
ČSSD	Czech Social Democratic Party
DFP	Danish People's Party
DG	Directorate General
DITB	Defence industrial and technological bases
DRA	Directorate of Religious Affairs
EADC	European Aerospace Defence Company
EADS	European Aeronautic Defence and Space
EBRD	European Bank for Reconstruction and Development
ECHR	European Court of Human Rights
ECJ	European Court of Justice
EEC	European Economic Community
EES	European Employment Strategy
ELF	Earth Liberation Front
EMU	Economic and Monetary Union
EP	European Parliament
EPC	European Political Cooperation
ERDF	European Regional Development Fund

ETA	Basque Homeland and Freedom
ETUC	European Trades Union Congress
EU	European Union
EUSR	EU Special Representative
EWCs	European Works Councils
FCC	French Constitutional Council
FCPA	Foreign Corrupt Practices Act
FI	Forza Italia
FN	National Front (France)
FPA	Foreign Policy Analysis
FPÖ	Austrian Freedom Party
FrP	Norwegian Progress Party
GAL	Spanish Anti-Terrorist Liberation Group
GATT	General Agreement on Trade and Tariffs
GATS	General Agreement on Trade in Services
GFCC	German Federal Constitutional Court
HCC	Hungarian Constitutional Court
ICC	International Criminal Court
ICT	Information Communications and Technology
IMF	International Monetary Fund
IRA	Irish Republican Army
JHA	Justice and Home Affairs
KFOR	NATO Kosovo Force
KSČM	Czech Communist Party of Bohemia and Moravia
LN	The Northern League
LPF	List Pim Fortuyn
LPR	League of Polish Families
MAB	Muslim Association of Britain
MDP	Muslim Democratic Party
MEPs	Members of the European Parliament
MSI	Italian Social Movement
NAPs	national action plans
NATO	North Atlantic Treaty Organization
NDP	German National Democratic Party
NGOs	Non-Governmental Organizations
NMS	Central and Eastern Europe new member states
NRMs	New Religious Movements
NUTS2	Nomenclature of Territorial Units for Statistics, the second level
OC	Organized Crime
OECD	Organisation for Economic Cooperation and Development
OMC	Open Method of Coordination

OSCE	Organization for Security and Cooperation in Europe
ÖVP	Christian Democratic Austrian People's Party
PAYG	pay-as-you-go
PC-CO	Committee of Experts on Criminal Law and Criminological Aspects of Organized Crime
PC-S-CO	Group of Experts on Criminological and Criminal Law Aspects of Organised Crime
PCT	Polish Constitutional Tribunal
PDS	German Left Party
PP	Spanish Popular Party
PRM	Greater Romania Party
PSD	Romanian Socialist Party
QMV	Qualified Majority Voting
RAF	Red Army Faction
RCC	Romanian Constitutional Court
RPR	Rassemblement pour la République [France]
RegLeg	Regions with Legislative Powers
SCT	Spanish Constitutional Tribunal
SFOR	NATO-led Stabilization Force in Bosnia and Herzegovina
SGP	Protestant State Reformed Party [Netherlands]
SGP	Stability and Growth Pact
SNS	Slovak National Party
TI	Transparency International
TRIPS	Trade Related Aspects of Intellectual Property Rights
UNHCR	United Nations High Commissioner for Refugees
UNICE	Union des Industries de la Communauté Européenne
UNMIK	United Nations Mission in Kosovo
UVF	Protestant Northern Irish Ulster Volunteer Force
VB	Belgian Flemish Interest
WEU	Wetern European Union
WFTC	Working Families Tax Credit
WMD	Weapons of Mass Destruction
WODC	Research and Documentation Centre of the Dutch Ministry of Justice
WTO	World Trade Organization

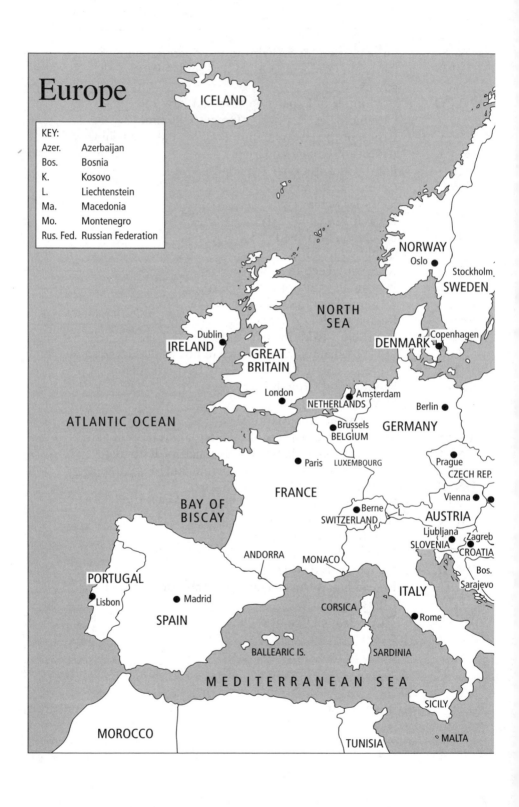

Europe

ICELAND

KEY:
Azer.	Azerbaijan
Bos.	Bosnia
K.	Kosovo
L.	Liechtenstein
Ma.	Macedonia
Mo.	Montenegro
Rus. Fed.	Russian Federation

NORWAY

Oslo ●

Stockholm

SWEDEN

NORTH
SEA

Dublin ●

IRELAND

Copenhagen

DENMARK

GREAT
BRITAIN

London ●

●Amsterdam

NETHERLANDS

Berlin ●

●Brussels

BELGIUM

GERMANY

ATLANTIC OCEAN

● Paris

LUXEMBOURG

Prague ●

CZECH REP.

FRANCE

Vienna ●

●

BAY OF
BISCAY

●Berne

SWITZERLAND

L.

AUSTRIA

Ljubljana

SLOVENIA

Zagreb ●

CROATIA

ANDORRA

MONACO

Bos.

Sarajevo

PORTUGAL

●Lisbon

● Madrid

SPAIN

ITALY

CORSICA

●Rome

BALLEARIC IS.

SARDINIA

M E D I T E R R A N E A N   S E A

SICILY

MOROCCO

TUNISIA

○ MALTA

Chapter 1

Introduction: Developments in European Politics

At the end of the Cold War people asked 'What is Europe?' with more than a hint of optimism and promise. History had ended, or so we were led to believe. Bipolar confrontation no longer divided the European continent. Liberal democracy was on the march. And it was possible to imagine a Europe that would be peaceful, dynamic, progressive – and whole.

Now we tend to ask 'What is Europe?' with a greater note of caution, some hesitation, and perhaps even a little fear. Europe may have a bright future in store. But, equally, it may not. Worse, Europe may turn out to be fragmented, conflictive, stagnant and in decline. Of course it is as easy to exaggerate a pessimistic image of Europe as it is to paint too rosy a picture. Yet when some Dutch politicians have to live in undisclosed locations, the ghettoized, immigrant-populated French suburbs have to be put under curfew, German political parties struggle to form a government, and electorates in Central and Eastern Europe continue to throw out one incumbent after another, it is hard to see whether it makes more sense to focus on the good or the bad.

What is clear is that European politics has changed dramatically since the fall of the Berlin Wall. What is also clear is that recent developments in European politics are now 'European' in the largest sense of the word. The one thing both euro-optimists and euro-pessimists can agree on is that it no longer makes sense to divide the continent into East and West when trying to map the pattern of events that is unfolding. No-one would suggest that the problems besetting different countries are everywhere the same. The unity of Europe as a concept does not require a convergence on common institutions, processes, cultures or aspirations. On the contrary, the countries of Europe remain individually distinctive in many respects. Despite these differences, however, the European countries share a common existence within Europe and a high degree of interdependence. Some challenges are

1

truly European in scope. Others may be more national, and yet with implications that ripple from one country to the next.

The enlarged European Union (EU) offers perhaps the most important institutional manifestation of the new post-Cold War Europe. The EU provides a collection of instruments for responding to common challenges with common policies. But it also provides a framework for managing the complex interdependencies between European countries. Whatever the advantages of the European Union, however, the EU is not Europe and EU politics is only a small part of the politics of Europe writ large. The referenda on the European Constitutional Treaty that took place in France and the Netherlands in May and June of 2005 make this point clearly. In neither country did the public vote specifically about the text of the consitutional treaty. Indeed, it would be difficult to explain the outcomes taking only EU (or even broader 'European') political considerations into account. The referenda were decided instead on the basis of national issues and national concerns about the European project.

The purpose of this volume is to analyse recent developments in European politics. We have structured the discussion into four Parts. The first provides a broad overview, and includes chapters on globalization, international politics, and the transformative influence of European integration. The second focuses more narrowly on government and the political process. It analyses the organization of democratic systems, the role of political parties, the problems of representation and voting, and the influence of sub-national territorial organization. The third Part digs deeper still, looking beneath the institutions to highlight developments in politics and society. It includes chapters on corruption, extremism, organized interests, judicial processes, and the relationship between church and state. Finally, we bring together the major challenges that the countries of Europe – and Europe as a whole – must face. In doing so, we focus our analysis on welfare, migration, organized crime and security.

The European state: integration and the world

The analysis begins with reference to globalization – the issue that has dominated debate in Europe more than any other. The challenge, of course, lies in separating out what is important in the debate from what is not, framing an appropriate response, and ensuring that the response is implemented. Other problems are nested within that challenge. Who decides what is important and what is appropriate? Who is responsible for the implementation of responses? And how can those responsible be held accountable for their actions when things do not work out as planned?

In Chapter 2, Erik Jones and Martin Rhodes focus on the economic dimension of the global challenge. They show how over the past half century the increasing flow of goods and services, labour and capital, have both enriched European countries and challenged them to survive and compete. They also look to the European response – both in the form of European integration and at the national level. They consider what can be done across countries, what can be done between them, and what must be left for individual governments to sort out. The underlying message is that 'Europe' is no panacea for the difficulties associated with globalization and the 'nation state' is more than just an institutional legacy from some long-past political age. On the contrary, European responses to globalization are often only effective when overarching European policies are paired with effective action at the national level. European economic integration is important, and increasingly so for all parts of Europe. Even so, national governments remain responsible for ensuring that policies are implemented and national political systems provide the most realistic arena for holding responsible politicians to account.

European integration is about more than economics and there is also a strong case for developing a coherent European response to the global challenge in foreign policy. In Chapter 3, Federica Bicchi, Karen Smith and Richard Whitman examine the development of European foreign policy cooperation alongside persistent and distinctive national foreign policy traditions. Although their analysis should not be confused with popular debates in the media about globalization today, European foreign policy has always had a global dimension and debate about globalization is inevitably skewed when important differences in national foreign policy traditions are left out. The trick here as in economics is to sort out what can realistically be handled at the European level and what must be left to individual countries. What Bicchi, Smith and Whitman reveal is that European foreign policy is constrained both by what European institutions can do and by what the voters in different European countries want them to do – or would be willing to support their doing.

Globalization encompasses one set of challenges to, or influences on, the countries of Europe. Europeanization offers another. As Tanja Börzel and Ulrich Sedelmeier explain in Chapter 4, the influence of Europe touches on all European countries in different ways and to different degrees. And they suggest that here, at least, a meaningful distinction between East and West can and should continue to be made. The countries of Western Europe that have long belonged to the

European Union (EU) have had more opportunity to upload their national preferences or practices into European-level policies – rather than simply downloading European legislation into their national frameworks of rules and institutions. By contrast, the countries of Central and Eastern Europe that have either recently joined the EU, or are waiting to join, have experienced Europeanization in only one direction – as a top-down imposition of EU rules and procedures into national political and economic life. But despite the differences between East and West, the lesson to draw from Börzel and Sedelmeier is consistent with the two chapters that precede it: European integration has changed the countries of Europe, but it has not necessarily made them more similar to one-another. On the contrary, national differences remain important in spite of the experience of Europeanization, and, moreover, in how Europeanization is experienced. Europe means different things in different countries, and national differences in relation to Europe persist as well.

The resilience of national differences and the nation state in the face of pressures emanating from integration and the world explain why we believe the analysis of developments in European politics should retain a strong comparative and institutional focus. Within that focus questions of responsibility and accountability retain a vital significance – both in our understanding of how countries work and in our anticipation of how they will adapt to an ever changing set of policy challenges.

Government and the political process

For all the uncertainty and unpredictability that have characterized European politics since the end of the Cold War, there remain some core features in the organization of democratic states. These features help structure national responses to the more challenging global environment. In particular, democratic states are fundamentally defined by systems of governance that process public policies and the existence of political parties and organized interests that shape the ways in which those policies will be developed and implemented. The chapters in Part II of this volume explore how these central elements of democratic organisation have been affected by and have responded to the more turbulent political landscape which has emerged in recent years.

In Chapter 5, Klaus Goetz analyses the principal relationships that structure and organize political power at the centre of democratic states. He lays stress on the interactions between executives and legislatures, between governing parties and the government itself, between chief executives and their cabinet colleagues, between ministers and the rest of the 'core executive', and between the executive and the administrative branches of government. Goetz demonstrates that while there is an inevitable tension both between and within many of these relationships, the way in which that tension is managed is neither consistent nor necessarily stable across European democracies. Although we would expect to see democratic states organised in such a way as to promote close integration between the core actors, in practice, effective integration of the core executive remains the exception rather than the rule – even where chief executives have extensive power resources and have sought to develop an institutional framework for coordination. As Goetz notes, the reality of governing from the centre is a messy business, with institutional structures constantly required to respond to contingent and unpredictable pressures. Thus, rather than a clear trend towards either a greater strengthening of chief executives through a process of 'presidentialization', or a counterveiling trend towards a 'hollowing out' of the centre, what we observe across European democracies is a series of piecemeal reforms to improve the efficiency of central state organization. Unsurprisingly, such reforms usually fail to resolve the tensions which characterize the core relationships at the heart of government.

Political parties are in many ways the defining organizations of democratic states, and their changing role and organization are analysed in Chapter 6. Ingrid van Biezen and Peter Mair contrast the emergence of political parties and party systems in the new democracies of Central and Eastern Europe with the pattern familiar from more established democracies in the West. Whereas the latter evolved from elite/cadre parties through mass parties, to catch-all parties and most recently cartel parties, their Eastern counterparts have so far failed to become strongly institutionalized, and are characterized by much weaker linkages with society. In short, parties in post-communist Europe have rarely been able to ground themselves solidly within the nascent democratic states. However, parties in both East and West are facing similar sets of challenges: they appear to be increasingly disconnected from wider society, and therefore have a reduced representative capacity; they are placing ever more emphasis on individual leaders, with whom they are increasingly identified; they are more closely connected with the formal institutions of state and thus ever more distant from their grassroots organizations and ordinary citizens – and are consequently seen as inhabiting their own, somewhat exclusive, world.

These various challenges present real risks for the nature of representation in contemporary European democracies. In Chapter 7, Gábor Tóka discusses basic concepts and models in the analysis of changes to party-based representation in the electoral arena. He analyses cross-national data about levels of citizen participation, the extent of identification with parties, electoral volatility, party system fragmentation and polarization, as well as the importance of established and emerging social cleavages in voting behaviour. Using a wide array of data, Tóka's chapter highlights some key differences in Europe regarding the centrality of parties in the democratic process, party system stability, and representational performance. He also discusses how variations between countries on these indicators have been influenced by institutional design and the duration of democracy. Tóka also revisits some classic models of party competition and party system configuration in light of the recent changes in, and geographic expansion of, European democracy. In contrast to the gloomier assessments which might emerge from the apparent undermining of representational linkages between citizens and parties, Tóka suggests that the possibilities for both choice and accountability have arguably increased in the current political environment – although the cues available to citizens in making that choice and holding politicians to account are more complex than when party systems were less fragmented and the policy milieu appeared less confused.

In Chapter 8, Michael Keating discusses how the growing complexity of the European political order has helped shape and influence territorial politics. As in the chapters that precede it, Keating's assessment highlights the need to avoid any linear interpretation of developments in territorial politics. Contrary to predictions that territory would diminish as a significant factor in modern societies – initially through the elimination of distinctiveness by dominant nation-states and latterly through the impact of globalization – Europe has witnessed the emergence of a 'new regionalism'. The key feature of this trend is a re-territorialization of politics at multiple scales: nation-state, sub-state, supra-national and trans-national. Regions, like other aspects of the emerging political order, operate in an increasingly interdependent environment. Keating underlines sharply contrasting (and even contradictory) developments both within and between Western and East-Central Europe. In most of the established democracies, the emergence of a distinctive regional policy at EU level since the mid-1970s diminished the role of nation-states as the drivers of territorial politics they once were. However, changes in the EU Commission's approach to regional policy in 2000 contributed to a very different trajectory in the new member states, where the role of central state executives in regional policy has been reinforced. As Keating clearly demonstrates, territory has been an ever-present factor in contemporary European politics and, indeed, has become increasingly significant.

Politics and society

The institutions of the nation-state matter insofar as they are used or perhaps even abused. Part III presents an overview of a variety of diverse challenges confronting Europe's liberal democratic systems, as well as focusing on the (re-)emerging role of a range of social actors. A key issue threatening the legitimacy of political institutions is the phenomenon of political corruption, as well as direct challenges by a variety of anti-system movements.

The problem of corruption is universal, and universally significant. In Chapter 9, Paul Heywood and Ivan Krastev analyse corruption as a threat to the rule of law and more generally to the legitimacy of the political system. The lower salience of ideological cleavages in post-Cold War Europe has enabled a stronger focus on the integrity of political elites, which in combination with changes in global communication technologies and mobilization by anti-corruption NGOs have increased the prominence of concern with corruption in public debates. Specific factors in post-communist countries which provided plenty of opportunity for corruption include the experience of a widespread system of favours that underpinned economic planning and made it easier for a less sophisticated form of bribery to find acceptance; rapidly emerging social inequalities and low public sector salaries; and the large-scale privatization of state assets. At the same time, anti-corruption campaigns themselves can have a negative impact on the democratic process. The instrumentalization of anti-corruption discourses by populist politicians can contribute to a de-legitimization of political elites and political institutions, and to a blurring of lines between political options. These dangers concern not only democratic consolidation in East Central Europe, but also the more established democracies of Western Europe.

Corruption threatens political institutions indirectly, by debasing their function. But there are more direct challenges as well. In Chapter 10, Cas Mudde analyses a variety of 'anti-system' movements that challenge key aspects of the liberal democratic systems in Europe. Despite high levels of diffuse support for democracy at the mass level across Europe, many citizens simultaneously reject certain key democratic institutions, which creates scope for anti-system movements to prosper. Mudde analyses four key challenges to European democracies: political extremism challenges democracy as such; political radicalism challenges only certain key liberal elements of the democratic system and most notably includes different forms of populism; religious fundamentalism, which can be found in all major (monotheist) religions in Europe, but is fairly marginal within European (party) politics; finally, terrorism, which is not so much defined on the basis of goals and ideas, but by the use of violent means. Liberal democracies face a dilemma in defending democracy against anti-system politics, especially whether to tolerate expressions of anti-democratic ideas. In the 1980s and 1990s, European states mainly focused on the extreme and radical right, often introducing anti-racist legislation, but only rarely banning parties. Since the attacks of 11 September 2001, the focus has moved to Islamic fundamentalism and terrorism, leading to the introduction of new counter-terrorist legislation, which has started to generate more serious political protests.

Issues related to corruption and extremism matter because they distort the relationship between politicians and voters. However, these are not the only groups that use political institutions. Hence this section also addresses concerns about the role of different actors, namely economic interests, the judiciary and organized religion. Sabina Avdagić and Colin Crouch discuss recent developments in the politics of representing organized economic interests in the policy process in Chapter 11. They identify changes in the general conditions of economic activity, as well as the internationalization and Europeanization of national economies as the principal challenges to the stability of established forms of interest-representation across Europe. These challenges are particularly pronounced for the different models of neo-corporatism (Scandinavian, continental, and state-led), as well as for the emerging hybrid types in East Central Europe, which appear increasingly remote from classical neo-corporatist patterns. However, despite these common challenges, there are considerable differences in the extent and character of the resulting change both between and within the two parts of Europe. There is no general convergence towards weak organized labour and decentralized, competitive modes of interest organization. While organized labour is weakening across Europe, within Western Europe this trend is much less pronounced in the Nordic countries, and it is generally more marked in East-Central Europe than in Western Europe. Rather than a general decay of corporatism, Avdagić and Crouch note its transformation, for example in a shift to sectoral level bargaining and a re-emergence, in specific circumstances, of national social pacts.

In Chapter 12, Zdenek Kühn analyses the role of constitutional courts in European politics. In contrast to a classical separation of powers, in which courts are not considered as political actors, a judicialization of politics in now a common phenomenon in Europe. The power of judges to review the conformity of law with constitutional requirements often gives courts a *de facto* veto power over important political decisions and has seen them increasingly assume the oversight function traditionally associated with parliaments in Western Europe. Notwithstanding national variations in the powers and composition of constitutional courts and procedural rules to start a judicial review, the possibility of bringing laws before the court is on the rise in Europe. A tendency to use constitutional adjudication as a means to continue battles lost in parliament also emerged quickly in post-communist East-Central Europe. However, in the less consolidated post-communist political systems, openly politicized courts can lead to serious political crises, as occurred in Romania in summer 2005 when the constitutional court, dominated by retired socialist politicians, sided with the opposition to obstruct reforms of the judiciary. In general, though – and despite mixed opinion in the legal profession on the desirability of a judicialization of politics – open and outspoken political defiance of court rulings are rare in Europe.

John Madeley focuses on the renewed salience of the religious factor in contemporary European politics in Chapter 13. Madeley points out that the key challenge for the state in its relations with churches, minority faiths and new religious movements involves how to delimit the role of public authorities. One of the most salient issues is the freedom of religious expression, which has been at the centre of public debates and court cases surrounding bans of Islamic headscarves in public institutions, notably in France, Germany and Turkey. Another key question concerns the equal treatment and standing of different religious organizations, since the majority of European states – in contrast to France – do not rigorously separate church and state. Finally, the state also has a role to play in promoting inter-religious tolerance and understanding. Madeley concludes that while the principle of religious liberty is by and large approved across Europe, religious equality by contrast has not been generally regarded as an important norm. The urgency of promoting religious harmony on the other hand has in recent years been reflected almost everywhere in initiatives aimed at drawing the sting of religiously-fuelled conflict, whether the threats emanate from extremist groups of religious fundamentalists or from movements of the extremist political right.

Challenges to the policy process

Having rounded out our survey of institutions and actors, it is possible to return to the question of how European countries are responding to the most important challenges of the day. Here, however, we choose not to survey the broad influence of globalization or Europeanization but instead to focus in on the specific challenges that European countries face in the domains of welfare, migration, organized crime, and international security.

In Chapter 14. Anton Hemerijck, Maarten Keune and Martin Rhodes analyse the diversity of European welfare states, the challenges they face and the reforms they have undertaken. They show that the standard division of Europe's welfare states into four families still holds, but that a fifth family – comprising the new EU member states – has hybrid characteristics, with some countries coming closer to Europe's 'liberal family' and others combining a Bismarckian legacy with more recent liberal reforms. Each family shares a common set of institutional features that make its members susceptible to the same problems and vulnerable to similar challenges: liberal systems have proven better able to generate employment, but suffer from greater inequality, continental systems have higher equality but lower employment, while their southern counterparts score poorly on both indicators. Only the Scandinavian countries enjoy the best of both worlds. This diversity contradicts attempts to present Europe in terms of a particular 'social model' except in terms of the broadest of principles. Attempts to develop a European policy for employment and social policy confront the same problem: common policies are ill-suited for welfare states, unless pitched at the most general level, while seeking to accommodate their diversity at the European level only produces policy fragmentation and superficiality.

After welfare comes immigration. In Chapter 15, Virginie Guiraudon and Elena Jileva analyse the evolution of immigration in Europe and current trends in immigration policy. They focus on the conditions under which immigrants are allowed to enter and stay in a given national territory and the ways in which countries try to deter or encourage immigration, exploring the factors that explain the different 'policy mix' between restrictive policies and moves towards openness. Labour market shortages and the effects of demographic change on welfare state financing and economic growth have led many European countries to actively recruit skilled and unskilled foreign workers. Positions towards foreigners without a work and/or residence permit vary, however, from the strengthening of internal controls and deportation policies to mass regularization campaigns. While immigration was once limited to Northern and Western Europe, this is no longer the case. In East and Central Europe, governments have had to set up the same set of immigration policies as in the West, even if their countries are staging posts for immigrants rather than final destinations. The authors also explore the extent to which there is a process of East–West convergence, the consequence in part by of EU-driven changes in the east and their indirect impact on migration trends in Central and Eastern Europe.

Organized crime is the subject of Chapter 16. Letizia Paoli and Cyrille Fijnaut demonstrate how several long-term processes and a variety of far-reaching and localized historical events have contributed to a radical change in European perceptions of the threat from 'organized crime'. Some of these are directly related to the activities typically associated with organized crime, including most notably the rise of the illegal drug and human smuggling industries, but others are related to them only indirectly, such as the fall of the Iron Curtain in 1989 and the completion of the EU's internal market and abolition of its internal border controls. In an effort to control organized crime, far-reaching legal and institutional reforms have been passed in all European states and *ad hoc* instruments have been adopted by the EU and the Council of Europe. Nevertheless, the fear of organized crime has been generated more by the growing sense of insecurity than by hard evidence that organized crime poses a serious transnational challenge. In reality, the authors argue, organized crime has been stigmatized as a 'folk devil' and has become a powerful political instrument to justify criminal law and criminal justice reforms at the European level. Meanwhile, there is a risk that attention is being diverted from the more disorganized, and localized variants of crime that are escaping police control in towns and cities in favour of ill-thought out transnational initiatives.

Last but not least is the problem of security. In Chapter 17, Rachel Epstein and Alexandra Gheciu focus on the ways in which post-Cold War challenges have led European states to reorganize their national defences internally and bolster their security externally. The end of the Cold War, and the collapse of the rigid militarized blocs, led many international relations experts and practitioners to question conventional security ideas. Building on the 'democratic peace' thesis, which holds that liberal democracies do not fight each other, analysts and practitioners argued that the best way to ensure security in the new era was by projecting liberal democratic values internationally. The authors argue that post-Cold War ideas about security have found expression in a series of untested policies and practices in Europe. They show that in response to the new international environment, Europe is blurring its internal and external security policies in multiple domains. A focus on transnational threats and conflicts beyond EU borders have led European states to make significant spending cuts in traditional areas of defence, allow transnational defence industry integration to proceed, and promote liberal democratic norms in the former communist Eastern bloc, principally via EU and NATO enlargement.

Looking ahead

Developments in European politics are moving in many different directions at once. Nevertheless, there are two themes that we would like to encourage readers to draw from this book as a whole. The first is that Europe is not the European Union. While we recognize the monumental influence that European integration has on the daily lives of Europeans both inside and outside the EU, that influence pales into insignificance when compared to the cluster of ideas, values, traditions and institutions that constitute national identities and cultures. Therefore, if we are to have any hope of understanding where Europe is going, we have to start by understanding the national states of Europe and the European nation-state system. Only by accepting the fundamental significance of European nationalism can we begin to appreciate the challenge of globalization, the scale of Europeanization, and the prospects for European development.

The second theme we would like to emphasize is that Europeans are different – one from another within countries, and one country from another between them – because they want to be different. Indeed, European diversity is a natural outcome of popular democracy. It is what Europeans want, it is what they have chosen, and it is what they have got. Having linked diversity and democracy, however, we do not mean to imply that the combination of the two is always a good thing. Insistence on diversity can easily shade into racist segregation just as democratic procedures can foster populist extremism.

If there is a fundamental challenge underlying developments in European politics, it can be described in terms of finding a balance between diversity and solidarity, democracy and moderation. This challenge is nothing new to Europe. The history of the interwar period could easily be cast in similar terms. What is new is the determination of groups and individuals across Europe to build institutions capable of striking a balance short of war. This determination is not universal. A few of the post-Soviet states are absent – most notably Russia. A few West European countries are absent as well, like Norway, Iceland and Switzerland. Nevertheless, it is possible to imagine a Europe that is peaceful, dynamic, progressive – and whole. But it will be not be automatic and neither will it be a gift to Europe from the outside world. On the contrary it will be hard work. It will call for sacrifice. And the task may never be complete. That is what developments in European politics are all about.

PART I

The European State:
Integration and the World

Chapter 2

Europe and the Global Challenge

Erik Jones and Martin Rhodes

At the start of the twentieth century, most Europeans believed that Europe dominated the globe. At the start of the twenty-first century, most fear that globalization will dominate Europe. Both views misinterpret what 'Europe' is all about. The twentieth century view overestimated the strength of European unity. When the countries of Europe turned on one-another in two world wars, their global dominance was among the first casualties. The twenty-first century view underestimates the strength of European diversity. Although globalization presents a challenge, the countries of Europe remain determined – and able – both to preserve their European identity and to retain their distinctiveness relative to one-another.

The purpose of this chapter is to explain the relationship between Europe and the wider world. However, the focus is on economics and politics rather than foreign affairs or international security. Our goal is to analyse how globalization challenges the countries of Europe and to explain how 'Europe' and European countries have developed in response. Because 25 European countries are now members of the European Union (EU) – the world's most powerful integrated regional economy – much of our analysis is devoted to analysing its capacities for successfully 'mediating' and channelling the forces of globalization. But we also make reference to non-EU European countries and their particular predicaments in the global economy.

This chapter has five sections. It looks first at the mechanisms behind globalization before proceeding to consider the European response and assess the strengths and weakness of action at the European level and the diversity of national responses.

The global challenge

The term 'globalization' connotes many different developments and processes and has become a leitmotiv of contemporary debate. It can

15

be used to capture the increasing speed and volume of communication, the spread of mass media, the growth of the internet, and the trade in goods, services, jobs and capital (Kearney, 2005). All of these things are important; in fact this book would never have been assembled without them. But the notion of globalization must be handled with care. Though it conveys a reality that needs to be understood, it is often used lazily by the media, as a means of avoiding blame by politicians and for personal aggrandizement by certain public intellectuals. All play on the fear of what lies beyond our control.

The global challenge to Europe is not globalization *per se*, but rather a more restricted subset of global linkages. It lies primarily in the domain of economics – and in the political implications of economic change. Globalization in this sense can be reduced to:

- trade (the movement of goods and services across national borders);
- direct investment (the purchase of factories or equipment abroad);
- capital flows (the movement of money across national borders); and
- migration (the movement of people across national borders).

Trade is important because it influences basic economic structures. Countries that trade with the world benefit from gaining access to what the world produces. But they must also produce what foreign firms and consumers are willing to buy – and at prices that they are willing to pay. In this way, trade necessitates adjustment (Millward, 1984: 212–31). West European countries joined the international economy at the end of the Second World War by focusing on specific areas of comparative advantage – luxury goods in France, machine tools in Germany, white goods in Italy, and so on. Their eastern counterparts have only recently emerged from state socialism and are still defining their positions in the international division of labour.

Trade also conditions evolution. In Europe, the impact is most clearly seen in manufacturing. European trade has grown dramatically since the early 1950s and Europe's economies have grown as well. But over time the share of European output that is devoted to manufacturing has declined. In 1970, manufacturing accounted for 31 per cent of GDP in Germany and 22 per cent in France. By 2004, those numbers were 20 per cent and 13 per cent respectively (for United Nations statistics, see http://unstats.un.org/). Comparative advantage made Europe wealthy, and the growth and spread of European wealth changed underlying comparative advantage.

Of course, part of the explanation for the relative decline in European manufacturing is that European firms have moved their manufacturing processes to other, lower labour cost countries, including those in Eastern Europe, and increasingly source their intermediate products from those locations – a subject that receives a great deal of attention from the media and politicians alike. Over half of Germany's increase in real output between 1995 and 2003 derived from manufacturing processes based on imported intermediate goods, explaining in part that country's loss of 8.3 per cent of manufacturing employment over that period, and the vigour of its national debate on the emergence of a 'bazaar economy' (EEAG, 2005: 39–50).

But too big an emphasis on the movement of jobs abroad ignores the larger influence that patterns of direct investment have to play in linking European countries to the wider world. Direct investment has to be understood with reference to the development of large multinational firms. Such firms invest in different countries by definition. But they do so to make profit and not to relocate jobs for the sake of relocation. As a result, European direct investment abroad is often necessary to maintain employment in Europe. Firms buy factories and equipment in other countries because without doing so they would be unable to compete. This is not just because European labour is too costly (and very often it is not, given the high levels of skills and productivity found in many parts of Europe). It is also because European firms need to diversify their access to raw materials or essential suppliers, or because they seek exposure to new ideas or technologies, or because they need to be closer (and more responsive) to foreign markets. Hence while it is true that some European jobs are going abroad, there is little evidence that domestic jobs in high wage European countries are being relocated on a significant scale to the low wage cost regions of the East and South (Konings and Murphy, 2004). That said, the availability of cheaper manpower and a relatively well-educated workforce in Central and Eastern European countries, is moderating demand and wages for less-skilled workers in the West.

By focusing attention on the multinational firm we can begin to explain two features of Europe's linkages with the outside world. First, the predominant flow of direct investment is not from Europe to the developing world, but from Europe to North America and the reverse. The sum of net foreign direct investment inflows into high-income countries that are members of the Organization for Economic Cooperation and Development (OECD) over the 1970 to 2003 period is four times as high as the sum of net foreign direct investment into middle-income countries and 47 times as high as the amount received by low-income countries (for World Bank statistics, see World Development Indicators On-line). Second, much of Europe's external trade in manufactured goods takes place within firms and not between them. According to estimates from the OECD (2002) for the period from 1996 to 2000, intra-industry trade accounted for 65 per cent of all manufacturing trade in Italy, 72 per cent in Germany and 78 per cent in France. Moreover, such high percentages exist across Central and Eastern Europe as well, with intra-industry trade accounting for 63 per cent of manufacturing trade in Poland, 72 per cent in Hungary and 77 per cent in the Czech Republic. Finally, both features – the concentration of foreign direct investment and the growth of intra-industry trade – have become more pronounced over time, along with the growth in trade and the decline in the relative share of manufacturing.

The movement of money across national borders takes place in response to trade and direct investment. Indeed, neither activity would be possible without the exchange of currency. Nevertheless, the volume of money moving across borders now greatly exceeds the requirements for trade and investment in Europe (or elsewhere). In 1999, for example, gross world capital flows were six times greater than net flows (Mathieson and Shinasi, 2001: 7–8). Some of this movement can be explained by the need of large financial movements to diversify their investment portfolios through the purchase of foreign shares or obligations. A larger share can be ascribed to the existence of small arbitrage opportunities that arise because of movements in interest rates, expected earnings, or economic forecasts. And at least some of the enormous volume of money moving across borders does so because of speculation.

The problem of capital flows is not that money moves for reasons unrelated to trade and direct investment. Rather it is that the movement of money – for whatever reason – can have a lasting impact on underlying patterns of trade and investment (whether foreign or domestic). Currency speculation has an obvious impact on relative prices both within countries and between them. But the portfolio reallocations of large financial institutions matter as well (Mathieson and Shinasi, 2001: 4). If large German pension firms decide to redistribute their portfolios away from a small country's government debt – because, for example, those firms decide that, say, Estonia is no longer an 'emerging market' and so start to look for higher-risk, higher-return investments elsewhere – the result may be felt on interest rates across Estonia. Bond prices will fall and interest rates will rise because portfolio managers upgraded a country's risk-and-return classification.

Capital flows and other changes in the global economy imply a potential for real economic volatility that is far removed from the day-to-day understanding of most people in any economy, especially in those economies that have made rapid transitions to democracy and capitalism over the last decade or so. But people do understand that their economic futures may be more viable if they move toward new and hopefully safer havens and opportunities. Where possible and where necessary, they will even seek to move across countries. And that is where migration comes into play.

The irony of globalization is that while travel across countries has become much easier, migration has not. Between 1990 and 1995, France received more than 350,000 immigrants. Between 1995 and 2000, that number was less than 200,000. German data for the same period are distorted by the process of unification. Nevertheless, the trend is still clear. Between 1990 and 1995, Germany received over 2.5 million migrants. From 1995 to 2000, it received less than 1 million. Within these numbers, the emphasis is heavily intra-European. Eight of the top ten countries sending migrants to Germany in 2003 were European (including Turkey and Russia). Of the non-European countries, one is China (ranked seventh), the other is the United States (ranked eighth) (for migration statistics, see http://www.migrationinformation.org/GlobalData/).

The economic changes implied by globalization can be summarized in terms of greater wealth, greater diversity and greater insecurity. Europeans have more available to them; but they are also expected to do more and to do so more flexibly. Moreover, much of the old certainty of the early post-Second World War era has been lost. It was delivered a solid body blow by the oil shocks of the 1970s and 1980s, and the rapid rise of new information and communications technology (ICT) in the last decade. The emergence of India and China as important producers of manufacturing goods, with increasingly high skills contents, have radically altered the parameters of international trade and comparative advantage. Jobs change more frequently; incomes rise and fall more quickly. Some groups – especially the highly skilled – prosper from the changes in comparative advantage induced by more intensive trade among nations. But others – notably those with poor education and with low or no skills – do not and have become the major casualties of technological upgrading in Western countries.

The political implications of these changes are both structural and distributive. The structural implications are most evident in relations between states and markets. David Cameron (1978) noted in the late 1970s that countries that are more exposed to the world economy tend to have larger public sectors and more generous welfare states. Cameron hypothesized that the state could play a vital role in cushioning the impact of world markets on domestic actors. What Cameron's analysis did not explore, is the impact that state institutions would ultimately have on economic competitiveness. Domestic actors became better insulated, but often at the price of becoming less flexible. And following the twin oil shocks of the 1970s and 1980s, when inflation, rising unemployment and burgeoning government deficits spread across Western Europe, the need to find a new mix between protection and flexibility became pressing everywhere (Ferrera, Hemerijck and Rhodes, 2001).

The distributive implications of these economic changes played out in terms of wage bargaining, taxes and transfers – the subject of analysis in Chapter 14. What is important to note here is that the traditional division between labour and capital was frequently overwhelmed by the cacophony of different and competing claims on income and welfare. Hence, even where trade unions and employers could agree to negotiate over how wages and profits would be distributed, such agreement was insufficient to preempt a larger social conflict over industrial restructuring and economic adjustment, producing a deeper sense of malaise among workers and citizens. In all European countries, the 1980s and 1990s were decades of massive shifts of employment between manufacturing sectors and from manufacturing to a growing services sector, with further declines also occurring in the continent's already much diminished agricultural sector.

In this context, migration takes on a political significance that goes well-beyond its economic importance. Some voters get upset about the loss of manufacturing jobs. Others take exception to both the presence of foreign firms and the decline of domestic production. All fear financial volatility and express dismay when prices move against them. But they reserve their worst outbursts against migration. Not all Europeans are xenophobic or racist; indeed most are not. Nevertheless, popular xenophobia and racism is colouring the politics of Europe in ever darker hues. As a result, European countries are making it more difficult for workers to migrate (Joppke, 2002). And politicians are coming to rue the migration that took place in the past.

Finally, it is important to acknowledge that this story of Europe's global challenge applies to all parts of the continent, though affecting it in different ways. Each country is engaged in its own social, political and economic adjustments to shifts in international comparative advantage. The problem of unemployment (or underemployment) is widespread, affecting Europe's large continental and southern countries worst, and its northern ones (the United Kingdom, Ireland and Scandinavia) least. Migration and immigration affect all countries. France has its 'Polish plumbers' (though very small in numbers, these migrant workers became a rhetorical focal point for the French opposition to the European Constitution in 2005), but Poland itself receives many immigrants from Russia, Belarus and the Ukraine. The point is not that the challenge of globalization manifests itself in the same way in every country. Neither is it that globalization is a problem everywhere for the same reasons. Rather, and more simply, it is that the global challenge is truly global – demanding responses at multiple levels, both national and European.

The European response

The European Union (EU) exists to a large extent to provide a buffer between the countries of Europe and the outside world. This is reflected in the origins of the EU as a common market or customs union, first in the European Coal and Steel Community, and then, after 1957, in the European Economic Community (EEC). When international trade was the most important feature of the global economy, during the mid-to-late 1950s, trade also emerged as the most important aspect of European integration. Nevertheless, such a coincidence was not self-evident. Many of the staunchest proponents of European integration thought that the establishment of a common trading regime would make for a false start. Instead they preferred to focus on more limited functional forms of integration, as in the areas of coal and steel or atomic energy. Opponents of European integration also saw trade as a weak starting point. When the common market was initiated in 1958, Britain responded with the creation of a free trade area. The difference between the two organizations lay precisely in their relation to the outside world. The common market implied a common external commercial policy. The free trade area allowed individual member countries to negotiate their own commercial relationships.

The existence of a common external policy marked a crucial difference and the common market exceeded all expectations in its promotion of European trade and welfare. In part the reasons were defensive. The European Economic Community (EEC) fostered the trade in manufacturing, but it also protected steel and (particularly) agriculture. To a greater extent, however, the EEC played a vital role in promoting European trading interests abroad, by speaking as one voice in multilateral trade negotiations within the General Agreement on Tariffs and Trade (GATT). Greater unity made it possible for European countries to assert their interests against the rest of the world and particularly the United States (Meunier, 2005). Over time, moreover, European integration became increasingly responsive to global challenges as they emerged. The increase in exchange rate volatility at the end of the 1960s brought forward the first plan to create an economic and monetary union. Although that plan ultimately failed, the ambition to find European solutions for global economic challenges remained.

As global linkages continued to deepen, European solutions only became more imperative. The rise in global capital flows in the mid-to-late 1970s encouraged European countries both inside and outside the EEC to pursue ever more elaborate schemes to stabilize the relative values of their currencies. And the emergence of powerful trade competitors in Asia during the late 1970s and early 1980s sparked concern about labour productivity and employment as well as a heady debate on the causes of 'Euro-sclerosis'. In turn, this provided a major spur to the negotiation of the 1986 Single European Act that led to the completion of Europe's internal market – the 'Single Market'. The capstone in these developments came with the formal liberalization of European capital markets and the drive to create an economic and monetary union (EMU). The 1992 Maastricht Treaty marked the transition from a European Community to a European Union, and ushered in the most remarkable experiment in regional economic institution-building that the world has ever known. The experiment continues. In 2004, a further ten countries from Central and Eastern Europe joined the EU and its increasingly liberalized market and also filed into line for EMU membership. Other nations further to the East (Romania and Bulgaria) are also anxious to join the EU club, and nations once at the core of the former Soviet Union (notably Ukraine) hold similar aspirations, even if there are no current plans for them to join. They all seek to consolidate their liberal political and economic transitions within a broader regional economic bloc.

Nevertheless, it would be a mistake to believe that the common market and the common currency together provide a comprehensive response to the global challenge. On the contrary, the architects of European monetary integration acknowledged that more work needed to be done. The Single Market had left significant areas untouched, such as network (phone, electricity and gas) and financial services, especially insurance. Moreover, while pan-European market liberalization boosted intra-European trade and services, and facilitated inflows of FDI, anxiety about the relatively poor state of European labour productivity, employment and GDP growth remained high. An immediate concern with regard to EMU was the inflationary consequences of bloated government deficits. Hence the Maastricht Treaty also included a set of convergence criteria that not only proscribe countries from running excessive deficits but also require that they demonstrate the ability to live with relatively low rates of inflation. The architects of the single currency were also worried about the social and economic costs of persistently high unemployment. Here, however, they were somewhat at a loss as to what 'Europe' could do. Most economists regard unemployment as a national or local phenomenon – not as a European problem *per se*. Hence, even if European policies might play a certain indicative role, the solution should be national or local as well (Viñals and Jimeno, 1996).

This focus on national and local solutions dovetailed with a third set of concerns about the combination of a single market and a common currency. The architects of Europe's monetary union recognized that only sustained market-structural reform within the member states could eliminate the problem of unemployment. Even more important, only sustained market structural reform could make it possible for a single monetary authority to chart a coherent policy across a diverse group of member states. The point was not that all countries had to look alike to share the same monetary policy. Rather it was that they should all behave alike so that the common monetary policy does not have persistently different consequences for different parts of Europe. Although European countries did not behave that way when the single currency was designed, it was important that they learn to behave that way for the single currency to function (Jones, 1998). The expansion of the EMU club to the new Central and Eastern European (CEE) member states of the EU will accentuate existing diversity and pose new challenges to the governance of the common currency Eurozone.

These additional elements in the European response to globalization emerged in piecemeal fashion starting with the 1997 Amsterdam European Council summit. There the heads of state and government of the European Union agreed to a 'stability and growth pact' to aid in the consolidation of fiscal performance across the member states. They incorporated an employment title in the treaty establishing the European Community, to set out a clear European ambition to help tackle the ongoing jobs crisis. And they recommitted themselves to implementing the various measures required to complete Europe's internal market. Such actions were viewed both as necessary to improve the functioning of the European Union and as a prelude to the EU's inevitable enlargement to the countries of Central and Eastern Europe.

The Stability and Growth Pact (SGP) provides a framework for the structural reform of member state fiscal accounts to augment the prohibition of excessive deficits that was set down at Maastricht. Over the medium term, the SGP calls on member states to achieve a fiscal position that is close to balance or in surplus. By implication, the goal is to achieve what economists refer to as a structural balance – meaning a matching of revenues and expenditures when the economy is operating at full employment. When fiscal accounts are structurally balanced, they will naturally run deficits during recessions and surpluses during booms. However, they should not run deficits that are inflationary and neither should they run surpluses that create a permanent drag on growth and employment (Jones, 2004).

The goal underlying this medium-term objective is to create a macro-economic environment within which prices are stable and interest rates are low. For firms, such conditions translate into greater predictability over longer time horizons, making it easier to plan and cheaper to invest. For workers, such macroeconomic stability should provide insulation against unexpected changes, it should offer more job stability, and it should give rise to greater employment prospects. Whether the rules that underpin this system – national debts within or approaching 60 per cent of GDP, deficits and inflation rates within 3 per cent of GDP – are equally relevant to the rapidly growing and still relatively poor CEE countries in line for EMU membership is a matter of considerable debate. Their growth rates and gaps in per capita GDP with the EU-15 would suggest that the tight monetary and fiscal constraints laid down at Maastricht may be less than appropriate for most countries in this group.

Nevertheless, the linchpin remains the effectiveness of market structural reform at the national and regional levels, and this holds for all 25 EU members states, both East and West. Here the European Union launched a number of initiatives starting with the November 1997 Luxembourg jobs summit and culminating in the March 2000 European Council summit at Lisbon. The various initiatives, processes and procedures that were developed are complicated. Nevertheless, the underlying rationale is straightforward. Only the member states can undertake effective market structural reform. The European Union as an institution cannot. Nevertheless, the EU has endeavoured to play a role. It has sought to encourage member states to help unemployed workers find jobs by encouraging active labour market policies, by setting benchmarks and targets for achievement, by monitoring progress at the member state level, by saluting achievement, and by publicizing failure (Rhodes, 2005).

What might work in the promotion of employment could conceivably work in other policy areas as well. The EU is seeking to play a role in the progressive liberalization of product and labour markets, even where it lacks the Treaty-based competencies it enjoys in competition policy for example. The Commission is especially active in trying to help tackle problems related to areas of discrimination, poverty, and social exclusion, where its powers are also less well-established in European law. Through pan-European funding and grants, it can promote scientific research and support more general forms of education, especially at the tertiary level.

These different roles for the EU in the structural reform of its member states were announced in March 2000 at Lisbon in the service of a common strategic objective – to make Europe the world's most competitive and dynamic knowledge-based economy by the end of the decade. EU heads of state and government agreed to meet annually in the spring to assess progress in the achievement of their reform objectives. They also began to emphasize the importance of establishing broad economic policy guidelines at the European level – guidelines which appertain both to the member states and to the European Union as a whole. And finally, they began to strengthen the links between economic policy coordination within the European Union and policy coordination between the EU and those countries participating in EU enlargement.

EU enlargement was a major policy initiative with implications ranging far beyond this discussion of globalization and European responses. Nevertheless, the global challenge did play a role in shaping the enlargement agenda as well. Not only did the process of enlargement promise to spread the economic advantages of European integration from West to East, but it would also stem the flow of migrants from East to West (Vachudova, 2005).

Taken as a package, the common market, the single currency, the Stability and Growth Pact, the Lisbon strategy, and enlargement begin to provide a reasonably comprehensive European response to the globalization challenge. Of course some elements were left out. Not all single market legislation has been implemented evenly across the EU. Not all market activities are conducted freely within Europe. Not all countries in the European Union participate in the single currency. Not all participants in Europe's single currency could be expected to live up to their fiscal commitments, and several have breached them in the last couple of years, revealing the limits of the EU's current system of economic coordination. Not all areas of market structural reform are as amenable to EU influence as others. And not all candidates for EU membership could be expected to join in 2004 or even in 2007. Nor may it be possible for the prospective CEE members of EMU to join on schedule before the end of this decade. However, such omissions do not vitiate the underlying intention of the policy measures. Even a flawed European response to the challenges posed by globalization is better than no European response at all. The challenge is to figure out what 'Europe' can do and what must be handled by the different European states.

What Europe can and cannot do

As argued above, the EU provides a buffer between its member states and the outside world. This is achieved first by providing a number of defensive mechanisms, and primarily in agriculture, where the Common Agricultural Policy, or CAP, has provided a consistent though increasingly controversial form of welfare and controlled adjustment for Europe's farmers – the numbers of whom have been significantly increased by the EU's eastern enlargement. A second part of the buffer takes the form of a more proactive carrot-and-stick approach to advancing Europe's modernization and adaptation to global forces. These mechanisms reveal both the strengths and weaknesses of 'Europe' as a model of regional integration. The EU is caught to some extent between defending the status quo and promoting the future, with much of its institutional system and budget still tied to the former. The consequence is considerable stasis in attempts to tackle some of Europe's most pressing problems, including, most notably, those which had already inspired the SEA, EMU and Lisbon agendas – that is, its poor economic and employment performance, or, to be more exact, the poor performance of some of its largest member states.

Taking defensive mechanisms first, the CAP is Europe's most powerful means of protective defence against the outside world and has always consumed the lion's share of the EU's relatively small budget, even if it has diminished as a proportion of spending over time. It helped reconcile farmers who had flocked to illiberal political philosophies in the 1930s to the newly-built democracies of the 1950s, and transferred earlier national farm support and protection policies to the European level. In the decades that followed, the CAP has successfully shielded European farmers from successive US demands for trade liberalization, and sustained the incomes of both small and larger farmers, initially through production subsidies, and more recently direct payments. The inclusion of agriculture in international trade agreements since the mid-1980s, beginning with the GATT Uruguay Round and continuing with the new WTO regime, has gradually helped push the EU towards less trade-distorting practices. But the CAP continues to depend on a heavily-bureaucratic system of government, enables national government to defend the privileges of its farmers, and channels the EU's scarce collective resources into one of the least productive parts of its economy (Rieger, 2005).

Conducting a common trade policy, which the Treaty of Rome placed firmly in the hands of the EU, is important for ensuring fair access of European exporters of goods and services to foreign markets, and in turn for generating growth in Europe itself. But the importance of the EU's strong national and sectoral agricultural lobbies, and their effective resistance to a thorough-going reform of the CAP, has also restricted the EU's room for manoeuvre in international trade policy. So too, at least until the late 1980s, did the support given by many

European governments to 'national champions' – large firms selected for special state tax, credit and subsidy treatment, in both traditional economic sectors and new technologies.

From the 1990s onwards, though, the gradual liberalization of the European economy under the Single Market Programme, coupled with the Nordic enlargement of the EU to the more economically liberal Sweden and Finland, allowed the European Commission to be less concerned with defensive measures, such as anti-dumping duties, and less likely to be involved in transatlantic spats over subsidy issues – though they continue to occur – and more devoted to multilateral, market-opening trade diplomacy. The EU's success as an exporter of services made it a keen advocate of international services trade liberalization, and the success of its own competition regime has spurred its active co-operation in developing international competition policies. The recent Agenda 2000 CAP reforms, which provided for a further shift from export subsidies towards non-trade forms or rural protection and support have facilitated engagement in the WTO's Doha development agenda. Nevertheless, in addition to severely restricting EU budgetary flexibility, continuing farm support schemes and still high agricultural tariffs limit the EU's credibility in WTO negotiations, especially with third world countries (Woolcock, 2005).

Turning to the EUs' carrot-and-stick approach to modernization and economic adjustment, the carrot comes most importantly in the form of structural fund support for Europe's poorer regions, either those that are economically less advanced, with low levels of income and high levels of poverty, as in the underdeveloped regions of existing member states (Ireland) and the countries who joined the EEC in the 1980s (Portugal, Spain and Greece), or regions of high unemployment and industrial decline. These funds have provided the distributive sweetener to both the EU's southern enlargement of the 1980s and its eastern enlargement in the 2000s. During that period the funds underwent a significant expansion and acquired a stronger Treaty foundation. They have also helped sell the major historical landmark shifts – the Single European Act and the Maastricht Treaty – to sometimes sceptical governments and electorates.

Nevertheless, they still account for only around a third of the EU budget, compared with around 50 per cent for the CAP, and their efficacy in mitigating growth disparities across the EU is in doubt: while some low income regions have grown faster (Ireland, the eastern German Länder), others (Portugal, Greece, Spain) have only grown just ahead of the average, and others (the Italian *mezzogiorno*) have shown no signs of convergence at all, GDP per capital is actually becoming more widely dispersed across the EU (Allen, 2005; Sapir *et al.*, 2004).

Sponsoring growth in the poorer regions of the CEE member states of the EU poses an even greater challenge, given the rapid increase in regional disparities and social inequalities in those countries since their emergence from state socialism in the early 1990s.

The stick comes in the form of market liberalization, achieved through European law put in place under the Single Market Programme and through competition policy. Legislation and free market rules are backed up by European Court of Justice and national court policing of the implementation of, and compliance with Single Market directives, concerning the mutual recognition of products and the unhampered flow of goods and services. As in commercial and agricultural policy, competition policy is one of the major areas of EU competence granted in the Treaty of Rome, and since the 1980s, the EU has operated a highly effective system of merger control (though not provided for in the Rome Treaty, it was introduced in the 1990s), has pressured governments to open up monopolies in public services, prohibits cartel agreements between firms that limit competition and has policed state aids in an effort to avoid a distortion of competition and conform with new international trade regime commitments. All form part of the more general European strategy of making the European economy more competitive in globalized markets. European competition norms have been translated equally as part of the *acquis communautaire* into the national regulatory systems of the new member states, which only a decade ago were state socialist regimes (Wilks, 2005).

What Europe does effectively is therefore largely determined by the nature of competencies awarded to the EU, and these are largely the consequences in turn of intergovernmental agreements that have succeeded in reconciling often divergent member-state preferences. The peculiar combination of market-opening, market-protecting and market-softening interventions discussed above is the result of the accretion of historical trade-offs. As a result, the EU has a protective system of agricultural support that is hard to reform alongside a fiercely liberal competition policy applied with great vigour by the European Commission. The price for success with the single market initiative and EMU was to some extent an expanded system of regional development aid whose legitimising and compensatory functions outweigh, however, its capacity to ensure a reduction of Europe's regional income disparities. Legal competencies and budget allocations decide where the EU's interventions will have most impact – for better or worse. Where neither legal competencies nor budget allocations are available, Europe's capacity for collective action is severely curtailed. This brings us back to the Lisbon agenda.

The Lisbon agenda and national sources of competitive advantage

As noted above, the aim of the Lisbon agenda is to make Europe a more-competitive, knowledge-based economy. But few of the core competencies listed above are clearly dedicated to that goal. Some – notably the heavy investment in agricultural income support and guarantees – may actively work against its achievement. Europe's engagement in international trade policy has helped secure foreign market access for its member states' products and services. The Single Market Programme set out to remove barriers to the intra-European mobility of capital, goods, services and labour, with the aim of boosting productivity and accelerating growth. The goal of EMU was to complete that process by providing a single European currency, which would reduce the costs of cross-border transactions and, via the Stability and Growth Pact, ensure the achievement of lower inflation and lower budget deficits. All provide an important framework and scope for greater economic dynamism and growth.

The problem is that signs of greater dynamism and growth have been few. As the Sapir Report on the European economic system, and other assessments of the EU's economic performance have pointed out (Sapir *et al.*, 2004: 27ff), the EU has strongly diverged from the United States (the traditional yardstick) in terms of employment and productivity, both absolutely and relatively over the last thirty years. EU living standards (GDP per capita) are roughly 70 per cent of US levels, approximately one-third of which analysts attribute to labour productivity differences, with the remaining two-thirds due to differences in the utilization of labour. These include differences in employment rates (which are well below the US-level in all European countries, apart from Ireland, the UK and Scandinavia, as discussed in Chapter 14) and hours worked per worker.

What explains this poor performance? The EU's productivity problems, and in particular the productivity downturn since the mid-1990s, have been attributed to three closely-related problems (Denis *et al.*, 2005): a concentration of EU countries' production systems in low and medium-technology industries, with declining productivity growth rates and investment levels; an inability to challenge the USA in the major areas of information and communication technology, reflected in the small size of the European ICT sector; and though the ICT production and diffusion are hard to measure, an apparent inability to reap the productivity benefits of ICT in a range of ICT-using industries. The CEE countries are in an even less favoured position given their recent transitions to capitalism, the collapse of traditional industries that could not survive outside the command economy, and their heavy dependence on foreign direct investment, which has been largely concentrated in areas of mass manufacture rather than leading-edge technologies (Kaczurba, 2000).

Even if policy areas susceptible to European intervention – especially trade openness, macro-economic stability and well-functioning product, labour and capital markets (in the latter there is still much to be done) – can play an important role in bolstering Europe's innovation capacity, Europe's productivity and growth problem derives in the first place from the nature of 'national innovation systems' which are largely beyond the reach of EU policy initiatives. The EU's national innovation systems are highly diverse, resistant to rapid change due to their complex institutional character and their core elements – research and development (R&D), quality higher education and academic research, university–business sector links, intra-firm networks for technology and knowledge diffusion, and a capacity for developing high technology clusters (OECD, 1997) – lie outside the traditional areas of EU competence and responsibility Improving innovation capacity by bolstering public and private R&D, strengthening education and enhancing the interaction between them would require a new means of generating institutional change in Europe. It is to this subject that we now turn.

National diversity is deeply embedded in the institutional structures of Europe's economies. As we now know from extensive research by the 'varieties-of-capitalism' school into the institutional foundations of comparative institutional advantage (Hall and Soskice, 2001; Hall and Gingerich, 2004) it is the institutional architecture of the economy that determines the behaviour of the firm by shaping strategic interaction. In turn, the nature of that strategic interaction will determine the way in which the broader economy is inserted into the international division of labour. Institutional complementarities deliver different kinds of firm behaviour, innovation and investment patterns.

Hence, in the liberal market economies (or LMEs) – for example the USA, Ireland and the UK, as well as the embryonic LMEs emerging from state socialism, such as Estonia – fluid labour markets fit rather well with easy access to stockmarket capital and the profit imperative, making firms the 'radical innovators' they have proven to be in recent years, especially in the United States, in sectors ranging from bio-technology through semi-conductors, software and advertising to corporate finance. The logic of dynamics in such countries revolves around the centrality of 'switchable assets' – of both capital and labour – whose value can be realized when diverted to multiple purposes. In the coordinated market economies (or CMEs) – such as Germany, Austria,

Switzerland, and the nascent CME of Central Europe, Slovenia (Feldmann, 2006) – by contrast, long-term employment strategies, rule-bound behaviour and durable ties between firms and banks underpinning patient capital provision predispose firms to be 'incremental innovators' in capital goods industries, machine tools and equipment of all kinds. In contrast to liberal market economies, the logic of the coordinated market economy revolves around 'specific or co-specific assets', assets, that is, whose value depends on the active cooperation of others.

These characteristics feed, in turn, into quite distinct patterns of innovation and specialization across nations. Hall and Soskice (2001: 41–4) present evidence to suggest that such specialization deepens over time. Hall and Gingerich (2004: 28–9) argue that high growth rates will depend on the degree to which there is either a high level of market coordination, as in the USA, or a high degree of strategic coordination, as in Germany. In those economies where there are incoherent mixes of the two – such as Italy, Spain, Portugal and France, as well as many of the CEE economies – long-run growth capacities are likely to be lower. Especially incoherent mixes of the core components of an economy (product markets, labour markets, financial markets and systems of education and skills provision), as found in certain CEE and former Soviet economies such as Poland and the Ukraine, will heavily constrain economic development and a full and balanced integration into the global economy (Stultz, 2005; Mykhnenko, 2006).

This suggests that there are at least two models of economic specialization and innovation in the EU, with different countries conforming to varying degrees to these two ideal-types. This national diversity suggests different capacities for adjusting to and specializing in the global economy that are not immediately susceptible to European policy manipulation. But what is important from the national innovation system perspective is that innovation and growth reflects not just different endowments in terms of labour, capital and the stock of knowledge, but also the role of strategic interactions, for example cooperative R&D agreements between firms, between firms and universities and the availability of venture capital for innovative, small-firm start-ups. In theory, these interactions can be enhanced in liberal market, coordinated and the mixed systems in between by improvements across various policy areas.

European national innovation assessments have been made across a large range of indicators revealing different levels of human resources for innovation (education attainment and employment in medium-high-tech manufacturing and services), degrees of creation of new knowledge (public and business R&D spending, high-tech patent applications and applications granted), capacities for the transmission and application of knowledge (small and medium-sized enterprise innovation, innovation cooperation and innovation expenditure), and success in innovation finance, outputs and markets (supply of venture capital, sales of 'new to market' products, internet access and use, ICT expenditures, and so forth) (European Commission, DG Enterprise, 2003). The results partly conform to the insights of the 'varieties-of-capitalism' approach: of the larger countries, Germany and the UK are ahead of France and Italy, though Italy is the best performing southern country. Finland, Sweden and Denmark lead overall, however, revealing their success in producing high levels of skilled employment in high-technology clusters. The new member and candidate countries, as a group, lag behind the EU on almost all indicators (*ibid.*). Although Slovenia, the Czech Republic, Hungary and Estonia lead the CEE group in terms of innovation policy mechanisms and capacities for generating new knowledge and technology diffusion, they all lost advantages in terms of the size of and capacity for R&D they inherited from the socialist era and suffer from highly inefficient national innovation systems (Radosevic, 2005).

Despite their national diversity and membership of different 'capitalist' camps, the core largest European economies – the UK, Germany, France and Italy – share a common failure, according to recent assessments (Denis *et al.*, 2005): an inability to refocus their R&D activities over the 1990s on high productivity growth industries such as ICT and potentially high productivity growth industries in pharmaceuticals and biotechnology, as well as certain service industries, including software and computer-related services. The share of total manufacturing R&D in high-growth ICT sectors in these four countries is much smaller than in the USA and decreasing over time, and all reveal a higher concentration of manufacturing R&D in non-ICT high-tech sectors.

Members of the EU's regional integration club may ultimately benefit from the EU's attempts to promote innovation and put in place a stronger institutional basis for economic development. But given the complex institutional arrangements and interaction effects underpinning these 'innovation systems', the EU's targets regarding spending on R&D and tertiary education will only have real effect if the quality of interaction between the different institutional elements of these systems is also improved. Denis *et al.* (2005: 48) calculate that if the Lisbon strategy's objective of an increase in the EU's R&D intensity from 2 to 3 per cent over the decade to 2010 had been set instead in 1990 for attainment in 2000, and if the EU had continued its trend investment in traditional high-tech industries (for example cars and chemicals), 'it would have gained relatively little in terms of closing the productivity gap with the US' (*ibid.*: 49). Tackling this situation effectively requires a major revision to the pattern of embedded policies at both the national and European levels. At the national level there must be a steady improvement in the articulation between advanced research systems and innovative sectors of the economy; at the European level there must be a rapid shift of resources away from compensatory policies, especially regarding agriculture, in the search for a new means of promoting research and development within member states. And the achievement of both requires the development of a more effective set of instruments for multi-level policy-making within the EU.

Conclusion

The increasing flow of goods and services, labour and capital, have both enriched European countries and challenged them to survive and compete. Even if they have also suffered massively from the social and economic costs of the transition from state socialism, the new members of the EU's economic integration club are slowly also benefiting from their access to the European and global economies. 'Europe' has spurred this process onwards, but its interventions offer no panacea for the difficulties associated with globalization. The 'nation state' remains an important site for policy-making and economic adjustment, and European-level policies cannot substitute for national initiatives and responsibilities in confronting the challenges of international competition. European responses to globalization are only effective when pan-European policies are paired with effective action at the national level. Success depends on finding ways to link European initiatives with national policies in facilitating economic change rather than preserving the status quo. A new balance between market-opening, market-protecting and market-softening policies at the European level has to be found. But so too has a new focus on effective economic adjustment within Europe's member states.

For the way countries are organized, and the way people in different countries view that organization, condition to a large extent the appropriateness of any economic response to the challenge of globalization. This is a central lesson of the literature on 'varieties of capitalism' and it is important for understanding how globalization affects all parts of Europe but is refracted by national institutions. No country is left unaffected by the challenge of increasing world economic integration – but that does not mean they should all respond in the same way, or even that they should become any more alike. The institutional logic of national distinctiveness suggests how national institutions and politics combine to form a strong and durable mix, and that combination must provide the basis for adjustment and change. European economic integration is important, and increasingly so for all parts of Europe. But the global challenge can only be met through a multilevel response.

Chapter 3

International Politics and European States

Federica Bicchi, Karen Smith and Richard Whitman

The international politics of European states have undergone profound changes in the last few decades, especially since the end of the Cold War and 9/11. During the Cold War, European states' foreign policies were heavily conditioned by which side of the Cold War divide they were aligned with – or by whether they attempted to stand-aside from superpower conflict by pursuing policies of neutrality. With the end of the Cold War, European integration has acted as the new key conditioning factor on states' foreign policies by transforming intra-European states' relations through the progressive enlargement of the European Union (EU) and by the attempt to build a collective foreign policy through the EU. West European countries first developed new forms of foreign policy cooperation under the shadow of superpower confrontation; these mechanisms were developed after the end of the Cold War and subsequently extended first to countries that had taken a neutral stance during the Cold War (with the accession of Austria, Sweden and Finland to the EU in 1995), and then to Central and East European countries with the 2004 EU enlargement.

All European states continue to pursue national foreign policies, but a distinction can be drawn between those countries that have joined the EU and those which are not members. For member states of the EU their national foreign policies are characterized by intensive bilateral and multilateral relationships with other EU member states and cover a wide range of issues that straddle domestic and international politics, a variety of national and European institutions, sectoral ministries and sub-national actors. Whether this *intra-EU* diplomacy has now gone beyond diplomacy as relationships between member states have been 'domesticated' is a matter of debate (Hocking, 2004). Alongside this intra-EU diplomacy, EU member states continue to pursue international politics individually, but also increasingly collectively, beyond the EU. For European states that are not members of the EU, their foreign policies are heavily determined by whether they aspire to membership of the EU, and even those European states not seeking membership the EU's economic and political strength heavily conditions their foreign policies.

Europe's international politics

Europe is a significant part, or sub-system, of a wider international politics from which it cannot be analytically separated. Europe contributes to over a quarter of global economic activity and is significant in the global political economy and the politics of the global environment. Europe is affected by the transnational and transborder phenomena identified in the other chapters in this volume on migration, crime and security, which have widened the range of issues that are now the subject of international politics and with which states need to grapple. The shift to the 'war on terror' since 9/11 has also caused European states to accommodate to this new focus of the USA as a key actor in international politics. European states are also significant actors within international political and economic institutions through membership of institutions such as the United Nations Security Council and the G-8.

Europe itself is characterized by the unique density of international institutions covering the region (see Table 3.1). The 55 member state Organization for Security and Cooperation in Europe (OSCE) includes the United States, Russia and Central Asia and demonstrates that the security boundaries of Europe extend beyond its geographical boundaries. The Council of Europe has the purpose of 'benchmarking' democracy, human rights and the rule of law in Europe and opens membership only to those who conform to a set of established European norms. A majority of European states are also in a military alliance with the United States through the North Atlantic Treaty Organization (NATO). These pan-European institutions operate alongside a significant number of sub-regional organizations in Europe, such as the Nordic Council. The European Union straddles the activities of all of these organizations and, in addition, organizes and regulates economic activity between its members, neighbouring states and beyond Europe.

European states operate within this dense institutional network which constrains and conditions the conduct of national foreign policies. Where such constraints and conditioning generate a process in which national policies converge through an increase in shared norms and interests in foreign policy, this is defined as 'adaptation' (Manners

Table 3.1 *European States: membership of international organizations*

Country	EU	Council of Europe	NATO	OSCE	OECD	WEU	UNSC	G8
Albania		x		x				
Andorra		x		x				
Austria	x	x		x	x	x		
Belarus				x				
Belgium	x	x	x	x	x	x		
Bosnia and Herzegovina		x		x				
Bulgaria		x	x	x		x		
Croatia		x		x				
Cyprus	x	x		x				
Czech Republic	x	x	x	x	x	x		
Denmark	x	x	x	x	x	x		
Estonia	x	x	x	x		x		
Finland	x	x		x	x	x		
France	x	x	x	x	x	x	x	x
Germany	x	x	x	x	x	x		x
Greece	x	x	x	x	x	x		
Holy See					x			
Hungary	x	x	x	x	x	x		
Iceland		x	x	x	x	x		
Ireland	x	x		x	x	x		
Italy	x	x	x	x	x	x		x
Latvia	x	x	x	x		x		
Liechtenstein		x		x				
Lithuania	x	x	x	x		x		
Luxembourg	x	x	x	x	x	x		
Macedonia		x		x				
Malta	x	x		x				
Moldova		x			x			
Monaco				x				
Netherlands	x	x	x	x	x	x		
Norway		x	x	x	x	x		
Poland	x	x	x	x	x	x		
Portugal	x	x	x	x	x	x		
Romania		x	x	x		x		
Russia		x		x				x
San Marino		x		x				
Serbia and Montenegro		x		x				
Slovakia	x	x	x	x	x	x		
Slovenia	x	x	x	x		x		
Spain	x	x	x	x	x	x		
Sweden	x	x		x	x	x		
Switzerland		x		x	x			
Turkey		x	x	x	x	x		
Ukraine		x		x				
United Kingdom	x	x	x	x	x	x	x	x

and Whitman, 2000) or 'Europeanization' (Wong, 2005a). This is not to suggest that national foreign policies in Europe are becoming homogeneous but rather that there is a distinctive 'system' of European international relations, which includes both the European and the national level (White, 2001; Hill, 1993: 322–3). The most salient element of the system is represented by the framework for coordinating foreign policies and producing common policies between EU member states, which is called the Common Foreign and Security Policy (CFSP). Reforms to the CFSP have been almost continuous, as the framework has been stretched to over four times the original number of member states involved in it. As a result, European foreign policy has expanded in scope and in depth: the original character of consultation among member states has developed into a 'coordination reflex' (de Schoutheete, 1980) and an increasing capacity to act collectively in certain areas and on given topics. However, member states continue to display a capacity to act on a national basis, along the lines of well-established foreign policy traditions.

Europe's national foreign policies

All states in Europe have retained the foreign policy-making and diplomatic infrastructure to pursue national foreign policies in international politics. European states do, however, have differing resources at their disposal and differing levels of ambition in international relations. 'Large' member states such as the UK and France, with extensive diplomatic networks and foreign policy-making infrastructure, pursue foreign policies which are global in extent and aspire to be first-order international actors active on all issues on the international agenda. By contrast, other European states seek 'role specialization' by making a distinctive contribution to international politics. For instance, Norway has adopted such a strategy of role specialization by acting as a neutral party in conflict resolution in the Middle East and Sri Lanka, whilst Ireland has been a significant contributor to UN peacekeeping missions.

Studying the foreign policies of European states presents the same problems as studying nation states' foreign policies in general. How can we assess the impact of changing international politics upon states in which distinctions between domestic and international politics are increasingly difficult to draw (and commonly referred to as processes of globalization) and in which international politics increasingly involves the actions of non-governmental actors as much as those of governments? What constitutes 'foreign policy' is becoming increasingly difficult to assess and raises challenges for foreign policy analysis (FPA), a sub-discipline of International Relations, that purports to understand and explain public policy projected beyond the nation-state (Webber and Smith, 2002). FPA places the *process* by which foreign policy is made and its *implementation* at the centre of its approach to understanding a state's foreign policy, by identifying the actors involved in foreign policy-making, the sources of influence at work on the decision-makers in the process of policy-making, how decisions are implemented and their outcomes. For European states, the Cold War created a considerable exogenous constraint on foreign policies. Consequently much recent analysis has focused on identifying the influences at work as European states have adjusted to the changed international politics of Europe, with a particular interest in the foreign policy of Germany (Hyde-Price, 2000; Maull, 2006).

There is the additional challenge when analysing the international politics of European states of comprehending the impact of international and domestic influences upon countries whilst simultaneously considering the impact of European integration. Undertaking the identification of such influences upon European states' foreign policies is generally done on the basis of single-country case studies, since assessing the mix of endogenous and exogenous factors necessary to comprehend a single state's foreign policy is a formidable task. This case study work tends to chart changes in the foreign policy orientation of European states across time and with a heavy focus upon the impact of countries' foreign policies as a consequence of EU membership and the intermeshing of national and EU foreign policy-making and implementation. The bulk of these single country case studies attempt to identify the distinctive impact of a process of Europeanization (see, for example, Wong, 2005b).

Comparative work has been undertaken to assess the degree to which European states' foreign policies demonstrate similar characteristics in terms of policy-making and implementation. Countries have been grouped to see whether, for example, meaningful comparisons can be drawn between small population member states (Tonra, 2001) or states that share similar geography (Kavakas, 2001). Comparative studies seeking to assess all of the member states of the EU are more scarce (Hill, 1996; Manners and Whitman, 2000). This is primarily because drawing comparisons between a 'micro state' such as Malta and a large post-colonial state such as the United Kingdom is problematic. Consequently much greater attention has been focused on the structures and mechanisms through which EU member states have sought to coordinate national foreign policies and to devise elements of a common foreign policy, explored below in more detail.

Whether the EU represents a constriction or an opportunity for the foreign policies of its member states is central to much analysis. Does EU membership have a determining impact on a state's foreign policy and/or does it provide a vehicle through which countries can pursue essentially national foreign policies? It is possible to talk about patterns of external relations that shape the way in which membership impacts on foreign policy actions (Manners and Whitman, 2000, chapter 1). A first discernible pattern is seen in member states which have an extensive network of external relations outside the EU, which affects foreign policy behaviour and the way in which these states interact with the EU and other member states. The two principal examples of this pattern are the United Kingdom and France, although it is far too simplistic to argue that this represents the only, or most determining, factor in explaining their foreign policies. For these two states the EU is more often perceived as a constriction on national foreign policy or simply as a means to amplify national foreign policy. The United Kingdom and France are also often bracketed with Germany as three members of an informal EU foreign policy *directoire* between whom there needs to be agreement in areas of foreign policy if the EU is to have a coherent collective position. The agreement between this EU-3 driving EU policy towards Iran's uranium enrichment programme is contrasted with their disagreements over the war in Iraq and, consequently, the failure of the EU member states to agree a common position.

A second pattern apparent among the member states relates to those that have a less extensive network of foreign policy relations than the United Kingdom and France, and which tend to work through the EU. In this pattern the countries involved often seek to work with the EU or defer most foreign policy prerogatives to it. It might also be argued that the EU presents an opportunity within which to hide difficult decisions, or the absence of any preconceived policy. Within this pattern of external relations are two types of member states – smaller states without the capacity or desire to engage in extensive external relations, and states which for historical reasons wish to enmesh themselves in a European rather than national system of foreign policy-making. Examples of the smaller state can be found in Portugal or Ireland. Examples of the 'European' state include Italy and Belgium, both of which seek EU solutions to difficult historical and domestic problems. An important additional point here is whether the EU can provide a balance between 'Europeanist' or 'Atlanticist' foreign policy trends which satisfy internal tensions. As has been the case for Spain, Italy, Greece, and to a certain degree Denmark, this second pattern of foreign policy can be viewed as a solution to the tensions between pro-European (read 'EU' or 'anti-US') and pro-American (read 'NATO' or 'anti-EU') forces within these countries. Clearly in this pattern of external relations, the EU is more often perceived as an opportunity for foreign policy action (or perhaps as an excuse for national foreign policy inaction).

A third pattern can be observed in those states which may not have an extensive network of foreign policy relations, but tend to work through other international organizations such as the UN, NATO or OSCE. Within this pattern a member state may seek to act independently of the EU or in concert with the EU in order to assist their foreign policies. Thus not all member states feel constrained to participate solely in EU foreign policy activity, and may well seek to avoid doing so because of the implications for further integration. This pattern of international rather than European foreign policy relations may also be related to the Cold War experience of a country, in particular its status as neutral or non-aligned. Additionally, this pattern of activity might be directly related to a multilateral foreign policy orientation within a member state. Examples of the 'international' pattern may be found in the cases of Austria, Finland and Sweden, all of which are actively engaged participants in the OSCE and UN. Examples of the 'multilateral' pattern may be found in the case of Germany which, through its *Sowohl-als-auch* approach, pursues its foreign policy through the EU, NATO, OSCE and the UN. In this type of pattern, EU membership represents not so much an opportunity or a constriction, but merely another forum for its foreign policy (as traditionally conceived).

For the EU member states, participation in the Union represents a mixed blessing for their foreign policy activities. On the one hand, it forces them to confront the rigidity or flexibility in their foreign policy-making within a European framework; on the other hand, it tends to underline the paramount role which non-traditional foreign policy (external or economic relations) has come to be assume in the twenty-first century.

What is clear is that EU membership involves asking some difficult questions of foreign policy practices, or the absence of them. The challenges and responses this presents can be considered by looking at notions of the 're'-formulation of foreign policy in terms of 'retreat', 'remove', 'rescue' and 're-nationalize' (Manners and Whitman, 2000). The first response is the attempt by member states to 'remove' many of the activities of foreign policy-making from state capitals to Brussels. It is important to note that this 'Brusselization' of foreign policy does not mean the wholesale communitarization of foreign policy-making and implementation within the European Union. Rather, it has been argued, the Brusselization of foreign policy-making is facilitated by the 'steady enhancement of Brussels-based decision-making bodies' such as the Political and Security Committee of the Council of Ministers, although some might wish to include decision-making within the NATO Headquarters, also located in Brussels (Allen, 1998).

The second response goes further than simple 'removal' by attempting to 'rescue' the foreign policies of member states by using membership of the EU as 'the means by which Member States made their positions less rather than more vulnerable' (Allen, 1996). In broad terms this second strategy goes far beyond the strategy of simple removal by Europeanizing a member state's foreign policy in an attempt to improve or strengthen its relations. From this perspective, the European Union is often presented as an intergovernmental mechanism for rescuing and strengthening the state and its foreign policy. (Laffan, O'Donnel and Smith, 2000) However, as has been made clear by other commentators, the extent to which Europeanization can 'rescue' foreign policy from the pressures of the supra-national, the sub-national, and the transnational needs to be questioned (Spence, 1999).

Another response to any perceived 'retreat' of member states' foreign policies is more recent and, for some, reflects crisis moments for CFSP, particularly in light of the embarrassing failures (shared with the most powerful state in the world) in the Balkans and over the Iraq war. This response would appear to be the 're-nationalization' of foreign policy as a means of dealing with the 'failure to progress' through the reassertion of 'traditional national foreign policies' (Hill, 1998). It is important to note, as they do, that even though 're-nationalization' is 'freely discussed' and a 'drift apart' has been noticed by some, 'vested interest' in the still early stages of CFSP makes this argument questionable.

The contrasting benefits of 'removal', 'rescue' or 're-nationalization' in response to a perceived 'retreat' depend on the viewpoints of those engaged in the foreign policy processes under discussion. For post-colonial states such as France, the United Kingdom, the Netherlands, Belgium, Spain and Portugal the use of development policy and external relations provides a convenient conduit for a 'rescue' of these relationships in the guise of a less historically 'loaded' EU policy. For smaller member states such as Denmark, Ireland and Greece the EU can represent a rescue of their non-security policies, but the pressure to 'remove' security interests to Brussels is fiercely resisted. For the (post-) neutral states of Austria, Finland and Sweden, the removal of aspects of their Cold War security stance to Brussels provides a means of overcoming domestic resistance, as well as seeing the human rights and development policies of the EU as a means to rescue, or at least advance, these issues on a larger stage. For the newest members of the EU in Central and Eastern Europe EU membership is about 're-nationalizing' foreign policy after the constraints on foreign policy action that existed as the consequence of being Soviet satellite states.

Foreign policy-making in the European Union

The processes through which European states have attempted collectively to formulate foreign policy have been in existence for over thirty years. In 1970, the then EC member states launched European Political Cooperation (EPC), a loose framework for cooperation on foreign policy issues. EPC was a separate framework from the Community, based on intergovernmental principles (namely unanimous voting). The Commission was only associated with EPC, the European Parliament (EP) played a marginal advisory role, and the European Court of Justice could not review EPC decisions. The rotating Council presidency managed EPC, and, often with the help of the past and future presidencies (composing the troika), presented EPC positions to third countries. Defence and security policy was rigorously excluded from discussion.

Such a loose framework was inevitably considered inadequate once history 'accelerated' in the late 1980s. There were quite high internal and external expectations that the EC/EPC would assume a greater international role with the end of the Cold War. The Maastricht Treaty thus replaced EPC with the Common Foreign and Security Policy (CFSP). Since Maastricht, the CFSP has been further reformed, in the 1999 Amsterdam Treaty and 2003 Nice Treaty – and often these treaty adjustments have followed reforms launched by European Council declarations and change 'on the ground'. The EU has come a long way since EPC, but the underlying tension between national interests and collective spirit has continued to influence the institutional framework for foreign and security policy cooperation.

Since EPC, there has been a gradual coming together of the institutions in the European Community pillar and those of the CFSP. There has also been a trend towards 'Brusselization', or locating CFSP decision-makers in Brussels itself rather than national capitals (Allen, 1998: 50, 54). The CFSP is, however, 'voluntary': while there is a hardening expectation that member states will act constructively to further their common interests and pursue common policies, foreign policy remains an area of intergovernmental cooperation. It is *not* an area where the member states have ceded authority over policy-making to central, supranational institutions, though they have increasingly strengthened the institutions and procedures that have been created in this area. Observers have argued that over time the CFSP has been 'institutionalized' and 'legalized' (see Smith, 2001, 2004). This has not necessarily, however, resulted in more common policies and less pursuit of national foreign policy interests: slow change there has certainly been, but not such that the 'capabilities–expectations gap' can be said to have been filled, perhaps because expectations that the EU will be an effective, influential international actor tend to be quite high (Hill, 1993). In the Iraq crisis of early 2003, the divisions between the member states over foreign and security policy were laid bare for all the world to see, but this is just the most recent spectacular example of the extent to which the CFSP does not constrain member states. The failure of EU member states to agree on fundamental reforms to the UN Security Council in 2005 was another, less dramatic, case: neither France nor the United Kingdom will contemplate giving up their permanent seats in favour of an EU seat, and Italy assertively countered Germany's attempts to become a permanent Security Council member.

Intergovernmentalism remains the principle guiding decision-making: although the reforms to the formal procedures have chipped away at the unanimity rule, in practice unanimity is still required. At the top of the pyramid of CFSP decisions there is the 'common strategy'. The European Council agrees common strategies, by unanimity, in areas where the member states have interests in common. A common strategy sets out the EU's objectives, duration and means to be made available to carry it out.

The Council then implements common strategies by agreeing 'joint actions' and 'common positions'; in so doing, there are provisions for voting by qualified majority voting (QMV). The Council may also approve joint actions and common positions separately, not as measures implementing a common strategy. In this case, the Council votes by unanimity, although it may decide unanimously to implement a joint action by qualified majority voting. Joint actions address specific situations where operational action by the EU is considered to be required. Common positions define the EU's approach to a particular matter of geographical or thematic nature. QMV can also be used for decisions to appoint special representatives (for example, to contribute to the Middle East peace process). However, a member state can oppose the use of QMV for reasons of important national interests (the national interest brake), and QMV does not apply to decisions having military implications. In addition, one or more member states can abstain from voting on a decision, without blocking it (the constructive abstention clause). But they must accept that the decision commits the Union and agree not to take action likely to conflict with it. If the member states abstaining from a decision represent more than one-third of the weighted votes, then the decision cannot be adopted.

In practice, these decision-making instruments have proved to be rather too inflexible to be of much use in what can be quite fast-paced decision-making in response to developments and crises. For example, the European Council has agreed three common strategies, on Russia

(June 1999), Ukraine (December 1999) and the Mediterranean (June 2000). But there has been much frustration with the common strategies: they are bland statements of broad objectives, merely restating what the EU is already doing. In early 2000, Javier Solana suggested several ways to improve common strategies: they must add value to what the EU is already doing, and should clearly set priorities. The Council largely agreed, though common strategies have not been used again since.

Joint actions and common positions are used much more frequently – for example, to impose economic, diplomatic and other sanctions on third countries, or to set out the EU's stance on particular topics. They tend to incorporate issues and instruments spanning all three of the EU's pillars. Alongside these, there are numerous European Council declarations and conclusions, assorted 'strategy' documents (proposed by the Commission and agreed by the Council), and CFSP declarations.

One of the most important European Council declarations is the 'European Security Strategy', agreed by the December 2003 European Council. This document can be viewed as a response both to the spectacular intra-European disagreements over the Iraq crisis in early 2003, and also to pressure from the United States for the EU to engage more with its agenda of preemptive action to counter traditional and non-traditional security threats. The European Security Strategy declares that the EU has three core strategic objectives: addressing security threats (terrorism; proliferation of WMD; regional conflicts; state failure; and organized crime); enhancing security in the EU's neighbourhood, by, for example, building relations with the Mediterranean and Eastern European states; and creating an international order based on 'effective multilateralism', which entails upholding international law and strengthening the United Nations.

So what do the institutions and procedures outlined above actually produce? And, most importantly, how does this system combine with well-established national foreign policies? The record is patchy and defies generalization. The daily production of new practices creates a continuously shifting balance between initiatives decided in Brussels and independent actions conducted by member states. There are, however, two main trends that emerge from the recent (and not so recent) history of EU foreign policy. First, the shifting international economic agenda has created opportunities for member states to limit the strong supranational flavour of EU external economic relations, which has implications also for the EU's foreign relations in general. Second, CFSP does not yet have a global reach, despite declarations to the contrary. The next section discusses the EU's external economic relations; the following one, the patchwork of EU policies.

Foreign economic policy-making in the EU

External economic relations are without doubt the most supranational sector of EU foreign policy (broadly defined). The Rome Treaty was a 'revolutionary document' (Meunier and Nicolaidis, 1999: 479) which created a single supranational entity with broad authority over all aspects of trade relations between member states and the rest of the world. The idea of the Common Market was based on the establishment of the Common External Tariff and its complementary Common Commercial Policy, regulating economic relations with non-members. The sector continued to evolve in a supranational direction through the late 1960s and early 1970s, as the European Court of Justice (ECJ) issued a series of rulings which established extensive powers of the then EEC and expanded the role of the Commission. By 1975, the issue of external economic relations was codified, and its supranational character exemplified by the Commission's powers to negotiate international trade agreements on behalf of member states. However, the first pillar's overall monopoly on external economic relations has reached its limits, and member states are struggling to maintain control of the new economic agenda and of the areas not yet covered by EC competence.

From the 1970s, the EC was increasingly recognized as a legitimate actor in international economic negotiations, both by third countries and in global bodies (Smith, 2004: 84). The tight coordination achieved by member states maximized the EC's economic pull. Member states were thus able to present themselves as a single bloc in international negotiations with other actors such as the US, or to participate in GATT rounds by presenting a single voice, expressed by the Commission. The relevance of these practices convinced Member States to maintain a unified stance also when they would have had legal ground to go it alone, as in the case of mixed agreements. It became customary that this type of agreement, which mixes areas under the competence of both the EC and member states, was in fact negotiated by the Commission on behalf of the member states, as the latter were well-aware of the benefits of the 'politics of scale' (Ginsberg, 1989).

The existence of a European foreign economic policy has had an impact on national foreign economic policies too, including the case of non-member countries. A clear example of Europeanization of foreign economic policies occurred after the fall of communism, when Central and East European countries shaped their national foreign economic policy according to the standards that the EC, together with the WTO and IMF, was promoting (Smith, 2004: 85). The EU is trying to foster a similar change in its neighbourhood, though with varying degrees of success. Countries such as Turkey and Ukraine, which nourish expectations of eventual membership of the EU, have displayed a willingness to adopt the EU principles of foreign economic policy, despite the temptation to combine them with, for instance, privileged relations with the USA.

The supranational trend in EU external relations is not without an intergovernmental counterbalance, as the substance of international economic exchange has expanded from trade in goods to trade in services. The traditional competences of the EU have centred on trade in goods, but more and more international exchanges are in the area of services and involve issues of intellectual property, on which member states have been free to pursue their own national positions. The timing of the shift can be aligned with the evolution of the GATT (Krenzler and Pitschas, 2001: 292). Up to the start of the Uruguay Round, the EU competences were broadly in line with the subject matters regulated by the GATT/WTO, whereas the beginning of negotiations on the GATS (General Agreement on Trade in Services) and TRIPS (Trade-related Aspects of Intellectual Property Rights) agreements brought member state representatives back to the negotiating table. The ECJ contributed to this shift in 1994, stressing the limitations to EC competences regarding trade in services. The negotiations leading to the Nice Treaty and to the Constitutional Treaty saw an attempt to extend EC competence to cover these new sectors, which however was only partially successful. Trade in services and intellectual property issues do now fall within the remit of the EU competences, thus limiting the need for mixed agreements, but are ridden with exceptions and limitations. This is an issue that is bound to remain at the top of the EU reform agenda.

The balance between member states and the EU on foreign economic policy thus portrays a situation in which a consolidated supranational monopoly over traditional forms of trade sits alongside a difficult cohabitation between Brussels and national capitals on the most pressing international economic issues of current times.

A European foreign policy?

With the existence of this infrastructure for cooperation on foreign policy the question arises as to whether there is an identifiable collective foreign policy in existence? Measured in terms of the number of decisions taken within the EPC/CFSP framework there is an upwards trend. Michael E. Smith (2004: 50–1) carried out a long-term analysis of EPC actions, based on data by Ginsberg (1989) and CFSP common positions and joint actions (thus excluding declarations).

The geographical spread of what the EU does in its external relations and in CFSP represents, however, a call for caution against sweeping supranational arguments about the EU's 'actor-ness' in the world. Though increasing, the EU's reach is far from global. Its limitations are evident both in its external economic relations and in its CFSP actions.

The EU has established economic relations with most non-member countries, but the politically problematic cases remain largely outside the EU foreign policy framework. At first sight, the EU record shows an impressive number of trade agreements in the form of preferential trade agreements, cooperation agreements, association agreements, and so on. These arrangements bilaterally regulate economic relations between the EU and non members, with a varying degree of preferential treatment accorded. In the vast majority of cases they also include political clauses about democracy and human rights, which are an integral part to the agreements and constitute the basis for political dialogues and assessments of the political situations in third countries. Countries not covered by this tight network of agreements are, however, the most politically salient cases in contemporary international affairs. Afghanistan, Belarus, China, Iran, Iraq, to mention but a few, are among the countries with which the EU has established no, or only partial, arrangements in terms of trade and political dialogue. In other cases, most notably the USA, the EU has put into place a high-level dialogue, but economic relations remain regulated by WTO general rules.

The regional scope of CFSP is similarly interesting. The EU has developed a set of regional policies which cover its relations with all parts of the world. The regional process to which the EU has devoted by far the most attention in recent times has been the accession of Central and East European countries. The process was crucial in anchoring the political and economic transition of these countries and culminated in the 2004 accession of eight of them (Czech Republic, Estonia, Hungary, Latvia, Lithuania, Poland, Slovakia, Slovenia), together with Cyprus and Malta, to the EU, while Bulgaria and Romania have been set for a second wave of enlargement towards the east (in 2007 or 2008). The process has brought new neighbours into contact with the EU, and has raised the stakes of the game with several partners. The EU has attempted to frame relations with its new and extended neighbourhood by proposing a European Neighbourhood Policy (ENP) in May 2004. The policy groups together several countries and is gradually subsuming the Euro-Mediterranean Partnership, which served as the venue for relations with southern Mediterranean non-members since 1995. Moreover, the ENP is intended also to address eastern neighbours (Belarus, Moldova and Ukraine) and Caucasian countries (Armenia, Azerbaijan, Georgia).

The ENP is not without problems, however, and has been complemented by other initiatives. Relations with Russia have been strained by the parallel expansion of the EU and NATO. Russia has shown little enthusiasm for the ENP framework, and the two partners are still striving to define priorities and actions for a complex bilateral economic and political relationship. The Balkans also represent a challenge for the EU, which has devoted to it not only an *ad hoc* regional policy under the name of the Stabilization and Association Process, but also several of its actions in terms of security.

Other regional policies address the African, Caribbean and Pacific (ACP) countries, which roughly group together former member states' colonies in a common project of development. The framework, which was established in the early days of the EEC, has since evolved. The most recent development took place in Cotonou, in 2000, which introduced some more specific differentiation among the countries involved and placed emphasis on conditionality and good governance. Relations with Latin America, which also date back to the 1960s, also include several sub-groupings in an overall regional dimension. The framework for relations with the USA, while not regional in scope, is yet another flourishing chapter of EU external relations. EU foreign policy is more directly aimed at its immediate (and turbulent) neighbourhood, while other areas, including not only Asia but also the Middle East, do not really fall within the scope of the EU's action.

This brief overview of the main trends in EU foreign policy thus gives a flavour of how complex the system of European international relations is. There are elements that suggest an important reach of the EU global stance. Traditional forms of trade fall squarely into the domain of EU supranational competences. Cooperation on external relations and especially in the CFSP framework shows several positive achievements since the end of the Cold War. Moreover, the EU has displayed a capacity to frame relations with countries from all over the world, at least at the conceptual level. At the same time, the reach of EU foreign policy is still patchy and far from global. New issues on the international economic agenda remain a contested subject of cooperation, relations with the most politically salient countries remain outside the framework of EU external relations, and when the EU does act, it tends to focus on its immediate neighbourhood or on its own internal functioning.

The question thus remains of the relationship between EU foreign policy and national foreign policies. Given this fragmented picture of the EU's international stance, member states retain several open options to express their national preferences. The 'solidarity clause' on matters of foreign policy, which was introduced with the Maastricht Treaty, has increased the pressure on member states to present themselves to the world with a single voice. But, as seen above, on several issues member states have preferred not to cooperate, or have conducted a discussion without reaching a consensus or a decision.

Conclusion

Is foreign policy cooperation within the EU framework exceptional? What distinguishes the European system of international relations from international cooperation on foreign affairs in other organizational settings? European states are unexceptional in that they are subject to the same challenges as other states seeking to grapple with processes of globalization that have simultaneously widened the foreign policy agenda and increased the role of non-governmental actors within international politics. However, the international politics of European states is also distinctive because of the additional impact of the structures and processes of European integration. In particular there is the question of what impact European foreign policy cooperation processes have on the structural characteristics of member states' national foreign policies. The picture described above, which at times suggests a conflictual relationship between national foreign policies and EU foreign policy, is not sufficient to grasp the extent to which the existence of EU foreign policy cooperation has changed the way in which foreign policy is conducted in Europe. The initial interest in cooperation over foreign policy has affected the behaviour of national representatives not only within such a framework, but also outside it, and, in turn, fed back into European cooperation. There is also an additional debate in the literature that has focused on the significance of EU foreign policy and on its 'added value.' Does the foreign policy output of the EU represent yet another foreign policy stance in an already crowded international environment, or is it something new and comparatively different from traditional national foreign policies? And if the latter, how can we define it?

Foreign policy decisions are taken by individuals and there is the question of the extent to which working together collectively on foreign policy issues there are socialization processes at work. This involves three elements: 'a greater familiarity with each other's positions; greater appreciation of the value of acting together to handle external issues; and acceptance of the idea that it is useful and appropriate for Europe to act as a single unit in world politics' (Smith, 2004: 59). Since the early days of the EPC, cooperation among European partners has benefited from recreating the environment more typical of a club than of international negotiations. Often in a secluded setting, diplomats exchange views and worldviews. A willingness to formulate common policy thus arises, at least partly, out of the socialization and identity-shaping processes that take place within the institutional framework for foreign policy cooperation. This raises interesting questions for analysis, particularly the extent to which new member states are assimilated and acculturated into the collective foreign policy-making processes. There has been speculation as to what extent the 2004 enlargement could wreck the development of 'community' feeling and solidarity within the EU because there will simply be too many member states with too many diverse interests for socialization to work. Would consensus-building take more time in a larger, more diverse group – which could frustrate some member states and tempt them to cooperate or pursue policies outside? EU foreign policy institutions have never been so strong as to be able to counter the centrifugal forces of national interests all the time. From the limited evidence so far, it is difficult to draw long-lasting conclusions.

European states do, however, attempt to keep some aspects of their foreign policy separate or private from the EU context. There are also tacit understandings between the member states on a range of relationships and interests they see as 'special' and beyond the realm of European consultation (Ekengren and Sundelius, 1998). There appears to be a dynamic, or a form of hierarchy, to these special issues which we may describe as four 'rings of specialness' (Manners and Whitman 2000). At the core of these rings of specialness is the *domain privé* which encompasses issues deemed 'national security' as they are central to the sovereign discourses of certain member states. The three clearest-cut policies of this *domain privé* are to be found in the sovereign discourses surrounding security issues and policies. Illustrative of such a security issue is the retention of nuclear weapons by France and the United Kingdom.

Outside of this inner ring of specialness lies the second ring of bilateral relations which are considered, by the participants, to be of special significance and therefore outside of 'normal' EU foreign policy discussions. These bilateral relations come in two varieties: those of 'special relations' (a form of strong bilateralism) and those of 'semi-independence' (a form of weak bilateralism). In terms of special relations, it is fairly common to focus on those traditionally between the United Kingdom and the United States (primarily in the defence field), decreasingly between France and Germany (mainly in the integration field), and increasingly Germany's relations with Israel, Poland and the United States. In terms of semi-independence, we can look at the Benelux cooperation, the Nordic relations (particularly in terms of Nordic roles in the UN), the relations of energy-dependent member states with suppliers (such as Italy with the Maghreb), and several member states on immigration issues (including both sending states, such as Italy and Ireland, as well as receiving states such as France and the United Kingdom). Whilst this ring of specialness based on bilateral relations is more dynamic than the previous inner ring, it still involves member states exempting from discussion those relations which are acknowledged outside of foreign policy actions.

The third ring of specialness, lying outside of bilateral relations, can be characterized as European multilateralism and consists of a mixture of issues which are regional, normative, or post-colonial in nature and which may be found to be a 'special issue' in the language of one or more member state. The regional issues are those foreign policy relations which have been significant for historical or proximity reasons, such as those that France, Spain and Italy have with the other (non-EU) Mediterranean states, as well as relations between France/United Kingdom and the Middle Eastern states. The normative issues are those foreign policy issues of significance for reasons of justice and equality, such as the issue of human rights for the Netherlands and Austria, and the question of developing countries for the Netherlands, Sweden and Denmark. Covering similar relations, although not necessarily for similar reasons, are the post-colonial issues which are held to be special for the United Kingdom and France (especially in Africa), Belgium and the Netherlands, Spain and Portugal. In all three of these areas of European multilateralism, attempts are made, by differing member states, to attach special meaning or importance to the issues under consideration. As might be expected, this ring of specialness is far more dynamic that the two inner rings and it is in this area that we might see the most interesting debates over foreign policy competence as all three issues seem destined to become more 'Europeanized' in the near future.

There is an outer ring of specialness, which is by far the most dynamic of the four, consisting of special relations and issues which are in a transitional phase and are usually in the process of being communitarized in one form or another. Those foreign policy issues which are the most difficult to place clearly within any one particular policy-making sphere are often to be found in this ring. These policies are considered special by perhaps one or more member states, but increasingly are being drawn into the European sphere. Thus, relations between Poland, Lithuania and Ukraine serve as an illustration, as well as relations which have a significant economic content to them, and relations which were formerly international in nature, but are now more interregional in reality.

Most member states have relationships and interests they consider 'special' and worthy of bilateral, rather than multilateral or EU foreign policies. Consequently it is difficult to talk of one clear-cut boundary between those policies which are 'Europeanized' or conducted through the EU, and those policies which are retained or excluded from the EU because of their 'special' status. Consequently debate about the nature of the international politics of European states will continue. European states are inseparable from the international environment that impacts upon their foreign policies and through which they seek to have influence individually and collectively. The preservation of the means to conduct national foreign policies alongside the evolving collective EU foreign policy arrangements creates the need to understand developments within, across, and between European states if the role of these states in international politics is to be fully comprehended.

Chapter 4

The EU Dimension in European Politics

Tanja A. Börzel and Ulrich Sedelmeier

This volume is about developments in European politics, rather than about developments in the European Union (EU). Still it would be misleading to consider the two as entirely separate. As the chapters in this volume show, many aspects of contemporary politics in Europe are influenced by developments at the EU level. Analysts use the term 'Europeanization' to denote the impact of the EU on the domestic sphere. Europeanization entails more than just a unilateral adjustment of the member states to EU rules. National governments participate in the making of EU rules. Member states download EU rules, but they also upload national rules and practices to the EU level. Furthermore, governments (as well as societal actors) influence EU policies to reduce domestic adjustment costs and also to engineer adjustment pressures strategically if they favour domestic change. Europeanization is thus best understood as a two-way process. Yet it is also clear that certain governments or particular societal actors are not always successful at influencing EU policies in a way that reflects their preferences. Either by design or through lack of influence, EU policies can be inconvenient at the domestic level. EU rules thus form a distinctive input into national political processes, and domestic politics cannot be adequately understood without considering the EU dimension.

This chapter surveys how EU-level institutions, processes and policies have an impact upon policies, institutions and political processes of European states. We start by outlining the key insights of the Europeanization literature with regard to the dimensions and outcomes of the EU's influences in its member states, and the mechanism through which such an impact occurs. While the EU dimension has been a long-standing feature of politics in the Western European member states, a key development over recent years is the EU's pervasive impact on the newer member states of East Central Europe. We therefore review the key characteristics of pre- and post-accession Europeanization in the candidates and new member states. We conclude that while the EU's impact constitutes indeed a significant part of European politics, this influence is far from uniform. It varies considerably across issues and countries, as well as between Western and Eastern Europe. Even with regard to specific policies, where the EU's influence has been greatest, it has not generally resulted in convergence across Europe. Thus, we cannot fully understand developments in European politics without understanding the influence of the EU, but there is no straightforward *a priori* guide to take the EU's influence into account; it has to be established in a careful empirical analysis of mediating factors that prevail in particular countries and issue areas.

The domestic impact of Europe on the 'old' member states

With the ever growing transfer of competencies to the European Union, students of European politics have become increasingly interested in how European integration has transformed the domestic institutions, policies and political processes in European states. Here we summarize findings on the outcomes of domestic change and present two causal mechanisms to account for the variation observed. Much of this analysis is adapted from Börzel (2005).

Dimensions and outcomes of member state Europeanization

Recent research demonstrates that Europeanization takes place, and yet the scope of change is far from clear. The EU's impact on domestic policy change appears to have been far greater than its influence on domestic politics and institutions. However, in light of more than 40 years of continuously expanding EU policy-making power, the degree of policy change induced by Europe still seems to be rather limited. Member states first of all seek to absorb EU policies by incorporating European requirements into existing policies. Member states also try to accommodate EU policies by adapting existing domestic policies without changing core features (Börzel, 2005: 58–60).

The domestic impact of Europe is mostly felt with regard to policy standards and policy instruments, while more entrenched administrative structures, policy styles and policy paradigms have been less affected (Jordan and Liefferink, 2004). Thus, EU policies have resulted in tighter environmental and social standards in all member states. They have also led to the introduction of new policy instruments, which are incentive-based and encourage societal participation in policy-making or prescribe cross-policy integration. For instance, EU air pollution standards made Spain cut its total emissions of major pollutants, such as sulphur dioxide and nitrogen oxide, by half within a period of less than 15 years (Börzel, 2003: 85–95)!

The environmental laggards are not alone in changing their policies as a result of Europeanization. The EU's 'access to environmental information' directive aims to broaden public access to environmental information in order to increase transparency and openness, thereby encouraging citizens and groups to participate more actively in the protection of the environment. It requires member state authorities holding information on the environment to make such information available to any natural or legal person at his or her request without having to meet the legal standard for 'direct effect'. This approach completely contradicts the German administrative tradition based on the confidentiality of information in possession of public authorities. The principle of restricted access to records grants the public access to information only in justified cases. Consequently, the implementation of the EU policy – fiercely opposed by the German administration – resulted in the introduction of a new policy instrument alien to German environmental policy (Börzel, 2003: 123–31).

While Europe has influenced virtually all policy areas, core economic policies such as the internal market, which eliminated tariffs and non-tariff barriers to the free movement of products, services, workers and capital, or monetary policy have been more profoundly affected. Such 'first-pillar' issues are more susceptible to European influence because they are subject to supranational policy-making. By contrast, the EU's reach into foreign and security policy and the justice and home affairs of member states is limited by the intergovernmental institutions of the second and third pillar.

Within the first pillar, the domestic impact does not systematically vary between market-making and market-correcting policies. Market-correcting policies, such as environment or social regulation, are certainly more likely to require direct policy changes by prescribing specific policy standards and policy instruments (Knill and Lehmkuhl, 1999). However, market-making – the removal of national barriers to foreign competition – has an impact on member state policies that goes right to the core. EU policies do not stipulate templates for deregulation and privatization. Even so, the liberalization of national markets has changed the dominant policy paradigm in member states like France, Germany and Italy, where the state used to be responsible for the provision of public utilities (Héritier *et al.*, 2001). Finally, some member states have undergone deeper policy changes than others. While this may vary across issue areas, the Southern European latecomers to the EU (Spain, Greece, Portugal) have generally been more affected (Jordan and Liefferink, 2004; Falkner *et al.*, 2005; Liebert, 2003).

While Europeanization as policy change has been significant in many cases, the impact on domestic institutions is more ambiguous. Some analysts find that domestic institutions have largely withstood Europeanization (Anderson, 2002). Others contend that the EU has federalized and pluralized the member states (Schmidt, 1999). The findings appear less contradictory when focusing on meso-level institutions.

National administrations have responded to the demands of EU membership by changing administrative structures or creating new administrative units in order to coordinate national input into EU policy-making or for the implementation of EU policies. However, such institutional adaptation differs significantly across countries and is mediated by preexisting institutions (Hanf and Soetendorp, 1998; Kassim *et al.*, 2000). That said, at least one finding seems to be uncontested: Europeanization has strengthened the central executive at the expense of parliaments despite their increased involvement in EU policy-making (Maurer and Wessels, 2001; Kassim *et al.*, 2000).

The politics of the member states seem to be the least affected by Europeanization but have also been least explored in the literature (Featherstone and Radaelli, 2003). There are many studies on how domestic actors seek to channel their interests into the European policy-making process (Greenwood and Aspinwall, 1998). Less has been done on the Europeanization of electoral and party politics (Gabel, 2000). Since the EU offers fewer opportunities and more constraints to parties than to interest groups, its impact on party systems of the member states has been limited (Mair, 2000; Ladrech, 2005: 328–33).

Even interest groups, many of which have made Europe part of their lobbying strategies, remain firmly embedded in their national systems of interest intermediation (Greenwood and Aspinwall, 1998; Eising, 2003). We hardly know anything about how the emergence of a European structure of political and societal interest representation impacts on processes of political contestation and interest aggregation in the member states. Mair (2000), for example, argues that Europeanization contributes to de-politicization, indifference and political disengagement. By contrast, Imig and Tarrow (2000) contend that European policy-making causes an increasing politicization at the domestic level.

Has Europeanization made the member states more similar? The EU does not prescribe a model to which member states have to adjust.

And, in the absence of a uniform EU policy model, we should not expect national policies to converge. Indeed, analysts have found little evidence for a general convergence of domestic institutions, policies and processes (Cowles and Risse, 2001; Featherstone and Radaelli, 2003). Often, EU policies constrain rather than bind member states in their policy choices (Featherstone, 1998). For example, EU directives are only framework legislation. As such, they grant member states the leeway to fit EU policies into their national arrangements. Hence, even when the EU creates common adjustment pressures, their effect is filtered through existing domestic institutions, policies and interests.

The mechanisms of member state Europeanization

How can we account for variations in the EU's impact across issues and countries? Most empirical studies find that a precondition for the EU's domestic impact is some incompatibility between European and domestic policies, processes and institutions. The 'goodness of fit' or congruence between the European and the domestic level determines whether we should expect domestic change in response to European policies, processes and institutions. Countries need to change only if European policies, institutions or processes differ significantly from those found at the domestic level.

Börzel (2005) identifies two types of incongruence. First, European policies might cause tension between European rules and regulations on the one hand, and domestic policies on the other. European policies can challenge national policy goals, regulatory standards, the instruments used to achieve policy goals, or the underlying approach to solving problems. Second, Europe can challenge domestic rules and procedures directly, or it can challenge the collective understandings attached to them. The less institutional congruence between the EU and domestic ways of doing things, the more requirements for institutional change and adaptation exist.

A misfit between European and national policy is the most common type of tension. For example, EU environmental directives caused problems in some southern member states with lower levels of environmental protection, but in particular areas – such as relating to drinking-water quality – also in Germany, where protection levels are generally higher. Member state resistance to adapting domestic policies usually violates European legal requirements. Even so, an incongruence between European and domestic policies, processes and institutions does not suffice to account for domestic change.

Whether misfit leads to pressure for domestic adaptation or not depends on the active intervention of actors, be it European or domestic. The European Commission can create adaptive pressure from above by opening infringement proceedings against a member state. Likewise, domestic actors can use the tension between European and national policy to push for changes from below. Finally, national governments can construct pressure for adaptation strategically by uploading their preferences unto the European level in order to introduce domestic reforms that have been difficult to implement because of opposition from domestic actors.

The different causal mechanisms for domestic change can be grouped under two alternative schools of institutionalism, one rationalist and the other sociological. Rationalist institutionalism describes the domestic impact of the EU as a process of redistributing resources among domestic actors and point to formal institutions as the main factors impeding and facilitating domestic transformations in response to European pressures. From this perspective, Europe is an emerging opportunity structure that offers some actors additional legal and political resources to exert influence and that constrains others from pursuing their goals. Such changes in opportunities and constraints empower some domestic actors over others. Those empowered will use the tension between European and domestic decisions, processes, and institutions to create pressure for domestic adaptation. The 'differential empowerment' may alter domestic policies and political processes as well as changing domestic institutions. For example, EU gender equality directives provided French and British women with new opportunities to push through reforms promoting equal pay and equal treatment at work (Caporaso and Jupille, 2001). Likewise, a coalition of German government and business actors used the EU's transport policy to push through a domestic market liberalization package that went far beyond European requirements (Héritier *et al.*, 2001).

Yet change is not automatic even when European developments modify domestic opportunity structures. Two institutional factors influence the capacity of domestic actors to exploit new opportunities or to avoid constraints. First, institutions or procedures providing for multiple veto points can effectively inhibit domestic adaptation (Haverland, 2000). The more power is dispersed across the political system and the more actors have a say in political decision-making, the more difficult it is to foster a domestic coalition capable of introducing reforms in response to European pressure. The number of veto points multiplies in federal member states where regions have the power to block legal and administrative change. In Germany, for example, regional governments (Länder) were able to withstand pressure in the case of the access to environmental information directive for more than five years. Coalition governments or corporatist structures for interest intermediation – like those found in Scandinavian member states – can also significantly slow down domestic adaptation.

Second, domestic actors are not able to exploit European opportunities if they lack the necessary capacity. Formal institutions can provide actors with the resources to benefit from European political opportunities and thus promote domestic adaptation. For example, the Equal Opportunities Commission in the UK – a public agency – helped women's organizations to use EU equal pay and equal treatment directives in furthering gender equality. In the absence of such a formal institution, French women were not able to overcome domestic resistance by (male-dominated) trade unions to implement EU policies (Caporaso and Jupille, 2001).

Sociological institutionalist approaches, by contrast, describe the domestic impact of the EU as a process of socialization and as an internalization of norms. Such causal mechanisms build on the role of political actors and on the facilitating role of informal institutions. They conceive of the tension between the European and national levels primarily in terms of the incompatibilities of norms and meaning between the European Union and the member states. Again, two factors mediate the degree to which misfit leads to processes of socialization by which actors internalize new norms and develop new identities: norm entrepreneurs and cultural understandings.

First, norm entrepreneurs mobilize at the domestic level to persuade actors to redefine their interests and identities in the light of new norms and rules by engaging them in processes of social learning. For example, in the case of the single currency, central bankers and like-minded national policymakers successfully advocated a monetarist approach that produced dramatic changes in domestic monetary policy, even in countries like Italy and Greece which had to undergo painful adaptation (Dyson and Featherstone, 1999).

Second, common cultural understandings can also influence the ways in which domestic actors respond to pressures for Europeanization. For example, it has been argued that Germany has a consensus-oriented, cooperative decision-making culture, which helps to overcome veto points by making it inappropriate to use them. Moreover, a consensus-oriented culture allows for the sharing of adaptive costs, which facilitates the accommodation of pressure for adaptation. Rather than shifting adaptive costs onto a social or political minority, the winners of domestic change compensate the losers (Héritier *et al.*, 2001). Another example, is the litigious culture in Germany that encourages its citizens to appeal to national courts for the deficient application of Community Law, while such a culture is absent in France where litigation is much lower (Conant, 2001).

The two schools of institutionalism appear well-suited to account for the differential impact of Europe on the domestic policies, political institutions, and political processes of the member states. So far, however, the Europeanization literature is inconclusive concerning which of the two models carries more causal weight. The next section examines the experience of the newer member states of Central and Eastern Europe.

The EU's influence on new members and candidate countries

There are some main differences in the Europeanization of the 'old' member states and the Central and Eastern European countries (CEECs) that joined in 2004. First, the CEECs have followed different historical trajectories than the advanced Western European democracies, in particular concerning their recent transition from communism. This should have significant implications both for the scope and the mechanisms of domestic impact. Second, while Europeanization has taken place in the context of EU membership for the old member states, the new members were exposed to adjustment pressures as candidate countries well before accession. Europeanization is a two-way process for existing member states insofar as they are involved in shaping EU rules. By contrast, candidate countries experience Europeanization as a process of unilateral adjustment underpinned by the EU's accession conditionality.

To be sure, since the CEECs made a choice to pursue EU membership, the process was not simply one of coercion or external imposition. In part, the pursuit of EU membership was a strategy by CEEC governments to induce and anchor domestic change. However, in contrast to earlier enlargements, the EU insisted on a strict, early, and comprehensive alignment of the CEECs with the *acquis communautaire* (the existing body of EU legislation, institutions and procedures) prior to accession. Successful alignment with the *acquis* was viewed as proof that the new members would be able to apply and enforce EU legislation after accession. Therefore, progress towards accession was tightly linked to progress with adopting the *acquis*. Moreover, the CEEC governments had to accept the EU's *acquis* in its entirety, without any scope to scrutinize whether each and every EU rule was appropriate in their specific socio-economic context. In the terminology of the literature on policy transfer, the Europeanization of EU candidate countries is thus not entirely voluntary but also includes elements of coercive transfer.

Of course, all EU latecomers in previous enlargement rounds were confronted with the need to adopt rules in the making of which they had not participated. However, in the eastern enlargement the adaptive pressure was much greater. Policy developments in the EU, such as the completion the internal market or the Schengen Agreement, have led to a massive increase in the *acquis communautaire*. Moreover, the specific post-communist socio-economic context created a particularly onerous starting situation. Experience with the operation of regulatory regimes of a market economy was completely lacking. Policy change and adjustments were required in virtually all areas of the *acquis*; and the very domestic institutions and administrative structures necessary for the application of EU policies had to be created, often from scratch. Finally, the EU demanded not only pre-accession adjustment in areas of the *acquis*, but also applied a far-reaching political conditionality. This conditionality included many areas in which EU institutions have no competences *vis-à-vis* the member states, such as minority rights, external relations with neighbouring countries, anti-corruption policies or the conditions of orphanages. Thus, the adjustment pressures for the CEECs were both much more intense and more extensive than in any previous enlargement.

The specific nature of Europeanization in candidate countries accounts for differences with regard to the dimensions, outcomes and mechanisms of the process. Given the breadth and scope of the EU agenda, the speed with which the CEECs had to adjust to Europe, and their openness to EU influence in the light of the post-communist transition process we would expect the domestic impact of the EU to be potentially more pervasive and profound. In the policy dimension, the EU requires more far-reaching adjustments in a broader range of issue areas. In the politics and polity dimensions, it directly affects much more fundamental principles of the political system. The Europeanization mechanisms in candidate countries are somewhat different, but at the same time, the general analytical framework to study Europeanization in the member states also works well.

Dimensions and outcomes of candidate Europeanization

In view of these particular characteristics of Europeanization of the new member states, many studies have expected to find a deeper domestic impact and stronger convergence with particular EU policy models than in the old member states (Grabbe, 2003: 306–8; Hughes *et al.*, 2004). Yet, their results show a mixed picture that does not completely confirm the expectations. Most scholars agree that 'enlargement is the main driving force and the main condition of effective EU rule export in this region' (Schimmelfennig and Sedelmeier, 2005a: 221). EU conditionality and the membership perspective provided a huge incentive for CEECs to adjust to Europe and to download EU policies in the various sectors. Moreover, EU rules and norms had to be adopted in a rather inflexible way with regard to the single market and the various sectoral policies. In this sense then, Europeanization strongly resembles a one-way street and top-down process.

At the same time, the Europeanization of CEECs confirms some of the findings of the literature on the experience of older member states. First, the EU's impact has been generally much stronger on policies, than on polities and politics. In the new members, this feature has been particularly pronounced. The EU's influence varied considerably across two main dimensions of Europeanization: the polity and politics dimension on the one hand and the policy dimension on the other. In the policy dimension, the EU's impact was pervasive. Before the EU started to spell out clearly its requirements from the mid-1990s, the CEECs adopted some EU rules, but such rule transfer was very patchy and selective. For example, the Czech Republic started to adopt EU-conform clean air policies as a result of transnational cooperation in the context of the 'Environment for Europe' process but most other CEECs did not (Andonova, 2003). However, once the EU made its accession requirements clear – starting in 1995 with a Commission White Paper on the alignment with the internal market – the adoption of EU rules increased strongly.

A second strong increase in the adoption of EU rules set in after the EU started accession negotiations with the CEECs. As the goal of accession came closer, the CEECs now also adopted EU rules in those policy areas where they had postponed alignment in view of the high costs. For example, in the area of environmental policy, Poland abandoned the clean-air policies introduced earlier, which had used US-style economic incentives, in order to implement EU-conform command and control instruments (Andonova, 2003).

In contrast to the EU's strong influence on policies, its impact in the polity and politics dimension was more varied. The EU's political conditionality exerted much more direct pressures on the institutions and principles of liberal democracy than in the member states. However, the influence of the EU was – on the whole – rather limited. In the democratic frontrunners, such as Hungary, Poland or the Czech Republic, the adjustment pressures emanating from the EU's conditions with regard to the principles of democracy, human rights, or minorities were too low to generate domestic change. In other democratic governments, such as in Latvia or Estonia, the EU's influence on minority rights was more discernible (Kelley, 2004). By contrast, for authoritarian or strongly nationalist governments – such as the Mečiar government in Slovakia, Croatia under Tuđman, or Milošević in Serbia – the adjustment costs were prohibitively high, as they threatened to undermine the regime's power base.

As long as such governments stayed in office, the EU's political conditionality thus remained largely ineffective. However, once such governments were replaced with more moderate and democratic forces, the EU did have an impact, and on current evidence, was able to lock-in democratic changes even if nationalist parties subsequently returned to power (Schimmelfennig, 2005; Vachudova, 2005). The Croatian Democratic Union (HDZ) under Ivo Sanader is an example of such a party that, first, moderated its programme to return to power, and then found that the progress towards EU accession under the previous government had created disincentives for departing from the path of complying with the EU's conditionality.

Even if the EU's impact in the polity dimension is uneven, the EU has been credited with a positive influence on democracy and anchoring fragile democracies and strengthening minority rights in the candidate countries (Pridham, 2005; Vachudova, 2005) – in stark contrast to the limited impact of EU institutions on member states in this area. The EU has also encouraged the development of a non-politicized civil service (Meyer-Sahling, 2004) and led to some degree of decentralization and regionalization, at least in comparison with the Communist legacy (Jacoby, 2004).

Yet at the same time, commentators have observed the EU's more ambiguous effects on undermining democratic processes – effects which are comparable to developments in the old member states. These effects include a stronger role for the executive to the detriment of parliamentary oversight and societal pressures, or territorial centralization (Goetz, 2005: 272). In the post-communist context, such detrimental effects might be exacerbated; for example, the EU 'could have a debilitating effect, arresting party developments by excluding from political competition those substantive, grass-roots, ideological policy conflicts around which western European party systems have evolved' (Innes, 2002: 101–2).

In sum, most studies on Europeanization in the CEECs suggest a differential impact of the EU. Variation is evident not only across countries and between the polity and policy dimensions. There has been little institutional convergence around a single European model of governance within the policy dimension either, where divergent endogenous interests prevailed over external pressures at institutional convergence (Goetz, 2005; Grabbe, 2003). Europeanization of the CEECs thus throws up some peculiarities with regard to the strong pressures for adaptation emanating from the EU, reinforced by conditionality. But the general picture emerging from the studies broadly confirms the existing literature on Europeanization, particularly the emphasis on the differential impact of Europe.

Europeanization mechanisms in candidate countries

The key elements of the analytical framework to study Europeanization in member states – goodness of fit and mediating factors identified by rationalist and sociological institutionalisms – also work well to explain the EU's influence in the new members. The particular post-socialist context of the new members means that the 'goodness of fit' of existing domestic policies with EU rules does not always provide a reliable yardstick for the extent of adjustment pressures that the CEECs experienced. While the misfit might have been considerable in most areas of market-making and regulation, the goal that governments pursued with socio-economic transformation was precisely to generate far-reaching domestic changes.

Thus, we have to consider that in many cases in which the CEECs adopted EU rules prior to accession, such adjustment was not the result of EU influence, but of a process that could be described as domestic lesson-drawing (Schimmelfennig and Sedelmeier, 2005c: 20–5). Policy failure and domestic dissatisfaction with the status quo, rather than external pressure, induced governments to look abroad for policies and rules that effectively solve similar problems elsewhere and are transferable into the domestic context. Significantly, in such cases CEEC governments rarely simply copied EU rules, but rather used various forms of emulation to adapt them to the national context (Jacoby, 2004). Such processes of emulation were most obvious in policy areas in which the EU did not demand adjustment, but certain CEECs none the less adopted rules from particular member states. An example is health care reform, in which CEEC elites drew on western European templates, yet the EU played a minor role in prompting reform (Jacoby, 2004: 45–64).

Other cases in which CEECs adopted particular EU rules in the early 1990s, long before the EU explicitly spelled out its accession conditionality, were nevertheless influenced by the EU. The CEECs engaged in anticipatory adaptation by choosing EU rules rather than rules from elsewhere in anticipation of having to adopt these rules sooner or later anyway as part of their objective to achieve membership (Haggard *et al.*, 1993). In such cases, the EU did not trigger the changes as such, but passively influenced the direction of such change (Vachudova, 2005). Yet even in cases in which domestic politics favoured a change from the status quo, a large misfit with EU rules usually meant that adjustment pressures were considerable.

In principle, the mechanisms for the EU's impact that rationalist and sociological institutionalist approaches emphasize in the case of member states also apply for candidate Europeanization. However, in this context, both the nature of the mediating factors and their causal relevance is distinctive.

As in the member states, rationalist institutionalism emphasizes that the EU changes the incentive structure and the domestic distribution of power. The key causal mechanism of Europeanization is the EU's accession conditionality. The EU provides the incentive of membership as a conditional reward for adopting and complying with its rules. Governments calculate whether the benefits of membership outweigh the domestic costs that arise from adopting the EU's rules. A number of specific factors then influence the calculation of costs and benefites, or in other words, impede or facilitate domestic transformation (Schimmelfennig and Sedelmeier, 2005a: 10–17).

An important factor was the clarity of the EU's conditionality. If the candidates were unsure whether certain rules are part of the EU's conditionality and what exactly they had to do if they chose to adopt them, it was unlikely that such rules would be (correctly) adopted (Grabbe, 2003: 317–23). For a long time, for example, the CEECs were unsure whether the rules of Schengen – which moreover continued to evolve considerably through the 1990s – were a precondition for EU membership. More generally, the EU attempted in the mid-1990s for the first time to provide an indicative inventory of the *acquis*. The Commission's regular monitoring reports from 1998 also served the purpose of clarifying the requirements.

Furthermore, it was unlikely that candidates would adopt EU rules if they did not believe that they would receive the reward of membership when (and only when!) they comply with the conditions. For example, the EU has to be able to verify whether its conditions have been met. In stark contrast to previous enlargements or the Commission's practice *vis-à-vis* full members, the EU has engaged in rather intrusive monitoring in the CEECs to prevent the candidates from exploiting information asymmetries. Another element of a credible conditionality is that the EU applies its conditionality consistently. Political favouritism of particular candidates decreases the incentives to comply both in the country in question and in other candidates, which cannot be sure that membership is awarded on the basis of merit. Mixed signals from different EU actors about the importance of specific rules – social policy is one example – is another disincentive to adopt such rules. The open disagreement among the member states in the run-up to the start of accession negotiations with Turkey are a key example how a lack of internal consensus can damage the credibility of conditionality, and is likely to be a disincentive for the Turkish government to undertake costly domestic reforms demanded by the EU. By contrast, for the eastern enlargement, the start of accession negotiations was a key factor increasing the credibility of conditionality, which increased the CEECs' compliance with EU conditions.

Finally, just as in the case of member states, domestic veto players who incur costs through complying with EU conditionality are a key impeding factor. With regard to the EU's political conditionality, such costs arise directly for individuals or parties in power; they are particularly high in states with authoritarian or strongly nationalist leadership. In other policy areas, veto players were not usually a decisive obstacle, despite potentially high costs. Societal interest organisations are generally weak in the CEECs and the strong domestic consensus in favour of EU membership allowed governments to subordinate those interests negatively affected.

In contrast to a rational calculation of costs and benefits made in response to the incentives created by the EU, sociological institutionalist approaches emphasize social learning as a key causal mechanism for the Europeanization of candidate countries (Schimmelfennig and Sedelmeier, 2005a: 18–20). In general, the positive identification of candidate countries' governments and societies with the EU was a factor facilitating the impact of the EU, as the EU was identified with a return to Europe after communism. Some cross-national variations notwithstanding, the EU generally enjoyed high legitimacy and positive connotations. Such identification with the EU often generated support for EU rules independently from the material benefits of membership and sometimes precisely prevented such concrete cost/benefit calculations.

By contrast, problems with the legitimacy of the EU's rules and conditions were detrimental to Europeanization through social learning. A basic legitimacy problem was that the candidates had no say in the creation of these rules that they were expected to adopt. Moreover, the EU asked the CEECs to comply with rules for which EU institutions have no powers to scrutinize full members, and compliance is problematic in some members, as with regard to minority rights or the situation of the Roma.

Just as in research on the Europeanization of member states, rationalist and sociological institutionalism thus identifies analytically distinct, partly competing, partly complementary, mechanisms and inhibiting or facilitating factors. However, in strong contrast to research on the old member states, which does not identify a dominant model for Europeanization, analyses of the candidates suggests that the patterns of EU influence can be explained predominantly in rationalist terms. A focus on cost-benefit calculations and veto players accounts well for variation in the effectiveness of the EU's influence between the polity dimension and the policy dimension. The prohibitively high adjustment costs of the EU's political conditions for authoritarian or strongly nationalist governments limited the EU's influence, while high costs of policy adaptation in particular areas were discounted against the aggregate benefits of membership by countries with a clear accession perspective. Rationalist institutionalism also explains well the temporal variations in the patterns of Europeanization in the policy dimension: from the mid-1990s, the clarity of the EU's conditions increased, and the start of accession negotiations increased the credibility of conditionality.

An analysis of the mechanisms of Europeanization in the new member states also has implications for the sustainability of the EU's impact after accession. Conditionality appears a highly effective mechanism of Europeanization in non-member states. However, it remains to be seen whether it also provides for sustainable compliance with EU rules once membership has been achieved. Post-accession compliance is much less of a problem for rules that were transferred to the CEECs as the result of social learning, since domestic actors have become persuaded of their legitimacy and appropriateness. By contrast, if EU conditionality was the underlying mechanisms, the changing incentive structure after accession matters. Such rules are more likely to remain contested domestically, and once the reward of membership is no longer conditional, inhibiting factors such as veto players and high adjustment costs might again become causally relevant.

The challenge of sustained compliance appears particularly salient, since in many areas of the *acquis*, the EU could only assess formal implementation (legal transposition), but not its proper application and enforcement, which often lagged behind. A key question is then whether the EU's compliance system can compensate for the lack of conditional incentives of the pre-accession period. One response of the EU was to create special safeguards that allow suspending some of the benefits of the internal market during the first three years of membership. Similarly, in the political realm, the Amsterdam Treaty introduced the possibility to suspend membership in response to 'serious and persistent breaches' of democratic principles. However, in many areas of the political conditionality that was applied during pre-accession, such as minority rights, EU institutions do not have any power *vis-à-vis* full members.

Thus, while the institutional and policy effects on the CEECs have been immediate and fast because of accession conditionality, the long-term outcome might be much more shallow and also reversible (Goetz, 2005: 262). Why should Eastern European countries lock in specific institutional arrangements given their generally weak state capacity and the enormous uncertainty surrounding enlargement (Grabbe, 2003: 318–23)? The strong and top-down accession conditionality could well have the unanticipated effect of hindering social learning and policy emulation.

Conclusion

Many key areas of European politics cannot be understood fully without taking account of the EU. The influence of the EU on domestic politics is particularly important in the policy dimension, especially in those areas in which the EU has strong policy-making powers. At the same time, the influence of the EU is far from uniform across countries, domestic institutions, and policy areas. In the new member states, which experienced Europeanization while still outside the EU, through its accession conditionality, the EU's policy impact has been stronger and less differential. In the polity dimension, the EU's impact has been generally less significant, but in a few countries, it had a substantial impact, for example on minority policies, especially in comparison to the older member states, even if it remains to be seen how durable domestic change remains after accession. While the EU has generated a certain extent of convergence of Central Europe with the western half of the continent, the general finding of the Europeanization literature is that the EU's impact on developments in European politics is highly differential, rather than inducing convergence on European models.

Furthermore, the convergence we do observe does not necessarily originate at the European level (Schneider, 2001; Wallace, 2000). The EU is not always the driving force, but complements and may enhance global, but also national trends that were already affecting the nation-states. Globalization in particular appears to be the major rival for Europeanization in driving domestic change. While some studies have attempted to separate effects of Europeanization and globalization (Verdier and Breen, 2001), it is often difficult to isolate the net effect of Europe and to disentangle it from other sources of domestic change not only at the global, but also at the national and local level.

While the impact of the EU is thus generally differential across countries and issues, and is certainly not the only source of externally induced domestic changes, it is a crucial dimension of contemporary European politics. The implication for students of European politics is that in order to understand developments in a given area of analysis, we need to be clear about the extent of adjustment pressures emanating from the EU and the absence or presence of mediating factors that facilitate or obstruct the translation of these pressures into domestic change.

PART II

Government and the Political Process

Chapter 5

Power at the Centre: The Organization of Democratic Systems

Klaus H. Goetz

Readers seeking to understand the development of the core institutions in contemporary European state may understandably feel confused. When it comes to analysing the trajectories of executive–legislative relations, governments and core executives, academic assessments differ sharply. At one end of the spectrum, scholars point to the demise of the nation-state, in the wake of which the traditional power centres have been progressively eroded. What we observe is a process whereby, as Rod Rhodes (2003: 69) has argued with specific reference to the UK, the 'state has been hollowed out from above (e.g., by international interdependence), from below (by marketization and networks) and sideways (by agencies)'. This haemorrhaging of powers and capacity takes different forms, including in particular, 'a loss of capacity at the heart of the state – in the core executive' (Saward, 1997: 17), which affects central government and the administration; and 'de-parliamentarization' as national parliaments cede many of their legislative functions and traditional rights to hold the executive to account. Somewhat less gloomy accounts note the growing diffusion rather than the simple disappearance of the erstwhile powers of the centre. Thus, public policy-making increasingly takes place in complex networks of supranational, national and subnational actors, who may be public, semi-public or private. The contemporary state is, accordingly, characterized by 'governance' rather than 'government', as the former centres of power are supplemented – and, in some cases, supplanted – by a host of other participants in the policy process, such as international bodies, non-governmental organizations or independent agencies.

At first sight, both of these scenarios contrast sharply with another popular argument, according to which Europe has been witnessing a growing concentration of powers. On the basis of a comparative exercise involving a range of European countries, Poguntke and Webb (2005) have recently suggested that there is 'ample evidence' (*ibid.*: 20) of a presidentialization of democratic politics:

> more power resources and autonomy for leaders mean that their capacity to act has been enhanced. They find it easier now to achieve desired policy decisions, to impose their will on collective actors like cabinets or parties ... presidentialized chief executives (and party leaders) increasingly govern past their parties and, equally important, past the most important social forces which support them. (*Ibid.*: 22)

Even if the discussion of European trends is limited to current members of the European Union ('the EU-25'), plus Bulgaria, Romania, Norway and Switzerland, manifest differences amongst these 29 countries limit the scope for any assessment of pan-European developments. Whilst the EU comprises the oldest nation-states, its members also include several states – including the Baltic countries, the Czech Republic, Slovakia and Slovenia – which have only recently (re-)gained their independent statehood and, in some cases, are still engaged in a process of nation-building. Parts of Europe may, indeed, be witnessing the decline of the nation-state, but others offer evidence of vigorous contemporary efforts at its creation or revival. It also needs to be noted that key concepts and approaches in the study of comparative European politics have been shaped by the Western European experience: their extension to Southern and, more recently, Central and Eastern Europe, is not unproblematic. Moreover, regardless of which conceptual and theoretical lenses are employed, they inevitably privilege certain insights over others. In short, part of the reason for the diverging and sometimes contradictory empirical assessments noted at the outset lies in unintentional 'selection bias'.

But there is also a more fundamental reason why the evolution of power at the centre is difficult to capture: developments across the five key relationships that underpin the organization of central power are less closely linked than is often assumed. These key relationships include those

- between the executive and the legislature, defining the type of representative democracy;
- between governing parties and government, defining the party–government nexus;
- between the prime minister, cabinet and cabinet ministers, defining the type of government;

- amongst ministries and between the latter and the centre of government, defining the type of core executive; and
- between the political and administrative parts of the executive, defining the politics–administration nexus.

Political parties, and especially the governing parties, make their presence felt in all five of the key relationships. Indeed, it is because of their omnipresence at the centre that parties play a crucial role in integrating the core state institutions. One of the chief criticisms levelled against the classical separation of power theory is, accordingly, that it neglects the role of political parties in modern democracies and has little to contribute to our understanding of how they really work. Thus, as far as executive–legislative relations are concerned, 'the debate suffers from an overdose of Montesquieu', as it 'treats "the" government and "the" parliament as two bodies that only interact as such' (Andeweg, 2003: 52).

However, omnipresence does not equal omnipotence. As will be argued below, although parties help to join power at the centre, they do not streamline democratic states in their image, despite occasional references in the literature to the democratic 'party state'. In part, such integration is limited by the prevalence of multi-party coalition government in Europe; regular changes of government; and the restraints imposed by opposition parties. More importantly, each of the key relationships follows to some extent its own logic, which cannot be subjugated to party interests. For example, whilst governing parties mitigate the institutional separation between government and parliament, executive-legislative relations are inevitably shaped by varying degrees of inter-institutional conflict, which cannot be reduced to a government–opposition dynamic. Similarly, whilst recent analyses of the relationships between executive politicians and senior officials provide evidence of growing political control over the 'commanding heights' of the administration (Page and Wright, 1999: 275), this trend does not equal straightforward partisanship by senior officials but rather a 'personalization of political trust' (*ibid.*: 277).

The following discussion examines the trajectories of power at the centre along the five dimensions introduced above. It underlines the irresolvable tensions between executives and legislatures; governing parties and governments; chief executives, ministers and the cabinet; ministries and the centre of government; and politicians and officials. Comparative analysis reveals that European countries continue to vary significantly in the manner by which they seek to manage these tensions. It also shows that even where strong leadership figures have made determined efforts at integrating the institutions at the centre so as to strengthen their own hold over the levers of power, close integration is the exception rather than the norm and is reliant on contingent factors that are largely beyond political control.

Representative democracy: two false dawns of presidentialism

The formal relationship between the legislature and the executive is the chief criterion for distinguishing different types of representative democracy. Definitions vary, but it is generally accepted that in presidential systems, the popularly elected president and his/her government are not dependent on the approval of a parliamentary majority. By contrast, in parliamentary systems, the government relies on the continued support of the governing parties in parliament (or, in the case of minority governments, at least a tacit approval by the majority of deputies), although parliament need not necessarily be formally involved in appointing the prime minister and government. A further variant, semi-presidentialism, was introduced by Maurice Duverger (1980) to characterize the French polity. Contemporary usage tends to define semi-presidential systems as 'the situation where a popularly elected fixed-term president exists alongside a prime minister and cabinet who are responsible to parliament' (Elgie, 1999: 13).

As set out in Table 5.1, only one of countries considered here – Cyprus – meets the formal criteria of a presidential system; all others are either semi-presidential or parliamentary democracies. The distinction between semi-presidentialism and parliamentarism, however, tells us little about the relative strength of the executive and parliament in the political process. For example, in semi-presidential France, parliament has long been regarded as subservient to a dominant executive, notably if the President's party and its allies also enjoy a majority in parliament, thus avoiding potentially tense 'cohabitation' between the President and a government led by a Prime Minister from a rival political party (Elgie, 2001). By contrast, Polish semi-presidentialism, which has been modelled on the French constitution, has gone hand-in-hand with an assertive legislature that pursues its own agenda and routinely amends government-sponsored bills (Goetz and Zubek, 2005). Similarly, whilst under the UK's parliamentary system, the government exercises a tight grip over parliament's legislative business, in Germany both the governing parties and, to a lesser extent, the opposition parties share in the process of legislative agenda-setting and the powers of the government to protect its legislation against amendments are very limited.

It should be clear from these examples that the presence of a directly elected head of state does not, in itself, spell parliamentary weakness. Where a directly elected presidency does not possess significant executive powers, as is the case in most semi-presidential systems, a popular mandate does not make the head of state into a rival of either the government or parliament. Conversely, although in parliamentary systems the executive cannot govern without the support or at least acquiescence of parliament, this does not necessarily make parliament or the governing parliamentary parties into the dominant partner in the relationship.

Two developments have, over the past 15 years or so, reignited a long-running debate about the respective merits and perils of presidential, semi-presidential and parliamentary forms of democracy in Europe (Lijphart, 1992). The first false dawn of presidentialism came with the fall of communism in Central and Eastern Europe at the end of the 1980s. In the immediate aftermath of regime collapse, it seemed as if presidential or semi-presidential systems, with powerful presidents who would enjoy significant executive powers, were set to take root in Central and Eastern Europe. Several of the post-communist countries opted for directly elected heads of state, and in the case of Poland and Romania, presidents were also endowed with substantial executive functions (for an overview of the constitutional provisions regarding the powers of the presidency in the early years of transition see Forum 1993/1994). Even where constitutional provisions clearly favoured a parliamentary system, indirectly elected heads of state did not easily settle into a largely ceremonial role. In Hungary, for example, during the early years of the presidency of Árpád Göncz (1990–2000), his office was 'shorn of its original intended powers but retain[ed] enough residual influence to stymie cabinet government and seize the initiative in some areas of policy' (O'Neil, 1997: 215).

Yet, from the mid-1990s, it became increasingly evident that the post-communist countries would follow the West European pattern of largely ceremonial presidencies, even where heads of state were popularly elected. The exceptional circumstances of transition politics – including instability in parliament, government and political parties – allowed entrepreneurial presidents to 'punch above their weight', but democratic consolidation progressively limited their room for manoeuvre. This dynamic could be most clearly observed in Poland, where the constitutional reform of 1997 stripped the president of significant executive powers. But in other countries, too, the president's political role became more circumscribed, a process that was often aided by constitutional courts adopting a restrictive interpretation of the presidency's power, as happened, for example, in Hungary.

Table 5.1 *Power at the centre: an overview*

Country	Head of State	Method of selection	Type of representative democracy	Head of Government	Appointment of Cabinet
Austria	President	Popular election; six-year term	Semi-presidential	Federal Chancellor appointed by President	Chosen by President on the advice of Federal Chancellor
Belgium	Monarch	Hereditary	Parliamentary	Prime Minister appointed by Monarch, then approved by parliament	Formally appointed by Monarch
Bulgaria	President	Popular election; five-year term	Semi-presidential	Chairman of the Council of Ministers nominated by President and elected by parliament	Nominated by Prime Minister and elected by Parliament
Cyprus	President	Popular election; five-year term	Presidential	President	Appointed by President
Czech Republic	President	Elected by parliament; five- year term	Parliamentary	Prime Minister appointed by President	Appointed by President on the recommendation of Prime Minister
Denmark	Monarch	Hereditary	Parliamentary	Prime Minister appointed by Monarch	Appointed by Prime Minister and approved by parliament
Estonia	President	Elected by parliament or Electoral Assembly; five-year term	Parliamentary	Prime Minister, nominated by President, approved by parliament	Appointed by Prime Minister and approved by parliament
Finland	President	Popular election; six-year term	Semi-presidential	Prime Minister, appointed by President, approved by parliament	Appointed by President and responsible to parliament

continued

Table 5.1 *Power at the centre: an overview (continued)*

Country	Head of State	Method of selection	Type of representative democracy	Head of Government	Appointment of Cabinet
France	President	Popular election; five-year term	Semi-presidential	Prime Minister, nominated by lower house, appointed by President	Appointed by President on the suggestion of Prime Minister
Germany	President	Elected by Federal Convention; five-year term	Parliamentary	Federal Chancellor elected by lower house	Appointed by President on the recommendation of the Federal Chancellor
Greece	President	Elected by parliament; five-year term	Parliamentary	Prime Minister appointed by President	Appointed by President on the recommendation of Prime Minister
Hungary	President	Elected by parliament; five-year term	Parliamentary	Prime Minister elected by parliament on recommendation of President	Elected by parliament on the recommendation of the President
Ireland	President	Popular election; seven-year term	Semi-presidential	Prime Minister appointed by President on nomination by lower house	Appointed by President with previous nomination by Prime Minister and approval of lower house
Italy	President	Elected by Electoral College; seven-year term	Parliamentary	President of the Council of Ministers appointed by President and confirmed by parliament	Nominated by President of the Council of Ministers and approved by President
Latvia	President	Elected by parliament; four-year term	Parliamentary	Prime Minister appointed by President	Nominated by Prime Minister and elected by parliament

continued

Table 5.1 *Power at the centre: an overview (continued)*

Country	Head of State	Method of selection	Type of representative democracy	Head of Government	Appointment of Cabinet
Lithuania	President	Popular election; five-year term	Semi-presidential	Premier appointed by President with the approval of parliament	Appointed by President on the nomination of Premier
Luxembourg	Monarch	Hereditary	Parliamentary	Prime Minister appointed by Monarch	Recommended by Prime Minister and appointed by Monarch
Malta	President	Elected by parliament; five-year term	Parliamentary	Prime Minister appointed by President	Appointed by President on the advice of Prime Minister
Netherlands	Monarch	Hereditary	Parliamentary	Prime Minister appointed by Monarch	Appointed by Monarch
Norway	Monarch	Hereditary	Parliamentary	Prime Minister appointed by Monarch with the approval of parliament	Appointed by Monarch with the approval of parliament
Poland	President	Popular election; five-year term	Semi-presidential	Prime Minister appointed by President and confirmed by lower house	Prime Minister proposes, President appoints and lower house approves
Portugal	President	Popular election; five-year term	Semi-presidential	Prime Minister appointed by President	Appointed by President on the recommendation of Prime Minister
Romania	President	Popular election; five-year term	Semi-presidential	Prime Minister appointed by President	Appointed by the Prime Minister

continued

Table 5.1 *Power at the centre: an overview (continued)*

Country	Head of State	Method of selection	Type of representative democracy	Head of Government	Appointment of Cabinet
Slovakia	President	Popular election; five-year term	Parliamentary	Prime Minister appointed by President	Appointed by President on recommendation of Prime Minister
Slovenia	President	Popular election; five-year term	Semi-presidential	President of the Council of Ministers nominated by President, elected by lower house	Nominated by Prime Minister and elected by lower house
Spain	Monarch	Hereditary	Parliamentary	President of the Government-Prime Minister elected by parliament on proposal of Monarch	Designated by President of the Government-Prime Minister
Sweden	Monarch	Hereditary	Parliamentary	Prime Minister elected by parliament	Appointed by Prime Minister
Switzerland	President	Elected by parliament; one-year term	Parliamentary	President elected by parliament	Elected by parliament
United Kingdom	Monarch	Hereditary	Parliamentary	Prime Minister appointed by Monarch	Appointed by Prime Minister

Despite the evidence of a curtailing of presidential powers in the new Central and Eastern European democracies, it has been argued that Europe is witnessing a progressive 'presidentialization of politics'. According to Poguntke and Webb (2005) – who draw principally on the experiences of Western European countries – one can observe 'structurally induced presidentialization' (*ibid*.: 21). This '*de facto*' presidentialization reflects 'the growth of leadership power and autonomy within parties and political executives, and the greater prominence of leaders in electoral processes' (Webb and Poguntke, 2005: 336). This 'shift from collective (or organizational) to individual power and accountability' is not normally 'induced or sustained by formal legal-institutional modifications'; rather, it occurs

> within the unaltered institutional frameworks of parliamentary, semi-presidential, and presidential systems. They make parliamentary and semi-presidential systems function more according to the inherent logic of presidential regimes, while they take the working mode of presidential systems closer to their logical conclusions. (*Ibid*.: 352)

The UK is often regarded as a prime example of this trend (Heffernan and Webb, 2005; see Burch and Holliday, 2004 for a detailed critique of this view). Thus, it has been suggested that long-term executive domination in Britain has been further reinforced during the premiership of Tony Blair since 1997, underpinned by 'democratic centralism' (that is, top-down control) within the Labour Party (Shaw, 2003). Despite some moves towards a consensus-style democracy along the federal-unitary dimension of political organization following devolution (Flinders, 2005), the predominant feature has been the rise of the 'British presidency' (Foley, 2000).

The UK does, though, offer unusually favourable conditions for the concentration of power, which are not replicated in much of the rest of Europe. In particular, a strongly disproportional, first-past-the-post electoral system, tends to produce dependable single-party majorities in parliament (it is worth noting in this context that in the UK elections of May 2005, the Labour Party won 356 out of 646 seats with just 35.3 per cent of the vote; by contrast, the Conservative Party, with 32.2 per cent, gained 198 seats). Moreover, there is a long-standing tradition of a near executive monopoly over legislative agenda-setting and control. Where these conditions do not hold, for instance where leaders need to rely on often fragile multi-party support, the opportunities for leadership autonomy are much reduced. It may also be questioned whether the comparative evidence of 'presidentialization' as understood by Poguntke and Webb, along the 'executive' and 'party faces' they identify is as persuasive as it seems at first. For example, scholars have pointed to a reassertion of legislatures in public policy-making in countries as diverse as Norway (Rommetvedt, 2005), Austria (Crepaz, 1994) or Portugal (Leston-Bandeira and Freire, 2003). Similarly, whilst Webb and Poguntke (2005: 343) note a 'clear-cut trend towards the growth of leaders' power within, and autonomy from, their parties', other observers such as Kitschelt (2000) have argued that party leaderships have become more responsive to their memberships over time, rather than less so. Finally, it is at least questionable whether electoral behaviour has, in reality, become significantly more leadership-centred than in previous decades (see Tóka, in this volume).

More generally, the presidentialization thesis highlights both the limitations inherent in the formal distinction between presidential, semi-presidential and parliamentary systems when assessing the distribution of political power, and also the ambiguities and potential for misunderstanding that arise from what in comparative politics is commonly known as 'concept-stretching' (Sartori, 1970). It seems clear that the mode of election of the head of state and the role of parliament in maintaining the government, though important, are not in themselves sufficient to assess the distribution of power at the centre. At the same time, adding complexity to the terms risks undermining their analytical usefulness altogether. This happens by seeking to take into account additional criteria, such as a leader's autonomy from his party; by speaking of presidentialization regardless of whether it is the president or the prime minister in whom executive authority is primarily vested; by treating the three types – presidentialism, semi-presidentialism, parliamentarism – as points on a continuum so that they differ in degree rather than in kind; and, finally, by allowing for informal 'presidentialism' within formally semi-presidential or parliamentary systems.

The party-government nexus: more than party government

The concept of party-government is frequently employed in discussing the nexus between parties and government. According to Katz's (1986: 43) influential definition, an ideal-typical party government comprises three elements: first, 'all major governmental decisions must be taken by people chosen in elections conducted along party lines, or by individuals appointed by and responsible to such people'; second, 'policy must be decided within the governing party, when there is a 'monocolour government', or by negotiation among parties when there is a coalition'; third, 'the highest officials (for example, cabinet ministers and especially the prime minister) must be selected within their parties and be responsible to the people through their parties'. Katz's definition clearly emphasizes the impact of parties on government; subsequent work, notably by Blondel and Cotta (1996, 2000), has sought to broaden the empirical and conceptual scope 'by an explicit analysis of the other side of the picture, that is to say the effect of governments on parties' (Blondel and Cotta, 1996: 3). Thus, they are interested in both the relative 'autonomy' and 'interdependence' of party and government and 'the direction of dependence', ranging 'from one extreme of total dependence of the government on the party or parties supporting it to the other extreme of total dependence of the party and parties on the government' (*ibid.*: 9). In line with Katz, they assume that these patterns can vary across the dimensions of appointments, policies, and what they term 'patronage'.

Thus, like the notion of 'presidentialization' as employed by Poguntke and Webb, party government is defined by several criteria and is a matter of degree. Placing countries with any precision along a continuum is accordingly no easy undertaking. Some generalizations are, of course, possible. Although non-partisan caretaker governments or governments of experts were formed quite frequently in the first years of post-communist transition (Müller-Rommel *et al.*, 2004), members of European governments, including the prime minister and members of the cabinet, are usually active party politicians with extensive experience in party and electoral politics. The recruitment of non-party politicians to ministerial office is rare. Party involvement in the formulation of government policy is also the rule, especially under the conditions of coalition government which predominates in Europe. As recent research on the workings of coalitions in Western Europe indicates (Müller and Strøm, 2000), political parties are at the heart of the negotiations leading up to the conclusion of formal coalition agreements and are strongly represented in mechanisms for conflict management, such as coalition committees and party summits, 'i.e. meetings of the leaders of the coalition parties, whether or not these hold portfolios in the cabinet' (*ibid.*: 583). Yet, whereas all this points to the close interlinkage between the government and the governing parties, the direction of influence – the central concern raised by Blondel and Cotta – remains uncertain.

As regards Western Europe, it has been suggested that the business of government increasingly reshapes the character of contemporary political parties. The notion of the 'cartel party', first put forward by Katz and Mair (1995), seeks to reflect the 'ascendancy of the party in public office' (Katz and Mair, 2002) and the linked rise in party leadership autonomy (see van Biezen and Mair in this volume). This characterization would seem to imply that it is governments that shape the programmatic profile of governing parties and their internal life rather than vice versa. With reference to the terminology employed by Katz in his discussion of party government, we would thus be witnessing the growing 'government-ness of parties' rather than the 'party-ness of governments'.

The changeable direction of influence is difficult to determine empirically, because it is a characteristic of party government that the prime minister and most cabinet ministers are also leading party figures and, in the majority of cases, members of parliament. It is therefore instructive to consider cases where these conditions do not hold. In the Netherlands (as in France, Norway and Sweden), the prime minister and cabinet ministers may not, at the same time, be members of parliament and ministers often do not have prior parliamentary experience. Yet, this clear differentiation of governmental and parliamentary roles goes hand in hand with a strong influence of party representatives on coalition formation and coalition management (Timmermans and Andeweg, 2000), suggesting a high 'party-ness of government'. In Poland, no such incompatibility rules exist, but for much of the time since the downfall of the Communist regime, successive leaders of the main governing parties have shied away from joining the government and have preferred to influence policy from within parliament. Unlike in The Netherlands, however, no elaborate machinery for managing the links between the government and the governing parties has developed (Goetz and Zubek, 2005). As a result, the governing parties and the government have tended to act with a high degree of independence. This situation resembles that which prevailed in Italy well into the 1980s, where 'the separation of responsibilities between parties and governments ... encouraged party leaders to pursue party goals without paying too much attention to the constraints (e.g. budgetary) which governments have to face' (Verzichelli and Cotta, 2000: 494).

Developments in Poland and several other Central and Eastern Europe countries show that managing the party–government nexus, whether through an arrangement that approximates party government as defined by Katz or by ensuring the 'government-ness of parties' (responding to the requirements of executive office), requires conditions that cannot be created at will (Dimitrov *et al.*, 2006). Under communism, central policy-making functions were concentrated in the Communist Party bureaucracy and the government acted as the 'agent' of the party. With the transition to democracy, this link between the state and the party was broken, and the new parties emerging in the competitive multi-party systems were primarily concerned with the representation of social interests rather than with the management of the state. At the same time, the influence of government over the parties diminished. This challenge to their governmental quality affected all parties, but it posed a special problem for the new non-communist parties, since they had no governmental experience and often defined their identities primarily in terms of opposition to the government. The early years of post-communism therefore witnessed the growing apart of governments and parties. Governments that had previously relied critically on the contribution of the Communist Party to public policy-making saw themselves confronted with parties that either tried to distance themselves from their previous record in government – in the case of the reformed communists – or had grown in opposition to the government. Political parties either had no experience of being parties in government or downplayed this role at the expense of their identities as parties in parliament. This led to a situation where governments frequently found that their supposed supporters in parliament behaved as if they were members of the opposition. It is not surprising, therefore, that as Nikolenyi (2004) has pointed out in an analysis of cabinet stability in the Czech Republic, Hungary and Poland, 'only in Hungary have political parties managed to maintain stable governments' (*ibid*.: 123).

Types of government: a strengthening of prime ministers?

Having considered the relationships of the government with parliament and political parties, we now turn to how power is organized within the executive itself. There are three basic models in Europe: the case of Cyprus, where the directly elected President heads the government; the case of a 'dual executive', in which the roles of president and head of government are separated, but the president enjoys more than residual executive powers (France is the most obvious example); and the most common case of a clear concentration of executive powers in the government. In the latter case, the key players include the chief executive as the head of government; the ministers; and the cabinet as a collective actor. With reference to their relative strength, it is customary to distinguish between prime ministerial government, in which executive power is primarily vested in the chief executive; ministerial government, in which most executive powers are delegated to individual ministers; and cabinet government, where the government as a collective actor determines executive action.

Government in Europe regularly involves the interplay of the principles of prime ministerial, ministerial and cabinet government; where countries differ is the relative weight accorded to each. Sometimes, as in Germany, the constitution explicitly seeks to balance all three principles (Goetz, 2003b). Thus, under Article 65 of the German Basic Law, the Chancellor determines and is responsible for the general guidelines of policy; ministers exercise independent responsibility for conducting the affairs of their departments; and 'the Federal government resolves differences of opinion amongst ministers' and decides on matters of political importance. But most constitutions stress the collective aspects of government. The purest form of collective government can be found in Switzerland, where the federal executive – the *Bundesrat* or Federal Council – is a strictly collective and collegial body, whose largely ceremonial chairmanship rotates annually amongst its seven members. But many other countries, too, vest most executive powers in the government as a collective, as in The Netherlands, where regulations ensure that 'all bills, all orders in council, specified appointments and in general anything that is politically controversial or involves major governing spending' should be decided by the full cabinet, so that 'the prime minister has little discretion in setting the agenda' (Timmermans and Andeweg, 2000: 380).

However, a constitutional preference for collective decision-making rarely leads to cabinet government in practice. Instead, government tends to work either along ministerial or prime ministerial lines (Blondel and Müller-Rommel, 1997; 2001). For much of the postwar period, Italy was a leading example of the former. The prime minister's role was both constitutionally and politically narrowly circumscribed and most decision-making powers were vested in the Council of Ministers. Yet, encouraged by the dynamics of coalition government and factionalism within the Christian Democrats as the main governing party, ministerial autonomy was pronounced, leading to frequent complaints about a lack of coordination between government ministries (Cassese, 2000).

More recently, the tension between constitutional norms that favour cabinet government and constitutional practice has been especially evident in the case of several Central and Eastern European countries (see Goetz and Wollmann, 2001; Dimitrov *et al.*, 2006). Thus, under communism, the central state consisted of a large number of ministries, including the sectoral ministries charged with administering the various branches of the economy, and a plethora of other central agencies. Many of the latter were formally attached to the Office of the Council of Ministers, but operated with great degrees of autonomy. Since the ultimate centre of power was the party and implementation was largely delegated to the individual ministries, there were few effective coordinating mechanisms within the government itself. In formal terms, the government was collective and collegiate, and its chairman had few prerogatives *vis-à-vis* ministerial colleagues.

Attempts to overcome this legacy have primarily taken the form of measures designed to buttress the position of the prime minister. In the case of Hungary, early constitutional reforms endowed the prime minister with powers closely modelled on those of the German Chancellor; thus, the prime minister may determine the members of the cabinet without seeking parliament's approval and can only be dismissed by a constructive vote of no-confidence. Combined with an early consolidation of democratic political parties and the party system and a willingness of party elites to assume executive office, the formal powers of the chief executive have encouraged prime ministerial coordination in government. Some Hungarian observers have even spoken of a 'presidential-style democracy in parliamentary guise' (Ágh, 2001: 871). Yet, in other countries, the formal position of the chief executive as 'first amongst equals' has been retained. Where the centrality of the prime minister has relied principally on personal power resources and has not been shored up by institutional reform, it has not lasted. This can been seen, for example, in the Czech Republic and in Bulgaria, where periods of strong executive leadership under the premiership of Václav Klaus (1992–97) and Ivan Kostov (1997–2001) respectively, have been followed by government infighting and conflicts within and between the governing parties. These examples also underline that where the governing parties have failed to accept the constraints associated with being parties-in-government, attempts to overcome executive fragmentation through a strengthening of prime ministerial authority have been unsuccessful. The result has been governments, which, whilst formally operating as cabinet government, are often characterized by ministerial autonomy and a lack of coordinated action.

Central and Eastern Europe provides limited support for a sustained rise in prime ministerial authority; but many observers have highlighted a shift towards more powerful prime ministers in Western Europe. The 'presidentialization' noted by Poguntke and Webb and their collaborators is, in fact, largely synonymous with prime ministerialization. Evidence of powerful chief executives is not difficult to find – be it Germany under Chancellor Kohl, the UK under Thatcher and Blair or the 'quasi-presidential premiership' in Spain (Heywood and Molina, 2000). There are also cases where a strengthening of prime ministerial authority has been clearly evident. Such a change can be observed in Italy, which as noted above, used to grant considerable discretion to individual ministers. Here, '[f]rom being scarcely even *primus inter pares*, with the status of little more than a mediator among the parties (and factions) that comprised his government, the prime minister has now evolved into by far the most prominent political figure in the nation' (Calise, 2005: 96).

But there are good reasons to doubt whether prime ministerialization is, in fact, a long-term trend. Constitutional provisions relating to the respective powers of the prime minister, ministers and the cabinet establish important basic parameters for the distribution of power within the government and are rarely subject to explicit amendments; but the power constellations to which they give rise are contingent on a range of other changeable factors. As van Biezen and Hopkin (2005: 124) have argued in respect of Spain during the post-Franco period:

> the status and autonomy of prime ministers have fluctuated over time, with no clear pattern or direction ... presidentialization has varied considerably throughout a period in which the main structural factors ... have either remained constant or moved in contradictory fashion ... Electoral strength, the personal appeal of the governing party's leader, and leadership control over the governing party organization, are key factors in presidentialization ... the variations in the exercise of presidential authority in Spain appear ... to rest on contingent rather than structural factors.

The same observation applies to most other European countries.

Core executives: power in co-ordination

A decisive influence on the distribution of power within the government is the organization of what has come to be known as the core executive, that is

> *all those organizations and procedures which coordinate central government policies, and act as final arbiters of conflict between different parts of the government machine* ... The core executive is the heart of the machine, covering the complex web of institutions, networks and practices surrounding the prime minister, cabinet, cabinet committees and their official counterparts, less formalized ministerial 'clubs' or meetings, bilateral negotiations and interdepartmental committees. (Rhodes, 1995: 12; emphasis in the original)

Mirroring the distinction between prime ministerial, ministerial and cabinet government, we can broadly identify three types of core executives: centralized-prime ministerial; decentralized-ministerial; and centralized-cabinet (see Dimitrov *et al.*, 2006). In centralized-prime ministerial core executives, a small number of key institutions and actors dominate the business of pulling together and integrating government policy. These institutions derive their authority – formal or informal – from the dominant position of the prime minister within the government and coordination is chiefly concerned with maintaining and securing the effective exercise of that authority. The prime minister's dominance in decision-making expresses itself in different ways: by the capacity to decide policy questions in any area in which he takes an interest; by deciding key issues that set the parameters for the remaining areas of government policy; or by defining a governing 'ethos' that leads to predictable and consistent solutions to most policy problems (Rhodes and Dunleavy, 1995: 15). This type of core executive is closely associated with a centre of government in the form of a prime minister's office that acts as the chief executive's vanguard. The British Prime Minister's Office (Lee *et al.*, 1998), the German *Kanzleramt* (Chancellor's Office) (Goetz, 2003b) and the Spanish Department of the Premiership (Heywood and Molina, 2000) serve as examples.

By contrast, in a decentralized-ministerial core executive, there are very limited government-wide coordinating mechanisms. Most ministers are almost entirely absorbed by the affairs of their department, and pay only intermittent attention to the policy problems confronted by their colleagues. Coordination at the level of government itself is weak; coordination largely takes places within individual ministries rather than between them. Under such conditions, the formal centre of government acts more as a registrar of decisions, which tend to reflect the priorities and preferences of individual ministries. One finds such centres of government in a number of post-communist countries such as Bulgaria, the Czech Republic or Romania. Another notable example used to be the Italian Prime Minister's Office, which, for much of the postwar period neither kept 'control of government policies' or maintained 'united government departments' (Cassese, 2000: 108). Thus, successive prime ministers were 'obliged to establish informal networks with experts and politicians ... outside the Premiership', whilst the cabinet was 'enfeebled by its lack of a supporting "staff" in spite of having a secretariat' (*ibid.*: 107).

Finally, in centralized-cabinet core executives, the number of specialized coordinating institutions is small and they may resort to hierarchy in their relationships with other parts of the executive. However, coordination is driven by considerations of effectiveness and efficiency in cabinet decision-making and of ensuring that both the prime minister and ministers adhere to the collective will of the government. The authority of the core executive is, accordingly, principally derived from cabinet. In such a system, the centre of government acts primarily as a guardian of collective responsibility rather than an instrument for the exercise of prime ministerial authority or, conversely, a government registrar. Countries such as The Netherlands and Denmark, with their traditional stress on collective responsibility, possess cabinet offices of this type.

Why is it important to distinguish between type of government, type of core executive and centres of government? The main reason is that they are, in many instances, less closely connected than might be expected (Goetz, 2003a). For example, as noted earlier, the German Constitution seeks to strike a balance between prime ministerial, ministerial and cabinet authority and the core executive is focused on achieving interdepartmental and interparty agreement under the conditions of coalition government. Yet, the centre of government itself – the Chancellor's Office – is unambiguously an instrument for the exercise of chancellorial authority rather than a guardian of collective responsibility.

Disjunctures of this type are especially likely in political systems that are undergoing major transitions. For example, in Bulgaria, after his UDS party had won a landslide victory in the parliamentary elections of April 1997, the new Prime Minister, Kostov, set about reforming the government structure through the Public Administration Act of 1998. The Act established for the first time a uniform organizational structure for central government. It re-emphasized the primacy of the council of ministers as 'a central collective body of the executive power with a general competence', but also sought to upgrade the position of the prime minister by giving him the right to initiate a decision to be taken by the council of ministers. Yet, the constitutional court later nullified this provision on the grounds that it violated the collegiate primacy of the council of ministers set out in the constitution. Thus, the cabinet principle continued to prevail. In the same vein, the Office of Government continued to be assigned and subordinated to the council of ministers as a collegiate body. Kostov could exercise personal and party-political dominance over his ministerial colleagues, and, thus, create a centralized-prime ministerial core executive that relied strongly on party-political coordination mechanisms. However, and this reinforces the point made earlier about the contingency of the concentration of prime ministerial power, this type of core executive did not survive his subsequent departure from office.

The politics and administration nexus: progressive party politicization?

The final key relationship at the centre of power that needs to be considered is that between executive politicians and officials. For much of the postwar period, the normative reference point for assessing this relationship has been provided by the ideals of the Weberian civil service, with its emphasis on professionalism and party-political neutrality. In the 1960s and 1970s, there were frequent warnings against the rise of 'technocracy' and 'bureaucratic government', which threatened to marginalize political decision-takers at the expense of unelected officials. By contrast, recent work on the policy process in Western Europe paints a very different picture. Thus, it has been argued that:

- public policy-making takes on an increasingly top-down character: politicians and partisan advisors set policy priorities, with a much reduced scope for bottom-up bureaucratic leadership (for a detailed account of the German case see Goetz, 2005);
- executive politicians rely ever more on external policy advice – whether provided by think-tanks or consultants – so that the erstwhile virtual monopoly of the senior civil service in providing policy advice is eroded;
- there is a growing 'deinstitutionalization or personalization of political trust' in the relationship between political and bureaucratic elites (Page and Wright, 1999: 277): 'increasing political influence in senior appointments suggests the possibility that membership of a "neutral" civil service is decreasing as a guide to trust among political elites . . . Instead, officials have to develop closer personal ties with political masters by acquiring political craft and confidence' (*ibid*.: 278); and
- politicization of the civil service has been increasing, because of (rather than despite) reforms ostensibly aimed at more effective management: 'reforms meant to weaken the role of political leaders have resulted in greater political intervention in the day-to-day management of government, and a weakening of depoliticized, professional managers within the public sector' (Peters and Pierre, 2004: 284).

Descriptions of the politics–administration nexus in post-communist Central and Eastern Europe highlight important parallels with those based on the Western experience (Verheijen, 1999; Goetz, 2001); in fact, the politics–administration nexus as it has evolved there since 1989 could be seen as an intensified version of Western trends. Thus, although not least in response to external pressure from the EU, civil service legislation was adopted in the new EU member states (Dimitrova, 2005), and party political influence on personnel policy is widespread, even where, as in Hungary, a career civil service was created very soon after the downfall of communism (Meyer-Sahling, 2004). Politicians are said to mistrust all but those officials whom they have personally appointed and a top-down approach to policy-making prevails, with politicians often bypassing the administration.

Such a picture of a civil service that plays an increasingly instrumental role and of civil servants whose careers come to rely on the goodwill of politicians ties in closely with arguments about the centralization of political power and the cartelization of political parties (see van Biezen and Mair, in this volume). The developmental trends in the politics–administration nexus that have been noted in both Western and Central and Eastern Europe are not without foundation – but we should be cautious not to overstate the apparent reassertion of political authority, the concomitant decline in bureaucratic autonomy, and party politicization. Two considerations, in particular, need to be taken into account. First, whilst political control over officials may have increased in the national context, there is ample evidence of the pivotal role of national officials in the EU policy-making processes, both in national capitals and in Brussels. Typically, senior national officials enjoy considerable autonomy in the EU context, especially if they come from countries where political conflicts over integration are of low salience and interministerial coordination of EU policy is weak (Kassim et al., 2000; Wessels *et al.*, 2003; Maurer *et al.*, 2003).

Second, the reassertion of political authority is not synonymous with party politicization. Of course, most government ministers in Europe are members of the governing parties and they typically combine party political and departmental roles (Blondel and Thiebault, 1991). But in the case of 'technical specialist' ministers, in particular, their executive office typically outweighs their party position. As Page and Wright (1999: 278) have pointed out, the growing importance placed on politicians' personal trust and confidence in their senior ministerial personnel does not just signal declining trust in the institution of the civil service: 'In the same way, a civil servant's membership of a political party may no longer serve as a guide to trust in countries where political appointments have traditionally been important'. One such case is Austria, which under the consociational arrangements of the postwar period had a heavily party-politicized bureaucracy. Yet, in the Austrian case, as 'loyalties of civil servants can no longer be taken for granted on the basis of their party affiliation, cabinet ministers fall back on two strategies . . . : the introduction of ministerial cabinets and the building up of personal loyalties of civil servants' (Liegl and Müller, 1999: 116).

The limits to integration

The last remarks point to a more general observation: whilst political parties pervade the key relationships at the centre, their capacity to mould power in their image is strictly limited. This is not just because European countries differ considerably when it comes to the hold that parties have traditionally exercized over the key institutions of the state. Thus, there

> are systems which are, or at some points were, fully-fledged 'partitocracies' (Belgium, Italy, and Austria), systems in which political parties play a central but not all-embracing role (e.g., Germany, Norway), and systems in which parties are less enduring organizations than vehicles tailor-made for the personal ambition of individual politicians, as has been the case in the Fifth French Republic. (Müller, 2000: 330)

Even in countries where political parties are strongly entrenched, they cannot resolve or fully suppress the tensions that are built into the key institutional relationships, let alone integrate the different dimensions into a streamlined, party-controlled formation.

As regards the relationship between the executive and the legislature, each has a specific role to perform in the political system, so that a degree of inter-institutional conflict is unavoidable. The executive may largely monopolize the preparation of legislation and may be able to shield government-sponsored bills from far-reaching amendments during the parliamentary law-making process (although it should be noted that there is great cross-country variation over such executive 'agenda-setting' and 'agenda control' – see Döring and Hallerberg, 2004). Nonetheless, parliament's function to hold the executive to account, although primarily exercised by opposition parties, regularly brings it into conflict with the government. This tension may be lessened, such as when the government can command a large solid majority in parliament; and it may be heightened, notably when governing coalitions break up mid-term; but it can never be suppressed for very long. The governing parties, under normal circumstances, help to contain this tension. As soon as we unpack the notion of 'governing party', a plurality of interests is revealed: that of the party, or, in most cases, parties in government; of the parliamentary party; of the national party organization; and of individuals and groups within each of them. As the discussion of the party–government nexus has shown, just as the interests of government and parliament can never be fully congruent, so the interests and identities of government and parties do not merge. This is especially the case in countries where governments change frequently, but parties remain.

Within government, shared party membership provides a common bond between the chief executive and most ministers – but this bond is often quite tenuous and departmental interests, in particular, tend to assert themselves powerfully. The party bond is qualified, in particular, because of the prevalence of multi-party coalitions and intraparty rivalry. The centrifugal effect of coalitions on the operation of governments is especially pronounced where ideologically opposed parties are brought together or where the likelihood of the coalition being continued after the next election is slim. Even in single-party governments, factionalism and intraparty rivalry may undermine governmental coherence. The ill-concealed power struggle between Prime Minister Tony Blair and his Chancellor (finance minister) Gordon Brown provides an example. Although, as Hennessy (2005: 9) argues, under the Blair–Brown 'dual monarchy' both men rule over fairly clearly defined 'policy fiefdoms', this does not apply to the case of the single European currency: 'both tend to think they are in the lead on Britain and the Euro, hence the tension usually builds up between their scrap-prone entourages when the currency question is at or near the top of the political weather-makers' (*ibid.*: 9–10). Moreover, ministers, however committed to the success of the government as a whole, inevitably become identified with, and act as champions of, their departments, and naturally may use the clout of their departments to advance their own career.

The conflict lines just noted also shape the workings of the core executive. Hard as some European prime ministers may have tried to enhance the coordinating capacity of the centre of government (Peters *et al.*, 2000), their offices are invariably outgunned by the ministerial departments. Amongst the latter, ministries of finance, in particular, often serve as superministries whose activities are difficult to monitor, let alone control, by the centre. The British Treasury, the Spanish Ministry of Economy and Finance, and the French Ministry for Economy, Finance and Industry are cases in point. Weak coordination from the centre is likely to be particularly pronounced where the powers of the prime minister to select and appoint his ministers are closely circumscribed, either by constitutional law, as in Bulgaria or Latvia (where the cabinet requires the explicit approval of parliament) or by political convention, as in most countries where the prime minister has little choice over the personnel nominated by the smaller coalition parties. Again, party-based coordination executive devices, such as coalition summits, may help to foster coherence in government (Wright and Hayward, 2000); but their role is, at best, to complement the formal core executive machinery.

Finally, executive politicians may try to use personnel policy as a means of controlling the ministerial bureaucracy; but their reliance on the administrative and technical expertise of officials for the successful discharge of their executive responsibilities ensures that partisanship only rarely becomes the principal criterion in senior appointments. Personnel policy helps ministers to increase the sensitivity of officials to the political requirements and constraints under which elected politicians operate; but if ministers were tempted to model the civil service in their party political image, they would undermine the technical expertise of the civil service on which their success of heads of department crucially depends. In sum, in each of the key relationships that constitute power at the centre, there are strong countervailing forces to partisan integration.

What follows from all this for the rival images of the development of power at the centre noted at the outset? Evidence of a 'hollowing out' of the centre is scarce; if anything, we can observe reforms in many countries aimed at increasing the effectiveness and efficiency of the central state. But, contrary to the 'presidentialization' thesis, these reforms do not primarily take the form of a personalization of the exercise of political power; nor are they principally aimed at, or do they lead to, the partisan integration of the central institutions. The reality is both more complex and more mundane. It is more complex in that reforms are typically piecemeal rather than overarching; fundamental reforms, such as the adoption of a new constitution in Finland in 2000 (Paloheino, 2005), which affect several dimensions of power at the centre at once and in a coordinated fashion, are very much the exception. It is more mundane in that these incremental reforms rarely challenge the basic tension-ridden principles on which power at the centre is organized.

Chapter 6

Political Parties

Ingrid van Biezen and Peter Mair

Political parties have become so firmly rooted in the established democracies and have so rapidly acquired relevance in the newer democracies of Eastern and Central Europe, that they are widely considered to be the key element in the organization of modern democratic polities. Despite little more than a century of involvement on the political stage of mass democracy, parties are believed to have become the crucial mechanisms for channelling political representation, for organizing government and the political institutions, and for ensuring the existence of democratic accountability. In many respects, the democracy of the twentieth century has become party democracy, while government has become party government. As Schattschneider (1942: 1) once famously asserted, 'political parties created democracy and modern democracy is unthinkable save in terms of the political parties'.

Increasingly, however, it is also argued that parties are beginning to fail – that they are weaker than they once were, and no longer have the capacity to fulfil many of the traditional functions once assigned to them (see Schmitter, 2001). Most immediately, there is extensive criticism of the performance and standing of today's parties, with accusations of corruption, incompetence and the pursuit of self-interest being levelled against many of the party leaders in contemporary government. Everson (2000: 106), for example, implicitly attacks party government by emphasizing the need to safeguard democratic goals 'from the predatory inclinations of a transitory political elite'. Similarly, March and Olsen (1995: 136–7) cast doubt on the value of party competition by suggesting that 'it is not self-evident that electoral political competition will necessarily produce leaders who represent the interests of the people well or who are competent to govern'. Although contemporary political parties may still constitute the key linkage to democratic governance, they are not necessarily believed to serve the broader public interest. On the contrary, they are often viewed as being predatory or incompetent, or even both.

97

While such anti-party critique is a long-established motif in writings on democratic theory (see for example Daalder, 1992; Sartori, 1976: 3–29), much of the more recent wave of anti-party sentiment stems from a growing disappointment with the ways in which parties now operate. Parties are losing legitimacy and relevance as vehicles of representation, as instruments of mobilization, and as channels of interest articulation and aggregation. Falling rates of electoral participation, and declining levels of party membership and organizational activism suggest that citizens are increasingly turning away from parties, while the burgeoning of interest groups and advocacy coalitions suggests that different means are now being used to transmit political messages. At the same time, however, parties have managed to retain more or less exclusive control over candidate recruitment and over the organization of parliaments and governments (see also Goetz, this volume). That is, they dominate the institutions of the polity, and continue to play a prominent procedural role. It is this growing disequilibrium, whereby parties have fastened their grip on the institutions while losing their grip on civil society, which lies at the heart of the present crisis of parties.

In this chapter we first review the long-term process of party development and adaptation in Western Europe, underlining the shift from the cadre party to the mass party, and then on to the catchall party and the cartel party. We then look at the contrasting pattern of development in East-Central Europe, showing how the parties in these new democracies have scarcely managed to move beyond the institutions, and how they have built only a relatively modest foundation in civil society. Finally, we look at the challenges facing contemporary parties in both West and East, and we show how despite their different trajectories of development, all parties now confront similar problems in trying to legitimize their governance.

Party development and adaptation in Western Europe

European political parties have gone through a process of considerable ideological and organizational change since their emergence in the latter half of the nineteenth century. The first embryonic forms of parties, which had appeared in the eighteenth century, were primarily followings of the aristocracy or local elites. Essentially cliques of notables, these early 'cadre parties' (Duverger, 1954) were primarily elite parties and existed as federations of small and relatively autonomous caucuses. Their strength depended not on quantity but on quality – that is, on the often powerful positions they occupied in society. Until

the extension of the franchise encouraged them to create more permanent party structures, cadre parties lacked a permanent organization
and were active only during election periods. Since the political elites
could rely on status and connections in order to be elected, there was
little need for well-structured intermediary political organizations to
support them. These parties were, as Katz and Mair (1995: 9) suggest,
basically committees of those who constituted the leadership in both
the state and civil society.

The mass party

With the introduction of universal suffrage it was no longer feasible for
parties to set themselves up on an *ad hoc* basis for each contest.
Instead, they began to acquire a permanent character, surviving beyond
the immediate election period. The parties that began to emerge under
mass democracy were based on tightly organized, permanent party
structures with extensive networks of local branches and high levels of
membership mobilization. These 'mass parties' first appeared in the
late nineteenth century and were primarily parties of civil society,
emerging from within the ranks of the still disenfranchised working
class as part of an ultimately successful struggle to gain political and
economic rights. Working-class parties – and in some European countries also Christian Democratic parties – were usually created *externally*: they first emerged as movements *outside* parliament and created
a coherent extra-parliamentary organization before competing in elections and acquiring parliamentary or governmental representation
(Duverger, 1954). Furthermore, mass parties were the first to explicitly
claim to represent the interests of one specific social group or class
rather than acting in pursuit of some sort of 'national interest'. Parties
were thus expected to act as agents of their social constituency.

The creation of a mass party with firm roots in civil society was often
a necessity for outsider groups who were trying to challenge the existing
economic and political order. An extensive membership organization
was also needed for financial reasons, with large numbers of fee-paying
party members compensating for a lack of private resources. The concurrence of political and economic (in the case of working-class parties)
or cultural (religious parties) demands also contributed to a close relationship between mass parties and collateral organizations, such as
trade unions or religious organizations. The democratic legitimacy of
the party, moreover, depended primarily on direct popular involvement
in the internal activities of the party, which implied the need for a nomi-
nally bottom-up party structure to provide channels of input from
below into the internal decision-making processes of the party.

In an attempt to increase commitment levels by their core constituencies, many European mass parties initially engaged in social activities for their supporters. Parties thus established a presence in the lives of their adherents which went well-beyond the political sphere. This contributed to the creation of a particular political subculture, which fostered a sense of belonging among party supporters and created long-term voter attachments, thereby generating a strong and durable linkage between parties and society. By narrowing the support market in this way, mass parties ultimately contributed to the freezing of the cleavage structures and the stabilization of party systems (Lipset and Rokkan, 1967).

The catch-all party

While Duverger (1954) associated the mass party primarily with socialist and social-democratic parties, he also expected a 'contagion from the left' to encourage parties across the political spectrum to adopt similar organizational structures. However, the emergence in the late 1950s and early 1960s of what Kirchheimer (1966) identified as the 'catch-all party' challenged this conception of political parties as representatives of predefined sectors of society and underlined the temporary nature of the mass party phenomenon. According to Kirchheimer, five core features characterized the shift from mass to catch-all parties: a dilution of ideological identity; a strengthening of the position of the party leadership; a reduction in the role of the individual party member; a reduced emphasis on the party heartland (defined in class or religious terms) and a greater emphasis on attracting as many voters as possible; building relationships with a wide variety of interests groups.

For the new catch-all party a coherent identity was more a liability than an asset. As parties started to appeal to the electorate at large rather than aiming to represent a specific class or social group, their strategies became more offensive as they sought simple electoral persuasion instead of partisan mobilisation. The focus of party strategy changed from what Parisi and Pasquino (1979) once defined as 'the vote of belonging' to 'the vote of opinion'. It was now voters rather than committed adherents which counted, even if these voters could turn elsewhere in the following contest. Furthermore, parties shifted from a 'bottom-up' to a centralized 'top-down' structure, with the elites playing an increasingly important role at the expense of the ordinary member. The traditional reliance of mass parties on collateral (religious or trade union) organizations was replaced by a more contingent and instrumental relationship with a larger variety of interest groups with weaker party ties.

The emergence of catch-all parties was the result of the ideological and organizational adaptation of the earlier mass parties to the changing external context. First, the postwar period was marked by significant changes in the social structure underlying the party systems. Technological innovation and economic modernization significantly reduced the size of the working class, while increased upward mobility blurred the traditional socio-economic boundaries, weakening the sense of collective identity based on the notion of class. Religious identities and practices were also subject to the erosion of secularization. Second, there were major changes in the resources available to parties, in particular access to modern techniques of mass communication and the beginnings of the provision of public funding. Both these factors facilitated a more top-down and catch-all approach and both offered party leaders the opportunity to bypass the traditional mass party model and appeal directly to the electorate, offering the benefits of a direct linkage in place of what previously was mediated by grass-roots activists. Politics also became more professionalized (Panebianco, 1988), with parties beginning to outsource key services to commercial organizations, whilst political consultants, policy experts and spin doctors took over many of the tasks once performed by volunteers or 'amateur democrats.'

As a result, politics has become increasingly about the competition between professionalized party elites, rather than involving the mobilization of socially distinct groups. Voters are no longer assumed to have longstanding partisan loyalties but are seen as free-floating and uncommitted, in principle available to any of the competing alternatives. While the mass party was firmly anchored within civil society, linking society with the state through the intermediary mechanism of the party organization, catch-all parties became autonomous from both society and the state. In the process of adaptation, the linkage between parties and civil society has become progressively weaker. Indeed, over recent decades West European democracies have suffered from growing popular withdrawal and disengagement from conventional politics. This can be seen from the declining turnout levels, increasing levels of electoral volatility, weakening of party identifications, and increasing partisan dealignment (Dalton and Wattenberg, 2000; Gallagher *et al.*, 2005: 288–96). It is perhaps most obviously seen in the substantial decline in the number of party members. By the end of the 1990s, the average ratio of party membership to the electorate across twenty (old and new) European democracies was just 5 per cent, compared to an average of almost 10 per cent in the older democracies in 1980, and nearly 15 per cent at the beginning of the 1960s (Mair and van Biezen, 2001; see also Table 6.1 below). By 1990, in other words, the parties were clearly losing their organizational hold on society and their capacity to engage citizens in the way they once did.

The cartel party

But while the linkage between parties and civil society may have been weakened in recent years, that between parties and the state appears to have strengthened. Katz and Mair (1995) have suggested that we are dealing here with something that is more than just professionalization, and that the changes wrought by the catch-all party have now progressed so far that they have led to the movement of parties from civil society towards the state. Parties no longer act as the representative agents of civil society, as in the age of the mass party, or as autonomous brokers between civil society and the state, as with the catch-all party, but become instead absorbed by the state and begin to act as semi-state agencies. This implies the emergence of a new type of party, the cartel party, which is characterized by the interpenetration of party and state, as well as by an increased tendency towards inter-party collusion rather than competition. In the era of the cartel party, the main parties work together and take advantage of the resources of the state – such as public subsidies, state-regulated media access, or party patronage – to ensure their collective survival.

Two key developments should be emphasized: on the one hand, parties are more dependent on the state; on the other, they are also increasingly managed by the state (see van Biezen and Kopecky, 2006). First, the introduction of state subsidies has made parties increasingly dependent on public money and state support. While parties in Western Europe traditionally relied on membership subscriptions and contributions from donors and affiliated organizations, state subventions have become a principal resource for parties in most countries today. Second, parties are increasingly managed by the state in that their activities are more subject to regulations and state laws. This increased involvement of the state in internal party affairs has contributed to a transformation away from the party as voluntary private association to the party as a special type of public utility (van Biezen, 2004). Whereas parties once drew their legitimacy from their capacity to represent the key constituencies within civil society, they now justify themselves by appealing to a conception of democracy which sees parties as an essential public good. Parties today, therefore, should no longer be understood in terms of their increasingly loose, contingent and temporal linkages with society, but rather in terms of their relationship with the state, which has assumed an increased importance both in terms of legitimacy and organizational resources.

Parties have also begun to strengthen their linkage to the state by prioritizing their role as governing agencies as opposed to representative organizations. With few exceptions, most substantial parties in contemporary democracies now get the chance to be governing parties. Parties have become more office-seeking, with power and status through government increasingly an end in itself as well as a normal expectation. This development has also produced a shift in the internal organizational structures of parties. With the erosion of the party on the ground and the enhancement of the institutional and procedural role of parties, there has been a shift in the centre of gravity from the extra-parliamentary party central office towards the party in parliament and government. What we see is 'the ascendancy of the party in public office', with the leadership of the party in parliament and in government assuming a more or less undisputed position of privilege within party organizations in the established West European democracies (Katz and Mair, 2002; Poguntke and Webb, 2005).

One final aspect of this process of cartelization involves the cooperation or collusion which now occurs between parties. During the heyday of the mass party, parties remained quite distinctive from one another. They mobilised separate constituencies, maintained distinctive organizational structures, and pursued independent policies and programmes in the interests of their own supporters. Today, parties fish in the same pool of voters, adopt similar professional and campaigning organizational techniques, seek consensus in terms of policy goals, and are sufficiently promiscuous to consider forming a coalition government with almost any other available party. Moreover, they share resources in the form of public subsidies, are subject to the same public regulations and party laws, and compete for attention in the same newspapers and television studios. Given such convergence in style and constraints, it is hardly surprising to find parties cooperating, and even colluding on particular political agendas. This process is also fostered by the sense of collective identity spreading across the leaderships from different parties, whereby they increasingly find more in common with one another than with their own supporters who live their lives beyond the institutions. The continued survival of the political elite can then become an end in itself, with the purposive intent that lay behind the original partisan mobilisation becoming of secondary importance. As von Beyme (1996: 151) has argued: 'A main problem of leadership in the postmodern party state is that the principal aim of a political elite – shaping the society by legislation and political action – is replaced in part by the goal of maintaining the advantages (power) of the in-group as a political class.' It is also in this sense that we can speak of a cartel of parties and of cartelised party systems.

Party emergence and development in East-Central Europe

How do the processes of party formation and development in the post-communist democracies compare with those in the established Western European democracies? On the face of it, it never seemed likely that the parties in these new democracies would follow a similar trajectory to that of their counterparts in Western Europe, running from cadre to mass party, to catch-all party, and eventually to cartel party. Although processes in the older democracies can serve as a useful reference point when charting post-communist developments, the beginning of the twentieth century was clearly distinctive in a social, economic and cultural sense, and the earlier models and paradigms are not necessarily the most appropriate to describe the process in the more recently established democracies. Indeed, the emergence of parties as strong movements of society, as opposed to agents of the state, is likely to have been an historically unique experience in Western Europe. In fact, in many of the post-communist European polities, the parties originated in the state institutions and grew from there (van Biezen, 2003).

However, even though the paths they have followed are different, we can expect to find substantial similarities between contemporary parties in East and West. That is, we can expect to find that the parties in the post-communist democracies will have missed out earlier stages of party development (Kopecký 1995) and will have made what Smith (1993: 8) has called an 'evolutionary leap' towards more the new West European models. That said, it is important to underline that the parties in post-communist Europe have arrived at this stage by following very different trajectories of development from those of the west.

Democratization and the parties

The first major difference involves the democratization process itself. Democratization in Western Europe at the beginning of the twentieth century usually meant expanding the inclusiveness of already established political systems, extending the political rights of participation in systems where an elected parliament and political parties competing for power were already in place. In contrast, democratization in Eastern and Central Europe occurred as a result of the collapse of the previously non-democratic regime. It thus required a wholesale restructuring of the polity and the very creation, rather than mere expansion, of a democratic and inclusive system of political contestation.

The democratic political system, in other words, had to be built virtually entirely from scratch. The same is fundamentally true for political parties. Free political organization was prohibited under the communist regimes, which typically restricted dissident political behaviour. This made it generally impossible for political organizations, other than the ruling Communist Party and its satellite organizations, to survive. It was thus not until the first democratic elections that parties in post-communist Europe effectively had the opportunity to organize. As a result, many parties contesting the first elections had only been created shortly before or during the transition, or sometimes only afterwards, emerging from the ranks of loosely organized and transitory opposition movements such as Civic Forum in Czechoslovakia.

As a consequence, post-communist Europe offers few examples of the sort of externally created parties that proved so important in the west. Many of the parties in post-communist Europe started out with almost no real presence on the ground, as the particular path towards democracy allowed for relatively little time to build the extra-parliamentary party organization prior to the first competitive elections. The context of post-communist democracies also provided few incentives to build strong popular organizations after the transition to democracy had been completed. As a result, many of the newly created parties were essentially top-down organizations, consisting primarily of small groups of national elites who first got together in parliament. In that sense, they can be considered as internally created. In many cases, moreover, parties appeared for a long time more or less confined to a parliamentary – and sometimes a governmental – existence and lacked an established organizational structure extending beyond these offices.

In contrast to many of the externally created parties (in particular socialist ones) in late nineteenth and early twentieth-century Western Europe, the parties in the new post-communist democracies did not regard a strong membership organization as an 'organizational necessity'. Indeed, a membership organization seemed to provide few benefits which would not be available from alternative resources. The parties in the new post-communist democracies, assisted by the availability of modern mass media, were more inclined to turn directly to the electorate at large. Strategies of electoral mobilization were generally perceived as more efficient for the creation of alignments with the electorate and as the most effective strategy to enhance the chances for party survival. Indeed, as noted above, electoral rather than partisan mobilization is also the strategy that is now increasingly preferred in the West. The difficulty of creating a strong sense of partisan belonging was further enhanced by the generally negative or hostile attitudes towards political parties that developed after decades of totalitarian rule – what Rose and Monro (2003: 54–9) refer to as 'a legacy of distrust'. This made political parties among the least trusted of the new democratic institutions, creating a further obstacle for the organizational penetration of society.

For all these reasons party organization on the ground in post-communist Europe tends to be weakly developed. Most parties have built only rudimentary organizational networks in the local constituencies and the level of party membership tends to be marginal, with the ratio usually falling below the levels recorded for contemporary West European democracies (see Table 6.1). The evidence over time reveals few signs of any significant increases in the level of membership, which suggests that small membership organizations are likely to constitute a more or less permanent feature of parties in post-communist Europe, as is also coming to be the case among the more established democracies.

Table 6.1   *National levels of party membership*

Country	Year	Total party membership as percentage of electorate (M/E)	Change in M/E ratio over time
Austria	1999	17.7	−10.8 *
Finland	1998	9.7	−6.1 *
Norway	1997	7.3	−8.0 *
Greece	1998	6.8	+3.6 *
Belgium	1999	6.6	−2.4 *
Switzerland	1997	6.4	−4.3 *
Sweden	1998	5.5	−2.9 *
Denmark	1998	5.1	−2.2 *
Slovakia	2000	4.1	+0.8 **
Italy	1998	4.1	−5.6 *
Portugal	2000	4.0	−0.3 *
Czech Republic	1999	3.9	−3.1 **
Spain	2000	3.4	+2.2 *
Ireland	1998	3.1	−1.9 *
Germany	1999	2.9	−1.6 *
Netherlands	2000	2.5	−1.8 *
Hungary	1999	2.2	0 **
United Kingdom	1998	1.9	−2.2 *
France	1999	1.6	−3.5 *
Poland	2000	1.2	n/a
Mean		5.0	

Notes: * Change since 1980; ** Change since early 1990s.

Source: Data from Mair and van Biezen (2001).

Organization and leadership

As a result, it is party officials and paid professionals rather than members who constitute the nucleus of the party organization and who perform the core functions of communication and electoral mobilization. More generally, party leaderships play a predominant role within the party organization and party politics tends to be highly personalized. This personalization of politics is a product of the combined impact of relatively weak party organizations and the pervasiveness of television. In the context of a newly democratizing polity and weakly institutionalized parties, the role of party leaders is already likely to be extremely important. Such high levels of personalization also follow from the availability and pervasiveness of modern means of communication and the professionalization of campaign techniques. Parties in the new democracies generally lack the human and financial resources to engage in labour-intensive and long-term mobilization of social support, and focus instead on rather short-term and capital-intensive means of attracting voters. Moreover, as levels of party identification and interest in politics remain comparatively low, a large proportion of votes are potentially 'up for grabs', accentuating the importance accorded to electoral campaigns. These campaigns necessarily involve a heavy use of television, which further facilitates the personalization of political contests. With the media accentuating the role of the parties' topmost echelons by encouraging voters to see elections as a choice between various leaders, parties then mobilize electorates on the basis of a very personalized appeal. The mass media have thus made a critical contribution to the process by enhancing the public exposure of the party leaderships and encouraging the creation of personalized (charismatic or clientelistic) linkages between parties and their voters rather than programmatic ones (Kitschelt, 2001).

While the institutional and organizational context of political communication may favour extreme levels of personalization in the new democracies of East-Central Europe, the personalization of politics is not exclusive to the post-communist context. Parallel developments can be found in the young democracies in Southern Europe, as well as in the longer established democracies. In Spain, for example, party politics in much of the democratic era was dominated by the leaderships of the charismatic González of the Socialist Party and the youthful Aznar of the Conservative Party. They were in charge of hierarchical and top-down party organizations with strong oligarchic tendencies, characterized by a high concentration of power in the hands of a small elite. The importance of these party leaders was such that it enabled them frequently to govern past their parties and indeed past the most important social forces that support them. Poguntke and Webb (2005) in this context speak of the presidentialization of politics. They argue that politics in most modern democracies reveals a development towards increasing power, resources and autonomy of the party leadership as well as increasingly leadership-oriented electoral processes. Because it is caused by structural changes rather than being dependent on contingent factors such as the exceptional charisma of the party leader, presidentialization is also likely to constitute a durable phenomenon of modern democracies, regardless of whether they are long-established or have only recently been created (for a contrasting view, see Goetz in this volume).

In post-communist Europe, moreover, the linkage between society and parties is much weaker because the foundation of the newly emerging parties did not normally rest on social divisions. Rather than politicized social stratification, party formation was often based on politicized attitudinal differences, in particular regarding the desirability, degree and direction of regime change (see also Tóka, 1998). The civic movements clearly illustrate these institutional origins. These movements mobilized public opinion by essentially embodying anti-regime sentiments and presenting themselves as an alternative against a delegitimized state. The first elections were thus often little more than a plebiscite on the legitimacy of the incumbent communist regime. As Schöpflin (1993: 259) has observed, 'the post-communist contest was not so much about policies as about polities. The key issues centered on the nature of the constitutional order and the rules of the political game, rather than the allocation of resources that makes up the standard fare of politics in established democracies.' Hence, because parties were not normally created as the representative agents of a pre-defined segment of society, the creation of a social basis for party politics was seen as something to be dealt with after the transition.

Parties and electorates

Another major contrast with the Western pattern of development is that the electorates in post-communist democracies are also different (Rose, 1995; Mair, 1997: 175–98). When the political systems in post-communist Europe opened up after decades of non-democratic rule, the large majority of voters had little or no sense of relevant party attachment. Since it requires at least some time for stable psychological attachments to parties to take root, partisan identities are weak in a context in which most parties have only recently been created. Furthermore, the cleavage structures underpinning the party systems are weakly developed and thus less likely to exhibit the same bias towards stabilization as in the established European democracies. As a result of the egalitarian ideology which had sought to transcend class, ethnic, linguistic, religious and other social divisions, communism had largely eradicated social stratification. This made it difficult for strong cleavage structures to emerge, in that it limited the possibilities for parties to appeal to specific social groups and create an 'electorate of belonging' by encouraging feelings of collective identity. Parties thus lacked natural constituencies in society.

Because the electorates are substantially more open and more than those of the established democracies, they are also more volatile and uncertain (see Table 6.2). While social and attitudinal divisions or ascriptive identities may well become the source of political conflict, the fluidity of the social structure and the relative lack of crystalliza-tion of identities suggest that such foundations are unlikely to consti-tute a stable pattern of alignments for some time to come – if at all. The lack of partisan identities or stable party preferences in the unaligned electorates, moreover, has encouraged the recently created parties to make a strategic choice for expansive electoral mobilization rather than defensive partisan mobilization. While mass parties in the old democracies generally started out as organizations of social forces that were demanding access to the system, parties in the new democra-cies were faced with the challenge of enticing citizens who already had rights of participation but who were often disinclined to exercise them.

Furthermore, because political parties are weakly anchored within society and weakly institutionalized as intermediaries between civil society and the state, they are unlikely to play a role similar to the mass party in Western Europe in the structural consolidation of the party systems. This is indeed suggested by the comparatively high indices of electoral volatility in post-communist East-Central Europe reported in Table 6.2. Average volatility – the aggregate net change in electoral support for the parties from one election to the next – was some three times higher in post-communist Europe than during the comparable periods in Western Europe. Only in the Czech Republic at the beginning of the new century do we find the lower levels of elec-toral volatility that tend to characterize most of the polities in Western Europe. In sum, with party membership at relatively low levels, and with parties on the ground relatively underdeveloped, the reduced importance of the partisan linkage is even more forcefully present in the context of the newly established post-communist democracies. It is an electoral rather than a partisan linkage that shapes the relationship between parties and society.

Table 6.2   *Electoral volatility in post-communist Europe*

	Electoral volatility levels*	
	1990s	2000–04
Czech Republic	19.3	11.5
Estonia	48.7	38.0
Hungary	26.9	22.5
Latvia	40.3	44.3
Lithuania	41.0	49.7
Poland	32.7	21.3
Slovakia	24.0	27.6
Slovenia	28.9	30.4
Mean (*n* = 8)	32.7	30.6
Western European Mean (*n* = 20)	11.3	11.0

* Note that these estimates of volatility are often roughly calculated due to lack of information about the precise relationship between some of the parties that contest sequential elections.

Source: Data from Gallagher *et al.* (2005).

Party funding

The relationship between parties and the state is proving less contingent, however. Indeed, it is now evident that parties in Eastern and Central Europe have developed more successfully, and consolidated more rapidly, as institutional rather than as social actors. In the post-communist context, it is their relationship with the state that constitutes the most significant dimension of the parties' organization. This leads to a further major contrast with the pattern in the west, and which lies in the widespread and immediate availability of public funding for political parties at the outset of the transition to democracy as well as during the early stages of party formation. Post-communist parties have grown up with public money: state subventions, as opposed to membership subscriptions and private donations, have provided most parties in East-Central Europe with the greater part of their income. This has decisively strengthened their linkage with the state and has reinforced the organizational styles already encouraged by the context of a newly democratizing polity. Crucially, while the introduction of public funding in Western Europe contributed significantly to the parties' shifting orientation from society towards the state, in the new democracies the financial dependence on the state came immediately in the wake of democratization. Indeed, for many parties in the post-communist context, the financial dependence on state support is such that the state tends to be the single most important financier of party activity. As a consequence, parties in the post-communist democracies are even more firmly entrenched in the state than their counterparts in the established democracies. The parties' financial dependence on the state, moreover, also appears to have removed a key incentive to establish a more structural financial linkage with society, contributing to the further marginalization of the party on the ground.

The extensive availability of public funds has not only created strong party-state linkages, but has also contributed to the further centralization of power within the parties. Parties in new democracies are primarily elitist organizations, although ones in which the locus of power is to be found within the extra-parliamentary executive rather than the party in public office (van Biezen, 2003: 214–18). This in sharp contrast to most parties in Western Europe, where it is the party in public office which occupies an increasingly predominant position. Parties in the more recently established democracies in East-Central Europe differ from their counterparts in the older democracies in combining a high level of accumulation of positions (or personnel overlap) between the party central office and the party in public office, on the one hand, and a concentration of power in the party executive, on the other. As a consequence, these parties are controlled from a small centre of power located at the intersection of the extra-parliamentary party and the party in public office. The reason for the dominance of the party executive in party organizations in the post-communist democracies should be sought in the desire to increase party cohesion and so reduce the destabilizing consequences of weakly developed party loyalties, high levels of intra-party conflict and instability, and a general lack of party institutionalization, all of which are an inevitable by-product of the volatile context of a new democracy.

Challenges to contemporary parties, east and west

Most West European democracies have by now experienced some sixty years of peaceful democratic development. Some of these democracies – such as Ireland, Sweden and the UK – have experienced even longer periods of sustained development, having managed to avoid either democratic breakdown or military occupation in the 1930s and 1940s. Others have had a more limited experience. Greece, Portugal and Spain effected a complete transition to democracy only in the mid-1970s, while Switzerland took the final step – granting women the right to vote in national elections – only in 1971. But even when dealing with these latter cases, we are dealing with polities, and hence also with parties, that have had a major head start on the new democratic organizations in post-communist Europe. Moreover, we are also dealing with parties that managed to establish themselves and their patterns of competition prior to the full onset of the media age, and prior to the wide-scale processes of individualization and particularization that have characterized the post-industrial political culture of the late twentieth-century. In Western Europe, parties have enjoyed more or less ample opportunity to establish strong organizational and institutional roots.

In post-communist Europe, by contrast, parties have rarely managed to ground themselves. The democracies are new, as are often the parties themselves. The institutional order remains unsettled, and the volatile social context offers few anchors with which to stabilise partisan preferences. From the beginning, party competition has ensued within a full-fledged media environment, and the availability of short-cuts in the process of reaching the electorate at large has discouraged a more consolidated party building process. For all these reasons, the parameters of party politics in post-communist Europe could be expected to be very different from those which prevail within the established European democracies.

In practice, however, and despite the different developmental paths that we have traced in this chapter, the contrasts between east and west are becoming less pronounced than might be expected. But this is not because the post-communist polities are somehow quickly catching up with their more established Western counterparts. Rather, it is because both sides are moving, and the party politics of post-industrial society at the beginning of the new century, whether looked at in the East or in the West, is radically different from what went before. The sharpest contrasts are therefore not necessarily those between the older parties of the West and the newer parties of the East, but rather those between both sets of twenty-first century parties, on the one hand, and the older mass parties and catch-all parties of the earlier postwar years, on the other.

What marks these new, twenty-first century parties out, and how do they differ from their predecessors in the older democratic regimes? Four features in particular are important here. First, parties are increasingly disconnected from society, and hence have a much reduced representative capacity. Indeed, when citizens wish to make their voices heard, they are more likely to turn to interest groups, advocacy coalitions or the media than to political parties. Citizens also turned to interest groups in the past, of course, especially when dealing with more specific and instrumental demands. In contemporary polities, however, the channel offered by interest groups and corporate representation now operates quite independently of the partisan channel, and in many ways offers an alternative or even a challenge to the process of interest intermediation that is offered by the parties (see Tóka, in this volume). In the past, particularly during the golden age of the mass party, interest groups tended to operate more often under the aegis of party, and as a complement to the partisan channel. In this sense parties have become more isolated, and more removed from societal demands.

Second, through the ascendancy of the party in public office or, as in some of the post-communist cases, the party in central office, the parties have become much more akin to the classic Schumpeterian notion of competing teams of leaders – organizations that are centred on, and identified with their leaderships, and that are increasingly subject to top-down rather than bottom-up controls. This is also a reflection of the process of presidentialization that Poguntke and Webb (2005) ascribe to modern democracies more generally, whereby the party organization fades into the shadow of the leadership in parliament and in government, and party identity becomes an outgrowth of the leader's identity. In this situation, in contrast to the processes associated with traditional models of party government, the capacity to win a position of party leadership flows from the ability to engender electoral success, rather than from a position of particular strength within the party itself.

Third, as has been emphasized throughout this chapter, parties are now much more engaged with, and much more likely to draw their terms of reference from, the formal institutions of the polity. Moreover, they are much more likely to extract from these institutions the key resources necessary for their survival – money, status, and the powers of appointment and patronage. In this sense also, they ask much less of civil society. The money that ordinary members once provided is now partially drawn from public subsidies and private or corporate donations. The work that ordinary members once carried out is now largely in the hands of professional campaigners, consultants and marketing managers. And the status that parties once derived from their involvement at the local level is now more likely to be achieved in the offices of the national parliament and government, or even in the television studio. If anything, party members, and the grassroots organizations that they sustain, have become more of a problem than a benefit for many mainstream parties. Indeed, among many newer parties, both in the West and in the East, scarcely any real effort seems to have been made to build up a party on the ground.

Finally, these are parties, or at least groups of leaders and professionals, who have much more in common with one another than they do with those who are not so fully engaged in political life. To paraphrase de Jouvenal, there is more in common between two professional politicians, each of whom comes from a different party, than there is between two party colleagues, one of whom is a professional politician. For this reason it is also sometimes plausible to speak of the emergence of 'a world of the parties', separate from that of the citizens or the voters (see Mair 1998). The idea that political parties - or political leaders or the establishment, or whatever - inhabit their own separate world is not a new one, of course. Often based on some conception of a 'political class,' it is a critique that has been a time-honoured rallying call for populist and extremist political movements since the very early days of mass democracy. What is different nowadays, however, is that it has begun to resonate far more widely than simply within these limited fringe circles. In fact, it has become increasingly common currency, both in popular discourse and in the media. More to the point, with the common style of professional campaigning shared by most of the parties, and with an ever-declining space for distinct ideological identities, it also seems to have a much realistic foundation, such that the various individual political parties - whether judged in programmatic, institutional or organizational terms - now genuinely seem to have more in common with one another than any one of them has with those sections of the non-party world from which they once emanated.

To a degree this situation has been forced on the parties. Social change, on the one hand, and the increasing uncertainties of the electoral market, on the other, have compelled parties to migrate to the safety of the institutions. But it also appears as a consciously preferred strategy that is aimed at ensuring organizational survival and maintenance. If their representative capacities weaken, one way in which parties can compensate is by emphasizing their procedural capacities, and also the essential role they play in the organization and leadership of the polity. But while such a strategy might work in the short term, it is unlikely to succeed in the longer run, and hence it risks provoking even more serious challenges in the future. The problem is that while the parties may be without rivals in their role as occupants of public offices, they no longer find it so easy to justify or legitimize this position. The parties may well be seen as necessary for the effective functioning of democracy, but this does not mean that they are liked or respected. Indeed, this syndrome is already evident, with parties now

Table 6.3   *The balance of trust in public and private institutions, EU15, 2003*

Institution	Balance of trust (%)*
Army	+42
Police	+39
Charities	+30
United Nations	+12
Legal system/judiciary	+10
European Union	+6
Religious institutions	–4
National Parliament	–4
Trade unions	–13
National Government	–16
Big companies	–28
Political parties	–59

* Figures report the net balance between those tending to trust (+) and those tending to distrust (–) the institution in question. In the case of parties, an average of 16% of those responding tended to trust parties, an average of 75% tended to distrust them, leading to the extreme figure of –59%.

Source: Data from *Eurobarometer*, *59.1*, 2003.

often being seen as the institution most susceptible to corruption (van Biezen and Kopecký 2006; see Heywood and Krastev in this volume), and being regarded as one of the least trusted institutions in the public eye. In the European Union, for example, parties enjoy far less trust than any other private or public institution on which opinions have been sought – less than even big companies or trade unions, and substantially less than institutions such as the army or policy, or even the United Nations and European Union (see Table 6.3). Indeed, levels of distrust in political parties are now so high that they are almost off the scale (see also Dalton and Weldon, 2005).

Conclusion

Ultimately, the key problem now being faced by parties in both the developed and the new European democracies in the twenty-first century is that of legitimizing their governance. Although this is perhaps easier in Western Europe with its long tradition of democratic party government and party democracy, and more difficult in Eastern Europe where forty years of communist control had already served to undermine the legitimacy of party-related activities, it is now becoming increasingly problematic in both areas. Unless parties are seen to represent as well as to govern, their governments will not easily be trusted. At the same time, because of social change on the one hand, and the depoliticization of decision-making on the other, parties find it increasingly difficult to play a representative role. Although they try to fall back on their institutional functions in order to justify their commanding role in the polity, they therefore find themselves less trusted as guardians of the public good, and they enjoy less popular confidence as governors. The age of party democracy may be passing, but the parties which are still in place have yet to learn to cope with these new realities.

Chapter 7

Elections and Representation

Gábor Tóka

In our everyday life, we commonly recognize elections as the most essential vehicle for the expression of citizens' political preferences. To be sure, the rule of law, a wide range of civil liberties and citizens' equality before the law are all valuable things on their own – and there can be more or less of them. But we categorically call countries democratic or otherwise depending on the presence of enough civic liberties to call their elections free and fair; enough equality to believe that in national elections all citizens were granted the same potential degree of influence; and enough rule of law so that the decisions of elected office holders define the rules of the game regarding any matter in the given country. Whether elections really establish a transparent, effective and credible system of representing citizens in the political process is, however, another matter. This depends, above all, on the shape of political parties and the party system. The political science literature of the last few decades is full of arguments about how the representational performance of parties declines due to social changes, political de- and realignments, a changing media landscape, and the rise of multilevel governance. While this chapter cannot review all these developments, it briefly assesses the health of electoral democracy in Europe.

The centrality of elections to citizen involvement in the democratic process

National elections are unrivalled in how close they get to allowing everyone to have an equal say in the determination of a political outcome – admittedly just a single one in every few years, but one that can shape or even determine all other relevant political outcomes in the country. Hence, it has been widely viewed with alarm that participation in elections declined in most European countries in the last thirty years. At the same time, non-electoral participation roughly doubled nearly everywhere in Western Europe compared to the 1950s (Topf,

117

1995). It also vastly increased in the former communist countries since the grip of the former party-states on society ended in the late 1980s. With the focus of citizen activity shifting towards non-electoral arenas, representative democracy may seem to have changed its character substantially.

Yet, as Table 7.1 shows, voting is still more widespread among citizens than the combined total incidence of the second, third and fourth most common form of political participation in Europe. The left column of the table shows the percentage of adults who, at the last millennium, ever participated either in a demonstration or a petition, or were members of a trade union. Across 36 European countries, the figures range from 21 per cent in Bulgaria and Hungary to 94 per cent in Sweden, with a modest average of 50 per cent. The middle column of the same table shows that about the same time, the percentage of adults voting in competitive national elections averaged, since 1945, from 50 per cent in Poland to 93 per cent in Belgium, where voting is compulsory. By and large, the turnout figures are well-above the cumulated figure for non-electoral participation for every single country save Sweden and the United Kingdom. Generally, long-established democracies show a smaller gap between the two percentages than new ones. Oddly, however, the only former communist countries where non-electoral participation is nearly as frequent as electoral participation are undemocratic Belarus and Russia, where union membership remains much higher than in Central Europe – though not nearly as high as in the Nordic countries.

Clearly, voting in national elections remains by far the most common political activity, especially in Southern and Eastern Europe where it largely lacks the assistance of other activities in assuring politicians' responsiveness to their electorate. But in the older and more affluent democracies of North-Western Europe, the frequency of all other political acts taken together is clearly catching up with voting. Does this reduce the role of voting in democratic representation? Maybe not: election results never offered as articulate a guide as other signals to what policies the electorate may support on particular issues. Moreover, the role of elections can hardly diminish as the chief regulator of access to political power in democracies, since non-electoral participation lacks the institutionalized guarantees of citizens' equality that the one person-one vote arrangement provides.

Declining electoral participation may well increase inequalities of political influence between age groups, classes, races, and so forth (Lijphart, 1997). Low and further declining turnout has made elections to the European Parliament particularly vulnerable to non-egalitarian tendencies and lacking in authority. The political science literature has

Table 7.1   *Differences between electoral and non-electoral participation across Europe*

	Total incidence of three most frequent types of non-electoral participation (%)	Voter turnout in elections (%)	Difference in favour of turnout
Bulgaria	21	81	61
Albania	32	88	56
Romania	22	73	51
Portugal	27	77	50
Hungary	21	67	46
Malta	46	88	42
Moldova	32	73	41
Estonia	28	68	41
Latvia	40	79	39
Spain	35	74	38
Ukraine	38	73	35
Slovenia	44	77	33
Bosnia and Herzegovina	29	60	32
Germany	55	85	31
Croatia	41	71	30
Luxembourg	60	90	30
Italy	62	90	28
Austria	64	91	27
Lithuania	28	53	25
Slovakia	63	85	23
Serbia	40	60	20
Macedonia	34	54	20
Czech Republic	64	83	19
Belgium	73	93	19
Poland	31	50	19
Netherlands	70	88	18
Russia	43	58	15
Greece	65	80	15
Finland	62	76	14
Belarus	50	61	11
Ireland	63	73	10
Denmark	79	86	7
Iceland	83	90	7
France	72	74	2
United Kingdom	80	75	−5
Sweden	94	87	−7
Switzerland	Not available	57	Not available
Norway	Not available	80	Not available

Notes: The turnout data are the number of votes cast in percentage of the voting-age popula-tion averaged across all national elections; communist-era elections in Eastern Europe are excluded. The column on non-electoral participation shows the percentage of adults who reported either to have ever participated in a demonstration and/or petition or to be a trade union member.

Sources: Turnout data, IDEA (Pintor and Gratschew, 2002: 78–9, 155 on Serbia); otherwise calculated from data in the 1999/2000 European Values Study (Halman, 2003).

started identifying the conditions that can ameliorate the problem by analysing the causal determinants of high turnout. As it turns out, nearly everything depends on the stakes in elections and the personal costs of voting. Sanctions for non-voting, the convenience of casting a ballot – for example, whether one can vote at weekends or by a mail ballot – as well as the clarity of alternative governmental coalitions and the expected policy and vote differences between them all go a long way to explaining both cross-national differences and changes over time in how many people vote (Franklin, 2004).

Thus, we do not need to invoke culture or society to explain why countries like Malta and Albania, where every vote has an unusually high chance to influence government composition in the context of intense competition between two major alternatives, has much higher turnout than Switzerland, where the frequent referenda and a stable coalition formula, reflected in the same grand coalition government over decades, deprive national elections of much political excitement. If true, then it may be possible to reverse current trends in voter turnout. It remains an open question, though, whether socio-economic development indirectly reduces turnout by (1) undermining ideological polarization between the parties, (2) creating ample competition to politics as a provider of social identities and mass entertainment, and (3) increasing the complexity of responsibility for political outcomes through new forms of governance, such as European Union (EU) structures. If socio-economic development does have this impact, then electoral democracy may never again be the same bastion of political equality as it was in Western Europe in the 1960s.

Party and party system institutionalization

In addition to free and fair elections, democracies also require what Sartori calls the 'representational transfer of power'. That is to say, elected officials are meant to be responsive delegates of citizens, and remain accountable to them. By and large, they ought to heed popular preferences and be subject to reward and punishment for their deeds from the electorate – otherwise democracy becomes a formal façade for elite domination rather than the everyday reality of popular rule. Indeed, the chances for genuine democracy may seem rather slim given how many choices every elected official faces every day, and how little time and energy citizens have for monitoring these choices.

Political parties and party systems are therefore essential for making responsiveness and accountability visible, credible and real (Katz, 1997; see van Biezen and Mair in this volume). Parties in democracies are best defined as groups of politicians contesting elections under a common label (Sartori, 1976: 63). They create continuity between elections: voters can hold a party accountable for the past record of its representatives, and anticipate the likely acts of its future representatives even if none of the incumbent legislators seeks re-election. Learning about hundreds of individual candidates would require far more time and attention from both mass media and citizens than either can allocate to politics. In countries like Poland, where legislators very often switch between parties in parliament, these 'political tourists' are condemned in general terms, but as individual members of a governing party can escape the electoral sanctions that other incumbents face for poor performance (Zielinski *et al.*, 2003). Scant citizen knowledge of even such trivial facts as the name of the candidates standing in their respective constituencies amply demonstrates the huge difficulties that mass democracy would face without parties (Norris, 2004). The downside of such a system is best revealed in the Russian lower house, to which most single-member districts sent independent deputies until the mid-1990s. A large majority of these seeming independents swiftly joined a government party shortly after being elected, apparently in exchange for particularistic favours (Moser, 2001), thus providing the appearance of democratic legitimacy to whoever controls the resources of the state.

Following the acts of a small number of relatively enduring parties makes the information requirements of democracy incomparably more manageable. Fellow party members can far more efficiently monitor ministers' and legislators' behaviour than citizens themselves. Given their shared interest in future electoral success and some broadly defined policy goals, fellow party members have the perfect incentive to sanction politicians for deviations from the party line as well as any obvious wrongdoing – even before the public would take notice. The demise of Margaret Thatcher over her European policies in 1990 was a case in point, as was the political retirement of a vice-president of the Hungarian socialists after his parliamentary interventions which appeared to support the interests of tobacco companies coincided with an unexplained increase in his personal assets.

Cohesive parties and a relatively stable party system are essential in making the selection of governments and policies relatively transparent. A crystallized party system, in turn, amounts to a predictable pattern of interactions among parties regarding what coalitions are possible, what are their ideological differences, and where issue-specific cooperation can occur. The domination of legislative outcomes by highly disciplined and relatively predictable parties may make parliamentary politics appear boring and robotically unresponsive to popular sentiments. But the only alternative is a chaotic and unstable give-and-take bargaining game between hundreds of individual deputies, or the more or less covered-up and non-democratic domination of the outcomes by skilful agenda-setters and/or moneyed interest.

Levels of party attachment in contemporary Europe

The functional centrality of parties to mass democracy does not automatically generate particularly strong citizen attachment to them. Party membership figures and the percentage of citizens feeling close to – or identifying with – parties have been declining in most European countries in recent decades, with only a few, mainly new, democracies offering exceptions to the trend (Dalton, 2002; Mair and van Biezen, 2001). As the first column of Table 6.2 shows, party membership now exceeds 5 per cent of the adult population only in some smaller European states: above all in the (formerly) corporatist Nordic states; in some intensely divided South European polities like Albania, Bosnia-Herzegovina, Greece, Macedonia, Malta and Serbia; and the formerly highly pillarized Austria, Belgium, Luxembourg and the Netherlands, where parties used to be just the centrepiece in vast organizational networks (pillars) of self-help, recreational and other organizations that represented members of the various political subcultures (socialist, Catholic and so forth) from 'cradle to grave'. Remarkably, the average membership rate of West European countries around the millennium was just a little over a third of what it was in the 1960s (Mair, 2005).

Partisan attachments are hard to measure in comparative terms owing to the difficulty of interpreting linguistic variations about the intensity of attitudes in survey responses. Yet, affective partisanship seems most widespread in the Nordic countries, and – depending on the wording of questions – is usually limited to a little less than half the electorate elsewhere in Europe (see the second column of Table 7.2).

However, a large majority of the European electorate consider political parties necessary. Between 40 and 86 per cent also believe that at least one party represents them reasonably well (see columns three and four). In a European-wide perspective, it is hard to imagine how any other type of organization – save possibly national governments in the context of supranational governance – could compete with parties in this regard. Not too surprisingly, though, polities with lower rates of party membership and partisan attachments also show generally lower approval of the representational performance of parties.

Since building party–voter linkages takes time, the new East European democracies lag behind the West and the South on all of these indicators. In the former communist countries, party membership

Table 7.2   *Attachment to political parties in Europe, 1996–2004*

		Percentage of the country's adult population who …			
	… are party members (3-survey average)	*… feel close to a political party (5-survey average)*	*… agree that political parties are necessary to make political system work (CSES1 data)*	*… say there is a party that represents their views reasonably well (CSES2 data)*	*… say there is a political leader who represents their views reasonably well (CSES2 data)*
Poland	1	40	61	40	40
Belarus	2		50		
Estonia	2	40			
France	2	51		59	60
Hungary	2	49	71	73	80
Lithuania	2		48		
Russia	2		53		
Germany	3	45	82	58	60
Latvia	3	44			
Portugal	3	59	63	56	59
Romania	3		76		
Spain	3	56	81	74	73
Ukraine	3		50		
United Kingdom	3	46	77		
Bulgaria	4			46	44
Croatia	4				
Czech Rep.	4	53	73	78	56
Italy	4	48			
Slovenia	4	35	57		
Ireland	5	44		77	77
Moldova	5				
Denmark	6	59	86	84	73
Malta	6				
Slovakia	6				
Serbia	6				
Belgium	7	46	63		
Bosnia-H.	7				
Finland	7	62		64	51
Greece	7	54			
Luxembourg	7	45			
Netherlands	7	55	85		
Switzerland	8	49	77	86	78
Sweden	9	63	78	78	64
Norway	9	56	88	82	72
Macedonia	11				
Albania	13				
Austria	13	52			
Iceland	17	54	75	64	56

Notes: All figures are percentages, calculated by the author from survey data collected between 1996 and 2004 (Halman, 2003; Jowell and the Central Co-ordinating Team, 2004, 2005; Sapiro *et al.*, 2003; Shively and the Comparative Study of Electoral Systems, 2003). Party membership and party identification data are averages across the sources, with missing national data points substituted with EM multiple imputations provided by the LISREL 8.54 package except if more than two-thirds of the time-points were missing.

rates tend to be one-third lower than in the rest of Europe; partisanship averages 44 per cent against 52 per cent elsewhere; only 60 per cent, on average, consider parties necessary (compared to a 75 per cent average in non-Eastern country) and just 59 per cent feel well-represented by a party. Nonetheless, at least outside undemocratic countries like Belarus and Russia, a convergence between Eastern and Western rates of cognitive and affective party attachments seems within reach in the not too distant future.

Implications of weak party attachments

Given current trends, this East–West convergence, should it happen, will occur at a significantly lower level of partisanship in the electorate than that which characterized Western Europe in the 1960s and 1970s. The scholarly literature is divided in interpreting this change. Some present it as a breakdown of time-honoured patterns of representation, producing increasingly random voting behaviour (Mair, 2005). Another school of thought sees behind the same facts the emergence of a politically more sophisticated and demanding electorate, which forces parties to be more responsive to citizen demands (Dalton, 2002). The only certainty is that weaker mass partisanship contributes to lower turnout and to greater swings of the vote from one election to the other than had been the norm in postwar Western Europe.

Another debate about possible party decline concerns the so-called presidentialization of modern politics (see Goetz in this volume). On the one hand, the increased complexity of governance, the centrality of leaders in coordinating agreements across national and supranational levels, a supposedly diminishing role for parties in policy-making, the decline of traditional social cleavages, and the increased personalization of news coverage in the media apparently strengthened the position of individual leaders as prime ministers and party leaders *vis-à-vis* their parties. These processes can be expected to downgrade the importance of collective actors, and increase the importance of individual leaders (Poguntke and Webb, 2005).

On the other hand, the very same leaders are – still, or even increasingly – just a temporary standard-bearer of the party that selected them, and which will dispose of them once their personal electoral appeal is gone. Hence, leaders are hardly an alternative to party-based representation. Indeed, as the last two columns of Table 7.2 suggest, citizens are more likely to find a leader who represents them well in those countries where party attachments are strong than in those where partisanship is weak. In only a few European countries are leaders as likely as parties to provide a sense of representation to citizens. These include semi-presidential systems (France and Portugal) plus Germany, Hungary and Spain, where the constructive vote of no-confidence rule contributes to prime ministerial dominance. Hence, it is probably institutional arrangements rather than the defect of parties that may elevate other agents than parties to a central position. But even where the ground is exceptionally fertile for the personalization of politics, as in Hungary, nearly as many citizens find an adequate representative among the parties as among the individual leaders. In spite of prime ministerial omnipotence, weak party attachments, the presence of charismatic leaders, ideological flip-flops and a chronic flow of financial scandals around their coffers, parties overwhelmingly dominate the Hungarian political process (Enyedi and Tóka, forthcoming).

Thus, it would seem that, to the extent that leaders on their own provide a sense of representation to voters, parties are not far behind. The reverse, however, is not necessarily true. In the Nordic countries and Switzerland, where the executive is clearly collegial and party attachments relatively strong, the parties are significantly more often seen as representative than the leaders are.

Yet, popular attachment to parties is clearly much lower in Europe's democracies today than it was thirty or forty years ago. The reduced or anyway weak authority of parties may in part be responsible for many recent reforms that limit party government. These measures include the increasingly frequent use of direct democratic methods, like the first-ever national referendum in the Netherlands with its famous 'no' verdict on the draft European constitution in July 2005; the spread of open-list systems, now also in Sweden, whereby citizens can signal not only the party they support but also which candidate of the party they wish to see in parliament; the introduction of primary elections to give voters a say about candidate nominations in Italy; and the widespread adoption of direct presidential elections all over Eastern and Central Europe except Albania, the Czech Republic, Estonia, Hungary and Latvia. Weak party attachments among citizens must also bear some responsibility for reduced electoral turnout and the declining predictability of election outcomes. However, these factors do not reduce the parties' ability to structure the choices offered in elections, and keep holders of public office accountable to their constituents. Details of policy-making are hardly under the impact of party manifestos – but it is questionable whether they have ever been (Budge *et al.*, 2001). Ultimately, therefore, it is probably unwarranted to say that parties are becoming less central agents of electoral representation than they appeared to be in earlier periods.

Increased volatility and its causes

Following an impressive degree of stability in West European party systems, 'earthquake' elections, which brought about previously inconceivable vote losses for some established parties and enormous gains for new parties with little known and untested political commitments, became commonplace across Europe from the 1990s onwards. Voter loyalties in the new Eastern democracies also proved far more fragile than had been the case in Germany, Greece, Italy, Portugal or Spain during their (re-)democratization periods. The most dramatic example was probably provided by Italy's 1994 election, which turned Silvio Berlusconi from media magnate to party leader and prime minister almost overnight. Arguably, though, this election was exceptional because of the extraordinary criminal investigations that removed from contention many leaders of the previously dominant centrist parties.

The Netherlands followed a more typical West European scenario. Following a gradual demise of the traditional Catholic, Protestant, Socialist and liberal pillars of Dutch political society, citizens' party attachments and the traditional class and religious cleavages weakened. From the second half of the 1960s onwards, inter-election vote swings between the parties considerably increased, and new parties emerged in the left-libertarian quadrant of the political spectrum. For example, the so-called Pedersen-index of aggregate electoral volatility (AEV) typically averaged about 5 per cent in the Netherlands for the first twenty years after the Second World War, only to jump to slightly over 10 per cent between 1967 and 1986 and around 20 per cent in the 1990s, when the major parties also converged around a broad consensus on neo-liberal socio-economic reforms. The drama of the 2002 election, which brought about a stunning 34 per cent, is remembered mostly for the politically motivated assassination of Pym Fortuyn, the leader of a brand new right-authoritarian party. Its lasting policy impact, however, occurred on the issue most closely associated with the meteoric rise of the late leader's party. All major parties, as well as subsequent Dutch governments, shifted significantly towards a more restrictive stance on immigration policies, which placed them arguably closer to popular preferences than they were before the 2002 electoral earthquake.

The Dutch developments encapsulate what many political scientists now believe to have happened all over Europe since the 1950s. As the traditional ideological and social divides gradually diminished between the social-democratic and communist-left on the one hand, and the Christian Democratic and market liberal parties on the other, party attachments weakened among citizens and electoral volatility increased. Socio-economic change and partisan dealignment created a market for new electoral appeals, especially amongst two groups, The first was a socially liberal, middle-class segment closely tied to the public sector and supporting environmentalism and gender equality, while the second constituted a right-authoritarian electorate mostly opposed to the internationalisation of markets, social liberalism, public-sector growth and high taxes, but supportive of certain aspects of the welfare state. Where traditional social democratic parties were prevented from appealing to the new left-libertarian electorate by the inertia bestowed on them by public office and their ties to trade unions and other traditional supporters, new left parties sooner or later filled that niche on the electoral market. Where the social democrats did move on to this market segment, they risked even further losses to the right in parts of their traditional working-class electorate. Similarly, where the traditional conservative and Christian parties developed a distinct appeal to the new right-authoritarian segment, they risked, like the Conservatives in Britain, even more dramatic losses to left-libertarian challengers among the middle class. However, where they did move to the right too cautiously or not at all, as was the case in Belgium and Scandinavia, the rise of new anti-immigrant and/or anti-tax parties was just a matter of time (Kitschelt, 1995). The net result of all these developments was, arguably, a marked drop in ideological polarization, class and religious voting, and party attachments; and a rise in electoral volatility as well as the fragmentation of party systems along old and new divisions.

In the scholarly literature some question whether class voting and ideological polarization really decreased. However, the above explanation is increasingly accepted as common wisdom. Table 7.3 summarizes where contemporary European political systems stand with respect to the key concepts involved in this account.

The data displayed in the table confirm that less ideological polarization among the supporters of the rival parties comes together with weaker party attachments, and prompts, through the latter, higher electoral volatility. This is borne out by the fact that partisanship levels are significantly and negatively correlated both with polarization and volatility, but the latter two are not significantly correlated with each other (correlations not shown). Volatility, in its turn, is also correlated with the effective number of electoral parties. Fractionalization and volatility are, presumably, interrelated – the more parties there are, the more movement there is between them, which in its turn creates chances for small and new parties.

Interestingly, though, levels of class and religious voting are unrelated to any other indicator appearing in Table 7.3. This suggests that social cleavages are probably not so important for cementing modern

Table 7.3 *Electoral fragmentation, polarization, alignment and volatility at the millennium*

	Effective number of electoral parties	Ideological polarization between party electorates	Class voting	Religious voting	Aggregate electoral volatility (%)
Greece	2.6	0.14	0.06	0.09	6.8
Portugal	3.1	0.08	0.07	0.07	5.9
Spain	3.2	0.1	0.34	0.14	8.6
United Kingdom	3.3	0.05	0.07	0.07	9.3
Austria	3.4	0.05	0.21	0.21	14.4
Bulgaria	3.5	0.14	0.29	0.58	51.9
Hungary	3.7	0.07	0.08	0.13	25.9
Germany	3.9	0.05	0.04	0.16	8.4
Sweden	3.9	0.14	0.15	0.16	14.8
Ireland	3.9	0.03	0.06	0.18	
Iceland	4	0.11	0.08	0.04	6.4
Luxembourg	4.6	0.07	0.05	0.17	8
Croatia	4.6	0.08	0.13	0.14	30.8
Poland	4.6	0.13	0.19	0.07	52.7
Macedonia	4.6	0.1	0.06	0.85	46.1
Czech Republic	4.8	0.12	0.1	0.21	19.8
Denmark	4.8	0.1	0.12	0.09	13.5
Netherlands	5.6	0.09	0.11	0.36	26
Slovenia	5.6	0.09	0.12	0.25	38.2
Finland	5.6	0.13	0.15	0.21	7
France	5.8	0.12	0.08	0.16	21.7
Romania	5.8	0.1	0.11	0.45	34.4
Estonia	6.1	0.07	0.15	0.06	41.1
Lithuania	6.4	0.18	0.11	0.18	49.1
Italy	6.5	0.16	0.06	0.18	24.4
Serbia	6.7	0.04	0.05	0.37	64.9
Latvia	6.9	0.06	0.06	0.06	57.4
Slovakia	7.2	0.08	0.1	0.14	44.8
Russia	7.9	0.06	0.13	0.04	50
Ukraine	8.1	0.16	0.17	0.13	59.2
Bosnia-H.	9.1	0.08	0.11	0.82	24.5
Belgium	9.1	0.09	0.12	0.25	13.9
Average:	*5.3*	*0.1*	*0.1*	*0.2*	*28.4*

Notes: Indicators of class and religious voting as well as ideological polarization were calculated by the author from the 19990/2000 European Values Study (Halman, 2003).
Ideological polarization is measured as the within-country standard deviation of the mean
left–right self-placement of each party's voters, with parties weighted by the number of supporters. The class and religious voting measures show the (1-Wilks lambda) statistics derived
from discriminant analyses of vote choice with manual work, education and income, and as
religious denomination and frequency of church attendance as independent variables, respectively. The data on electoral volatility and the effective number of electoral parties is the
average across two subsequent legislative elections around 1999/2000, and were computed
from election results as reported by Mainwaring and Torcal (2004) and various sources on
the internet.

party systems as they have often been thought to be. Some party systems like those of Greece and Portugal now display considerable stability despite the weakness of class and religious voting in these countries. Conversely, denominational differences between Moslems and orthodox Slavs in Bosnia, Bulgaria, Macedonia and Serbia seem to anchor some party alignments firmly in ethno-religious identities, but appear to do surprisingly little to cement voter loyalties in the party system as a whole. Instead, countries of ethno-religious heterogeneity, clustering mostly in the bottom half of Table 7.3, tend to end up with a far more fragmented party system than relatively homogeneous countries like Greece, Portugal, Austria, Hungary, Germany, Sweden and Iceland. Fragmentation, in its turn, facilitates weakened partisanship and further volatility.

Accountability in volatile electoral contexts

As can be seen in Table 7.3, party systems tend to be somewhat more fragmented and dramatically more volatile in new democracies than in older ones. In the former communist countries, the cross-country average of electoral volatility is about three times higher than in the rest of Europe, and the average effective number of parties, based on the fractionalization of citizens' votes rather than those of seats in parliament, is about 6 compared to 4.6 elsewhere. While hardly a surprise, this raises further questions about the quality of the democratic process. What is in doubt is not so much the centrality of East Central European parties in electoral and parliamentary politics: in fact, they often seem to dominate political agenda-setting and decision-making to a far greater extent than their counterparts in Western Europe (Enyedi and Tóka, forthcoming). But extreme swings between parties in such ideologically polarized party systems as the Bulgarian, Lithuanian or Ukrainian may create unpredictability and short-termism in public policies, and limit the system's capacity to aggregate popular preferences coherently.

The apparent increase in erratic election results also raises doubts about the capacity of Western party systems to represent coherently the underlying policy preferences of citizens. First, as the seat share of an average parliamentary party becomes smaller and the range of conceivable coalitions increases, the mathematical chances diminish that vote gains for a party directly translate into increased presence in governmental office. Second, the more parties there are in parliament and especially in government, the more difficult it becomes for citizens to apportion credit and blame to parties for their performance.

Recent studies on the impact of macro-economic conditions such as growth and unemployment rates on the political fortunes of governing parties have explored these arguments in considerable detail. They find that in multiparty systems, where the dispersion and sharing of executive power undermines direct accountability to the electorate, economic conditions have a lesser impact on the vote for governing parties (Anderson, 2000; Powell and Whitten, 1993). At the same time, however, parties' prospects of hanging on to governmental office are far more sensitive to economic conditions in multiparty than in majoritarian democracies (Cheibub, 1998). Presumably this is because of the stronger indirect accountability of executives in the former systems, which is established through less spectacular but apparently more effective system of checks and balances than direct feedback from the electorate.

Thus, it would be premature to conclude that there is a loss of accountability as a result of the greater fragmentation of European party systems and the slightly shorter lifespan of governments. In fact, it was the very same trends that actually made electoral accountability a reality for all politicians and governments. Back in the 1950s and 1960s, several European party systems saw long-term governmental dominance of one side – social democrats in much of Scandinavia, and of Christian democrats (in various coalitions or on their own) in large parts of Continental Europe. Some parties could not be left out of any conceivable government, while others seemed permanently relegated to the opposition benches. The erosion and diversification of traditional cleavage structures, the rise of volatility, and party system fragmentation might all have complicated policy linkages between citizens and parties. But the same trends certainly allowed for more frequent and more comprehensive alternation between government and opposition in the 1990s, and a much faster access for relative newcomers to governmental office, than what was the norm forty years ago. The consequences are not necessarily bleak.

Change of what?

The most influential typologies of European party systems charted a world that by now seems long gone. The number of European democracies has at least doubled since the 1960s, when the historically 'frozen' party systems of the time managed to accommodate both the class divide and secular–clerical cleavages. These systems, together with the end of the Cold War, helped to incorporate and assimilate into the democratic process the (former) supporters of non-democratic alternatives on both the right- and left-wing ends of the political spectrum. Consociational democracy gave way to party competition as usual in Austria and the Netherlands. Two-party systems practically disappeared from the map, and so did the one-sided social democratic hegemony in Scandinavia. Among the democracies that have been emerging in Europe since the early 1970s, none has turned into a true two-party system, and yet all except the still undemocratic Belarus and Russia developed regular and straightforward alternation between left- and right-wing parties in government from very early on. As a minor exception, Bosnia-Herzegovina – born and tied together as an international protectorate, not entirely unlike Belgium in the nineteenth century – developed consociational arrangements as a result of the Dayton Accords, which promoted power-sharing between its ethnic blocks, although constitutional provisions are currently under review.

The ideologically polarized, immobile multiparty systems that blocked wholesale alternation in governmental office in postwar Italy and France – and, on some account, also in Finland and Denmark – also disappeared. Among the new democracies, only Spain in the late 1970s and the Czech Republic about a decade later showed some potential for maintaining un-coalitionable, anti-system opposition on both the left and right of the spectrum. Their dynamics, however, were never the same as that of classic polarized multiparty systems, and they soon moved in the opposite direction.

The variation in European party systems in terms of the number of parties is still very large today (see Figure 7.1), and in quantitative terms it is probably larger than at any time before in history. However, it is not clear any longer what major qualitative differences in political dynamics can be expected from the mechanical difference between three- and four-party systems, or between five- and six-party systems. Writing during the 1960s and 1970s, Giovanni Sartori (1976) noted a distinction between polarized and moderate multiparty systems. In the first type, government is more or less perpetually controlled by a centrist party facing ideologically extreme, anti-system opposition on both ends of the left–right spectrum. As a result, the pattern of competition is 'centrifugal'; parties engage in irresponsible outbidding and ideological wars, rather than a competition for the middle ground. In Sartori's reasoning, extremely fragmented multiparty systems are prone to develop in this direction whenever a single ideological dimension regulates friend–foe relations between the parties. In Sartori's moderate multiparty type, ideological polarization remains much more muted, because either (a) two relatively moderate blocks compete for governmental office; or (b) the number of parties remains moderate and, thus, they all need to maintain the loyalty of a relatively diverse electorate; or (c) multiple dimensions of identification and policy competition divide the numerous parties, such that each can carve out a safe and

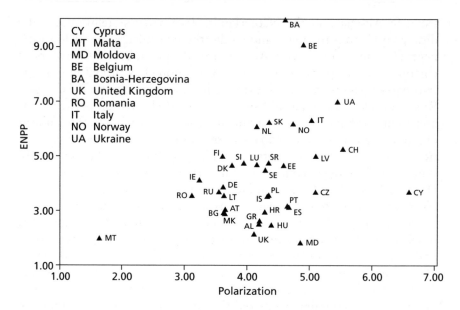

Figure 7.1 *Fractionalization and polarization of European party systems around 2003*

Notes: Ideological polarization was calculated by the author from the PPMD elite survey data set (Benoit and Laver, 2005), as the within-country standard deviation of the mean left–right self-placement of each party by groups of experts in 2003, with parties weighted by the number of supporters. Party system fractionalization is measured here with ENPP (the effective number of parliamentary parties) in the last election prior to mid-2003.

unique electoral niche for itself without adopting an extreme position on the main ideological divide.

What has changed since the 1970s is partly the way political scientists understand multiparty systems. Empirical research motivated by new theories of party competition and voting explored how a relatively large number of parties, each emphasizing a slightly different set of issues rather than confronting each other directly on a single dimension of ideological differences, maintain a distinct electorate in each West European country, and build reasonably meaningful policy linkages between electoral preferences and government activity (Budge *et al.*, 2001; Iversen, 1994). Around the same time, studies of coalition government discovered surprisingly powerful ways in which fragmented party systems structured by multiple dimensions of ideological differences can lead to fairly stable and centrist governmental policies, due merely to their merciless competition for votes, office and policy on the one hand, and the typical institutional arrangements of legislative committees, parliaments and cabinet governments on the other (Laver and Schofield, 1998).

Looking at Figure 7.1, we can observe that more fragmented party systems do indeed result in ideologically more polarized party systems. We can probably discount the results for Cyprus (CY), Malta (MT) and Moldova (MD), three small countries for which the available elite survey data on ideological polarization may feature unusually high measurement error. Then, only the two consociational ethno-federal states, Belgium (BE) and Bosnia-Herzegovina (BA) stand apart with high levels of party system fragmentation, but relatively limited left–right ideological polarization. The rest of Europe seems to line up nicely along a single continuum running from the somewhat less fragmented and less polarized party systems clustering between the United Kingdom (UK) and Romania (RO), towards the more fragmented and highly polarized systems in Italy (IT), Norway (NO), and the less obviously democratic Ukraine (UA). What is interesting is that all these endpoints in the distribution feature predominantly centripetal party competition and straight alternation between left and right-wing governments: the configuration that political scientists usually deem most favourable for creating accountable and responsive governments.

Changing cleavage structures

Another thing that has changed since the 1970s is the world itself. Not only did polarized pluralist systems totally, and anti-system oppositions largely, disappear, but the ideological divisions underlying European party systems also became slightly more multidimensional following a modest decline in the hold of traditional cleavages and the emergence of new social and political divides over immigration, social liberalism, environment, regionalism, European integration and the impact of global competition on domestic markets. At the same time, party systems became slightly more fragmented. All this probably increased the range of possible inter-party coalitions, which appears to be confirmed by the acceptance of hitherto inconceivable coalition formulas in Austria, Germany, Ireland, Italy and the Netherlands in the 1990s, and in Greece a little earlier. In terms of government formation, the new East European democracies seem to fit the same emerging pattern of relatively open, multidimensional competition, but with a strong left–right pattern of alliances between the parties.

Thus, many building blocks of the Lipset and Rokkan model of cleavage structures still hold true. The socio-economic left–right divide still homogenizes European party systems. Not so surprisingly, therefore, the large majority of Members of the European Parliament (MEPs) in the European Parliament can be conveniently accommodated in just two party groupings: the Christian-conservative European People's Party and the social democratic Party of European Socialists. Only latecomers to nation-building – like Ireland, Slovakia and probably Macedonia today – nurture an unambiguously different 'national' issue dimension that cross-cuts the left–right divide and yet serves as the chief determinant of coalition alternatives. Unusually deep ethnoreligious divides – even where they are organized into party alternatives as in Belgium, Bosnia-Herzegovina, Bulgaria, Finland, Macedonia and Romania – tend to be bridged, rather than deepened, by governmental coalitions.

It also remains true that patterns of historical development have curiously lasting effects on the cross-national variation of cleavage structures. Religious divisions play a marginal role in both the Nordic Protestant and the Eastern Orthodox countries where a single church clearly and unambiguously became a state-church a long time ago: Sweden and Russia are probably the key examples. In other religiously homogeneous countries, where the church tended to coalesce with public authority for long historical periods, but without achieving broad national acceptance of this outcome, the religious–secular divide remains not only salient in politics but also largely overlaps with the modern socio-economic divisions between left and right. The classic examples include France, Spain and now Poland, but non-Catholic countries can also develop in the same direction, as shown by contemporary Turkey.

Religiously heterogeneous countries, like Germany, Hungary, Lithuania, the Netherlands and Switzerland, still maintain a moderately salient clerical–secular divide that at least partly cross-cuts the socio-economic divide and leaves relevant liberal parties occupying an unambiguous position, typically to the right of Christian-democrats on economics, and close to – or even to the left of – the social democrats on social liberalism.

Yet contemporary analysts of cleavage structures are less impressed by the persistence of the patterns discovered by Lipset and Rokkan forty years ago, than by the apparently declining impact of religious denomination and social class on voting behaviour (Knutsen, 2004). At the same time, they note that even if class voting declined, as most claim, there is really no sign that citizens' views on socio-economic issues traditionally dividing left and right would impact on their vote choice any less than before. Quite the contrary, in the last few decades the party choices of (West) Europeans have come to reflect their values more unequivocally, and on a wider range of issue dimensions, than before (Knutsen, 1995). Again, the evidence points to possible improvements, rather than a decline in the capacity of European party systems to articulate and aggregate popular preferences on issues. A parallel development is noticeable in how parties rely ever more on private polling and focus groups to assess possible electoral responses to new policies or leaders. Whilst seemingly downgrading the value of elections as providers of feedback from voters to parties, these devices derive their popularity with parties exactly from the fact that they allow them to match electoral preferences better than ever before.

Conclusion

One view on the ongoing changes in party-based representation in Europe stresses that the decline of traditional cleavages, the withdrawal of citizens from parties, the growing dominance of the 'party in public office' over party headquarters undermines representational linkages between citizens and parties. Probably the most influential statement of this position has focused on the emergence of cartel parties (Katz and Mair, 1995). The current chapter has looked only at readily quantifiable developments and they seem to support a far more upbeat interpretation (Kitschelt, 2000). Contemporary party systems, with their increasingly fragmented character, niche-marketing techniques and multidimensional structures of policy divisions, may make it harder for citizens to choose among the alternatives and hold parties accountable – certainly harder if they rely solely on their social group identities as a possible cue to vote choice. Yet, as long as citizens live up to this challenge, the above developments allow citizens to convey more information about their policy preferences through the ballot than was the case a few decades ago. At the same time, in a European-wide perspective, the electoral accountability of government parties has arguably increased. Whether the choices offered in national elections are more frivolous and insubstantial today than forty years ago is a question that this chapter cannot address, and nor can we investigate the issue of citizen representation at the European level. Yet these potentially troubling questions appear to have little to do with parties and voters. In the world of the latter, the only danger that we might foresee here is that substantially more choice for citizens may indirectly generate slightly less political equality between them if fewer people are inspired to take advantage of that choice.

Chapter 8

Territorial Politics in Europe

Michael Keating

It is notoriously difficult to integrate territory into the study of political science. On the one hand, all politics takes place somewhere, so that in one sense all politics is territorial. On the other hand, political science since the Second World War has concentrated on finding universal theories and models, applicable everywhere. As Prezworski and Teune (1970) memorably put it, the aim of a satisfactory explanation is to 'eliminate proper names' in favour of universally-applicable variables such as economic factors, industrial structure or class and religion. In this view, politics might vary from one place to another, but only because the balance of social and economic factors happens to be different, not because of anything intrinsic to territory itself. So one region may be predominantly agricultural and another industrial, or one may contain a large middle class and another be predominantly working class. Once we allow for the incidence of these factors, territory in itself disappears as an explanation for anything.

A slightly different but related argument is that territorial differences may matter in 'traditional' societies but not in 'modern' ones. Such differences as we find are therefore attributed to retarded development. Durkheim (1964: 187), a founder of modern sociology, argued that 'we can almost say that a people is as much advanced as territorial divisions are more superficial.' Karl Deutsch (1966: 80) similarly argued that states as they developed would assimilate their territories, eliminating distinctiveness. In limiting cases where this was impossible, the deviant territories would secede to form states of their own, leaving 'sovereign governments which have no critical regional or community cleavages'.

Other scholars, drawn from political science, history, sociology, and political and social geography, see the question as more complex. Territory does mould politics but in subtle and differentiated ways. First, it is indeed true that the distribution of social and economic variables across territories is different, so that there are industrial areas, agricultural areas, working-class areas and so on. Second, however, is

136

the interaction effect among these social and economic factors, which in combination produce something more than the sum of their parts. Industrialization in a Catholic region, for example, might not be the same as in a Protestant or secular one. Third, the interaction of factors over time may produce and sustain distinct institutions, norms and cultural practices that survive the immediate conditions of their own creation. Social scientists use the term 'path-dependency' to describe the way in which conditions and institutions in one period will influence behaviour in the next period. Historians go further and show how history itself is re-written and re-interpreted to produce a continuing dialogue between the present and the past. European integration, with its questioning of the state as the basis of all political authority, has also questioned the old visions of the mature, integrated state as the natural outcome of political evolution. It is notable that at one time neo-functionalist theorists of European integration sought to explain and predict the process using similar tools to the theorists of national integration. Gradually, national differences would disappear across Europe just as territorial differences had supposedly disappeared within states. More recently, however, scholars have drawn attention to the complexity of the European order and the way in which authority is being reconstituted at multiple levels, above the states, below them and across them. At the same time, they are questioning old accounts of national integration to show that territorial politics never really went away. Indeed, to understand territorial politics in the present, we need to know how states were formed in the first place and how they maintained their territorial cohesion for so long.

State and nation-building

Early modern Europe was home to a variety of political arrangements, and it was not historically ordained that the nation-state format should prevail (Osiander, 1994; Spruyt, 1994; Tilly, 1990). There were empires, which rose and fell. There were large land-based states based on military power, taxation and control of territory. There were city-states and provinces astride trade routes, able to survive because of their economic capacity (Venice, the Baltic cities, the cities of Flanders) or alliances (such as the Hanseatic League). Elsewhere, as in Germany and Italy, aristocratic provincial states survived into the modern era. By the nineteenth century, however, the nation-state was dominant in the western part of the continent and in the course of the twentieth century it spread throughout Europe. In the era of mass warfare there seemed little other way to ensure security. This did not, however, mean that a single model prevailed everywhere. In particular, we can distinguish between those states that are the product of the consolidation of territories and those that have resulted from the fragmentation of empire. Generally speaking, the former dominate in Western Europe (France, Spain, Germany, Italy, the United Kingdom) and the latter in Central and Eastern Europe, although there are exceptions. The Scandinavian nations did not become a single state but rather fused and split over the centuries. Portugal did not long remain part of Spain and diverged as it turned to its overseas empire. Belgium emerged as a buffer state from the remnants of empire. Poland was a large landward state before its partition and subjection to empire.

The most sustained effort to trace these patterns systematically (at least in Western Europe) was made by Stein Rokkan with his conceptual map of Europe, showing patterns of integration on the key dimensions of the economy, identity and the political system (Rokkan, 1980; Rokkan and Urwin, 1982, 1983; Flora *et al.*, 1999). The crucial events shaping these are the religious revolution (the Reformation, to which we might add the Catholic-lay cleavage of the nineteenth century); the national revolution (in the form of nation-building strategies); and the industrial revolution. These together produced the nation-states of Europe but not in perfect symmetry since the three effects did not always coincide perfectly, leaving territorial cleavages within and across states. There was a substantial number of 'peripheries' which were never quite integrated into consolidated states. These were located at the edges of the state system on the fringes of Europe; or on the borders at the interface between state-building projects. Some of these survived as independent polities, including small states like Luxembourg, Iceland or Finland and micro-states like Andorra. Others were incorporated within larger states but never quite assimilated, as with Catalonia, the Basque Country or Scotland. All this ensured that territorial politics survived within the modern state. More recently, Caramani (2003) has extended the Rokkanian scheme to Central and Eastern Europe, noting the absence of nation-state building and the fragmentation of territories and group borders.

None of this happens automatically. The states of Western Europe have sought, over the centuries, to unite and integrate their territories and to forge them into nations. Two forms of integration are critical. Functional integration involves control of territory, the creation of national markets, taxation systems to extract revenues, a uniform national bureaucracy and later on a national welfare state. Normative integration is the process of creating common values, language and culture and forging a single national identity. Some instruments, such as education or the welfare state, may serve both purposes. These have proven remarkably effective, notably in France, but some territories are less easy to assimilate. Atlantic peripheries including Ireland, Iceland and (partially) Greenland and Faroe have broken away. Other peripheries remain in an uneasy relationship with the host state. Interface peripheries in Belgium and the Alps are still in political flux. More critically still, new peripheries and centres emerge and old ones reappear regularly, in response to changes within the territories, in the state and in the transnational order. National integration is thus not a once-for-all or a unidirectional process punctuated only occasionally by break-aways. It is a constant of political life which states must face. The myriad and complex ways in which they do so has given rise to a literature on 'territorial management', strategies used by states to keep their territories on side (Rokkan and Urwin, 1982; Urwin, 1998; Keating, 1988).

Culture, economy and politics

Territorial politics is multidimensional but, to simplify, we can identify three critical elements. The first is to do with cultural differentiation and the survival of distinct identities. Terminology here is very difficult, since most of the language used is value-laden. Often the phenomenon is referred to as 'ethnic' politics, referring to self-identifying groups. Objections to this term are that ethnicity is a vague term and covers both territorially-based and non-territorial groups including migrant populations. The term 'ethno-territorial' is also used, which limits it to territorial groups but still begs the question of what is an ethnic group. My preferred term is nationality politics, since we are talking here of groups who do not feel that they belong entirely within the nation-state as constituted. Such groups come in two forms. Stateless nations are groups who see themselves as a distinct nationality but have no state of their own, being contained within a state (or sometimes more than one state) dominated by another nationality. This is the case of Scots in the United Kingdom, or of Basques and Catalans in Spain. National minorities are groups within a state who identify with the titular nationality of another state. This would include Hungarians in Slovakia, Danes in Germany or Irish nationalists in Northern Ireland. These categories, it should be emphasized, are by no means rigid. Identities are often fluid and contextual and people may hold more than one at the same time. This rough typology, however, allows us to note that stateless nations are most often found in Western Europe, where the consolidation of the state system has absorbed some groups who have not been assimilated into the dominant state identity. In Eastern Europe, by contrast, the main issue concerns national minorities, since the creation of states by the fragmentation of empires has not, and cannot ever, produce perfectly homogeneous states with nobody stranded on the 'wrong' side of the border.

The second dimension of the territorial question is economic. Neo-classical economic theory predicts that in a single market, whether national or European, economic conditions will tend to converge. Poor areas with high unemployment will see an outflow of workers looking for jobs and an inflow of capital to tap the available labour. Wealthy areas will see the reverse. In practice, factors of production are not so mobile, and in a modern economy there are good reasons to think that regions that are already wealthy will attract most capital and have the best infrastructure and research base. The resulting uneven development will have political consequences, although it is not possible to predict exactly what they will be. People in the poor regions may feel alienated from national politics and parties, or alternatively may seek deeper integration in order to secure resources from the centre. In the wealthy regions, people may sustain the state that has produced their well-being, or may try to disengage from their poorer co-nationals by seeking more autonomy. Changes in the international and state economic system may influence this calculation. So in the nineteenth and early twentieth centuries regions that had been central in an open trading system sometimes became peripheral in closed national markets. In the early twenty-first century, these national peripheries may again become central points in a European trading system.

The third dimension is political. Regional actors including political parties may formulate demands for territorial autonomy, cultural recognition or other forms of special treatment. In some cases, territorial parties have emerged, while in others the state-wide parties must include regional demands within their policy prospectus.

Territorial management strategies undertaken by European states sought to address all three dimensions of state politics in three ways. One was to provide access to central government for regional interests. Even the most centralized systems of government often produced territorial intermediaries whose task was to link centre and periphery and assuage territorial pressures. A well-documented case is France, where the prefects, sent from Paris to govern the provinces, had to bend policy to local needs and particularities. The political class was territorially integrated through the accumulation of mandates whereby individuals could hold central and local office simultaneously. Centralization thus paradoxically generated new forms of local power (Grémion, 1976). Territorial intermediaries also existed in Spain, Italy and the United Kingdom, while in Germany the federal system was organized on cooperative lines so as to integrate national and territorial issues (Keating, 1988).

A second strategy of management was to make policy concessions to regional interests, especially in economic matters and cultural issues. In the nineteenth century, tariff policies were often used to protect key sectoral/territorial interests and coalitions of interests. The alliance of Ruhr ironmasters and the big grain farmers east of the Elbe has been recognized as a key force in imperial Germany after unification in 1870. Unified Italy of the same era has been explained as an alliance of the northern bourgeoisie and southern landowners, with some side-payments for the northern industrial proletariat, but excluding the peasantry of the south. Following the Second World War, governments, faced with problems of underdevelopment in some regions and obsolescence in others (notably in the older industrial areas of the United Kingdom), put in place ever more elaborate mechanisms to manage their spatial economies by diverting investment to areas of need. At a time of overall full employment, this was presented as a positive-sum policy, in which the needy areas would benefit from added investment, the booming areas from the relief of pressure, and the national economy from mobilizing resources in peripheral areas that would otherwise remain idle. The broad aim was to reintegrate declining areas into national economies, while preparing to face European competition and the opening of global markets. Policies, initially based on fiscal incentives and grants and on planning controls, gradually became more sophisticated as governments engaged in spatial planning (especially in France, Scandinavia and the Netherlands) and sought to build 'growth poles' around key sectors. Policy was overwhelmingly top-down, aimed at integrating the regions into the national economy but, as strategies became more elaborate, governments sought partners on the ground, among local political and economic elites.

Until the second half of the twentieth century, states were much more reluctant to concede cultural diversity or recognize national pluralism. France was again the archetype of the centralizing state, assimilating its diverse cultures and languages into a single one, a policy pursued with less success by the weaker states of Italy, Spain and Belgium. As a result, few of the non-state languages and cultures survived as high-status vehicles used across the spheres of daily life, the economy, the education system or the bureaucracy. In the imperial systems of Central and Eastern Europe, there were only sporadic efforts at cultural assimilation, such as the Russification campaigns in Finland or attempts to promote German in the Habsburg empire. In contrast, Hungary, when it gained autonomy in 1867, followed the

Western model of assimilation, seeking to construct a nation state. The national revivals of the nineteenth century across Central and Eastern Europe then promoted their own languages among peoples who had not already been educated in the state languages, generating a plethora of competing demands.

The third strategy is to concede political autonomy to the regions. Germany has a long federal tradition aimed at balancing territorial interests within a national state but in other countries regional decentralization only emerged in the last quarter of the twentieth century. We examine its impact below.

The new regionalism

So there is nothing new about territorial politics and nothing new about predictions that it will disappear. From the late 1990s there was again talk of the deterritorialization of politics, this time not because of the rise of the nation-state but because of globalization and the communications revolution (Badie, 1995). Once again, however, there is a strong counterpoint to this literature in the 'new regionalism' (Keating, 1998). The central tenets of this are that politics has not been deterritorialized but reterritorialized at multiple scales, including the sub-state, the supra-national and the trans-national; that the concept of territory has been loosened so that not all functional systems need have exactly the same territorial boundaries; that regions are emerging both as systems of action and as actors; and that they must be placed not just within the context of the state, as in the traditional literature on territorial management, but within the broader global and European order.

The dimensions of this process are once again economic, cultural and political, to which might now be added the welfare state. Economic change must be understood in a global and European context and in its immediate local and regional context, and not just within the framework of the nation-state (Scott, 1998; Storper, 1997). Growth in a modern economy no longer depends on traditional factor endowments such as access to raw materials or proximity to markets, but on innovation, entrepreneurship, adaptability and the capacity of economic actors to balance market competition with the cooperation necessary to provide public goods. These are characteristics not of individuals but of territorial societies. According to this view, we are seeing the rise of regions not just as locations of production but as systems of production, each finding its niche in global markets. Some go even further, arguing that regions are now pitched into a competition for capital, technology and markets and so obliged to equip themselves with the necessary institutional apparatus, or to decline. Not all academic observers accept this idea (Lovering, 1999), but it has become a powerful theme in development policies, widely shared among regions and promoted by the European Commission.

In the new conditions, the nation-state no longer serves as a frame for territorial development and the old top-down regional development policies have been abandoned. Investors cannot be forbidden from investing in booming regions, since they can just move out of the country altogether. The old bargain, whereby wealthy regions transferred resources to poorer ones knowing that the money would come back with orders for their goods, no longer holds. So national regional development policies, in which regions are seen as complementary within national economies, have given way to policies led by the regions themselves, as competitors within national and European economic space.

Welfare states have been quintessentially the product of the nation-state (see Hemerijck, Keune and Rhodes in this volume). Welfare systems, intended to redress the disequilibria produced by capitalist development, have tended to have the same reach as those markets. The social solidarity on which they draw is heavily dependent on a shared sense of destiny or community. The elaborate administrative mechanisms required have been available only to the nation-state. Yet as markets have internationalized or regionalized, welfare states have come under pressure to differentiate regionally. Active labour market policies, at the interface between welfare and economic policy, have often been assigned to the regional level where the relevant labour markets can be identified. Management and rationing of health care is increasingly regionalized. It may even be that, in certain cases, territorial solidarities at the regional level may be rivalling the state level, especially where there is a strong historic or cultural identity.

Culture has similarly been de-territorializing and re-territorializing. Modern technology may enable people sharing the same culture to communicate at great distances, but in practice maintaining a distinct culture and language requires control of territory. This is because it relies on day-to-day and informal encounters and on the existence of educational, administrative, judicial and other systems to sustain the culture and language in high status uses. So we find, in places such as Flanders, defence of the language has increasingly relied on territorial regulation within a defined space rather than on individuals dispersed across the wider state territory.

Politics is changing scale in a variety of ways. Politicians are using the theme of inter-regional competition as a basis for rallying support in the face of weakened class or ideological motivations. Historic identities are revived or even invented as a basis for political mobilization. Interest articulation is also shifting scale alongside the functional systems around which it is organized. So trade unions, while still essentially state-wide in their focus, have been drawn into local and regional campaigns against plant closures or in favour of development. Business groups, similarly national in scope, have engaged with local and regional development plans. Welfare advocates have been resensitized to the existence of territorial disparities resulting from competitive development and to the need for regionally and locally-sensitive strategies for social inclusion and reinsertion of marginalized people into the labour market.

States have responded to these pressures through institutional change. Across Europe, states have put in place a tier of government at the 'meso' level, that is, between central and municipal government (Sharpe, 1993). The aim is to address both the economic and the cultural/nationality dimensions of the territorial question. The first moves go back to the 1960s experiments in regional planning and diversionary regional policies. These were accompanied by institutional arrangements linking national and local actors, the public and the private sector. In France, Italy, Belgium and the United Kingdom they took the form of regional planning councils and boards, while in the German federal system they were incorporated into the Joint Tasks framework for handling joint federal-Land policies. This 'functional regionalism' was an effort to recognize the regional dimension to policy while maintaining centralized plans and strategies, and to incorporate local collaborators, without conceding power. It was also intended to insulate economic development and planning from broader political influences, so as to allow a concentration on growth without interference from local elected politicians concerned with distributive matters. Such depoliticization did not work since inevitably development policy raised broader issues and excluded groups wanted to be included. Members of the regional development boards and agencies, caught between central and local pressures, rapidly became disillusioned. So in most cases, these evolved into elected regional governments, with the national framework for co-ordinated regional policy giving way (at least in part) to decentralized and competitive development plans. During the 1980s and 1990s a similar process started in welfare states, as regional governments were used for planning and rationing welfare services, notably in health care, replacing previously unelected or intermediary bodies.

Since the transition to democracy, the states of Central and Eastern Europe have recognized the same functional logic for a regional tier of action and faced similar dilemmas over the extent to which it should be politicized and elected. All have put into place systems of regional planning, with some institutional mechanisms and an effort to co-opt local economic and social actors into the implementation of development strategies. Poland was the first to move to elected regional government, followed by the Czech Republic and Slovakia, but Hungary has repeatedly postponed this step. The move towards strong regional government has further been frustrated by the influence of the European Commission, which at one time seemed to favour it and then changed tack (see below).

Regional devolution has also been used to address the nationalities question in Western Europe. Belgium has gradually transformed itself into a federal state, with both regions and language communities and a tendency for the territorial regions to predominate. Spain after the transition gave autonomy to the 'historic nationalities' of Catalonia, the Basque Country and Galicia, a process that rapidly spread to the rest of the country. In the United Kingdom, Scotland, Wales and Northern Ireland have varying degrees of autonomy. Territorial concessions have also been made in various interfaces such as the Äland Islands (Finland) and South Tirol (Italy). Even France has proposed various forms of special status for Corsica. The states of Central and Eastern Europe, by contrast, have been extremely reluctant to make this kind of accommodation, since they still fear for the integrity of the state in the face of secessionist and irredentist claims.

European integration and territorial politics

European integration has also served to enhance the importance of territorial politics within states but has had significantly different effects in the old and new member states. Market integration has made it more difficult for states to manage their territorial economies, stimulated interregional competition in the single market, and given incentives to regional actors to organize their region better to compete. European sectoral policies in areas like agriculture, fisheries, steel or coal have an uneven territorial impact, provoking territorial lobbies. More generally, European integration serves to undermine national systems of interest accommodation, since states no longer have the powers to respond to sectoral demands – but without putting in place an effective pan-European system of interest groups. One result is a certain territorialization of interest articulation, as sectoral groups work through regional governments and interest coalitions. European integration also undermines national systems of centre–periphery accommodation and regional government, since it is member states who are represented in the Council of Ministers. This means that when competences devolved to the regions are in turn Europeanized, national governments can re-enter the policy arena through the Council of Ministers. In response, regions have demanded, and obtained, mechanisms to represent their interests in Europe.

The EU's own regional policy started in 1975 after the accession of the United Kingdom with a double logic (Hooghe and Keating, 1994). It was intended to counteract the adverse effects on regions of market integration, and to compensate the UK for the fact that it was a net contributor to the budget. This policy logic and intergovernmental logic have long been in tension and until 1988 the latter prevailed. Funds dispensed under the European Regional Development Fund (ERDF) were received by national governments, which regarded them as compensation for their own national regional policies rather than passing the money on to the regions. In 1988, however, a major reform doubled the size of the funds, grouped the ERDF with the European Social Fund and the Guidance section of the Agriculture Fund into the Structural Funds instrument, and sought to make this into an instrument of genuine European policy rather than a mere intergovernmental compensation mechanism. European-wide criteria and a single European map of eligible areas were established, regions were to be involved in the management of the funds in partnership with the Commission and national governments, and the principle of additionality was to ensure that the money was passed on to the regions. For a time it seemed as though the Commission might take over the role being vacated by states in spatial planning and redistribution, but it was not successful and the funds have remained an object of contention. While it is impossible to measure their real impact, they are still an object of symbolic contention, allowing regional politicians to claim that they have bypassed the state and got money from Brussels. They may have mobilized regional interests around the relevant programmes, but these are usually of a local or sectoral nature, so serving to divide rather than unite regional interests. Perhaps their greatest significance lies in the way the Commission has used Structural Fund programmes to diffuse new ideas about regional development policy, including the fashionable concepts of endogenous development, decentralized policy, and social partnership. In this way, European regional policies have encouraged the emergence of regionalism in Western Europe.

In the early years of transition in the countries of Central and Eastern Europe, it appeared that Europe would have the same effects. A strong impression was given that, to be a good European state, it was necessary to have regional governments and, in particular, that this was a condition for benefiting from the Structural Funds (Hughes *et al.*, 2003, 2004). Poland was an early mover, establishing elected regional governments in 1999. Around 2000, however, there was a dramatic change of tactics on the part of the Commission as responsibility shifted from Directorate General (DG) Enlargement to DG Regio and a date was set for the accession of the ten new members in 2004. Now they were told that the only structural requirement was to delineate regions at NUTS2 (the second level in the Nomenclature of Territorial Units for Statistics) in order to generate information for Structural Fund designation, and to have in place some administrative capacity at this level in order to implement programmes. Fund management and policy-making, however, should be at the central level. There should be as few regional or sectoral programmes as possible, and spending should be concentrated on hard infrastructure projects. There appear to be a number of reasons for this. One was the need to spend money in the two years remaining of the Structural Fund programmes between 2004 and 2006. Another was concern about the absence of administrative structures at the regional level, and worries about corruption and clientelism if programmes were to be divided. Having shifted from decentralized to centralized policies, however, Commission officials then sought to rationalize their stance by pointing to the success of Portugal and Ireland, which had managed the Funds centrally in the 1980s and 1990s (although at the time the Commission had been urging these countries to decentralize). So while Europe is on balance a decentralizing force in the old member states, it has served to reinforce state centralization in the new ones.

Europe has had similar, contrasting effects on the nationalities question in the old and new member states. This is less for what the EU has done than from the new context which the European project provides. Across much of Western Europe, nationalities movements have embraced European integration as a way of transcending the old dilemmas of statehood and secession. Instead of seeking national independence or union with co-nationals in other states, they have looked to the loosening of the state concept itself and the opening of borders to forge new mechanisms for self-expression and autonomy. For some movements, like the Esquerra Republicana de Catalunya (Catalan Republican Left), the goal (usually long-term) is independence within a united Europe, as the old states fade. Others, like the Scottish National Party, see independence within the existing European Union as feasible. Others again have embraced a more radical, post-sovereign conception of politics in which the whole idea of an independent state has been abandoned in favour of insertion as a self-governing community into an evolving multilevel polity (Keating, 2004). At the same time, nationalities movements have become more territorially consolidated, allowing them to play on new regionalist themes, emphasizing the need for an economic project within Europe as much as formal political autonomy.

Similar trends are visible in east and Central Europe, but they are weaker. National minority movements have sought openings into Europe as a substitute for irredentism, but they are not as clearly territorialized as in the West. This is not a matter of chance or the distribution of 'ethnic' populations, but rather because in Western Europe we have seen a process of region and stateless nation-building which the prevailing circumstances did not permit in the east. National minority questions did feature in the negotiations for accession to the European Union but the EU was very reluctant to prescribe forms of internal government to candidate countries. So it tended to stress minority rights rather than self-government, and individual rather than collective rights. Although minority protection was one of the Copenhagen Criteria which accession countries had to meet, this was not incorporated into the *acquis communautaire*. This ensured (as was clearly the intention) that the 15 old member states would not be subject to similar obligations.

The result is a contrasting approach to nationalities questions in the two parts of Europe. In the old member states, there has been an increased acceptance of territorial autonomy and a new form of accommodation within the regionalist mode. This is not universal or uncontested and France still holds out, but it can be seen as an evolving practice. In Central and Eastern Europe, on the other hand, states, with European encouragement, have preferred to deal with minorities questions as matters of individual rights.

Building regions

The new regionalism, like the old territorial politics, can be measured by the three dimensions of economics, culture/identity and politics/institutions. At one time economic regions were defined by the existence of homogeneous production systems, specialized in one product (such as agricultural regions or heavy industrial regions). Now they are more often identified as more or less integrated production systems, with dense internal linkages and some shared external interests. They have been identified in many parts of Western Europe, where they may be at the regional or the local scale and may cross state boundaries. It is more difficult to identify such systems in Central and Eastern Europe under the conditions of transformation to a market economy. The overall picture there appears to conform to the old centre–periphery model, with large disparities between capital cities and other areas, showing the importance of the location of political power and a tendency to clustering. Elsewhere, the penetration of foreign investment has brought industrial development but only as the end of European or global supply chains, with foreign plants poorly anchored into local economic structures.

The second dimension concerns identity and culture. There has been, in Western Europe, a territorialization of identities and self-determination claims on the part of stateless nations and national minorities. This has allowed nationalist movements to adopt new regionalist themes and strategies, seeking a place within the new territorial political economy and European regional dispensation.

The third dimension is political and institutional. The large states of Europe all have some form of meso or regional level of government (although in the United Kingdom it does not apply within England), but with very different forms, powers and resources. The smaller states tend to be unitary, but sometimes with strong municipal government.

Putting these dimensions together, we can produce a new regional map of Europe. This is a Europe in which, for the first time in centuries, there are, over most of its space, no military threats and so no military borders. The states are still there and powerfully shape social, economic and political life, but borders are no longer barriers in the economic and cultural sense. It shows some places where the economic, cultural and institutional meanings coincide, others were they largely overlap, and others where they are still quite distinct. It shows the most distinctive regions lying at the periphery, and at the interface between state-building projects, just as in the Rokkanian analysis. We see trans-border economic regions, often fostered by EU initiatives, and cultural regions spanning more than one state, even though the state context still shapes them on each side (as in Catalonia, the Basque Country or the Tirol). There are even powerful suggestions of historic continuities or revivals, when we compare the famous 'blue banana' invented by French economists to describe the new zone of prosperity with the historic trading routes of the early modern period, from southern England, through the Low Countries and the Rhine Corridor to northern Italy.

If we look at regions from inside, considering each individually, we must note how they are built as up as economic, cultural and political spaces, as networks, then as institutions (Keating, 1998). There are cases, such as the French or Italian regions, of administrative bodies with a degree of autonomy and powers, but which do not correspond to political spaces or to the new patterns of economic dynamism (Trigilia, 1991). Until 1999, Scotland was a political space, but without its own autonomous institutions. There are cultural and linguistic regions, like Catalonia or the Basque Country, that span state boundaries. In France, this disjuncture may not be accidental – critics allege that the boundaries of the regions were drawn up precisely to break up historic regions like Britanny, Normandy or Languedoc and weaken regionalist potential. Regions are the work of political and cultural entrepreneurs, working in the context of social and economic change and within a state system that is very much alive. Here we do see a difference in different parts of the continent, not for essentialist or deep historical reasons, but because of the evolution of the state and region since the Second World War. In Western Europe, regionalism has developed over a long period and in some cases the various meanings of region have been brought into line through region-building or 'stateless nation-building'. We have seen the gradual transformation of functional regionalism into political regionalism and then to regional government. Central and Eastern Europe has not had this experience and the meanings of regionalism may be more distinct. During the transition the tendency was to a fragmentation of local government, to break up the old Communist units and give politicians new power bases, rather than to regional consolidation. Western European governments have gradually seen in regionalism a new mode of territorial management allowing them to accommodate cultural and historic demands, to decentralize regional development policy and to rationalize and manage the welfare state. Of course, they are still sensitive about sovereignty and show strong tendencies to recentralize at many times and places, but generally regionalism is not seen as a threat to the state. Central and Eastern European governments have been very conscious of the weakness of statehood and reluctant to decentralize. Federalism is taboo and there are constant fears of secession and irredentism.

Regions as actors

Regions, as noted, can be recognized across the dimensions of the economy, culture/identity and politics/institutions. They may be seen as territories on which external forces impact, altering the distribution of wealth and opportunities. They are arenas in which politics takes place, with the bargaining, competition and compromise that goes with it. They may also, under certain circumstances, become actors within state and transnational systems. There is a danger here of reification, of treating regions as unitary actors with defined interests, when the reality is that they are composed of diverse groups with multiple interests. Yet these may have the capacity to formulate a common territorial interest and to promote it externally. The role of regional actors in the past was conceived within the framework of the nation-state but internationalization and the rise of transnational institutions now enlarges this framework, opening up a world of 'paradiplomacy' in which regions act in the international area. Again, there are the familiar three dimensions. Regional actors may seek economic benefits in the form of inward investment, technology and markets. They may seek to promote and export their culture in alliance with like-minded territories elsewhere. In other cases the goals may be overtly political, to enhance their autonomy and influence by gaining access to international arenas.

The most intense external activities of regions, however, are in the European Union, which presents threats and opportunities on all three dimensions. The single market, left to its own devices, appears to accentuate territorial disparities, which in turn has led to an elaborate set of policies (the Structural Funds) aimed at combating these. Enlargement increases these disparities further, both between the old and new member states and, as importantly, within the latter. Disparities in the old member states were between centre and periphery; rural and urban areas; and old and new industrial districts. In the new member states the main disparities are between capital cities and the rest of the country; rural and urban areas; and eastern and western regions, especially close to the respective borders.

On the cultural dimension, regions have feared for the survival of lesser-used languages and smaller cultures in the single market. They have been active in trying to secure cultural exceptions to market rules and in pressing for broader recognition of the plurality of the Union, going beyond the member states.

Politically, European integration has taken powers away from regional governments, upwards to the EU or back to national governments since it is these that are represented in the Council of Ministers. The European single market, largely based on the model of competitive development, gives an advantage to regions which are well-organized to exploit local synergies and to operate within national and European networks. Europe also provides an arena for stateless nations and strong regional autonomist movements to project themselves beyond their states without going all the way to separatism. There has thus been a certain convergence between minority nationalism and regionalism, around projects for autonomy and building a capacity for action within the new European networks (Keating, 2004).

There are three types of channel for regions to operate within the European Union. The first and most important is via the national government. Since the Maastricht Treaty, states with regional governments have the option of being represented in the Council of Ministers by a regional minister. The clause has been used in Germany, Belgium, Austria and the United Kingdom and is being extended to Spain. The strongest position is that of the Belgian regions and communities, who have a veto over the Belgian negotiating position in matters of their competence. In Germany, the *Länder* decide the position by majority vote if needed in the Bundesrat, while in the United Kingdom the central government has the last word. Since none of new member states have the necessary constitutional provision, there is no regional representation in the Council of Ministers. In these and other cases, regions must rely on their political influence with the centre.

There is a variety of channels of direct access. Many regions have established offices in Brussels and employ lobbyists and consultants. There is a vibrant inter-regional network in which regions can establish alliances and coordinate strategy. The most important formal instance is the Committee of the Regions (CoR), set up by the Maastricht Treaty and whose rights of consultation have progressively been extended. Its main weaknesses are that its role is consultative only, and that its membership is so heterogeneous, including municipalities as well as different kinds of regional government. In recent years, the stronger regions have bridled at these restrictions and sought a parallel form of organization or special recognition for themselves. The most prominent forum for this is the group of Regions with Legislative Powers (RegLeg), including representatives from Germany, Austria, Belgium, Italy and the United Kingdom, who have pressed for a formal recognition of the regional level, greater consultation over Commission proposals, guarantees for their competences from European intervention, and a greater role in implementing EU directives. They have, however, gained little support either from other members of the CoR or among the states and their demands were not adopted by the Convention on the Future of Europe. Another division which has weakened the regional cause is between those regions (including some German *Länder*) who want to limit the scope of EU law, and those who still see the EU and the Community Methods as a way of extending their own power at the expense of their host state.

The regions that are most effective in EU policy-making are those that are already well institutionalized and integrated into national systems of policy-making. Europe cannot therefore be used to compensate for weakness in national arenas or to bypass the nation-state. Here again, differences emerge between old and new member states as well as within each category. The new member states do not, as we have seen, have strong systems of regional government and Europe has not helped such systems to emerge. No Central European region, for example, qualifies for membership of RegLeg. The latter therefore seem set to remain objects of regional policy rather than actors within it.

Conclusion

Recent years have seen an increased recognition of the importance of territorial politics in Europe, and also of the complexities of the subject. This chapter has focused on regions as the level that has responded most to processes of state restructuring and transnational integration, but change is also visible at the level of cities, of neighbourhoods, and of emerging spaces such as the French have tried to capture in the concept of the *pays*. Territorial politics is shaped by the new international economic context, but attempts to reduce it to an economic determinism (such as that of Ohmae, 1995) fail to understand the multiple dimensions of the phenomenon. Rather it is the complementary logics of economics, culture and politics that make up the new regionalism and account for its varieties.

It is common to refer to the emerging complex European order as a system of 'multilevel governance' (Hooghe and Marks, 2001). The debate on 'governance' and whether it is a useful concept at all goes beyond the scope of this chapter (Pierre, 2000; Pierre and Peters, 2000; Rhodes 1996; Bevir and Rhodes, 2003). If it does have value, it seems to refer to a distinction between a system of social regulation in which there is an authoritative point of control (government) and one based networks through which actors coordinate their behaviour without hierarchical control (governance). This concept is applied most commonly to Europe (given the absence of a state at that level) and to the regional level. Yet at the regional level we can see a tendency over time to move from a system of functionally-specific administration, agencies and *ad hoc* interventions, to elected governments. This is not surprising. Given that functions are being handled at the regional level, that resources are present there and that economic and social problems can in some cases be more effectively addressed there, politics naturally follows, with the demand that these be subject to democratic control and opened to competition. We may, therefore, be seeing a move from governance to regional government and not, as often claimed, the other way around. It is, however, partial and confined to certain states. Elsewhere, territorial restructuring has led to a greater focus on the cities. Other territories again have been penetrated by new external influences without the ability to respond by forging their own institutions; this is especially the case where the various meanings of region (economic, cultural and political) do not coincide.

We have noted the persistence of older territorial cleavages and their reappearance in modern times; but also the emergence of new ones. Common influences have refracted differently across the continent as a result of domestic politics and conditions. There is some continuing division between the old and new member states, partly as a result of historical factors and the circumstances of state-building, but also stemming from more recent experiences.

Political science in recent years has moved back from the universalising ambitions of the postwar era, which aimed to explain behaviour all over the world as stemming from the same factors or combinations of factors. There is more recognition of the context of politics, of the weight of history and institutions and of dominant norms and practices. Regions and localities are the sites of many of these historical memories, norms and practices, not as an unchanging set of values but as a flexible framework within which social, economic and political questions are understood and addressed. Territorial politics never really went away but it is only in recent years that its importance has fully been appreciated.

PART III

Politics and Society

Chapter 9

Political Scandals and Corruption

Paul M. Heywood and Ivan Krastev

It could be argued that in Europe today, corruption has replaced communism as democracy's most dangerous perceived enemy. Just as the communist threat was often seen as coming from within through infiltration ('reds under the bed'), so corruption is also held to undermine democracy through its corrosive impact. Across many European democracies, both long-established and more recently created, a stream of high-profile corruption-related scandals since the early 1990s has contributed to a sense of de-legitimization of the political process. Notable examples have occurred in Italy, where corruption scandals led to major electoral reform, France, Spain, Germany, Belgium and virtually all the democracies of East-Central Europe.

In fact, Mishler and Haerpfer (1997) have argued that, at least in the case of post-communist societies, 'corruption has replaced repression as the main threat to the rule of law'. They suggest that the level of corruption is a more important determinant of support for 'undemocratic alternatives' than the country's democratic tradition, its current level of freedom or economic performance. In fact, it has been argued that in the post-communist context corruption causes the 'political damage' of 'undermining the purpose of public institutions' or diminishing popular support for democracy (Karklis, 2002). Whilst the situation is not so extreme in the established democracies, European publics nonetheless list the spread of corruption among the major problems facing their societies. As Dogan (2001) has argued:

> a ... wealth of data indicates that in most countries a large proportion of people are dissatisfied with the real functioning of the system, that they mistrust basic institutions and social organizations and that they have lost confidence in the 'political class' ... One cannot emphasize strongly enough the corrosive effects of corrupt behaviour on the loss of confidence in institutions.

In a sense, corruption is portrayed in the public discourse of many European societies in terms of what Cohen (1972) called 'moral panic', which is said to exist when a particular condition comes to be defined as a threat to societal values and interests and when its nature, consequences and solutions are presented by influential elites in 'a stylized and stereotypical fashion'. It could be argued that the 1996 call by the then President of the World Bank, James D. Wolfensohn, to combat the 'cancer of corruption' and the subsequent promotion of the 'good governance' agenda have both contributed to the sense of moral panic. This is in no sense to diminish the significance of corruption, nor its damaging impact on democratic politics, but rather to highlight the way in which corruption rhetoric has been instrumentalised for political ends. This chapter explores the reasons for the growth of interest in corruption in contemporary Europe, arguing that it does not simply reflect an increase in how much corruption is taking place. After a brief discussion of how corruption is defined, the chapter goes on to look at the costs of corruption, the reasons for its increased prominence in political discourse, the relationship between party finance and corruption, and how different forms of corruption have fed into the emergence of anti-corruption campaigns which – paradoxically – may actually pose threats to democratic stability.

Defining corruption

Rather than engage in a lengthy discussion of different definitions of corruption, on which there is an extensive literature, we adopt the widely used and parsimonious definition that – in its broadest terms – corruption is an abuse of public office for private gain (Heidenheimer, 1999; Rose-Ackerman, 1999). In practical terms, it often results in the development of 'a network of illegal exchanges' (della Porta and Vannucci, 1999: 20–1), which can become self-sustaining and entrenched. However, there are various different manifestations of corruption, ranging from grand-scale systemic (usually associated with a country's political leadership) to routine everyday (usually associated with bureaucracy and public officials). Examples of grand-scale corruption include *kickbacks* organized by political parties in power, for instance by setting up front-companies to charge banks and businesses for fictitious consultancy in return for privileged access to policymakers; *toll-gating*, whereby an illegal fee is charged for the granting of public licenses; and the creation of '*reserve (slush) funds*', which are generally used by political leaders to purchase favours. Routine or 'petty' corruption, which is very widespread in former communist countries, involves paying bribes to public officials, usually to access services which should be provided without charge.

Corruption is thus not just about straightforward bribery and personal enrichment, important though those elements undoubtedly are. Our principal focus in this chapter is specifically on *political* corruption, and here we follow Claus Offe (2004) who defines political corruption in terms of actors in the public sphere employing the powers of office for private and self-serving ends, especially through the 'selling and buying of public decisions'. Daniel Kaufmann (2004) also stresses the need to distinguish between different forms of corruption, and notes an increase in the 'purchase' of laws, regulations and policies as a recent trend, known in its more extreme forms as 'state capture' (see p. 171 below). Such short-circuiting of due process in decision-making is particularly insidious, since it attacks the very foundations of accountability upon which democracy rests. The key agents through which purchase of decision-making usually takes place are political parties, which are widely seen as the crucial mechanisms for channelling representation and ensuring political accountability (see van Biezen and Mair in this volume). That so many recent corruption scandals in Europe have involved political parties underlines why there is such concern about the damage being done to democratic legitimacy by high profile examples of malfeasance within the political class.

The costs of corruption

Concern about corruption is not driven just by moral repugnance. Recent literature on corruption (see World Bank, 2000: 18–24) has reached several conclusions about the direct and indirect impacts of corruption on the economic well-being of society, using both theoretical arguments and empirical case studies.

First, corruption hurts economic growth. It does so by undermining investments and by distorting the allocation of resources towards inefficient ends, driven more by corrupt rent-seeking opportunities than by any rationale based on economic productivity or growth – hence the existence of so-called 'white elephant' projects, often associated with poor standards in construction and safety (Cartier-Bresson, 2000). Corruption also means that the rules of economic activity are arbitrarily enforced, that property rights are insecure, and that the administrative capacity to provide services is diminished, all of which translates into a highly uncertain business environment (World Bank, 1997: 18–20). Uncertainty in turn raises the costs of private investment and damages the growth of productive capacity. At the same time, corruption undermines the effectiveness of public investment (Tanzi and Davoodi, 1997) – it leads not just to higher public investment expenditure, but also to lower productivity of such investment. Corruption also hurts prospects for foreign direct investment, put off by concern at the misappropriation of funds (World Bank, 2000: 23, note 2). In addition, corruption decreases the efficiency of resource allocation by introducing severe distortions into the price system (Shleifer and Vishny, 1993: 599–617) and, by creating incentives for lower budget revenues and higher budget expenditures, generates unsustainable fiscal positions (Tanzi and Davoodi, 1997; World Bank, 2000: 21–2) which result in high inflation and again in lower effectiveness of the price system. The impact on the price system results in a misallocation of resources towards sub-optimal uses. Ultimately, low investments and poor allocation of resources spell low growth in the long run.

Second, corruption not only hurts citizens' long-term welfare, but it does so in an unfair way. The costs associated with corruption fall primarily on the weakest and most vulnerable groups in society. Societies in which corruption is widespread experience more poverty and higher inequality than those where there is only limited corruption. This is due not only to lower growth, but to the fact that corrupt governments are effectively financed through regressive, rather than progressive taxes, that they cannot successfully establish and maintain social safety nets, and that they divert resources away from investment in human and social capital, both of which are important for reducing poverty and inequality (Gupta *et al.*, 1998; World Bank 2000: 20–1).

Third, corruption is a key factor in the erosion of trust in institutions, and therefore damages the social fabric more generally. That corruption leads to lower revenues and higher expenditure justifies people in thinking that they are paying more for less. Moreover, those who foot the bill – mainly the poor and the disadvantaged – get almost nothing from the services they are in fact financing. Logically, this leads to a very low level of public trust in state organs and in political leaders, thereby further reducing the capacity of the state to provide welfare-enhancing services (Shleifer and Vishny, 1993; Gupta *et al.*, 1998; Tanzi and Davoodi, 1997; Tanzi, 1998; World Bank, 2000: 21–2).

Fourth, as della Porta (2000) has persuasively argued, the spread of corruption over time generates a vicious circle in which widespread corruption undermines confidence in the government and public officials and thereby encourages the search for ways to bypass or short-circuit the official state machinery; in turn, the readiness to pay for privileged access to services which should by rights be provided free of charge, or at least without favour or discrimination, generates further incentives for public officials to engage in corrupt activity and thereby further undermines trust and confidence in the political process. As in postwar Italy, public officials may wish to be seen as inefficient, since that will increase their scope for charging a premium price to perform what should be routine duties. In this way, corruption and poor governance feed off each other in a self-sustaining manner.

Fifth, there is increasing concern – particularly in the former communist countries – about the links between the spread of corruption and the rise of organized crime and, indeed, terrorism. For instance, an official report by the Russian secret services documented that widespread bribery in the Russian police made it possible for Chechen terrorists to smuggle in the explosives used in the 2002 attack on a Moscow theatre. Elsewhere in Europe, separatist organizations such as ETA in Spain or the IRA in Northern Ireland have long imposed so-called 'revolutionary taxes' on local businesses, enforced via the threat of kidnap or assassination, whilst the Mafia (and national variants thereof) is believed to be responsible for much organized crime in a wide range of countries, but especially in Russia, Ukraine and other transition economies in East-Central Europe. The link between corruption, crime and terrorism is one which has generated major international concern since 9/11. Indeed, it can be seen as further contributing to the 'moral panic' in political discourse, noted above.

Explaining the increased visibility and salience of corruption

Corruption, though, is hardly a new phenomenon; on the contrary, it has existed to a greater or lesser extent in all societies and at all times. So, the obvious question is: how can we explain the recent emergence of global interest in corruption? What has happened? Do we have more corruption today? Or do we have corruption which is more harmful? Over the last decade, social scientists have sought to explain the prevalence of high level political corruption, with economists in particular using large-*n* factor analysis to identify the principal correlates of corruption. These have been variously identified as religious structure (specifically Catholicism), a legal tradition based on civil law, sustained low levels of economic development, federal rather than unitary state structures, lack of democratic tradition, and economic protectionism (La Porta *et al.*, 1999; Treisman, 1999; Paldam, 2001; Gerring and Thacker, 2004). However, such findings tell us little about the specific causal relationship between these factors and the actual incidence of corruption across different countries.

Two main analytic frameworks have been developed to explore why corruption occurs. On the one hand, some analysts have stressed the importance of cultural factors in generating a climate that is conducive to corruption: according to this view, influenced by the rise of 'social capital' theory, historic patterns of socio-political development generate particular modes of social interaction. Of particular importance is the emergence of generalized trust, which is seen as playing a crucial role in promoting healthy and productive exchanges between citizens and thereby stable economic development. Such patterns of development, linked to high levels of generalized trust, characterize the established, Western democracies. By contrast, the post-communist democracies have struggled to develop the kind of positive social capital which promotes trust and therefore economic development, falling victim instead to the kind of self-sustaining vicious circle of corruption and bad governance described above. The analytical difficulty with this approach relates to causal direction: does poorly developed social capital lead to corruption and bad governance, or is the level of social capital itself a reflection of the quality of governance?

On the other hand, it has been argued that high level corruption, like all other forms of corruption, is more accurately understood as a function of specific incentives (Rose-Ackerman, 1999). According to this view, the likelihood of corruption emerging in any given setting reflects a complex interplay between incentives and opportunity structures: since opportunities for corruption exist in nearly all forms of exchange transaction, the key issue centres on what kinds of incentive exist, and why they sometimes result in actual instances of corruption and other times do not. The analytical difficulty here lies in specifying the precise functioning of incentives, which will vary from individual to individual according to their particular make-up. Economists may argue that 'everyone has their price', and that incentives are therefore primarily financial, but even if such a cynical (and contestable) view is accepted it remains the case that the price will not only differ, but will also be influenced by a host of intervening variables – for instance, sense of personal morality, peer pressure, custom and practice, perceived likelihood of discovery, potential sanctions and so forth. Our view is that an incentives-based approach to explaining corruption is more persuasive than one based on cultural factors, but we also need to look at specific institutional and contextual factors to understand why corruption seems to have become such a prominent issue in contemporary European politics. We can identify six factors which have contributed to the increased visibility and salience of corruption.

First, the end of the Cold War also brought to an end the period of political hypocrisy it had created in the first place. Following the collapse of the Soviet Union, there was no longer any reason for Western democracies to support corrupt dictators who had sought to use anti-communism as a legitimizing rationale: it was neither necessary nor credible to turn a blind eye to corruption under the pretext of security issues. The end of the Cold War also effectively ended the great ideological confrontation between capitalism and communism in both the developed and developing world. When asked to explain the success of the operation *Mani Pulite* ('Clean Hands') in Italy, former President of the EU Commission, Romano Prodi, used just one word – 'Yalta'. What he meant was that end of the geo-strategic political framework established by Yalta helped convince Italian businesses that paying the 'party tax' to lock out the communists was no longer legitimate.

In fact, the end of communism gave rise to an unanticipated challenge to the very legitimacy of the democratic states which had 'won' the Cold War. Deprived of this great ideological clash, citizens in the established democracies began to focus their attention on the integrity of the political class. An 'Americanization' of European electoral politics, with an increased emphasis on US-style presidential contests, saw the old economy of 'selling ideology' replaced by the new economy of 'selling leaders'. Debate about moral values and the personal integrity of political leaders captured the public imagination, and general elections in particular saw ever more references to the personal attributes of the candidates for top office as a key factor in appealing for votes. According to a British diplomat (Theil and Dickey, 2002):

> Not so long ago, candidates were elected in much of Europe on the strength of their policies and platforms . . . These days it's personality that counts. The effect on European parties has been not so much to discourage corruption as to mask it, even to encourage it. With the new emphasis on TV blitzes, capped teeth, dyed hair and 'up-close' portraits of aspiring first couples, it takes much more money to win these days.

In particular, previous scandals involving the party in government led to opposition leaders emphasizing their own trustworthiness as a marked contrast to the alleged dishonesty of the incumbent governments – high-profile examples include José María Aznar's campaign against Felipe González in 1996, Tony Blair's against John Major in 1997 (and, indeed, Michael Howard's against Blair in 2005), Gerhard Schröder's against Helmut Kohl in 1998, Jean-Marie Le Pen's against Jacques Chirac in 2002, and – notably – José Luis Rodríguez Zapatero against Aznar in 2004. Moreover, the – albeit brief – success of populist politicians such as Pym Fortuyn, Jörg Haider and Christoph

Blocher has been attributed to a reaction against the perceived corruption and incompetence of mainstream politicians, reinforced by growing concerns about physical insecurity and immigration as key policy areas rather than questions about taxation and redistribution.

Also linked to the end of the Cold War are some issues which have contributed to the new anti-corruption sensitivity specifically in Eastern Europe. Following the political transformations unleashed by the fall of the Berlin Wall in 1989, the old system of exchanges of favours that typified the communist period was replaced by a rather less sophisticated form of bribery. Eastern Europe effectively made the transition from a 'do me a favour' society into a 'give me a bribe' society. The eruption of social inequality that took place in the post-communist countries as a result of so-called economic shock therapy was difficult to explain in terms of rewards for entrepreneurship and hard work. The emergence of a new rich and a new poor, together with the unexplained circumstances of success and failure, led people to believe that corruption was the only credible explanation. As will be seen in more detail below, massive privatization was the other critical factor increasing the incentives for corrupt behaviour. If we simply look at the scale of wealth redistribution that has taken place in the countries of the former Soviet bloc since the early 1990s, it becomes easier to understand the seeming fixation with corruption in East-Central Europe (World Bank, 2000).

A second factor which has contributed to the growing attention being paid to corruption relates to changes in global communication technologies. In a world where 'infotainment' has become a major growth industry, and in which investigative journalism seeks to generate high-profile news stories, corruption scandals offer a potent mix of newsworthiness and sensationalism. Moreover, the exponential growth of access to information and communication technologies (ICT) means that today, just by the click of a mouse, people can learn about the latest corruption scandals in all corners of the world. Not only are there several high-profile websites devoted to exposing corruption – such as those run by the World Bank, the OECD, Transparency International, The Corner House, and others – but corruption is also a major topic in the 'blogosphere', the news and opinion websites known as blogs.

Linked in some senses to these ICT developments, a third factor relates to the role of civil society and public awareness campaigns organized by NGOs to mobilize anti-corruption sentiments. Civic advocacy has been partially responsible for making corruption a problem not just in corrupted countries, but also for those corrupting them. In particular, the emergence of Transparency International (TI)

as a highly visible international NGO dealing with corruption has significantly shaped the anti-corruption agenda. The publication of TI's
annual Corruption Perceptions Index (CPI) each October has become a
major international news event, which not only attracts considerable
attention, but has also become the standard reference point for
assessing levels of corruption across the world.

A fourth factor, of particular relevance to former communist states,
is that the spread of democracy itself has contributed to revelations of
corruption. This is not to argue that democracies are by definition
more or less corrupt than non-democratic regimes, but democratic governments have to face the verdict of the ballot box. Electoral competition may increase the likelihood that acts of corruption will be
exposed, as opponents seek to gain advantage through whatever means
are at their disposal – although, during the Cold War period, a tacit
understanding between the political class and other social actors
(notably, the media) ensured that some corruption scandals were not
exposed in the way they would later be once democratic 'victory' over
communism had been ensured (Pujas and Rhodes, 1999). Of particular
significance in the exposure of corruption was the developing independence of the judiciary in countries such as Italy, where the impact of
the 'Clean Hands' operation also helped mobilize support for the
newly accorded prominence of the fight against corruption (Heywood,
Pujas and Rhodes, 2002).

Fifth, increased mobility and the new global market have also contributed to corruption's greater visibility. In the words of Vito Tanzi
(1998):

> globalization has brought individuals from countries with little cor-
> ruption into frequent contacts with those from countries where cor-
> ruption is endemic. These contacts have increased the international
> attention paid to corruption, especially when some companies
> believed that they were cut out of some contracts because the
> winning company has paid a bribe.

The sixth factor contributing to the current focus on fighting corruption is the prominent role played by multinational companies, which
have moved from being viewed as major sources of corruption to
posing as fighters against corruption. In the words of George Soros
(*Financial Times*, 1998), 'There is always somebody who pays, and
international business is generally the main source of corruption.'
Multinational companies have long used bribery to win contracts or
favourable terms, especially for public sector construction works and
the supply of military equipment. Indeed, until recently, bribery was

seen as a normal business practice, which was even tax-deductible in states such as France, Germany, the Netherlands, and Norway. It is noteworthy that in Bulgarian, all French, German and English words for doing business have the connotation of performing a corrupt act.

In the 1960s and 1970s, foreign investors saw corruption as a useful way to open up and modernize the economies of developing countries. Corruption was used as an instrument to break the protectionist barriers that were imposed by the governments of the post-colonial states. And multinational companies were able to exert persuasive influence through their financial power, their value often dwarfing the GDP of those developing countries in which they sought to invest. However, two significant changes have combined to alter the perspective of many multinational companies. First, the US Foreign Corrupt Practices Act (FCPA) of 1977, designed to prevent corporate bribery of foreign officials, represented a significant (if flawed) step adopted in the wake of the Watergate investigations by the Security and Exchange Committee, which revealed widespread payments by US companies to foreign governments – notably the so-called Lockheed scandal, in which the US company had bribed Japanese government officials to buy its aircraft. The FCPA made the issue of corporate corruption prominent, but it was not really until the anti-protectionist stance of the World Trade Organization (WTO) came to assume hegemony that the need to combat corruption in international business transactions was widely recognized by most developed countries. The FCPA provided the model for the 1997 OECD Anti-Bribery Convention, which was designed to support WTO initiatives – but, despite reasonably widespread ratification of the Convention in Europe, it is too early to assess its real effectiveness.

In practice, protectionism has become an unaffordable luxury for most governments. Indeed, in the transition economies of Central and Eastern Europe, protectionism is simply unthinkable. Their dependence on IMF loans and competition for foreign direct investments has forced them to open their economies and adopt non-protectionist legislation. It is this new open environment, rather than the FCPA and the OECD Convention, that has been the major reason for multinationals' change of mind on corruption. Compared with properly regulated markets in goods and services, corrupted markets are characterized by the very high value of local knowledge. In order to corrupt public officials and to win contracts, it is not enough just to offer the biggest bribe in the biggest brown-paper bag. The market in corruption services is clandestine and closed, and in order to be competitive in it, players need to know when, to whom and how to give a bribe. Local businesses are much better positioned in this market because they are plugged into the existing networks and possess local knowledge. In other words, a corrupted business environment is much more favourable to local businesses than to foreign investors. Unlike the Lockheed scandal which prompted the FCPA, the major corruption scandals in Eastern Europe in recent years have not concerned multinationals paying bribes to win contracts, but rather multinationals losing contracts or seeing their property rights undermined. Corruption in the commercial world today is a hidden form of protectionism.

Corruption and the cost of politics

Money and corruption are, of course, intimately related. So, too, are money and politics. The increased visibility of corruption has inevitably shone a spotlight on the issue of political finance – and in particular the key role of political parties as the principal nexus between money and politics. Indeed, party-related corruption has been a central feature of several high-profile scandals which have emerged over the last two decades in European democracies – from the Flick scandal of the early 1980s in West Germany and the ongoing investigations into funding of the French RPR, to the 'hundreds of political funding scandals' in Central and Eastern Europe (Walecki, 2003). Such corruption has involved not just the search for illegitimate sources of revenue, but also extorting bribes, appointing party members and followers to lucrative positions in the public sector, and channelling money to the pockets of party leaders.

Corruption connected to party funding is thus a common feature across both Western and Eastern Europe. However, as will be seen in more detail below, the problem is particularly acute in the transition economies. The key question is why political parties should be so closely linked to corruption: to use the framework suggested earlier, what have been the main incentives for parties and how have they related to any changes in opportunity structures? We can point to three specific incentives for parties to accrue more money. First, it is widely believed – though with little systematic research so far to prove the assertion (Pinto-Duschinsky, 2002: 82) – that politics has become an ever more expensive business. As indicated by van Biezen and Mair in this volume, political parties remain the key linkage between the public and politics and play the lead role in mobilizing voters, selecting candidates for public office, and organizing election campaigns. All of these activities cost money: parties need to pay for staff, office space, advertising, equipment, transport and so forth. Second, the availability of 24/7 access to news means that parties are on a more or less permanent election footing. As recognized by the UK's Committee on Standards in Public Life, the belief that elections can only be won through vast expenditure mainly on advertising has 'put enormous pressure on party fundraisers to devise imaginative ways of attracting donations' (Neill Committee, 1998). The temptation therefore exists for parties to spend as much as they can, often exceeding formal campaign spending limits. In short, in democratic politics corruption is a mechanism to raise campaign money and control loyalties that can be critical for electoral success (della Porta and Vannucci, 1999: 22–3).

Third, as the pressure on political parties to spend more money has grown, so some more traditional sources of income have started to diminish. In European democracies mass parties are in decline; nowhere do political parties generate sufficient income through membership dues to cover their costs – indeed, most major parties in developed democracies run significant levels of debt. Moreover, some of the traditional financial links that parties of the left used to enjoy – notably, links between social democratic parties and trades unions or between communist parties and the Soviet Union – have either been significantly weakened or have dried up altogether. Thus, the incentive exists for parties to seek out new funding sources, and all have increasingly turned to the business and financial sector as a key source of income. Links between these sectors have become closer, reflected in the emergence of so-called 'business politicians' and the 'revolving-door' – the appointment of corporate executives and lobbyists to public posts and the movement of government officials into positions in the private sector.

Examples abound of such appointments, notably concerning EU Commissioners. For instance, Martin Bangemann, a member of the disgraced Commission which resigned in 1999 amidst accusations of fraud, immediately joined the Spanish telecommunications giant, Telefónica, having been responsible in the early 1990s for EU information and telecommunications policies. Other commissioners who joined private-sector companies in areas related to their EU responsibilities include former President of the Commission, François Ortoli (Elf, which itself was subsequently embroiled in a major corruption scandal), and Peter Sutherland (BP and Goldman-Sachs). And, despite increased sensitivity to the revolving-door issue, and the existence in many countries of 'cooling-off period' guidelines or special appointments commissions, it was stated in December 2005 that the outgoing German Chancellor, Gerhard Schröder, was to join the North European gas pipeline project agreed just three months earlier between the state-controlled Russian energy giant, Gazprom, and several German companies.

A predictable response to the problem of parties seeking ever more funds is to regulate the use of money in politics. Nassmacher (2003) has identified the 'magic quadrangle' – transparency, accounting, practicality and sanctions – as the core to regulating finance and monitoring party funding, alongside civil liberties and a free media. It is also widely believed that state funding of political parties can help reduce the propensity to corruption, particularly when allied to spending limits. Yet, when we look at two of these indicators– the existence of direct public funding and of disclosure laws (Table 9.1) – what is striking is not just that the vast majority of countries in Europe already have some form of state funding (though the amount and basis for calculation varies widely); more significant is that the only three countries which do not have disclosure laws are Finland, Sweden and Switzerland, all of which are seen as having very low levels of corruption (see Table 9.2). Indeed, Sweden has no maximum limit on donations to political parties.

Moreover, Sweden has been slower than many other European countries to embrace the WTO-inspired turn to deregulation linked to major policy initiatives such as privatization. It is significant that in both the established democracies, and most especially in the transition economies, the sale of state assets to the private sector has generated major new opportunities for corruption. Indeed, large-scale privatization is widely seen as one of the key explanations for the rise of corruption during the post-communist transitions in Eastern Europe. Political parties, of course, were deeply implicated in privatization-related corruption scandals, seen not just as responsible for implementing the policy but also suspected of deriving direct or indirect benefit. Theoretically, and in the long run, privatization is promoted as a corruption-reducing policy (Kaufmann, 1997). But in practical terms, and especially in the short run, privatization often increases the level of corruption. In spite of evidence from established democracies on links between privatization and corruption, economic restructuring in Eastern Europe – whether through so-called shock therapy as in Poland or through more gradual reform as in Hungary – placed privatization at its very heart. Experience from the established democracies pointed to clear risks: in the case of the UK, the *Financial Times* quoted police in 1996 stating:

> the overwhelming majority of corruption cases in Britain are connected to the award of contracts. Compulsory contracting-out in local government, and the new Private Finance Initiative have produced an explosion in the number of such deals.

Table 9.1   *State funding and disclosure laws in Europe*

	State funding	Disclosure laws
Austria	Yes	Yes
Belgium	Yes	Yes
Bulgaria	Yes	Yes
Czech Republic	Yes	Yes*
Denmark	Yes	Yes*
Finland	Yes	No
France	Yes	Yes
Germany	Yes	Yes*
Greece	Yes	Yes*
Hungary	Yes	Yes*
Ireland	Yes	Yes*
Italy	Yes	Yes*
Latvia	No	Yes
Lithuania	Yes	Yes
Macedonia	Yes	Yes
Malta	No	Yes
Moldova	No	Yes*
Netherlands	Yes	Yes
Norway	Yes	Yes
Poland	Yes	Yes*
Portugal	Yes	Yes*
Romania	Yes	Yes*
Russia	Yes	Yes*
Slovakia	Yes	Yes*
Spain	Yes	Yes
Sweden	Yes	No
Switzerland	No	No
Ukraine	Yes	Yes*
United Kingdom	No	Yes*

* indicates that individual donations must be declared.

Source: Compiled from data in Pinto-Duschinsky (2002).

In France, the system of privatizing public utilities through contracting-out – *gestion délégué* – 'led to widespread corruption, overcharging for services and weak control over the privatized companies' (Hawley, 2000: 3). In Austria, Belgium, Italy and Spain, leading politicians have been accused of accepting bribes from private companies in relation to the sale of public assets.

In the transition economies, the incentives for quick enrichment via privatization were so high that corrupt behaviour became almost unavoidable. The Polish Minister of Privatization, Janusz Lewandowski, gave an ironic but telling description of the process: 'Privatization is when someone who does not know who the real owner is and does not know what it is really worth, sells something to someone who does not have any money' (Dunn, 1999). Lewandowski's definition touches on three problems with the post-communist privatization processes. The first relates to the pricing of the ex-state property – a difficulty which has also affected various privatizations in the established democracies (Grout *et al.*, 2001). The prices of the socialist enterprises differ dramatically in the eyes of the market and in the eyes of society, leading to the widespread complaint that the states have been selling off their assets too cheaply.

A second problem relates to the buyers. Domestic buyers for large, and even middle-sized, enterprises did not exist in Eastern Europe. 'Real' socialism had not created a society of equal prosperity, but at the outset of the transition many still believed that it was a society of equal poverty. In the initial years of transition, therefore, some citizens were able to get access to credit and become buyers, whilst the (mis)fortune of the majority remained aligned with that of the selling state. For that majority, it was the past of the new owners that intrigued them much more than the future of the privatized enterprises. And the third problem is that the very process of privatization was conceived by many as a form of corruption *per se*. The absence of effective controls over 'black' and 'grey' privatization practices acted as a catalyst to the rise in popular reaction against both corruption and the newly emerging financial elites. In a 12-month period, one Czech study identified 33 cases of personal gain from privatization, totalling some 25 billion Czech crowns, but which resulted in only two prosecutions (Miller *et al.*, 2001). The Bulgarian economist Roumen Avramov (2001) identified 'the privatization of profits and nationalization of losses' as the major formula for creating the private sector in post-communist Eastern Europe. State assets to be privatized function as 'natural resources' in the early stages of transition and it is not surprising that post-communist regimes displayed some of the characteristics of the so-called 'oil democracies' of Latin America, Africa and the Middle East.

Administrative corruption and state capture

Recent research on corruption has stressed the need to distinguish between different kinds of corruption, which not only have different causes, but also different impacts. All corruption is damaging, but there are important distinctions to be drawn between countries where corruption has become embedded and virtually all-encompassing, involving state politicians and the public administration, and those where corruption is primarily confined to local politics and where there is only the occasional high-profile scandal at national level. Although open to challenge in terms of both design and underlying methodology, and despite the fact that it does not make explicit distinctions between different forms of corruption, TI's Corruption Perceptions Index offers an indicative guide to those countries in Europe where corruption is most deep-seated. Table 9.2 shows clearly that, at least in terms of perception, corruption is significantly more of a problem in the former Soviet-bloc countries. Only five of the established Western democracies – Malta, Portugal, Cyprus, Italy and Greece – ranked below 7.0, which is usually taken as the cut-off for 'least corrupt' countries, whereas the best score achieved amongst the transition countries was 6.4 in Estonia. Nine countries were accorded a score of 3.4 or below, placing them in the 'most corrupt' category.

The difference between the established democracies and the transition economies is significant. Although corruption is a concern across Europe, the nature of that concern differs markedly: whereas in most of Western Europe, corruption scandals have contributed to the loss of confidence in public institutions (above all, political parties), in the more recently democratized states corruption has assumed an altogether more far-reaching dimension. Concern about corruption is becoming a powerful policy narrative in much of Eastern Europe, the explanation of last resort for a whole range of failures and disappointments in the fields of economics, politics and even culture.

Of particular concern is corruption which entails the purchase of public policy decisions. As the former chair of Transparency International, Peter Eigen, has argued, contemporary political corruption is less about personal enrichment than about 'the purchase of access to policy-makers, and political parties are the prime target in this game' (Transparency International, 2000). The World Bank report *Anti-Corruption in Transition* (2000) distinguishes between administrative corruption and state capture. The former refers to deliberate distortions in the implementation of laws and regulations, involving 'grease payments', bribes and various other forms of extortion. This kind of corruption is found, to a greater or lesser extent, in all states. However, it is state capture – 'the actions of individuals, groups, or firms both in the public and private sectors *to influence the formation* of laws, regulations, decrees, and other government policies to their own advantage as a result of the illicit and non-transparent provision of private benefits to public officials' (World Bank, 2000: 16) – that poses the most significant danger to the proper functioning of democratic institutions. State capture can involve various institutions (such as the executive, the legislature, the judiciary, regulatory agencies) and

Table 9.2   *CPI 2005*

Country rank (out of 159)	Country	2005 CPI score
2	*Finland*	9.6
4	*Denmark*	9.5
6	*Sweden*	9.2
7	*Switzerland*	9.1
8	*Norway*	8.9
10	*Austria*	8.7
11	*Netherlands*	8.6
	United Kingdom	8.6
13	*Luxembourg*	8.5
16	*Germany*	8.2
18	*France*	7.5
19	*Belgium*	7.4
	Ireland	7.4
23	*Spain*	7.0
25	*Malta*	6.6
26	*Portugal*	6.5
27	Estonia	6.4
31	Slovenia	6.1
37	*Cyprus*	5.7
40	Hungary	5.0
	Italy	5.0
44	Lithuania	4.8
47	Czech Republic	4.3
	Greece	4.3
	Slovakia	4.3
51	Latvia	4.2
55	Bulgaria	4.0
70	Croatia	3.4
	Poland	3.4
85	Romania	3.0
88	Bosnia and Herzegovina	2.9
	Moldova	2.9
103	Macedonia	2.7
107	Belarus	2.6
	Ukraine	2.6
126	Russia	2.4

Note: 'Western' European countries in italics.

Source: Compiled from data in TI Corruption Perceptions Index (CPI) 2005 (http://www.transparency.org/cpi/2005/cpi2005.sources.en.html#cpi).

may be attempted by a range of different actors, including private firms, political leaders or sectional interest groups. It is in regard to state capture that we see the clearest differentiation between Western and Eastern Europe, with the more established democracies less susceptible to the kind of overt attempts to buy and sell control that have been evident in some of the transition economies.

Corruption can also be used directly as an electoral resource. A striking illustration relates to the loans-for-shares scheme implemented in Russia in 1995. In the autumn of that year, public opinion polls indicated that the re-election of President Yeltsin seemed a mission impossible. His approval ratings were desperately low, and public rejection of his politics and personality was overwhelming. In order to be re-elected Yeltsin needed a powerful political constituency and to this end, the loans-for-shares schemes was developed. According to Chrystia Freeland (2000: 162, 173):

> the loans-for-shares deal was a crude trade of property for political support. In exchange for some of Russia's most valuable companies, a group of businessmen – the oligarchs – threw their political muscle behind the Kremlin ... The complicated two-step plan implicitly bound the economic fortunes of the future oligarchs to the political fortunes of the Yeltsin administration. In the autumn of 1995, the businessmen received stakes in Russia's most valuable companies only in trust. The final, formal transfer of ownership would not take place until the autumn of 1996 and in 1997 – after the presidential elections. When he signed the decree, the Kremlin chief bought himself the constituency which a year later would guarantee his re-election.

It is understandable in the light of such activities that public mistrust of and cynicism towards the political class as a whole, and parties in particular, should have risen so markedly in recent years across all of Europe – but most especially in the transition economies.

The costs of corruption-centred politics

Concern over corruption has reached unprecedented heights in recent years. In both Western and Eastern Europe, corruption has become a major focus for policy-makers, political reporters and academic researchers. Yet, across Europe, anti-corruption campaigns seem to be running out of steam. As they become more familiar, corruption scandals lose their power to shock and so act as catalysts for reform; instead, the pervasiveness of scandals can create the sense that corruption is endemic in politics. Indeed, there is something of a silent consensus that the war on corruption has failed to obtain the expected results, particularly in the transition economies:

Though still in the early stages of development, the experience of anticorruption programs to date has produced mixed results ... Ambitious anticorruption campaigns in several countries have floundered at the implementation stage. Key structural reforms have been blocked by powerful vested interests. In some cases, politicians have hijacked the anticorruption agenda and used it to attack their rivals. (World Bank, 2000: 15)

A study sponsored by the European Bank for Reconstruction and Development (EBRD) has indicated that implementing the anti-corruption package advocated by international financial institutions has failed to affect levels of corruption in the transition countries.

One issue which has not received much attention in the literature is the possibility that anti-corruption campaigns can have a negative impact on the process of democratic consolidation. A seemingly ineluctable tendency of anti-corruption campaigns is the constantly expanding definition of corruption. If at the outset of such campaigns the suspicion is that corruption is almost everywhere, subsequently the suspicion develops that corruption is almost everything. Ultimately comes the conviction that almost everybody is corrupt. The fear of being accused of corruption effectively paralyses government officials and the major objective of policy-makers becomes that of searching for policies that look clean regardless of what other disadvantages they may have. Making 'transparency' the ultimate policy objective helps explain why governments have recently favoured privatization 'by auction' even when the evidence is clear that such an approach can have a damaging impact on infrastructural development. For governments, it has become more important to prove their 'honesty' than to pursue more appropriate economic options.

A second disadvantage of anti-corruption campaigns is that they have contributed to a blurring of the lines between different political options. Corruption-centred politics in a way is the end of politics: it moralizes policy choices to the extent that politics is reduced to a choice between corrupt government and clean opposition. The risk of such a development is that it 'depoliticizes' political judgement. As Warren (2001) states, 'when the trustworthiness of the candidate overrides agreement on the issues, the vote does not reflect a judgement about public affairs, but is something more like a defensive reaction against a system that has, for all practical purposes, been written off as captured by other interests'. Corruption-centred politics is thus one of the explanations for the transformation of East-European democracy into what have effectively become protest vote democracies.

If the trend has been starker in several transition economies than in the established democracies of Western Europe, there are nonetheless grounds for concern in the latter too. One development of note has been the rise of populist parties, which in turn has seen mainstream parties often adopt a more populist style in response (see Chapter 10). Fieschi and Heywood (2004) have distinguished between 'traditional' populists and 'entrepreneurial' populists: whereas the former (for instance Jean-Marie Le Pen and Jörg Haider) base their appeal on the standard rhetoric of offering an anti-system alternative, the latter (for instance, Silvio Berlusconi or Pym Fortuyn) seek to 'play' the system in a more knowing fashion, almost making a virtue of its rotten state. For both traditional and entrepreneurial populists, the public sense of disillusionment with politics – whether expressed through outright mistrust or growing cynicism – is essential to their success. And that disillusionment is largely driven by a focus on corruption-related scandals, which contribute – as stated at the start of this chapter – to a loss of confidence in political institutions.

In turn, then, a third potential disadvantage of current anti-corruption campaigns is that, through an ever increasing delegitimization of the political elite and public administration, they can serve as a disincentive to non-corrupt actors entering those spheres. Such an outcome makes it easier for the corrupted to continue to exercise their perverse influence within political institutions. The claim that politicians are corrupt by definition, therefore, is dangerous for the democratic process, but nonetheless appears to have significant support in many European countries.

Conclusion

Does all this mean, then, that we should pay less attention to the issue of corruption? It does not. However, what this chapter has sought to highlight is that we need to be alert to three factors in particular when analysing corruption. First, there is a need to distinguish between different types of corruption (grand versus routine, public versus private sector, personal versus institutional and so forth) and seek to identify their particular causes and characteristics. Second, it is essential to ensure that anti-corruption campaigns are more carefully focused, based on a better understanding of how corruption incentives and opportunities work in practice, so that specific measures can be more appropriately targeted. There is no 'one size fits all' model of good governance, no ideal form of state organization, which will counteract corruption in all cases: what works in some circumstances may produce undesirable outcomes in others. Third, there is a need to keep concern about corruption in proportion: in the established democracies, this means that the reporting and use of political scandal needs to be handled responsibly; in the transition economies, the problem is much more acute since corruption is far more widespread and deep-rooted. However, there is a real risk that the near obsession with corruption in many of the former communist countries may undermine democratic development by destroying trust in the political class as a whole. Ultimately, for all the current international concern about corruption, anti-corruption initiatives stand the best chance of succeeding when they are genuinely led from within countries – supported both by public opinion and the honest elements within the political class - rather than imposed from outside.

Chapter 10

Anti-System Politics

Cas Mudde

In the afterglow of the fall of the Berlin Wall, Francis Fukuyama famously proclaimed 'the end of history'. Similarly, politicians and scholars alike argued that liberal democracy had now become, in the words of Juan Linz and Alfred Stepan (1996), 'the only game in town' – at least on the European continent. However, developments since 1989 have shown that these commentators might have spoken too soon, or at least too strongly. Throughout Europe dissenting voices remain, some from the distant past, some rather newer.

Despite the absolute triumph of democracy, at least in name, various movements continue to challenge key aspects of the contemporary European democracies. Within a liberal democratic context, one could label these 'anti-system' (for example Capoccia, 2002; Sartori, 1976), in the sense that they challenge some of the fundamental institutions or values of the liberal democratic systems of Europe. Two basic sub-types of anti-system movements in Europe can be distinguished, depending upon the specific elements of liberal democracy they challenge. Extreme movements challenge the essential idea of democracy, that is the sovereignty of the people. In contrast, radical movements challenge only certain key liberal elements of the system, such as the constitutional protection of minorities or the separation of institutional powers. Thus, extremists are truly anti-democratic, whereas radicals 'only' challenge liberal democracy.

This chapter first discusses briefly the developments in system support and opposition at the mass level. The bulk of the chapter encompasses an analysis of the four key challengers to European democracies, including their character, development and explanations for their rise. The third section discusses the various ways in which European democracies have responded to these challenges, with a particular focus on the role of the European Union (EU). Geographically, the prime focus is on the 25 member states of the EU, although references to other European countries are included when relevant. The chapter concludes with a short assessment of the role and (possible) future of anti-system politics in the new Europe.

Mass support for the liberal democratic system

Decades of mass survey research in established European democracies confirm the common view that everyone is a democrat now. No less than 82 per cent of citizens in the 15 old member states of the EU believe that democracy is the best political system (Eurobarometer, 47.1, 1997). This is not much different in the new post-communist democracies, including those that have not yet joined the EU, where only limited support for non-democratic alternatives exists (see Rose *et al.*, 1998). Despite this, contemporary democracies are confronted with a 'democratic paradox' (Dahl, 2000): many citizens combine a high level of support for democracy as a system with disdain for some key democratic political institutions. It is this tension that anti-system movements seek to profit from.

On the basis of survey data a picture emerges of continuing high levels of diffuse support (Easton, 1965) for democracy, but at the same time fairly low levels and intensities of specific support. In Eurobarometer studies, diffuse support is measured by the question: 'On the whole, are you very satisfied, fairly satisfied, not very satisfied or not at all satisfied with the way democracy works in (your country)?' Despite considerable movement in certain periods, notably in 1999–2001, the situation in the 15 old members states of the EU has not changed much in the past 15 years (see Figure 10.1).

In both 1990 and 2004 the largest group (around 45 per cent) of the EU-15 citizens were 'fairly satisfied' with the way democracy functioned in their country, while a large minority was 'not very satisfied' (around 30 per cent). Only a small minority was 'very satisfied' (around 10 per cent) or 'not at all satisfied' (around 15 per cent). In short, we can conclude that a small majority of Europeans expresses diffuse support for the national democratic system, though only moderately so. However, there are significant national and regional differences. Most importantly, the average level of diffuse support for democracy in the 15 old member states was 57 per cent, compared to just 33 per cent in the 10 new member states (Eurobarometer, 63, 2005). While few people are very satisfied, only slightly more are very unsatisfied; in other words, mass level support for (extreme) anti-system movements politics is fairly limited.

Although the democratic system still enjoys overwhelming support in theory, and large support in practice, this is not the case for several

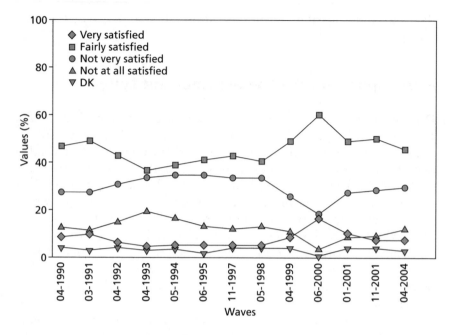

Figure 10.1 *Average diffuse support in the EU-15, selected dates 1990–2004*

Source: Data from
http://europa.eu.int/comm/public_opinion/cf/subquestion_en.cfm

of its key institutions. Most importantly, parliaments, governments and parties are facing (sometimes sharply) increasing scepticism in almost all European democracies (Pharr and Putnam, 2000). According to Eurobarometer surveys over the past decade, average levels of trust for key national political institutions within the EU-15 were just over 40 per cent for parliaments, just under 40 per cent for governments, and well under 20 per cent for political parties. The severity of the lack of trust in political parties, the most important political actors in European democracies (see Gallagher *et al.*, 2005), was made painfully clear in the aftermath of 9/11, when the parliament and government enjoyed a short-lived rise in trust (51 per cent and 48 per cent, respectively), whereas political parties remained at their low level of 18 per cent (Eurobarometer, 56, 2001). In 2004, the EU-average dropped further, mostly because of the inclusion of the more sceptical new member states: 32 per cent of all EU-citizens trust theit parliament, 28 per cent trust their government, and just 14 per cent trust political parties (Eurobarometer, 61, 2004).

The four main challenge(r)s

It is not always easy to divide the different anti-system movements into a few clear and recognizable sub-groups, as they represent very different shades and colours. Rather than trying to devise a wholly new, perfect classification scheme, I will group the challengers on the basis of both their prime ideological core and their practical manifestations. This leads to four separate categories, which are partly overlapping in both theory and practice: political extremism, political radicalism (including populism), religious fundamentalism, and terrorism. Within these broad categories, various sub-types can be distinguished. Rather than trying to be exhaustive, this chapter introduces only the most relevant subtypes and refers selectively to some key actors.

Political extremism

Even though Europe became an almost uniformly democratic continent during the twentieth century, many will remember it first and foremost as 'The Age of Extremes' (Hobsbawm, 1994). More than the continuing spreading of democracy, it was the political extremism of the right (fascism) and left (communism) that left its bloody mark on Europe (and beyond) in the past century.

Political extremism is here understood as political ideas that are undemocratic in the sense that they challenge the sovereignty of the people. Usually, the literature distinguishes different forms of extremism on the basis of the two key categories of political ideology: left and right. While much can be said about the content and usefulness of this terminology, here the terms are defined in line with Norberto Bobbio's famous distinction: the left considers the key inequalities between people to be artificial and negative, to be overcome by an active state, whereas the right believes that the main inequalities between people are natural and not to be changed artificially, for instance by the state (cf. Bobbio, 1996).

The extreme right reached its zenith in the first part of the twentieth century, with Italian fascism and German National Socialism as its most notorious and gruesome representatives. With the end of the Second World War, fascist regimes ceased to exist, although right-wing authoritarian governments did manage to survive in some southern European countries (Greece, Portugal and Spain) until the 1970s. In most of postwar Europe extreme right parties have been completely marginal, with the possible exceptions of the German National Democratic Party (NPD), during certain periods, and the Italian Social Movement (MSI). Given the almost complete consensus on the preference for democracy at the mass level, these parties are shunned by voters. Indeed, a majority of the population in Europe supports the banning of 'fascist parties'. In reality, only very few extreme-right parties are banned, even though most European countries do have legal provision to do so (see below).

Insofar as the extreme right is still relevant in contemporary European politics, it is through the violence with which it is often linked. Particularly since the 1980s, 'extreme-right violence' has become a serious public order problem in a number of European countries, most notably the Czech Republic, Germany, Slovakia and Sweden. While 'racist' violence is often linked to 'skinheads' and extreme-right organizations in the media, most known perpetrators do hold racist or xenophobic views but are not activists in these organizations (see Wahl, 2003). Nonetheless, various countries have reacted with repressive measures against extreme-right (youth) organizations, including international groups like Blood & Honour (B&H), which has led them to go (even further) underground and localize their activities.

The high point of the extreme left in Europe was the period 1945–89, when the eastern part of the continent was ruled by communist regimes, and related parties fared well in various Western countries (notably Finland, France, Greece, Italy). Since the fall of the Berlin Wall in 1989, most extreme-left parties have either transformed into social democratic or democratic socialist ones, or they have ceased to exist. However, unlike on the right, some extreme-left parties seem to have escaped relegation to the political margins (see March and Mudde, 2005; Moreau *et al.*, 1998). Large unreformed communist parties still exist within various post-Soviet states, notably Moldova (PCRM), Russia (KPRF) and Ukraine (KPU), while smaller communist parties gain significant election results (5–10 per cent) or else are part of larger coalition blocs and governments in France (PCF), Greece (KKE), Italy (PCI and RC) and Slovakia (KSS).

Still, it is important to note that while most contemporary European communist parties might still refer to revolutionary socialism as their ideological basis, in terms of their actions their extremist credentials are far less obvious. In some European countries they constitute more or less reliable coalition partners in democratic governments. But even in the case of semi-permanent opposition parties, most communist parties belong at the very least to the category of 'semi-loyal' opposition. A good example is the Czech Communist Party of Bohemia and Moravia (KSČM), one of the largest openly communist parties within the EU with almost 20 per cent of the vote. The party has recently replaced its old-style leader, Miroslav Grebeníček, with the more modern and moderate Vojtěch Filip, in a clear attempt to become *koalitionsfähig* for the Czech Social Democratic Party (ČSSD).

In addition to (Soviet-style) communist parties, a broad variety of other extreme-left organizations continue to exist. In essence, most of these organizations belong to one or more of the many permutations of Maoism and Trotskyism. In terms of electoral politics, these parties are irrelevant, if they even compete in elections; notable exceptions include three Trotskyist parties in France (for example Bell, 2002). At the non-party level, some extreme-left organizations are still able to mobilize large numbers of people, although they pale in comparison to the demonstrations of the late 1960s and early 1970s. Moreover, Trotskyist groups in particular have tried to regain significance through their old strategy of infiltration and acting as front organizations within the 'new fringe' (see below).

Political radicalism (especially populism)

As suggested above, political radicalism is not anti-democratic *per se*, but anti-liberal democratic. In other words, radical opposition is situated within democracy, whereas extreme opposition places itself beyond democracy. There are various types of political radicalism, but the most relevant in contemporary European politics is undoubtedly populism. While populism can be democratic, it is essentially anti-liberal and anti-constitutionalist (see Mény and Surel, 2002; Canovan, 1999). Within the ever-growing debate on the correct meaning of the term, various key features of populism are found in most definitions. In line with the emerging consensus, populism is here defined as a (thin) ideology that considers society to be ultimately separated into two homogeneous and antagonistic groups, 'the pure people' versus 'the corrupt elite,' and argues that politics should be an expression of the *volonté générale* (general will) of the people (Mudde, 2004).

In contemporary European politics populism is mainly associated with the right, that is with political parties like the Austrian Freedom Party (FPÖ) of Jörg Haider, the French National Front (FN) of Jean-Marie Le Pen, or the Norwegian Progress Party (FrP) of Carl Ivar Hagen. Although many authors group these parties together into one category of 'the' (populist) radical right, it makes more sense to distinguish at least two sub-categories: the populist radical right and neo-liberal populism (Mudde, 2006; Betz, 1994). While both groups share the core feature of populism, they differ significantly in their world-view; most importantly, the former is fundamentally collectivist, whereas the latter is essentially individualist.

The core ideology of the populist radical right combines three features: nativism (a combination of nationalism and xenophobia), authoritarianism and populism (Mudde, 2006). Some of the most prominent party representatives of this sub-category include the Belgian Flemish Interest (VB), formerly Flemish Bloc, which enjoys the support of one-quarter of all Flemish voters and one-third of the electorate in Antwerp, the biggest city of Flanders and Europe's second-biggest harbour; the French FN, whose leader Le Pen made it into the run-offs of the 2002 presidential elections in France; the League of Polish Families (LPR), whose 7–8 per cent electoral support is closely linked to the Catholic-nationalist sub-culture in Poland; and the Greater Romania Party (PRM), whose leader Corneliu 'Vadim the Righteous' Tudor gained 30 per cent of the votes in the run-offs of the 2000 presidential elections in Romania.

One of the most significant developments of the past two decades has been the transformation of the populist radical right 'from the margins to the mainstream' (Hainsworth, 2000). Within the 25 current EU member states, three have had populist radical right parties in their government at least for a period: the FPÖ and the recent Haider-split Alliance for Austria's Future (BZÖ) in Austria (2000–02 and 2002–05), the Northern League (LN) in Italy (1994 and 2001–05), and the Slovak National Party (SNS) in Slovakia (1994–98). In addition, the Danish People's Party (DFP) has been a vital supporter of the Danish minority governments since 2001.

The neo-liberal populist sub-category has a core ideology that combines populism with neo-liberalism, the latter mainly defined in economic terms. Even more than the populist radical right, neo-liberal populist parties are associated with their leaders. In many cases, the parties are not much more than personal entourages of the leader, which generally causes great problems in sustaining their initial electoral success. Consequently, some of the most spectacular 'flash parties' – that is, party political one-hit-wonders who score huge victories in one election and virtually disappear in the next – can be found in this family: for example, the Dutch List Pim Fortuyn (LPF), the eponymous party of the murdered flamboyant 'pink populist', or the German *Schill-Partei*, named after its leader, *Richter Gnadenlos* (Judge Merciless) Ronald Schill. However, in some cases charismatic leadership can be combined with long-time political success as well: the best example is the Italian *Forza Italia* (FI), the party of media tycoon and two-time Italian Prime Minister, Silvio Berlusconi.

While the two groups of parties show some striking similarities, in terms of ideology and electorate, they are far from identical. In fact, their main similarity is to be found in functional terms. With some degree of simplification, one can argue that populist radical right and neo-liberal populist parties operate largely as functional equivalents in Europe. Like Christian-democratic and conservative parties, they rarely feature prominently in the same party system, but they perform roughly the same role in their respective party systems. Populist radical right and neo-liberal populist parties function first and foremost as right-wing challengers to the political establishment. Whereas both groups target all mainstream parties for being corrupt and outdated, and exploit economic and xenophobic tensions in their propaganda, populist radical right parties tend to have a more xenophobic discourse, while neo-liberal populists focus more on economic arguments.

While these are the two most visible populist actors of contemporary Europe, the phenomenon is by no means limited to the right. Most notably, social populists have gained some significant electoral results in recent years, including the Scottish Socialist Party in the UK, the German Left Party (PDS), or the Polish Self-Defense of the Republic (*Samoobrona*). Social populists combine a core ideology of socialism and populism, although their socio-economic policies often resemble more old-style social democracy then real socialism (March and Mudde, 2005). To a large extent, they profit from the popular dissatisfaction with the right-wing turn of social democratic parties in Europe, both in the East and West.

In addition, populist rhetoric and policies have been expressed by parties of the mainstream, be they right, left or centre. With some degree of exaggeration, we could argue that Europe is currently experiencing a populist *Zeitgeist* (Mudde, 2004), in which populism is prevalent in politics as well as in many other aspects of life. Anti-establishment sentiments and positive references to 'common sense' are pervasive features of the discourse of many parties and politicians, including both government and opposition leaders. For example, the former Vice-Premier of Flanders, the socialist Steve Stevaert, regularly claimed to follow 'the wisdom of the people' rather than the advice of academics. Similarly, former British Conservative Party leader William Hague claimed to defend 'Middle England' against 'the condescending liberal elite' of New Labour. This is not to say that we are all populists now, but it is important not to limit assessments of the use and relevance of populism to the usual suspects on the right.

One of the more heated debates within European politics is about how mainstream parties should deal with radical parties. That this is not just a matter internal to individual states was shown most dramatically in the case of the 'EU boycott' of the first Austrian government of Wolfgang Schüssel. In 2000 the Christian Democratic Austrian People's Party (ÖVP) broke the unwritten *cordon sanitaire* around Haider's FPÖ, and formed a coalition government with it. This led not only to the scorn of the Austrian (left-wing) opposition, including then

President Thomas Klestil, but also to political sanctions from the 14 other EU member states of that time (see Merlingen *et al.*, 2001). The sanctions prompted much resistance within Austria and amongst the EU-14. After some seven months, they were lifted unconditionally and without any changes within the FPÖ-ÖVP government, as a consequence of the so-called 'Wise Men Report'.

Another aspect of the discussion on the way to deal with radical parties focuses on the lessons to be drawn from government participation by these parties. On the basis of some spectacular cases, at the national level notably the FPÖ and the LFP, some argue that radical parties should always be taken 'into the fold' of government, believing that they will inevitably implode both electorally and organizationally. However, there are some less spectacular examples of radical parties surviving government participation as well, such as the FI and LN in Italy and the SNS in Slovakia. At the same time, while a formal or informal *cordon sanitaire* might have led to the marginalization of radical parties in countries like Britain and the Czech Republic, it has done nothing to stop the unprecedented electoral advance of the Belgian VB. Consequently, the debate about the best way to deal with radical political parties continues to preoccupy (and divide) politicians and public in many European countries.

With regard to radical non-party organizations, the term 'new fringe' is used here to capture the plethora of more and less organized groups and movements that do not easily fit within the classic left–right spectrum. The new fringe includes the (now almost traditional) issues of the new social movements of the 1970s, like peace and the environment, but also more recent concerns, including animal rights and globalization. Obviously, such a broad and diverse category entails individuals and groups with a broad variety of positions *vis-à-vis* liberal democracy. The vast majority of groups and activists within the new fringe is democratic, just a tiny minority is radical or even extreme in actions or ideas; examples include ecological authoritarian intellectuals or anarchists like the *Autonome* and the 'Black Bloc'.

Here we are concerned exclusively with the radical component of the new fringe, that is with those actors and ideas that challenge fundamental aspects of liberal democracy without questioning democracy *per se*. Within the new fringe one finds radical forces in almost all major movements, ranging from animal rights to anti-globalization or from ecologism to anti-war. In part, their critique resembles that of more classic radical left forces, that is challenging certain liberal features that are believed to prevent ecological and social justice (for example private property), but other complaints are specific to the new movements (for example the call for legal personality for animals).

While the height of the new social movements was in the 1970s, the new fringe continues to be a visible and relevant aspect of European politics, particularly in western parts. This is especially the case for the anti-globalization movement, even though this 'movement of movements' combines a wide myriad of at times conflicting ideologies and interests (see Starr, 2000). As a consequence of their popularity, some new fringe issues and organizations are targeted by external actors. Particularly within Trotskyist circles, establishing front organizations or infiltrating existing organizations represent key strategies to extend their influence beyond traditional circles. So far, there have been more failures, such as the attempted infiltration of the German branch of the Association for the Taxation of Financial Transactions for the Aid of Citizens (ATTAC), than clear successes, like the British Anti-Nazi League (a front organization of the British Socialist Workers' Party).

While the direct political influence of most new fringe movements remains fairly marginal, they do have weight with certain decisions and decision-makers. For example, the relatively large demonstrations of the anti-globalization movement, and the support from prominent intellectuals for groups like ATTAC, have clearly influenced the debate on globalization, most notably within left-wing parties. A first symbolic victory has been gained recently with regard to the so-called Tobin tax, the suggested tax on all currency trade in Europe, which has become a *cause célèbre* for the global anti-globalization movement. Having already been endorsed by prominent left-wing leaders in Latin America, such as the presidents of Brazil (Luiz Inácio Lula da Silva) and Venezuela (Hugo Chávez), the Belgian federal parliament approved a bill in 2004 stating that the country will introduce the Tobin tax if all other countries in the eurozone agree to do the same.

Religious fundamentalism

Religion plays a role among some political extremists, notably from the right, yet for religious fundamentalists it is obviously the main basis of their ideology. Religious fundamentalism can be defined as the belief that religious values are the most fundamental, thus overriding democratic values or human rights in case of opposition. Fundamentalism is of course not linked to one specific religion; in fact, it can be found in all major (monotheist) religions in Europe.

Not all religious fundamentalists are political. In fact, many religious fundamentalists prefer to separate themselves mentally and physically from the 'sinful' and 'impure' world around them, taking no part in politics whatsoever. A good example of such a religious fundamentalist group is the Jehovah's Witnesses. Others are essentially non-political, but become involved in politics to defend their existence and privileges, such as the Church of Scientology. And there are religious fundamentalists who are not just explicitly political, but are violent too. These latter groups will be discussed under the heading of terrorism below. In this section, the focus is on religious fundamentalists who are active within conventional European politics.

Not surprisingly, given decades of secularization, religious fundamentalism is fairly marginal within European politics. In some countries Christian fundamentalists do play some role within mainstream politics. Probably the only relevant Christian fundamentalist party in contemporary Europe is the Protestant State Reformed Party (SGP) in the Netherlands. Although it never challenged democracy in practice, the party still supports the introduction of theocracy. In addition, some Catholic fundamentalist groups are influential in non-fundamentalist parties, such as the Christian-Solidarity faction in the French FN, *Opus Dei* in the Spanish Popular Party (PP), and *Radio Maryja* with regard to various Polish right-wing parties (notably various successors of Solidarity, including the LPR). In addition, Orthodox fundamentalists play an important role in the politics of various post-communist countries, such as Bulgaria and Russia.

While Christian fundamentalism is clearly on the decline, other forms of religious fundamentalism are gaining ground in Europe, most notably within the immigrant communities. Hindutva fundamentalism has been exported from India to the Hindu community of the United Kingdom, where it has taken root among mostly younger second and third-generation immigrants (see Bhatt, 2000). A similar development is taking place among some Sikh youth, who find refuge in fundamentalist Khalistan movements (see Biswas, 2004). However, given the relatively moderate size of these communities in the United Kingdom, let alone in the whole of Europe, these movements remain fairly marginal in political terms.

The situation is somewhat different in the case of Islam, which has become Europe's second religion over recent decades with some 23 million believers. As in all major religions, the vast majority of Muslims are not fundamentalist. And even of the small percentage of those who hold fundamentalist beliefs, only a tiny minority is politically active (approximately 1 per cent of all Muslims). These so-called 'Islamists' organize mainly in non-party organizations, such as the Muslim Association of Britain (MAB) or Islamic Community *Milli Görüs* in Germany. In recent years, some Islamist political parties have been founded in Europe, though so far with little success in elections; for example, the Muslim Democratic Party (MDP) in Belgium and the Netherlands. Their political relevance within the larger community remains small, but they do add further fuel to the already widespread Islamophobic attitudes in post-9/11 Europe. Moreover, Islamic fundamentalists can be dominant within larger Islamic communities, notably in the so-called *banlieues de l'Islam* (Kepel, 1997) of some major European cities (for example Hamburg, Leeds, Paris, Rotterdam).

Terrorism

Whereas the first three categories were mainly defined on the basis of goals and ideas, terrorism is at least in part defined by its chosen methods. Even if we leave aside the normative platitude that one person's terrorist is another person's freedom fighter, terrorism is notoriously difficult to define. Already in 1988, Alex P. Schmid and his collaborators found no less than 109 different definitions, including 22 major features, and this was well-before the recent boom in terrorism studies (Schmid, 1988). In a recent assessment of this major work, the continuing existence of conceptual confusion was confirmed (Weinberg *et al.*, 2005). While accepting the possibility of overlap with definitions of political violence, a very basic working definition is employed here: terrorism is the organized pursuit of political goals by violent means.

Up until a few years ago, terrorism was a big problem for a small group of European countries. The most violent postwar period in this respect was the 1970s, which saw a broad campaign of left-wing terrorism around groups like the Red Brigades in Italy and the Baader Meinhof Group in West Germany. In the 1980s, political and media focus shifted more to the right, particularly in countries of the former Eastern bloc (including East Germany). However, even though 'right-wing' violence has been a significant problem in various European countries in recent years, there have been few cases of right-wing terrorism. One of the few exceptions has been Sweden in the 1990s, when small neo-Nazi cells were involved in terrorist acts, though mainly killing each other. Speculations about a Brown Army Faction in Germany, referring to similarities to the left-wing terrorist Red Army Faction (RAF) of the 1970s, have so far proven exaggerated and unsubstantiated, even in the former communist Eastern part.

In addition to political terrorism of the left and the right, some European countries have been faced with a threat of territorial terrorism (see Hewitt and Cheetham, 2000). Obviously, the most affected countries in this respect are Spain and the United Kingdom, which have for decades been haunted by terrorist attacks from separatist groups like Basque Homeland and Freedom (ETA) and the Irish Republican Army (IRA), as well as from 'retaliations' by 'loyalist' opponents, such as the Spanish Anti-Terrorist Liberation Groups

(GAL) and the Protestant Northern Irish Ulster Volunteer Force (UVF). In recent years the death toll of separatist terrorism has decreased significantly within these countries, with the recent pledge to disarm of the IRA serving as a highpoint. That said, ETA is still active, despite suffering heavy operational losses as a consequence of counter-terrorist actions by Spanish (and French) security forces, while Corsican separatists have become increasingly violent within France.

Since the 1980s, some (Western) European countries have also been confronted with so-called 'single-issue terrorism', focusing mainly on animal rights and ecological issues. The most important terrorist group in this respect is the Animal Liberation Front (ALF), which operates in various European countries, but is only truly active in a few. While the ALF is linked in the media mainly to sympathetic actions, such as the liberation of furry animals from breeders, the group has a dark side too. In countries like the Netherlands and, most notably, the United Kingdom, ALF activists have been involved in terrorist attacks against both properties and people. These attacks have involved the torching of companies and laboratories, which were believed to mistreat animals, the vandalizing of cars and homes of people involved in animal testing, and even the threatening of their families (including the children). In comparison, ecological terrorists, such as the Earth Liberation Front (ELF), have been relatively inactive and moderate, with the exception of spiking trees in Britain and the USA (see Wall, 1999).

Whereas the political terrorism of the twentieth century has been a threat in only some European countries, at least for most of the postwar period, religious terrorism seems to have become the scourge of all of Europe, and far beyond, at the beginning of the twenty-first century. Since the horrific attacks of 11 September 2001, European democracies have felt threatened by 'Islamic terrorists', often referred to simply as 'the al-Qaeda network'. How deadly this threat can be for European democracies, has been shown in the murderous attacks in Madrid (11 March 2004) and in London (7 July 2005). In addition, experts claim that at least fifteen major terrorist attacks have been prevented on European soil in the four years after 9/11.

Not much is known about the internal life and structure of Islamic terrorist organizations. While parts of the media and some governments insist on creating a picture of one well-integrated movement, 'the al-Qaeda network', most experts reject this image as a (dangerous) simplification. Acknowledging the prime significance of the al-Qaeda group and its leader, Osama bin-Laden, both in terms of inspiration and structural support, they differentiate between the threat constituted by the largely foreign al-Qaeda network and the various domestic Islamic terrorist groups and networks.

Militant Islam has been present within immigrant communities in Europe for decades, but it has been given a new dimension in the light of the 'successes' of the al-Qaeda network. Whereas 'Jihadists' used to look for foreign organizations and battlegrounds in the past, some are increasingly turning inward. Rather than joining some Mujahideen group in Afghanistan, Bosnia or Iraq, these youths form their own cells and organizations in their native country with the aim of attacking domestic targets. An example of such a domestic group, despite the alleged significance of a Syrian national within it, is the Dutch *Hofstadgroep*, one of whose members (Mohammed B.) murdered the film producer and Islam critic Theo van Gogh on 2 November 2004.

While the threat of Islamic terrorism is not limited to countries with a large Islamic population, given the international connections of the 'movement' (particularly the al-Qaeda network), the growth of domestic Islamic terrorism clearly is. Consequently, European countries like France, Germany and the United Kingdom feel particularly vulnerable to the development of domestic Islamic terrorist groups. Security officials in various European countries warn of the increasing militancy of Muslim youths and of the development of domestic terrorist groups. However, the situation should not be exaggerated. According to the German Federal Bureau for the Protection of the Constitution (*Bundesverfassungsschutz*), only 1 per cent of the approximately 59,000 Muslims in Germany are members or sympathizers of an Islamist movement. Of these, just a tiny minority are considered potential terrorists. While little is known about the characteristics of these potential terrorists, experts believe them to be mainly well-educated, middle-class, second-generation immigrant males.

There is little doubt that Islamic terrorism is the main terrorist threat of the immediate future, both inside and outside Europe. But its effects have already been significant, not just directly (notably the human devastation of the terrorist attacks), but mainly indirectly. Since 9/11, all European democracies have introduced new anti-terrorist laws and practices. While the implications for liberal democracy are not always easy to discern, there is little doubt that many of these measures are at least challenging the spirit of liberal democracy, if not the very essence of it.

The liberal democratic response

Unlike authoritarian regimes, liberal democracies have a particular problem in dealing with anti-system politics. The key dilemma is how to defend democracy against anti-democrats without becoming anti-democratic. A particular problem is the question of how to deal with movements that pursue anti-system ideas with democratic actions – as anti-system actions, that is political violence, are illegal in all liberal democracies. Should anti-system movements have the (democratic) right to pursue their anti-democratic goals? Or do democracies have the (democratic) right to use 'anti-democratic' measures to protect themselves?

With regard to responding to non-violent anti-system ideas, two opposing models of response can be distinguished, at least in theory (see Eatwell and Mudde, 2004). In the first model, often branded the American, all political ideas are tolerated and treated equally, whether pro- or anti-system. In the second, known as the German model, political mobilization on the basis of anti-system ideas is considered illegal, irrespective of the way it is done. It is probably easiest to see the two models as the poles of one dimension, with most countries somewhere in between (including Germany and the USA).

In the final two decades of the last century, European democracies mainly focused on anti-system challenges from the extreme and radical right. Whereas most extreme-right and racist acts of violence could be prosecuted under existing legislation, the expression of extreme-right and racist ideas often needed a new legal framework. In part as a consequence of international treaties (United Nations) and cooperation (EU), European democracies are converging increasingly in their anti-racist legislation. Nowadays, almost all EU member states are far closer to the German than the American model; this even holds true for the post-communist states, which initially tended to be far closer to the American model (see Mudde, 2005).

But while legal provisions might become increasingly similar within the EU, significant differences in the way these provisions are implemented continue to exist. For example, whereas anti-democratic parties are illegal in many European countries, only a few have actually banned such parties. Many East European countries banned communist parties in the first years of post-communism, but most have since lifted that ban. In Western Europe, countries like Austria and the Netherlands have banned extreme-right parties; the National Democratic Party (in 1988) and the Centre Party'86 (in 1998), respectively. Even within a single country important regional differences may exist in terms of the state response to anti-system actions and ideas. This is so not just in the typical case of the united Germany, but also in many post-communist countries.

One of the most debated cases in this respect has been the failed attempt to ban the extreme right NPD (see Flemming, 2003). In Germany, the Minister of Interior can ban anti-democratic organizations, but only the Federal Constitutional Court (*Bundesverfassungs-gericht*) can ban political parties (see Kuhn in this volume). Although the NPD had been threatened with a ban many times before, it took until 2000 for the German state to finally make good on its threats. However, the court case soon became entangled in the so-called 'V-*Männer Affäre*'; several NPD members, whose pronouncements had played an important role in the case against the party, had been working at the same time as informers (*V-Mann*) for the German secret service. After months of legal procedures, and heated debates in the media and between politicians, the Court finally ruled against the legal case to ban the NPD in 2003, largely because it could no longer clearly distinguish between genuine NPD leaders and V-men.

At least since the attacks of 9/11, the primary focus for defending democracies has moved from the extreme right to Islamic fundamentalism and terrorism. It is still too early to assess the full significance of this change, including the lasting consequences and effects of the post-9/11 measures for the state of liberal democracy within Europe. However, it seems that Europe is experiencing not just a quantitative but also a qualitative development in terms of the nature of its democratic defence. Not only have most western democracies increased the number of acts and ideas that are deemed illegal, including 'the glorification of terrorism', and increased the severity of their punishment, some of the fundamental values of liberal democracy have become challenged by the self-professed defenders of that very system (see Heinz, 2004; Haubrich, 2003).

European democracies are transforming slowly but steadily from the model of the *Rechtsstaat* (legal state) to that of the *Sicherheitsstaat* (security state) (Braml, 2004). While in the legal state all citizens are equal before the law, in the security state some have fewer rights than others. Initially, the limitation of legal protection was almost exclusively applied to foreign nationals, particularly alleged Islamic fundamentalists from non-Western countries. But some countries, including the United Kingdom, have started to apply measures of limited legal protection also to the own citizens. For example, one of the most crucial principles of the rule of law, that someone is innocent until proven guilty, has been replaced in some cases by the obligation to prove one's innocence. And even the illegality of torture no longer seems to be beyond debate, at least in the USA (see Goldberg, 2005), although European democracies have so far 'limited' themselves mainly to using information acquired by torture in other countries.

While the first provisional counter-terrorist measures were temporary, and little contested, recent permanent laws have given rise to more serious political protest. A good example of such a contested counter-terrorist measure is 'detention without trial', one of the most radical aspects of the Anti-Terrorism, Crime and Security Act 2001 (ATCSA), introduced by the UK Labour government shortly after the 9/11 attacks (see Fenwick, 2002). After heated debates, the Law Lords ruled that the principle of detention without trial is illegal and unacceptable. Giving in to political opposition from Labour backbenchers, Prime Minister Tony Blair removed the controversial point from the government's permanent anti-terror law in 2004. However, in the aftermath of the terrorist attack on London in 2005, the UK government reintroduced the proposal to hold terrorist suspects for up to 90 days without charge.

As most of these developments are very recent, and (to some extent) the result of very dramatic terrorist attacks and panic reactions by both the elite and the masses, the contemporary and future significance cannot yet be assessed properly. Many questions will remain open for some time to come: Will European democracies transform fully into states of security? Will the measures now developed to defend democracies from the international threat of Islamic terrorism be applied as well to other anti-system challengers? Will the European Union be able to develop a common model of defending democracy; and if so, which model will it choose? Irrespective of the answers to these questions, one thing is beyond discussion: European democracies are increasingly converging towards a more proactive and restrictive model of defending democracy.

Anti-system politics in Europe: an assessment

Given the societal context of strong diffuse support for democracy, as outlined above, it comes as no surprise that extreme, anti-democratic movements enjoy little mass support in contemporary Europe. Whereas political extremism was the main anti-system challenge of the twentieth century, political radicalism has become the main anti-system force of the twenty-first century. The major contemporary anti-system movements do not so much reject democracy *per se*, but challenge some key features of liberal democracy instead. The key anti-system movements are populist parties, so far mostly of the right (that is liberal and radical right), which have proved very effective in influencing the mainstream discourse (rather than the policy).

Since the terrorist attacks of 9/11, most European democracies have started to see Islamic fundamentalism as the main threat. Although much of the terrorist threat is external, that is coming from groups and individuals from non-European countries (mostly Islamic Asian and

African countries), European states have introduced many legal and extra-legal measures to curb the perceived danger from domestic Islamists and 'Jihadists'. While this process is still very much in progress, a development from *Rechtsstaat* to *Sicherheitsstaat* seems detectable. This means that in addition to a democratic paradox, European democracies are experiencing a democratic defence paradox: while anti-system politics has never been so weak, in terms of intensity of ideas and level of mass support, the response by European democracies has never been so strong, in terms of both legal and extra-legal actions.

Chapter 11

Organized Economic Interests: Diversity and Change in an Enlarged Europe

Sabina Avdagić and Colin Crouch

A wide range of organizations and associations seek to represent the interests of their members within the national public sphere, as well as at the European level. Contemporary organized interests in Europe comprise, on the one hand, various groups representing specific economic interests within production or consumption spheres, and on the other, groups whose primary or direct interests are non-economic and who concentrate instead on issues such as the environment or gender equality. This chapter is focused on one segment of the arena of organized interests, namely on functional economic interests represented by organizations of business and labour. The significance of these actors in contemporary interest politics stems not only from their size, organizational capacity and long-standing structures, but also from the fact that they have been traditionally the key players in shaping distinct models of interest representation and thus different types of political economies in Europe.

In what follows we discuss recent developments in the organization and politics of organized economic interests in the old and new EU member states. We first sketch distinct forms of interest representation, and then examine some of the principal challenges to the stability of those forms, and in particular of neocorporatism. Finally, we show that despite the common challenges associated with general changes in the conditions of economic activity, and internationalization and Europeanization of national economies, there are considerable differences in the extent and character of the resulting changes both between and within the two parts of Europe.

Forms of interest representation

The contemporary literature distinguishes between three main forms of democratic interest representation: pluralism, statism and (different types of) neo-corporatism. It is also necessary to draw attention to a fourth form, which though not in itself democratic, is found widely and increasingly in many democratic polities, namely the unitary form of industrial relations.

Pluralism is a form of interest politics in which a variety of groups and organizations freely compete for political representation of their interests, mainly by relying on various lobbying tactics to influence policy outcomes. Rather than directly intervening, negotiating or collaborating with organized interests, the state's role is limited to providing legislation and ensuring competition between autonomous organizations. Relations between fragmented organizations of business and labour are highly voluntaristic and mainly workplace-based. This model originated in the USA, and within Europe it has been associated with the UK.

Statism denotes a pattern in which a proactive state plays the principal role in policy formulation. The impact of organized interests in the process of policy-making is minimal, and limited only to a small number of organizations directly selected by the state. State intervention in industrial relations is pronounced, particularly in issues such as minimum wages, the extension of collective agreements, and the settlement of labour disputes. Bargaining between polarized interest organizations can occur at different levels, with the central level involving a particularly strong role of the state. This pattern has been traditionally associated with the French regulatory state.

Neocorporatism is a form of interest intermediation in which the state shares authority with a limited number of typically hierarchically ordered, well-articulated, non-competitive and broadly based private-interest organizations who actively participate in both policy formulation and implementation (Crouch, 2000; Schmitter, 1974). Interest associations usually have an encompassing character, that is their national peak organizations represent in an effective way such a high proportion of the workforce that they cannot easily separate their organizational interests from those of the society as a whole. They therefore abstain from exclusively furthering their narrow interests, and ensure that their members conform to public policies that are in the general interest – in the sense that their activities do not create negative externalities (Olson, 1982). Rather than competition, neo-corporatism is characterized by coordination within associations and cooperation among them. Depending on the type of neocorporatism (see below), social partners regularly engage in either national or sectoral-level collective bargaining (especially over wages and incomes policy, employment conditions or labour market policy) that serve as the key instruments of macro-economic management.

Several types of neo-corporatism can be distinguished. The Nordic or Scandinavian model is usually associated with a high degree of consensus and coordination between strong and cohesive interest organizations. Encompassing trade unions, in particular, have been the main pillar of this model, while the state has traditionally played the role of a mediator. Well-established tripartite structures serve as a channel for linking collective bargaining with macroeconomic considerations.

Another type of corporatism – usually referred to as the continental European social partnership model – rests more heavily on a comprehensive system of legal regulations defining the terms of free collective bargaining between well-organized and highly coordinated associations of business and labour. Here, the role of the state has been more indirect than in the Nordic model; collective bargaining is highly coordinated and occurs predominantly at the sectoral level. This model has been prevalent in Germany, Austria and the Benelux states.

Finally, a state-led corporatist model characterizes systems in which social partners are considerably weaker and corporatist institutions, although sometimes extensive, need continuing state support. In the first decades after the Second World War this form of corporatism was evident in some countries that subsequently transformed into the continental social partnership model, such as Austria and the Netherlands. In general, however, this model is usually associated with state-led corporatist attempts in the post-authoritarian Spain and Portugal, and to a lesser extent Greece. The consolidation of political democracy in these countries, however, made governments less dependent on social partners. A search for social pacts has continued to be a component of the politics of interest representation, but with no strong consolidation of corporatist arrangements as had happened at earlier periods in North-West Europe (Molina, 2004; Rhodes, 1997; Schmitter and Grote, 1997). Similarly, state-led formation of national-level corporatist structures was visible in the Central and Eastern European countries (CEECs) following the collapse of communism. As in Southern Europe, the main purpose of these structures in the immediate post-transition period was to preserve social peace and strengthen the legitimacy of the new democratically elected governments (Avdagić, 2005; Schmitter and Grote, 1997). Subsequently, however, the consolidation of corporatist-type institutions has proved to be even more problematic than in Southern Europe, and their role in macroeconomic management more limited. Characterized by the generally weak social partners and an underdeveloped sectoral level (save for Slovenia and to a lesser extent Slovakia), this hybrid type of neocorporatism displays very little coordination between different bargaining levels. With the uncoordinated, enterprise-level bargaining becoming predominant across the CEECs, these systems appear to be increasingly remote from the classical neocorporatist pattern.

Finally, the fourth form of interest representation, while usually found at a sub-national level, is increasingly common in contemporary capitalist democracies. This is the unitary form of industrial relations (Fox, 1966), where employers do not permit their employees to have any autonomous organization at all. While this prevents organized interest representation on the employee side, organization by business interests is not inhibited. This is the predominant form of interest representation in many regions and industries in the USA, France, the UK, Spain and most CEECs. In all these countries unions are able to organize in some other regions and industries, producing a national system in which the organization of 'the two sides of industry' is visible and even significant. However, there are likely to be systematic blank spots in its coverage, and a related weakening of the representation of labour interests.

As the above account implies, elements of these different forms of organized interests can be found in various combinations across countries. It is, for example, entirely possible for many firms to assert a unitary position (allowing no organization among their employees) within a country otherwise characterized by strong collective bargaining; or for neo-corporatist patterns to exist in export industries while pluralist bargaining without wage restraint exists in industries not exposed to foreign trade. However, there is a tendency for characteristic national patterns to emerge. This is because nation states have had considerable autonomy in deciding the kinds of interest representation patterns that they will accept within their societies. In general, some states (for example, Germany or the Scandinavian countries, though in very different ways) accepted the role of organizations of interests in governing society, but would determine what kinds of interest they would permit to take on this role. In other cases (France and the UK are two, again diverse examples) states guarded their domestic sovereignty more jealously. This in turn affects the way in which the organizations then develop (for a detailed account of the emergence of these different patterns in Western Europe from the late nineteenth century to the end of the twentieth, with the roots of different state traditions being traced back to the early modern period, see Crouch 1993).

Pressures for change

The last two decades have presented considerable challenges for nationally specific forms of economic interest representation in Europe. These challenges relate to: general changes in the conditions of economic activity; the role of internationalization in the context of these changes; and the specific form of internationalization embodied in Europeanization. All of them have profoundly affected the organization of labour and business.

General changes in the conditions of economic activity

Several broad challenges for established patterns of interest representation can be identified here. To start with, technological innovation puts pressure on firms to change their production strategies so as to achieve higher flexibility and better quality with lower costs. In this process firms need to reorganize not only their supplier chains and modes of financing, but also their shopfloor relations, requiring more highly skilled labour and more flexible terms of employment. By driving a more general reconfiguration of labour markets and occupational structures, the advancement of technology has an important effect on interest organization of both labour and business.

Similarly, structural economic changes, such as the substantial shifts of employment from manufacturing to the service sector and to smaller production units, indicate a significant reconfiguration of the traditional organization of work and production. Given that large industrial enterprises have been traditional strongholds of trade unionism, the decline of manual employment is likely to result in the weakening of organized labour.

A weakening of interest associations is further reinforced by intraclass divisions that have emerged along several sectoral lines. One of the most prominent is that between the tradable goods and services sectors (that is, those whose products can be traded internationally) on the one hand, and the 'sheltered' sectors (in particular non-traded services and the public sector) on the other. Faced with an increased international competition and the generally slack labour markets, unions in the tradables sectors have often backed their employers in their quest for higher competitiveness. This means that they have shown more willingness to accept wage moderation and significantly higher wage differentials than unions in public non-tradables. In this sense, we can talk about the erosion of the traditional class solidarity. In many economies (major exceptions being the Nordic countries) the organization of labour has been far easier to achieve in public services than private ones (many of which are also non-tradable). The current greater ease of organizing cross-class alliances in the tradables sector has therefore frequently led to public services becoming the major sites of industrial conflict. Given that this largely leaves out the organized interests of private employers, the conflict paradoxically becomes one between public employees and their fellow citizens who are the users of their services. Because they are eroding the traditional class basis of interest politics, these developments have serious implications for the established patterns of interest representation. Contemporary interest politics faces more complex requirements, as it needs to accommodate several new cleavages that have emerged across occupational and sectoral lines. This change would seem to threaten the corporatist systems most directly, as this pattern is accustomed to non-competitive interest associations.

Finally, most significant of all has been a change in the nature of the 'game' being played in relations among the interest organizations, and between them and government. Under Keynesian demand management there were constant inflationary pressures. National governments were committed to sustaining full employment, and this made it likely that employers' associations and unions would reach wage agreements that exercised upward pressure on prices, as they would assume that government would intervene to prevent the consequences of a fall in demand and the increased unemployment that would follow a rise in prices in a pure market economy. The central purpose of corporatist arrangements of all kinds was to persuade employers and unions to see that in the long run this would cause general damage to the national economy in question. Although this kind of restraint was particularly difficult for unions to achieve – as it meant not exercising their full power in the organized labour market – there were clear circumstances in which it could and did happen (see Crouch, 1993; Katzenstein, 1985; Olson, 1982). If inflation could be contained, Keynesian demand management and the full employment guarantee could be maintained alongside strong interest organizations. There was a positive-sum collective outcome available, if the organizations possessed the organizational capacity and the motivation to seek it out.

The post-Keynesian economy provides a more difficult scenario, because it presents its participants with considerably greater uncertainty. The greater difficulty that governments experience in guaranteeing full employment and stable domestic markets is itself a source of that uncertainty, but the collapse of Keynesianism had been in turn the result of growing uncertainties that made demand management more difficult to achieve. The most important sources of these will be discussed below. The overall result has been to shift the nature of the game to one over the distribution of uncertainty. Whose lives will be made more insecure, and whose less, by these uncertainties? While there continue to be, as with the inflation game, positive-sum outcomes, the uncertainty game also has multiple equilibrium outcomes that are zero- or even negative-sum. If capital becomes stronger in the global economy (as we suggest below that it does), it can press for labour to bear a large share of uncertainty in product markets by accepting reduced work security and reliability of wages. Organized business might also lobby politically for greater price stability to be achieved through reductions in pensions and social security payments, which in turn reduce security for the workforce. At the same time, unions may seek to protect the conditions and security of 'insider' established workers (more likely to be union members), at the expense of marginalized outsiders. These latter usually include a disproportionate number of young people, women and ethnic minorities. For instance, to take an example found particularly in Spain, a protection from redundancy of existing workers, despite uncertain product markets, can be achieved by giving only temporary contracts to most new employees. There are many other possibilities. In general, the weaker parties in any situation will be forced by the stronger to bear the brunt of uncertainty. The identity of the weaker parties may be determined by position in the hierarchy of the corporation, in the labour market, or in the politics of relations among organized interests.

The role of internationalization

The growing internationalization of economic activities and intensified market competition, have posed similar pressures on national economies and in most cases required their substantial adjustment. With growing economic interdependence and an increasing need for deflationary policies, governments could no longer rely on aggregate monetary and fiscal instruments to enhance economic performance. The combination of these pressures and the perceived failure of Keynesian demand management encouraged European governments to adopt various measures aimed at the deregulation of trade, financial and labour markets, privatization and cutting budget deficits. Since these policies encourage the reinforcement of market mechanisms, they limit the role of interest associations in the policy-making process. Thus, the impact of internationalization and its associated policy shift is likely to have most detrimental consequences for the corporatist systems, traditionally rooted in the joint regulation of the economy. In particular, the bargaining position of labour has become significantly weaker: deflationary policies have led to higher unemployment, while deregulation and privatization have undermined the largely 'union-friendly' national enterprise in large manufacturing. This in turn has resulted in a decline of union membership. These developments combine with those discussed above to further convert conflict in industrial relations into that over the allocation of insecurity burdens.

Patterns of interest representation are also affected by another consequence of trade and financial integration: the increasing role of mobile capital. Increasing internationalization changes the opportunity structure of the firm such that individual large corporations can shop around the world for more favourable regulatory conditions, harsher conditions for labour, and lower costs of production, thus escaping not only their domestic institutional frameworks, but often also their own associations. It is another form taken by the conflict over allocating the burden of insecurity. Given that corporatist systems have been traditionally supported by strong and cooperative associations of labour and business, these developments are also particularly likely to undermine this form of interest representation. Statist systems are also challenged and weakened by individual firms escaping domestic regulations and 'going global.' New exit options available to capital indicate the possibility of a shift to more voluntarist modes of interaction, in which individual companies rely on direct lobbying rather than representation of their interests through employers' associations.

The impact of Europeanization

The EU's effect on national patterns of interest representation is twofold: by affecting both policy and institutional developments, the process of Europeanization presents constraints as well as opportunities for organized economic interests.

From the Single European Act to the achievement of Economic and Monetary Union (EMU) and the subsequent Growth and Stability Pact, the process of European integration has put increasing strains on domestic arrangements and demanded significant policy adjustments. Given the central goal of increasing competitiveness, national economies had to move towards neo-liberal policies, restructure their social welfare policies and cut down expenditures. In addition to deregulation and privatization, EMU requirements further delimit the scope of national autonomy over policy choices, in particular over monetary and fiscal policies, which have been the traditional instruments of the corporatist macro-management. Similar to the pressures of internationalization discussed above, these policy developments affect national systems of interest representation by increasing the bargaining power of capital relative to that of labour. Depending on the strength of labour and the type of national institutions, these developments can encourage either managerial unilateralism, or the inclusion of labour in the reform processes, but under terms that are significantly less favourable to its interests than during the Keynesian era.

The institutional impact of the European Union (EU) on national patterns of interest representation is both direct and indirect. The former refers to the increase in the EU's legislative powers, and to the construction of EU-level structures for collective bargaining. The strengthening of the EU's legislative powers signifies the upward shift of competencies from the national level. The result is a number of directives that have to be transposed into national legislation, some of which directly affect national patterns of interest intermediation (most notably those concerning labour law). In addition, the construction of EU-level structures for collective bargaining adds another level of interest representation. For instance, the European Social Dialogue – involving European-level associations of labour and business, namely the European Trades Union Congress (ETUC), *l'Union des Industries de la Communauté Européenne* (UNICE), and *le Centre Européen des Entreprises à participation Publique et des entreprises d'intérèt économique générale* (CEEP) – is a corporatist-like structure at the European level, which was intended to give social partners a formal role in social policy legislation. In parallel, new structures were established to facilitate negotiation of voluntary agreements at the sectoral level, and representation at the company level (in the form of the European Works Councils, EWCs). Furthermore, the European Employment Pact called for the initiation of macro-economic social dialogue between the European Central Bank, national governments and social partners. The European Employment Strategy and the Open Method of Coordination also envisage a formal role for social partners in the negotiation and implementation in different policy sectors.

By providing new opportunities for representation above the national level, these structures were expected to benefit social partners particularly in those cases where they are often sidelined in the policy process, as in pluralist and statist systems, as well as in the new member states where – despite the existence of formal corporatist structures – their influence seems to be marginal. In some cases, most notably France, this development indeed has resulted in a wider consultation with organized interests at the national level than was the case in its traditionally statist pattern. Some limited achievements have been also noted at the sectoral level, especially in the metal, chemicals and finance industry where unions and employers have been willing to subordinate their national rivalries and engage in exchange containing clear elements of a weak Euro-corporatism (see Pochet, 1999, 2002;

Dubbins, 2002). On the whole, however, the practical results of most EU initiatives have been modest. For instance, the EWC Directive did not harmonize national systems of workplace representation as the functioning of these bodies depends mainly on industrial-relations practices of their companies' country of origin. Achievements at the supranational level have been also limited. The European Social Dialogue, for instance, has resulted in agreements on issues that are either uncontroversial (for example unpaid parental leave) or do not go much beyond codifying existing practice at the national level (for example part-time work) (Streeck, 1998). Simultaneously, the macro-economic social dialogue functions merely as an informal forum for outlining joint opinions on common challenges.

Hence, far from furthering genuine corporatist practices at the European level, the new structures seem to facilitate a type of exchange that, at least to this date, has been mainly symbolic politics. This is not really surprising, as it relates to certain paradoxes in the current stage of the Europeanization process. On the one hand this presents a model of policy style of consultation, participation, dialogue among organized interests; on the other, the ends being sought are those of increased marketization of labour issues – a process that strictly speaking excludes these practices. Governments and organized interests in established member states are better able to cope with these contradictory demands than are those in the new members. The former have encountered different elements of the package at different times, as the emphasis of European policy has changed and wavered. They also start with a base of advanced market institutions. The new members from the former state-socialist states, however, are presented all at once with all components of the *acquis communautaire* and the construction of market economies.

Finally, a more indirect impact of the EU on national patterns of interest intermediation concerns new possibilities for interest representation that are not directly envisaged in legislation and formal procedures, namely lobbying the European institutions. A dramatic increase of interest-group presence in Brussels over the last decade indicates strong lobbying activities. Big businesses, in particular, are well-represented at the European level – the European Round Table of Industrialists being one of the most influential (van Apeldoorn, 1999). Apart from some employers' groups, sectoral producer associations and individual big firms, various non-governmental organizations (NGOs), environmental and consumers' associations are engaged in informal lobbying practices. With the exceptions mentioned above, traditional social partners, however, find it difficult to build solidarity and outline common interests above the national level, since their activities and functions are constrained primarily by national industrial relations institutions which differ considerably across the member states.

Diversity between and within old and new member states

Given that all European economies have been subject to the above-mentioned challenges, some have predicted the emergence of a uniform trend across countries. This would entail a weakening of organized labour, a significant decentralization of collective bargaining, and a shift from negotiated, corporatist practices towards more competitive, pluralist modes of interest representation – in short a convergence towards disorganization (see Lash and Urry, 1987).

The picture in reality, however, is much more complex. First, while recent unionization trends indeed suggest a weakening of organized labour in most EU countries, there remain striking differences in unionization levels across Europe (see Table 11.1). While the Nordic corporatist countries still display the highest unionization rates (above 70 per cent), the lowest figures (below 15 per cent) are found in France, Poland and Spain. Apart from the extraordinary cross-country diversity, these figures also reveal a broad difference between, on the one hand, West European countries, and on the other the CEECs. The latter generally have significantly lower unionization levels, though there are some clear exceptions to this tendency (in particular, Slovenia and Slovakia, and within Western Europe, France and Spain). The difference between the two regions is especially clear with respect to the speed of the decline in union membership, with the unionization in the new member states declining at a much faster rate. In part, this is a consequence of the abolition of compulsory union membership that existed during the communist rule. Other factors include a generally negative image of the unions in the new democracies, and particularly their low effectiveness in protecting the interests of their members during the process of economic transformation.

Second, even though distinct signs of decentralization have been evident everywhere, the result has not been a universal shift to uncoordinated bargaining and employer unilateralism. As Table 11.2 indicates, it is the sectoral rather than enterprise level that continues to be the dominant level of wage bargaining in most West European economies (apart from the UK and France). The situation, however, is rather different in the CEECs where – despite the existence of peak-level tripartite structures – wages are predominantly determined at the enterprise level. The weakness or virtual absence of bargaining at the

Table 11.1 *Organization rates of trade unions and employers' associations*

	Union density				Employers' org. rates c. 2000
	1990	*1995*	*2002*	*Change (%), 1995–2002*	
Sweden	80.0	83.1	78.0	-0.7	55
Denmark	75.3	77.0	73.8*	-0.5	52
Finland	72.2	78.0	71.2*	-1,1	60
Cyprus¹	..	..	70.0		60
Malta²	54.4	56.0	62.8	1.3	..
Belgium	53.9	55.7	55.8*	0.1	72
Slovenia	..	..	41.0	..	100
Ireland	51.0	47.1	35.9*	-1.9	60
Austria	46.9	40.7	35.4	-0.8	100
Slovakia	78.7	57.3	35.4	-3.1	65
Italy	38.8	38.1	34.0	-0.6	51
Luxembourg	44.8	38.7	33.5*	-0.9	80
UK	39.3	34.1	30.4	-0.5	40
Greece	32.4	29.6	26.7**	-0.7	70
Czech Rep.	78.7	46.3	25.1	-3.0	35
Portugal	31.7	25.4	..	-0.5	58
Germany	31.2	29.2	23.2	-0.9	63
Netherlands	25.5	25.7	22.1	-0.5	85
Latvia	..	..	20.0	..	30
Hungary	..	63.4	19.9	-6.2	..
Estonia	90.6	31.6	16.6*	-2.5	35
Lithuania	..	..	16.0	..	..
Spain	14.7	16.3	14.9**	-0.4	72
Poland	..	32.9	14.7*	-3.0	..
France	10.1	9.8	9.7*	-0.1	74
EU-25***	..	32.6	26.4*	-1.0	
EU-15***	32.8	31.0	27.3*	-0.6	
EU-10***	..	42.7	20.4*	-3.7	

Notes: *2001; ** 1999; *** weighted averages (in the case of missing data, the nearest year is taken into account); ¹ excludes Turkish Cypriot part; ² includes pensioner members (10%); .. no data available.
Source: Data from European Commission (2004).

sectoral-level in the CEECs is directly related to the weakness of employers' organizations. The lack of the private sector in communism meant that independent employers' associations were virtually non-existent. After the collapse of communism, these associations were slow to emerge, remained relatively fragmented and organizationally weak. There are no precise and comparable time series on the employers' rate of organization (as measured by the proportion of the workforce covered). However, available data clearly indicate that – notwithstanding some outliers, such as Slovenia, which has the obligatory membership in the chambers of commerce and industry – these rates are generally much lower in the CEECs (see Table 11.1).

The upshot is that the coverage of employees by collective agreements is also much lower than in Western Europe (see Table 11.3). The weighted average for the old member states is 78 per cent, for the new members (including Cyprus and Malta) only 35 per cent. Moreover, the bargaining coverage has been steadily declining in the CEECs throughout the 1990s. A clear exception again is Slovenia where the bargaining coverage has been stable and universal due to the obligatory membership of chambers. A more significant variation is visible within the old member states. Not only do they differ in terms of the extent of bargaining coverage (compare, for instance, the UK with Austria and France in Table 11.3), but also in terms of the general trend, with the coverage increasing throughout the 1990s in Sweden, Denmark, Finland, the Netherlands, Portugal and Spain, remaining stable in Austria, France and Belgium, and declining in the UK and Germany (European Commission, 2004).

Finally, despite the common pressures discussed above, the outcome has not been a universal decay of corporatism, but rather its transformation. While many traditionally corporatist countries (for example Sweden, Germany, Austria) have undergone a decentralization of collective bargaining during the late 1980s and 1990s, this decentralization was not accompanied with considerable disorganization. Instead, these countries still display a high degree of coordination of bargaining activities, albeit one that largely has shifted to the sectoral level (Traxler, 1995). Agreements reached at this level are then binding for company-level bargaining. This pattern, therefore still constitutes a variant of corporatism because it involves a significant voluntary coordination.

Another important development that goes against the disorganization thesis is the more recent reappearance of state-sponsored wage coordination in the form of national social pacts (for example Ireland, the Netherlands, Finland, Italy, Portugal, Spain, and among the CEECs, Slovenia). In terms of functions, however, this form of central-level coordination is significantly different from its traditional predecessor. Under the current economic regime, where a heavier reliance on the corrective capacity of market forces has coincided with tight monetary policy and the generally slack labour markets, the terms of corporatist exchange have significantly changed in that they favour the

Table 11.2 *Levels of wage bargaining, 2003*

	National	Sectoral	Company
Belgium	***	**	*
Finland	***	**	*
Ireland	***		*
Slovenia	**	**	*
Greece	**	**	*
Netherlands	*	***	*
Denmark	*	***	**
Portugal	*	***	*
Spain	*	**	**
Slovakia	*	**	**
Hungary	*	*	***
Germany		***	*
Austria		***	*
Sweden		***	*
Italy		***	**
Cyprus		***	*
Luxembourg		**	**
France		*	***
Czech Republic		*	***
Estonia		*	***
Latvia		*	***
Lithuania		*	***
Malta		*	***
Poland		*	***
United Kingdom			***

Notes: *** = principal or dominant bargaining level; ** = important but not dominant level; * = existing level of bargaining.
Source: European Commission (2004).

interest of capital over that of labour. In a nutshell, the classical Keynesian, demand-side corporatism has given way to competitive, supply-side macro-coordination. This is why the new social pacts differ significantly from corporatist agreements that prevailed in the 1970s. Rather than being concerned explicitly with social and redistributive issues, the new pacts are about meeting EMU requirements and improving external competitiveness. Wage restraint negotiated through these pacts is seen as a functional equivalent of the now unavailable option of currency devaluation in the quest for improving competitiveness of national economies. While both types of pacts are likely to involve conflict over the distribution of uncertainty and difficult

Table 11.3 *Collective bargaining coverage, employers' organizations and union density*

	1–10	11–20	21–30	31–40	41–50	51–60	61–70	71–80	81–90	91–100
Austria				U						Cov, E
Slovenia										Cov, E
France	U									Cov
Belgium						U		E		Cov
Sweden						E		E		Cov
Finland						E		U	Cov	
Netherlands								E	Cov	
Spain			U					E	Cov	
Denmark		U				E		U	Cov	
Luxembourg								Cov, E		
Ireland			U	U		(Cov), E				
Portugal			U			E		Cov		
Germany			U				Cov, E			
Greece							(Cov), E			
Cyprus						E	Cov, U			
Malta						(Cov), U				
Italy				U		E	Cov			
Slovakia				U	Cov		E			
Poland		U			Cov					
UK			U	Cov, U						
Hungary		U		Cov						
Czech Rep.			U, Cov	E						
Estonia		U	Cov	E						
Latvia		Cov	U	E						
Lithuania		Cov, U								

Notes: Cov = bargaining coverage non-standardized; E = employer organization rate (private sector); U = union density rate; (Cov) = estimate of coverage rate based on employers' organization rate (Greece, Ireland) or union density (Malta).

Source: European Commission (2004).

debates over employment levels, the new pacts are also likely to entail reductions in public spending that weaken the security guarantees of the welfare state. In this sense, they are much less favourable to labour than the corporatist deals from the 1970s. This general move to neoliberal policies notwithstanding, the very fact that the policy adjustment has been brought about in so many cases through corporatist-type negotiations suggests that contemporary interest representation in Europe is far from resembling the pluralist, or disorganized pattern.

Where 'disorganized decentralization' (Traxler, 1995) was most evident is the UK – a country that never had a strong corporatism, and had been through the first and most thoroughgoing European neo-liberalization during the 1980s. This process resulted in the collapse of multi-employer bargaining, an erosion of collective bargaining coverage, and a weakening of organized labour through legislative changes and an increasingly strong employer unilateralism (Thelen, 2001). By the late 1990s there was a limited return to some Keynesian-type policies, with government, unions and employers' organizations engaging in a reasonably amicable pluralism based partly on the fact that all three had been weakened by previous neo-liberal policies.

Most CEECs also display significant disorganizing tendencies and a generally weak coordination, albeit one that paradoxically has evolved alongside peak-level tripartism. The latter, however, has had little impact on overall macroeconomic management. Tripartite agreements and social pacts from the early 1990s could hardly be described as negotiated policy adjustments tailored to improve coordination at different levels. Instead, these early post-transitional agreements usually had a purpose of legitimizing new governments and neoliberal policies designed by their expert teams. Alternatively, they presented one-off responses to specific problems, particularly when the latter entailed threats to social peace, as was the case in Poland in 1993, and to a lesser extent in Hungary in 1992. Only rarely did they entail explicit trade-offs that were to be regularly monitored, such as the one between wage freezes and employment guarantees at the onset of transformation in Czechoslovakia. Gradually, however, these largely system-legitimising agreements have been phased out, even though the formal structures for peak-level tripartism have remained in place. Subsequent tripartite negotiations have had generally little influence over wage developments as central-level agreements (apart from those on the minimum wage) are only non-binding recommendations for the lower levels. Given the weakness of the sectoral level (see above), and a scanty coordination among and within interest associations in these new capitalisms, wages are determined predominantly through uncoordinated bargaining at the enterprise level.

One exception is Slovenia, which seems to be developing a neo-corporatism modelled on neighbouring Austria. Here, bi-annual central-level agreements serve as explicit guidelines for the sectoral and enterprise level, and the coordination between different levels is regularly monitored. With this exception, however, the prevailing system developing in the CEECs seems to be unitarism: employers accepting almost no day-to-day role for unions, and lacking effective organization themselves. However, this sits awkwardly alongside formal rights to collective bargaining, and some occasional attempts at central-level agreements that imply some degree of neo-corporatism. Whether these latter attempts have any more than paper value tends to vary as economic conditions and the political preferences of governments change.

In sum, disorganizing and liberalizing trends have been on the whole much more pronounced in the CEECs than in the old EU member states. This is evident not only with regard to the abovementioned organizational characteristics of interest associations and the form and functioning of collective bargaining institutions, but also with regard to the sharpness of the neo-liberal policy turn. The stagnant economies of the old Soviet bloc had at least offered workers security: guaranteed employment, reliable if low wages and social benefits. The sudden removal of this protection was the biggest single shock to meet employees in this part of Europe when they encountered the realities of an entrepreneurial economy. The shock was to be that much greater, not only because they were entering the capitalist economy during its most prolonged turbulent period since the Second World War, but also because their weak economies had to confront exceptional degrees of adjustment that involved comprehensive institutional changes and a simultaneous adoption of several neoliberal policy packages. In this sense, the burden of insecurity accompanying a global shift to the new policy regime appears to be even greater than in Western Europe.

The different outcomes in the two parts of Europe are certainly influenced by the variation in the starting points of these economies. Given that the CEECs experienced a total collapse of the political and economic system, it is only natural to expect that the change in interest representation and economic policies would be much sharper than in Western Europe. However, the fact that the extent of decentralization and liberalization in many cases has surpassed that of Western Europe indicates that the divergence in the economic starting points offers only one part of the explanation. The second part is institutional. As with any institution, the adjustment and reconfiguration of the main industrial relations institutions depends on their age (Pierson, 2004). Older institutions are considerably more difficult to change, not only due to inertia and powerful vested interests keen to preserve benefits that such institutions provide to them, but also due to the existence of institutional complementarities. The latter term refers to complex functional interdependencies that exist between different institutions in an economy – such as between industrial relations, systems of skill formation, and corporate governance – and which are usually referred to in the literature that distinguishes between coordinated and non-coordinated or liberal market economies (Crouch and Streeck, 1997; Hall and Soskice, 2001). Since many institutions of the nationally embedded political economies are tightly coupled, a considerable change in one set of institutions would require the adjustment of the related institutional area.

This is not to say that interest representation and industrial relations institutions in Western Europe are resistant to change. Quite the contrary, all have been subject to different degrees and types of change over the last two decades (Streeck and Thelen, 2005). But the existence of institutional inertia, vested interests and institutional complementarities that characterize long-standing and well-entrenched institutions has made this process more gradual, so that many of the basic parameters of the industrial relations institutions in West European countries still reflect historical class compromises (Crouch, 1993; Streeck and Yamamura, 2001). In contrast, when institutions are new – especially in cases where a system experiences a wholesale replacement of institutions as in post-communist Europe – they are likely to be less entrenched, and therefore less resistant to change. Put differently, the absence of strong institutional inertia and institutional complementarities indicates a weak capacity of new institutions to constrain and structure actors' behaviour. In such cases, the scope for strategic action is much wider, so that the functioning and the adjustment of the new institutions is more likely to reflect current power games between the actors than the institutionally established modes of interaction (Avdagić, 2005). Given the weakness of organized interests in Central Europe and the existence of governments largely committed to neo-liberal reforms, it is not surprising that the economic adjustment has taken a stronger neo-liberal turn and that the main industrial relations institutions reflect less coordinated practices than in many West European countries.

These general differences between the old member states and the CEECs notwithstanding, it is evident that the common challenges have not led to uniform outcomes within the two parts of Europe either. This is particularly evident among the old member states, where responses range from a shift to unitarism to the profound transformation of the classical corporatist pattern that involved either a voluntary shift to the sectoral level, or state-initiated re-centralization in the form of social pacts (see Regini, 2000). The reasons behind different responses to similar exogenous pressures in the advanced European capitalisms lie in the country-specific institutional arrangements, established modes of interaction, and the organizational capacities of collective actors. Differences in these arrangements affect the degree and type of change such that similar pressures can produce different outcomes and sustain cross-country differences.

Conclusion

Recent and current changes in the conditions of economic activity (in technology, economic structure and intra-class cooperation); in economic internationalization; and in Europeanization, are together challenging the established patterns of interest representation that had been familiar in Western Europe since the Second World War. At the same time, they are presenting severe challenges to the infant patterns of the new EU member states in Central Europe.

In the West, systems of industrial relations that developed during the period when manufacturing industry dominated economies have often been ill-equipped to cope when private services sectors have become dominant. In both Western European countries and in those in the former communist part of Europe, internationalization is imposing major challenges of adjustment while also shifting the balance in relations among organizations in favour of employer and business interests. European integration plays a paradoxical role in relation to this, both encouraging the marketization processes associated with internationalization (and hence a weakening of the role of organizations, particularly of labour), and insisting on dialogue and negotiation that gives these organizations a major role.

In this context, the main content of interactions among governments and organizations representing employers and employees shifts from the Western preoccupation with inflation of the first three postwar decades to a struggle over the allocation of the burdens of economic insecurity. This unbalances some systems, turning institutions like those of Germany from being protectors of a national economic interest to defenders of the interests of organized insiders. In the CEECs infant systems of autonomous interest representation have encountered a triple version of this shock: in addition to the common experience of all existing industrial societies, they face having weak economies that experience exceptional insecurity; and they must leave behind their background of considerable, if low level, security of the state socialist period.

The general picture is one of organized interest systems in difficulty, with labour weakening as a participant within that. There are exceptions: the Nordic countries; and within Central Europe, Slovenia, which has acquired a set of stronger institutions, more closely resembling some of those in the West than its neighbours. These exceptions repay closer study, as they demonstrate the scope for institutional variety within general trends, and sometimes also the role of particular actors and strategic decisions.

Chapter 12

The Judicialization of European Politics

Zdenek Kühn

Alexis de Tocqueville, a French visitor to the United States of the mid-nineteenth century, noted that the power 'peculiar' to American judges to set aside a law on the grounds of its unconstitutionality

> gives rise to immense political influence. In truth, few laws can escape the searching analysis of judicial power for any length of time, for there are few that are not prejudicial to some private interest or other, and none that may not be brought before a court of justice by the choice of parties or by the necessity of the case. (Tocqueville, 1945: 106)

In the nineteenth century this power was truly 'peculiar' only to American judges. However, judicialization has become a global phenomenon in recent decades. In Western societies, constitutions now play a key role in legitimizing governments, and the judicialization of politics has become a common European phenomenon. The courts in Europe today hold in effect a sort of veto power over many important political decisions.

The purpose of this chapter is to explain this process and the underlying philosophy of the 'New Constitutionalism', which has become one of the most significant mechanisms of holding governments to account. After discussing classical conceptions of judicial power in Western Europe and the changing nature of political control, the chapter looks at the role of judges in Eastern Europe. There then follows an assessment of the role of constitutional courts in national politics, and the growing significance of supranational courts, before the final section looks at current critiques of the judicialization of politics.

The original conception of judicial power and its transformation in Western Europe

The eighteenth-century separation of powers was constructed in strict terms. There were supposedly clear lines between the legislature making law, the executive enforcing law, and the judiciary interpreting law, and these lines were established in order to provide a system of checks and balances in which no one branch of government could dominate another. The power of judges to review laws enacted by parliament for their conformity with higher standards, embedded in the constitution, was unimaginable. In fact, '[o]f the three powers . . . the judiciary is in some measure next to nothing' (Montesquieu, 1766: Book XI, Ch. VI: 228). Accordingly, 'the national judges are no more than the mouth that pronounces the words of the law, mere passive beings, incapable of moderating either its force or rigor' (*ibid.*: 232). The original liberal idea behind these theories was to limit judicial discretion and thereby, limit the state's power to interfere with private business. This concept of the judiciary was justified by reference to the influence of the overly powerful French judicial authority prior to 1789.

The notion that the legislature makes the law, the executive enforces it, and the courts ensure that it is applied still seems to prevail in much contemporary mainstream political discourse. According to this perspective, the legislature and executive are political actors, while law courts take an 'apolitical' legalistic position in interpreting the law. The fact that it is not the judge but the law which decides the issue is a crucial factor in maintaining judicial legitimacy. In this sense, judicial language is constrained by legal rules and doctrines and the maxims of statutory construction. However, the original conception of a separation of powers in which a more powerful executive and legislature are counterposed to a 'weak' judiciary have been radically transformed over recent decades. Indeed, conventional understandings of how political control is exercised in parliamentary democracies – primarily through parliamentary oversight – have increasingly been revised in light of the fact that 'judicial control of governments has gained ground virtually everywhere in Europe' (Helms, 2005: 86). In order to understand how judicial control has come about, we need to focus some attention on the broader issue of political control and especially the question of legislative oversight.

Although it could be argued that the focus on parliamentary control of government has always been overplayed in the literature on representative democracy, it remains the case that traditional approaches tend to focus on parliaments (and electorates) serving as the main check on executive power. More recent work has focused on the need to adopt a more 'realistic' view which incorporates other actors, particularly private sector actors (Helms, 2005). However, it has always been the case that the nature of parliamentary oversight has varied across Western Europe, according to a range of factors including the degree of decentralization, the nature of committee structures and the discipline of political parties (Heywood, 2002: 160–4). In general terms, though, whilst the nature of parliamentary control has remained relatively constant – with different patterns emerging according to the degree of collegiality in executive organization – it is also true that the widespread emphasis on majority rule has seen a diminution in the reach of such control. A growth of executive dominance over so-called 'reserved domains' (generally economic and foreign policy) has seen a parallel decline in the capacity of parliaments to exercise effective oversight (von Beyme, 2000: 81–8).

Thus, it is unsurprising that judicial review, especially as exercised through constitutional courts, should have come to assume increasing prominence in West European democracies. The notion of a 'weak' judiciary has in turn become harder to sustain. Amongst other factors which have contributed to this development, it was recognized that, despite the expectations of some eighteenth-century thinkers, law was not, nor could it ever have been, easily deducible from legal texts. Interpreting the text to some degree means making that text.

Moreover, the conception of the restrained and weak judiciary seems to be intrinsically connected with nineteenth-century concerns around political stability and limiting state intervention so far as possible. Therefore it could not survive untouched the collapse of the model which it served. The remodelling of the state, the growth in its powers, and the building the welfare state fundamentally transformed the conception of state and law. The government ceased to be limited to those few issues that liberals believed the state was good for. As the role of the state increased, the role of the judiciary followed this development. Special administrative courts were established by most European countries to protect citizens against misuse of power by the growing executive branch.

The principle of adherence to the letter of the law endorsed via a 'weak' judiciary was discredited by the realization that law might sometimes be grossly unjust, as happened during the Nazi or communist eras. Some influential scholars even linked the horrors of the Nazi machinery to an overly restrained judiciary. Although these claims are now generally considered overstated, a growth in the role of the judiciary, 'the least dangerous branch', was nonetheless supported as a result. A strong judicial power was no longer viewed as a danger to democracy, but rather as an enhancement of democracy through a more appropriate system of checks and balances. Judges being granted insufficient power came to be considered as dangerous for democracy.

Last but not least, Europe has increasingly moved towards the model of 'conflict society', where most conflicts are ultimately decided in law courts rather than through the informal processes of the past. Law has replaced 'old' ideologies (especially religion) and, consequently, according to some observers, the judiciary has become 'the twenty-first century equivalent of the twelfth-century papacy' (Badinter and Breyer, 2004: 4).

The role of judges in Eastern Europe before 1990

The growth of Western European judiciaries presents a striking contrast to the decline of the judiciary in the Soviet bloc. While the powers of the communist state became absolute, the judiciary was excluded from decision-making in complex issues relating to politics, such as constitutional review or judicial review of the legality of administrative actions.

The caseload of a typical communist judge was rather simple and unimportant. Complex issues of international litigation, or of administrative, constitutional or commercial law, did not really arise in the socialist state – or else the task of resolving them was transferred from courts to other bodies. Thus, the political impact of judicial decisions was negligible. Even the repression of dissidents was effected mostly by extra-judicial means, without any judicial interference.

Constitutional review was unthinkable during communism and the Western constitutional courts were ridiculed. Although constitutional courts were established in what was then Yugoslavia in the 1960s and in Poland in 1985, these courts – facing the limits imposed on them by authoritarian governments – did not gain any major political influence until the fall of the communist rule. Oversight capacity in Eastern Europe has therefore been generally weak, the legacy in large part of the Soviet system in which parliaments and other bodies had very limited oversight role over the executive.

The 1990s in post-communist Europe saw a shift towards judicialization and the creation of a conflict society. The judiciary has seen its old competences restored, including the power of judicial review of administrative acts. Most importantly, however, constitutional courts have been established in all post-communist states. Indeed, judicial review has become even more important given the relative immaturity of parliamentary structures and party organization in the transition countries, which have resulted in poorly developed systems of parliamentary oversight. A lack of party cohesion, as well as public scepticism towards the institutions of government, has further undermined 'horizontal' accountability exercised by the legislature over the executive. Unlike in Western Europe, where legislative oversight has declined over time relative to the role of other public and private-sector agencies, the transition countries have generally failed to develop strong systems of parliamentary control in the first place. Hence the significance of constitutional courts in particular.

Constitutional courts in Europe

The US Supreme Court already in the early nineteenth century proclaimed the principle 'essential to all written constitutions, that a law repugnant to the constitution is void', and that courts have to set aside such a void law (*Marbury*, US SC 1803: 180). In Europe until the mid-twentieth century, the situation was different and the idea of parliamentary supremacy was uncontested. Most European states viewed their constitutions as the basic laws establishing the distribution of powers among various branches of government. As basic rights were rarely directly enforceable by the judiciary, constitutions laid down only procedural constraints on the government.

It was not until the end of the Second World War that the idea became firmly established that the constitution should put substantive constraints on the legislature. In this new conception, constitutions are made on behalf of the people, and establish basic and inviolable principles of the polity. Politicians are only temporary agents of, and elected by, the people, which is why constitutions should restrain the possible range of action of politicians in power. This is why it became necessary to grant some institution with the power to annul an unconstitutional law. Following a modified American idea of judicial review, it was generally agreed that this empowered body should be of a judicial nature. The 'old constitutionalism' based on parliamentary supremacy died out and the 'new constitutionalism' of the empowered judiciary emerged from this paradigm shift (Stone Sweet, 2000: 20–21, 37).

The idea of constitutional review has won widespread approval in recent decades. In most of Europe, a constitutional court is now seen as essential to democracy and the rule of law, reflected in the fact that almost all European countries after the fall of totalitarian or authoritarian regimes established constitutional courts. In the 1990s, respect for the constitutional judiciary was so entrenched that it was virtually inevitable that constitutional review would be implemented in post-communist Europe. In the early twenty-first century, constitutional courts existed in Austria (established in 1920, re-established 1945), Germany (1951), Italy (1956), France (1959), Spain (1981), Portugal (1982), Belgium (1985), Poland (1985), all successor countries of former Yugoslavia, Hungary (1990), Bulgaria (1991), Romania (1992), Albania (1992), the Czech and Slovak Republics (1993), the Baltic states and all European post-Soviet Republics (the early 1990s), and Luxembourg (1996).

In order to understand the European constitutional courts, it is important to outline differences between American and European model of judicial review. In the American model legislative acts might be set aside for their unconstitutionality by all courts, lower courts being subsequently bound by the final precedent of the Supreme Court. As opposed to this decentralized model, the European model is centralized. This means that law might be annulled for its unconstitutionality only by a specialized tribunal – the constitutional court, whereas regular (ordinary) judges cannot exercise this sort of judicial review. The constitutional court is a special body, which is not part of the judiciary proper and does not adjudicate regular cases. On the contrary, its sole function is (subject to different exceptions in different states) to protect the constitution.

The reasons for centralized constitutional review as opposed to decentralized judicial review were numerous: political emphasis on the exceptionality of constitutional review; distrust in the very nature of European ordinary career judges who were seen as unlikely to protect the constitution vigorously enough; the impossibility of replacing all post-fascist or post-communist judges at once, resulting in the need to create an institution of 'positive deviation'; and the absence of a formal system of precedent in continental Europe.

Most European systems give parliamentarians (be they deputies or senators) the power to bring laws before the court. This for all practical purposes means that the law is often reviewed by the constitutional court even before it has been applied in real-life cases (this type of review is called 'abstract' as opposed to 'concrete' review). In the US system of judicial review, by contrast, the existence of an individual dispute is a necessary condition to review the law.

The practice of constitutional review

The possibility of bringing a law before the constitutional court has been increasingly used in Europe. In France, both deputies and senators were granted this power in 1974. In the period 1974–80, 46 laws were brought to the Constitutional Council (FCC) by parliamentarians (6.6 laws per year), in 1981–87, this number doubled to 92 laws (13.1 laws per year, one-third of the total passed by parliament). Over half of the referrals ended in laws being partially or fully annulled by the FCC. The early 1980s coincided with the major political reforms of the socialist government, and the counter-attack by rightist parties via referrals to the FCC. The FCC defended property rights and significantly altered or even blocked some laws, most importantly nationalization of bank sector (Stone, 1992: 140 ff.). The judicialization of politics intensified further in the late 1990s and the early 2000s, with a record of 25 referrals in 2003.

In Spain, where the possibility of referring a law to the Spanish Constitutional Tribunal (SCT) is vested in more institutions, numbers are similar. After five years of becoming accustomed to its existence, politicians began to use the SCT more assiduously and between 1986–90 20 referrals annually were sent to the SCT (103 in total). In the first decade of the SCT's existence, 23 per cent referrals have been made by the parliamentary opposition and 31 per cent by the national government. At the same time, in the era of establishing regional governments, growing frictions and decentralization of Spain, autonomous regions made 42 per cent of the total number of referrals and the SCT 'has become a kind of permanently constituted forum for the clarification and revision of the constitutional rules governing Spanish federalism' (Stone Sweet, 2000: 64–5, 107).

The annual number of parliamentary referrals to the German Federal Constitutional Court (GFCC), the most influential European constitutional court, is much smaller at less than three (a total of 110 over its first 40 years), which might be explained by the existence of a strong upper house of the Parliament (the *Bundesrat*), other mechanisms to avoid passing laws which might be deemed unconstitutional, and the fact that constitutionality of laws might also be challenged, as in Spain but not France, by referrals from ordinary courts and complaints by individuals. If all mechanisms of constitutional review are taken together, the GFCC has reviewed some 20 per cent of all federal laws over 40 years, annulling almost every fourth law reviewed. Issues like financing political campaigns, broadcasting laws, or the separation of state and religion are typical areas in which the GFCC has left a deep impact (Landfried, 1995). For instance, in controversial rulings, the GFCC has set limits on the display of religious symbols (like crucifixes) at state schools in order to protect neutrality of the state.

The tendency to use constitutional adjudication as a means to prolong or even revise political battles lost in parliament soon found its way into post-communist political systems. Constitutional review in some post-communist systems is even more open to such use because, as in the Czech Republic or Poland, there is no time limit during which laws can be referred to the court by members of parliament. The Romanian Constitution gives its Court a unique power to adjudicate *ex officio* on any initiative which is deemed to entail a revision of the Constitution.

In the Czech Republic, to take one example, the number of parliamentary referrals between the fall 1993 and the end of 2004 was close to ten annually. Of these laws challenged, every third law was either totally or partially annulled. Of the major decisions made by the Czech Constitutional Court (CCC), particularly noteworthy was a substantial expansion in the process of restitution (the return of property nationalized by the communists) and lustration (the process of managing the participation of former communists in the public administration). That the CCC can significantly influence political competition has been demonstrated by decisions on the financing of political parties: when funding has been limited to those parties which enjoy parliamentary success, political competition has been more restricted than when all parties are eligible for support if they receive a percentage threshold of votes, regardless of whether they secure any deputies.

The Polish Constitution set out a list of institutions eligible to challenge laws before the Tribunal (PCT) which is the most extensive in Europe (see Table 12.1). The PCT's most controversial direct intervention has concerned the banning of abortion. However, the most open system of constitutional review is undoubtedly the Hungarian Constitutional Court (HCC). All citizens enjoy the right to challenge laws regardless of whether they are directly affected by them.

This unusual regulation has given rise to over 1,000 petitions annually to annul laws, mostly by private individuals and non-governmental organizations. In consequence, the HCC has considered almost all important social issues, including the death penalty (annulled), abortion (upon which strict conditions were placed), or the punishment of communist crimes (modified). The HCC also struck down post-communist social welfare reform because it conflicted with abstract constitutional principles like the protection of legal certainty. This led to widespread doctrinal criticism of the Court's overt and uncontrolled activism as well as the fact that the HCC effectively made the communist welfare system irreversible (Sajó, 1999).

From these data, it appears that the number of parliamentary referrals is similar to the more litigious West European examples mentioned above. The key difference between the established democracies and the post-communist democracies, however, is the possibility of actors other than politicians referring laws to the court. Some European constitutional courts give individuals access to the court via so-called constitutional complaint if they claim that their basic rights have been violated and only once all other routes have been exhausted. If we focus solely on constitutional review, the workload of the Constitutional Court in Romania is some one hundred times that of its Hungarian counterpart and two hundred times higher than most West European constitutional courts. The question must be asked whether such a system is beneficial for the development of democracy, especially given concern about the unrestrained judicialization of politics (discussed further below).

German ordinary courts were required by the GFCC to be openly involved in adjudicating between competing rights. The GFCC has become 'deeply involved in the work of the ordinary judges' which 'led the latter to behave much like the former' (Stone Sweet, 2000: 117). Similar trends are taking place throughout Europe, which effectively means that it is no longer the case that politically important cases might be found only in the constitutional courts. In post-communist Europe, the process of constitutionalization of the ordinary judiciary has been somewhat slower; however, it is clear that the German trend of including the ordinary judiciary in the 'new constitutionalism' is becoming more widespread.

Constitutional review and political reaction

It would be wrong to describe European judges as usurpers of power. It often happens that when constitutional courts show self-restraint, they receive criticism for not fulfilling their constitutional task. A recent example is provided by the issue of the ban on Muslim veils in Germany. A Muslim female applicant was refused employment at a state school because she insisted on wearing a veil. In deciding on her constitutional complaint, the GFCC refrained from a clear-cut judgement on whether and under what circumstances Muslim veils could be prohibited and instead delegated a final decision to Germany's legislatures. In response, the GFCC was criticized for its self-restraint. Judicial intervention is sometimes attractive for politicians as a means of settling issues they consider undesirable to be solved through open public debates, 'primarily because they present no-win political dilemmas' (Hirschl, 2004: 39).

The expansion of the 'new constitutionalism' has also led to a proliferation of 'rights rhetoric' and court-influenced rhetoric is now used more generally in political discourse. In most countries, proposed bills must address the issue of constitutionality. Political debates have increasingly assumed a juridical-like flavour, with parliamentarians making arguments through reference to legalistic debates and to precedents of constitutional and international courts. Major political parties and governments across Europe employ constitutional specialists, who advise them how to avoid constitutional problems, how to attack laws before the constitutional court, or how to defend their constitutionality (Stone Sweet, 2000: 104–5).

Constitutional decisions can be overridden only by constitutional amendments, which happen rarely due to the complicated process usually involved. Most constitutions require amendment by various forms of super-majority, some require approval by referendum, and others even protect some provisions from any change whatsoever. A rare recent instance of constitutional change occurred in Italy. After a newly introduced American model of adversarial criminal procedure had been hampered by decisions of the International Criminal Court (ICC) in the 1990s, the constitution was amended to place adversarial American-style values of criminal law into the very heart of the constitution (Pizzi and Montagna, 2004: 460).

Open and outspoken political defiance of constitutional courts is rare in Western Europe. For instance, in face of the GFCC's vast authority, German politicians avoid criticism, leading some scholars to comment on 'the excess of deference by members of Parliament toward the court' (Landfried, 1995: 314). In contrast, post-communist politicians often ignore or ridicule constitutional jurisprudence. Legislatures have on occasion enacted laws even when similar legislation was deemed unconstitutional by previous court decisions. For instance, the Czech Parliament repeatedly reduced judicial salaries, despite repeated rulings of the CCC which declared this practice unconstitutional.

Due to growing judicialization at the trans-national level, national governments find themselves more constrained to obey constitutional rulings. The European Court of Human Rights (ECHR) found that several PCT rulings had been ignored by the Polish legislature in relation to rent control. Moreover, the ECHR found rent control as practiced in Poland to be in conflict with the right to property, because low rents deprived landlords of reasonable profit (thus it followed the PCT reasoning). The ECHR further criticized Poland for non-compliance with the decisions of its own constitutional court (*Hutten-Czapska*, ECHR, 2005). If Poland refused to obey the ECHR's ruling, the Polish state would face severe sanctions.

Appointment and election of constitutional justices

The judicialization of politics necessarily gives rise to the politicization of the judiciary. Appointments to constitutional courts are

Table 12.1 Composition and powers of European constitutional courts

	Germany (1951)	Italy (1956)	France (1959)	Spain (1981)
	Federal Constitutional Court	Const. Court	Const. Council	Const. Tribunal
Number of judges	16	15	9	12
Appointment (election) by	Bundestag elects 8, Bundesrat 8, both by 2/3 vote	National govt. appoints 5, nat. Council of Judiciary appoints 5, parliament elects 5 by 2/3 in joint session	President appoints 3, President of National Assembly 3, President of Senate	National govt appoints 2, nat. Council of Judiciary 2, Congress and Senate each elect 4 by 3/5 vote
Term	12 years	9	9 years	9 years
Qualification	40–68 years of age; 6 must be former federal judges; all qualified lawyers	All judges with 20 years of experience or tenured professors	none	Judges, professors of law, lawyers, civil servants, 15 years of experience, well known judicial competence
Who can start judicial review of constitutionality of laws	Federal government; Land governments; 1/3 of the Bundestag (all within 30 days following adoption of law); ordinary court*; individuals†	National government (against regional laws); regional governmetns (against national laws); Ordinary court* (all within 30 days of adoption)	President; President of National Ass.; President of Senate; 60 deputies of Nat. Ass.; 60 senators (all within 15 days following adoption)	Prime Minister; Pres. of Parliament; 50 deputies; 50 senators; heads of autonomous regions; (within 90 days following adoption); Ordinary court*; Individuals †
Individual const. complaints against decision of public authority?	Yes	No	No	Yes

	Poland (1985)	Hungary (1990)	Romania (1992)	Czech Rep. (1993)
	Const. Tribunal	Const. Court	Constitutional Court	Constitutional Court
Number of judges	15	11	9	15
Appointment (election) by	Lower house (the Sejm) elects; nomination by 50 deputies of Sejm or its presidency	Parliament by 2/3 majority‡	President appoints 3, the lower chamber elects 3, Senate elects 3	President appoints and Senate confirms
Term	9 years	9 years (one re-election possible)	9 years	10 years (renewable)
Qualification	Excellent knowledge of law; 10 years in legal profession or academic activity	Jurists of outstanding theoretical knowledge, or 20 years practical experience	Lawyers, high professional reputation, 18 years of experience in legal field or academics	40 years, 10 years experience in legal profession
Who can start judicial review of constitutionality of laws	President (within 21 days following adoption); Marshalls of both chamber of parliament; Prime Minister; 50 deputies; 30 senators; Prosecutor General; Chief Justices of Supreme Court and Supreme Adm. Court; Ombudsman; President of Supreme Chamber of Control. If law relates to their activities: units of local self-government, national organs of trade unions, employers, and occupational organizations; churches and religious organizations; National Council of Judiciary Ordinary court* (all without any time limit)	President (before promulgation), each individual	President; presidents of chambers of parliament; 50 deputies; 25 senators; Government Supreme Court; Advocate of the People (all before promulgation); Individuals†; ordinary court*	President; 41 deputies; 17 senators; ordinary court*; individuals†
Individual const. complaints against decision of public authority'	No (unless the constitutionality of the law applied by that public authority is in question)	No (unless the constitutionality of the law applied by that public authority is in question)	No	Yes

* If the court hears the case where the allegedly unconstitutional law shall be applied (subject to some exceptions), if the law has been applied in that individual's case; † After exhaustion of all remedies (subject to some exceptions), if the law has been applied in that individual's case; ‡ Candidates proposed by the special parliamentary committee consisting of one member each from the factions of parties represented in Parliament.

openly political, especially if compared with the non-political appointments of most European ordinary judges. While in the latter system appointments are based on technical prerequisites, constitutional justices are scrutinized by political process. Because constitutional justices are generally seasoned lawyers, scholars or politicians, they have clear backgrounds and records of mature opinions, which allow for appointments to be made by major political parties in the hope of influencing in their favour the composition of the constitutional court. At the same time, however, this political dimension gives justices the legitimacy needed to engage actively in decision-making and assert counter-majoritarian logic in the protection of basic rights.

The nature of investiture varies throughout Europe, ranging from the appointment by heads of state and heads of government, or election by parliament (usually by qualified majority), to the 'American' system of presidential appointees approved by the house of parliament (see Table 12.1).

European constitutional justices are usually appointed for a limited and relatively short time, most often nine years. In this way, the body which holds the power of appointment or election exercises ultimate control over the court. In contrast, the possibility that justices would become estranged from the current political mainstream over the course of time always exists in the system with life-tenure (such as Austria or Belgium). Most European justices are law professors, though many are linked in some way with political parties, be it as members or advisers. The second largest group of justices come from ordinary courts. This highlights the 'apolitical' nature of constitutional courts and reinforces their legitimacy.

The French Constitutional Court, by contrast, is staffed by retired politicians or their close collaborators. For instance, in summer 2005 seven of the nine French justices were either former top politicians or their associates. Although such an openly politicized court might work well for France, such an approach is problematic in more unstable post-communist countries. For instance, Romania – which follows the French example of staffing the court by political figures, in this case associated with the socialists (PSD) – saw political crisis erupt in summer 2005 after several rulings by the RCC had sided with the PSD (at the time in opposition) and blocked reform of the Romanian judiciary. An editorial in a leading daily criticized the RCC's composition: 'the leadership made a big mistake in leaving an institution that is extremely important for Romanian democracy in the hands of PSD' (*Romania Libera*, 11 July 2005).

European countries without constitutional courts

The existence of constitutional courts is widespread, though not universal, across Europe. In the United Kingdom, governed by the constitutional principle of parliamentary sovereignty, judicial review of parliamentary legislation is impossible. Recently, however, the British judiciary was empowered by the Human Rights Act of 1998, which established a sort of soft judicial review of laws to test for compliance with the European Convention of Human Rights. According to the 1998 Act, legislation must be implemented in such a way as to be as fully compatible as possible with the rights established by the Convention. Although British judges are not empowered to annul acts of Parliament, the next section shows how accession to the EU has given them significant additional powers.

There are few European countries which follow the system of decentralized judicial review exercised by all courts. All Scandinavian nations, where until recently judicial review did not exist or was not practiced, opted to follow the decentralized model – most recently in Finland in 2000. Up to now, Scandinavian courts have shown their legislatures high respect, especially if compared with activist constitutional courts. For instance, Swedish courts strike down laws only very exceptionally, consistent with the Swedish Constitution which states that parliamentary acts may be set aside only if their conflict with the constitution is 'obvious and apparent'. Generally, Scandinavian political parties oppose further judicial empowerment, and are certainly against the introduction of a constitutional court.

However, even legal systems without formal constitutional review often develop some form of substitute and the judiciary still decides important questions of law and politics. For instance, creative decision-making by the Dutch Supreme Court has intervened in numerous political issues, including the right to strike, drug policies, euthanasia and abortion. These interventions have often influenced subsequent laws enacted by Parliament, and further politicization of the Dutch judiciary followed with increasing political involvement in judicial appointments (Ten Kate and Van Kopen, 1995: 373, 375).

European supranational courts and the application of European law

A very powerful impetus in the judicialization of national politics has come about through European integration. The enforcement of EU law is decentralized and all national courts are expected to enforce EU law even against their national legislatures.

The European Court of Justice (ECJ), the EU's supreme court based in Luxembourg, has been provided with important competencies to adjudicate disputes between institutions of the EU, and between these institutions and member states. In addition, the ECJ responds to cases referred by courts in member states – which in fact represents its most common activity, one which has proved crucial not just for the EU's expansion but also for the further judicialization of national politics. In response to national courts, though without any explicit basis in the EC Treaty, the ECJ has reasoned that the 'spirit, the general scheme and the wording' of that Treaty required that European law has direct effect in and primacy over national law. Thus, already by the early 1960s, the ECJ had moved the European system from its originally envisaged international and intergovernmental framework closer to a supranational and constitutional design (Stein, 1981; Weiler, 1994).

In its subsequent activities, the ECJ further continued to strengthen the enforcement of EU law in national legal systems through the empowerment of national judges. For instance, the ECJ decided that the member state shall be held responsible for damages suffered by individuals when states failed to transpose EU directive. This state responsibility should be adjudicated by national judges. At the same time, however, the ECJ carefully refrained from interfering with sensitive national issues, such as abortion in Ireland.

The reason that national courts are empowered by the application of EU law can be explained through comparison with the United States. In the USA there is, apart from state courts, a special hierarchy of federal courts (with the Supreme Court at the top) whose primary task is to enforce federal law. The fact that there is only one European court also effectively means that EU law must be enforced by all national courts. The national courts must protect EU law, its market freedoms and the individual rights of citizens. As a matter of EU law, therefore, all national judges (and not just constitutional courts) have the power to set aside national legislation for its non-compliance with EU law.

In interpreting EU law, the ECJ often provides substantial leeway for the national courts and formulates only abstract principles which are subsequently enforced by the national courts, which are invited to consider competing domestic policies and values. All European judges thus inevitably face legal problems with a vast political impact. For instance, national judges have had to decide whether a given national regulation amounts within an EU context to prohibited quantitative restrictions on, say, imports and exports; they have even had to pronounce on the legality of Sunday trading laws in the United Kingdom.

Similarly, the ECJ has held that national measures do not constitute prohibited indirect sex discrimination if they are justified by objective factors: the member state, as the author of the allegedly discriminatory rule, has to show in judicial proceedings that the rule in question reflects a legitimate aim of its social policy and that it could reasonably consider that the means chosen were suitable for attaining that aim. The British House of Lords ruled that a specific national law which gave the right 'not to be unfairly dismissed' only to those employees who have been employed at least two years affected a considerably smaller percentage of women than men. However, it was still not indirect discrimination according to the House of Lords, because British law was adopted in order to increase employment and reduce the unwillingness of employers to take on more employees (Fredman, 2002: 114). These examples show that European law has brought about new aspects of judicialization to fundamental questions of domestic politics.

Until now, the relation between the ECJ and national courts, and the decentralized application of EU law through national courts, has proved to be surprisingly workable in the old EU-15. In claiming direct effect and the primacy of EC law, the ECJ opened up national legal systems to private litigants: 'private actors, motivated by their own interests, provided a steady supply of litigation', pushing their national courts to refer the issue of EC law to the ECJ; 'as the domain of EC law expanded, this dialogue intensified, socialising more and more actors – private litigants, judges and politicians – into the system, encouraging more use' (Stone Sweet, 2000: 165). It is too early to judge whether the judicial systems in the new EU Member States are already adjusting to the EU legal system and its specific logic of judicialized politics.

Another and different level of judicialization with respect to the EU has come about through the set of cases where constitutional courts redefined their national identities in respect to the EU. The lead was taken by the GFCC in the so-called 'Maastricht' decision which protects German sovereignty and delineates the limits of the EU activity. National politicians sometimes 'play the constitutional card' during negotiations at the EU level, claiming that a draft of European legislation they oppose is likely to be found unconstitutional by their constitutional court (Kumm, 2005: 281). In the early 2000s, during the process of ratification of the European Constitutional Treaty, constitutional courts intervened in many member states including the new members of East-Central Europe.

European Court of Human Rights

Alongside the European Union, another factor promoting judicialization which has developed through the Council of Europe is the

European Court of Human Rights (ECHR), located in Strasbourg. The ECHR's principal task is to protect the 1950 Convention of Human Rights. The reform of the system of human rights protection in the late 1990s strengthened its overall judicial character when it established, in contrast to the earlier system, direct and easier access to the Court itself.

Since it was first established at the end of the 1950s, the ECHR has decided a number of hotly contested political issues, including measures taken by the UK government against terrorism in North Ireland, expropriation of royal property in Greece, suffering by victims of the Russian war in Chechnya, or the Turkish reprisals against the Kurds in the ongoing civil war in Eastern Turkey. Many of the ECHR's decisions contributed to further judicialization by penalising those states which did not allow full judicial review of public administration (Sweden, Netherlands, and most post-communist nations). A rapid increase in the number of Council of Europe member states (from 25 in 1989 up to 46 in 2005) led to the ECHR becoming overloaded, and a competing system at the EU level organized via the European Court of Justice has placed question-marks against the long-term viability of the ECHR in the twenty-first century.

Critique and defence of the judicialization of politics

The all-pervading judicialization of European politics has supporters as well as opponents. While the former celebrate the judicialization as the victory of democracy, the latter worry about increased judicial activism lacking legitimacy. In the words of Landfried (1995: 322), 'It is the competence of Parliament to shape politics and policies.'

Some scholars favour the American variant of judicial review over its European centralized counterpart. In their view, the very fact that parliamentary opposition groups in Europe have an easy route to the constitutional court casts some doubts on the legitimacy of the European model, since parties which have lost the argument in Parliament can deeply influence the political agenda by appealing against the constitutionality of legislation. In contrast, the US courts cannot decide constitutional issues without specific a case to consider and abstract motions are generally unthinkable. While the American model is legitimized by real-life litigants, the European model of judicial review – where the law to be scrutinized has often never been applied – finds it harder to establish a claim to legitimacy (Sadurski, 2002: 176–7).

For others, judicial review in itself is deeply suspicious. Since juridical categories are hardly self-explanatory, the resultant 'indeterminacy of the constitutional interpretation' is worrisome. As there is no controlling method which can effectively constrain judges, legal justification is of secondary and mostly rhetorical importance. Constitutional judges might therefore impose their own values and opinions, using legalistic arguments to mask an undemocratic and partisan process.

On the other hand, more mainstream European scholars have praised constitutional courts for their 'centrist' tendencies, emphasizing the courts' importance in moderating radical tendencies, protecting minority interests, and 'pacifying' politics. Political parties are well-aware of constitutional restraints from existing precedents, and this awareness contributes to a form of self-limiting ordinance when preparing parliamentary legislation.

It seems that both camps in this critique of legitimacy differ in what they understand democracy to mean. On the one hand, the empowerment of the judiciary is criticized because when a political question becomes a legal one, all except judges and lawyers are excluded from decision-making and political debate is shaped by a small group of legal experts, employing technical jargon: '"They the Jurists" are granted an elevated status in determining policy outcomes at the expense of "We the People", laypersons who make up the vast majority of the populace' (Hirschl, 2004: 187). The judicialization of politics in effect weakens majoritarian democratic institutions by granting authority over decisions to 'privileged and unrepresentative elites' (Tate and Vallinder, 1995: 527).

On the other hand, it is argued that powerful courts deciding on important political issues does not necessarily lessen the level of freedom and democracy: 'If we understand democracy to mean not majority rule in itself, but majority rule under appropriate conditions, then it does not compromise but rather protects democracy when effective means are deployed to secure those conditions' (Dworkin, 2004: 74). Democratic systems without properly functioning checks and balances might turn into 'illiberal democracies', where majoritarian forces have control over too much power (Zakaria, 2003). Constitutional courts are by definition counter-majoritarian: they protect individual rights as outlined in the constitution, even if the violation of such rights is backed by the majority.

Even if one leaves aside the problem of legitimacy, there is still 'the institutional problem'. According to many scholars the courts are poorly equipped for law-making. By contrast, parliaments are structurally designed to make laws which reflect political priorities and social change. Whereas parliaments are dynamic elements of the legal system, making law 'by a process of trial and error', courts are conservative, adhering to their own precedents and disregarding their sound-ness and capacity to function in real life (Landfried, 1995: 322). Judges are poorly equipped to decide on issues of economic organization or social spending. Without effective restraint, judges are able to block or impede the whole-scale economic reforms, as happened under the socialist administration in France in the 1980s, when the FCC's deci-sions on the rights of private owners led to the costs of nationalization rising by 30 per cent. In Hungary during the 1990s, the HCC for some time prohibited reforms of outdated communist welfare system.

Another strand of critical scholarship has sought to analyse the reasons for the expansion of judicial power, arguing that 'rights rhetoric' is merely a façade behind which lie the real reason which is to preserve the hegemonic status quo. Judicial empowerment is thus explained as 'the by-product of a strategic interplay between three key groups: first, threatened political elites who seek to preserve or enhance their political hegemony' and 'to insulate certain policy prefer-ences from popular pressures'; second, 'economic elites' trying to pursue their neo-liberal agenda; and third, 'judicial elites'. If one takes into account the social background of judges, it is easy to explain why they 'tend to adhere to an agenda of relative cosmopolitanism, open markets' and formal (as opposed to substantive) equality (Hirschl, 2004: 43–4, 213).

Public support

Another issue needing explanation is the wide support for constitu-tional courts and the judiciary among the general public. It seems that European societies both in the East and the West strongly support their high courts, with average positive evaluations of more than 50 per cent, reaching nearly 70 per cent in Germany, Denmark and the Netherlands. Constitutional courts usually enjoy much higher level of public trust than do parliaments (Ginson *et al.*, 1998). It is noteworthy that European elites back their courts. In some states a sort of constitu-tional patriotism resembling that of the USA has emerged, as is the case in Germany, where as a result of the country's history the constitu-tion has come to be viewed as the embodiment of basic societal values and principles.

European legal scholarship is generally supportive of constitutional courts, seeing their activity as apolitical. Even critical commentaries tend to analyse judicial decisions in purely legal terms, which keeps this literature from the attention of most political scientists. Pursuing group interests by litigants is reconstructed as defending constitutional rights by legal scholars. The fact that courts are major policy-makers is largely neglected. All this further legitimizes courts because it supports the all-embracing idea of the court being composed of unbiased judges who do not make, but rather interpret, laws.

The very question of to what extent judges make the law and to what extent they 'only' interpret the law remains controversial. Some scholars claim that judicial activity inevitably requires judicial law-making which is hardly distinguishable from regular law-making by the legislature. In contrast, others argue that judicial interpretation, although necessarily creative, qualitatively differs from law-making by the legislature. On the one hand, law-making by the legislature requires reference to broader policies; on the other hand, judges use principles (Dworkin, 1977: chs. 2 and 3). That is why the former equates to real law-making, whereas the latter is much closer to specifying already existing rules and principles. With some degree of oversimplification, it might be said that mainstream European scholars see judicial interpretation as distinct from law-making.

The fact that such views predominate helps explain the high level of public support for constitutional courts. The mass media usually present judicial opinions in a very different way to how they report, for instance, parliamentary votes. Unlike parliamentary debate, judicial deliberation takes place in closed chambers and judicial opinions are written on behalf of the court as a whole. Moreover, dissenting opinions which would openly reveal differences within the court are rarely used, and in some European countries they are even prohibited. The names of justices are mostly unknown, even to European lawyers. Perhaps for this reason the nomination process to constitutional courts in Europe, apart from some exceptions, is not a major media event, in contrast to the United States where lengthy reports of hearings in the Senate of Supreme Court nominees appear on front pages of major newspapers.

Conclusion

In Europe at the outset of the twenty-first century, politics has become profoundly judicialized and the judiciary has become heavily involved in issues which used to be traditionally assigned to politics. This process has occurred very rapidly in much of post-communist Europe following the collapse of communism, though the level and the nature of judicialization still shows some specific features there. Contemporary politicians are indeed constrained in their range of possible actions by potential court intervention. Therefore, politicians are effectively required to internalize constitutional jurisprudence into their own decision-making.

Courts worldwide increasingly show little reluctance to adjudicate issues which were considered 'purely political' only few decades ago (Miller, 2004). A typical example is *Bush* v. *Gore* (2000) which in fact decided who would become President of the USA. In many European states where the courts act as guardians of the rules of fair campaigning, they would not hesitate to quash the results of an election if a candidate (in judges' opinion) violated these rules.

If in the long run the judiciary comes to represent a serious obstacle to widely accepted social reforms, that would most likely undermine the process of judicialization and lead to a new era of judicial self-restraint, as occurred in France after 1789. However, for as long as the process of constitutional review is generally considered 'one of the most powerful barriers that has ever been devised against the tyranny of political assemblies' (Tocqueville 1945: 107), the judicialization of politics is likely to continue.

Chapter 13

The State and Religion

John Madeley

One of the more remarkable developments in politics across the world around the turn of the twenty-first century has been the resurgence of the religious factor; while only a few have spoken of a revival of religion itself, the renewed political salience of issues related to religion and its place in public affairs have been noted by many (Kepel, 1994; Westerlund, 1996). In the 1990s Samuel Huntington warned of a coming clash of civilizations, each of which was defined in large part by its religious heritage, while others pointed to the role of deep religious-cultural differences in the Middle East and the emergence of militant Islamism onto the world stage, or to the role of religio-political action groups in the domestic politics of many countries, including the USA (Marty and Appleby, 1994; Huntington, 1996). Nor has Europe, despite its reputation for secularity, been immune to these global trends.

For theorists of secularization from Max Weber onwards Europe long represented the model of a secular future that awaited all societies and cultures as and when they educated their citizens, modernized their systems of production and distribution, progressively urbanized their populations and greatly increased material prosperity and welfare as conventionally measured. The final and complete separation of the spheres of church and state, religion and politics, whereby the concerns of religion were relegated from the public to the private realm, was regarded as a necessary, often desirable and, in any event, inevitable concomitant of these processes. Even though developments in other parts of the world seemed to defy some of these expectations, the advancing tide of secularization appeared unstoppable in Europe: as levels of orthodox religious belief and observance continued to decline in the late twentieth century, church–state issues seemed increasingly to become non-issues, and Christian Democracy, the principal vehicle for the translation of the religious factor into Europe's mainstream politics, exhibited many of the symptoms of decay and dissolution (Broughton and ten Napel, 2000; Norris and Inglehart, 2004).

A series of interconnected changes over the last 25 years has, however, had the combined effect of raising, instead of lowering, the political profile of religion in Europe as elsewhere: the end of the Cold War, brought about in part by the mobilization of religious forces, for example in Poland; the revival of traditional, and the introduction of novel, religions in Eastern Europe and the emergence of exotic and disturbing NRMs (New Religious Movements: colloquially 'cults' or 'sects') in Western Europe; the outbreak of bitter ethno-religious conflicts particularly in the former Yugoslavia; the development of a new agenda of religiously sensitive issues touching bio-ethics and gender relations; the massive increase of migration flows into and across the continent and the controversies arising in the increasingly multicultural environments which resulted: all contributed to the generally unexpected re-emergence of political issues with religious resonances. Nor did the start of the new millennium lead to any diminution; instead, the 9/11 attacks on New York and Washington, carried out in the name of militant Islam, and their ramifications through the so-called 'War on Terror' only had the effect of greatly magnifying the attention paid to the impact of the so-called religious factor (Soper and Feltzer, 2003).

Analysing the interaction between politics and religion

In the European context the renewed political salience of the religious factor has been registered in a disparate series of challenges to a distinctive model of church–state–society relations, which had first taken on its distinctive form in the Western part of the Continent in the decades after the Second World War, where it had promised to provide a relatively stable and durable context for the composition of old religio-political quarrels (Robbers, 1996; Ferrari, 1999). In addition to unsettling challenges to the model in its place of origin, there have been the attempts of the post-communist regimes of Central and Eastern Europe to adopt and adapt it in ways which are sensitive to diverse sets of local conditions.

For convenience this chapter surveys the political impact of the disparate challenges to church–state–society relations under three headings reminiscent of the principal slogans of the 1789 French revolution, a key secularizing moment of modern European political history: liberty, equality and fraternity. Each of these principles or values in fact sits awkwardly with the European model of church–state–society relations, partly because its basic outlines developed at a time before so many other, non-church religious traditions, centring for example on mosques, synagogues, temples and other institutions, had emerged with the effect of greatly extending the range of religio-cultural pluralism. Expanded pluralism was a principal source of the new challenges which emerged on the back of issues related to individual and collective religious freedoms (liberty), of controversies affecting the relative standing of religious institutions, organizations and communities (equality), and around the increasingly urgent necessity of promoting good relations between the different world religious traditions (fraternity).

Reviewing the issues which have arisen in terms of religious liberty, equality and fraternity recapitulates the sequence in which they were first addressed in Europe over the modern period, whether one dates that from the Peace of Westphalia in 1648, or from the French Revolution of 1789 itself. First came the struggle to establish religious freedoms in the context of what had once in almost all cases been confessional states, a struggle which led to the first full elaboration of liberal principles (Habermas, 2004). Only then did there follow more or less long-lasting campaigns to institutionalize egalitarian arrangements in the field of religion, to be followed, finally, by the still-evolving concern on the part of the public authorities to promote amity and comity between the representatives of religious traditions. The fact that the three values as applied to the field of religion are potentially rivalrous, and that it is not possible to maximise any one without prejudicing the chances of maximizing at least one of the others, reflects the difficulties of the enterprise; it also helps to explain why – at the margin at least – there remain significant variations between the different national systems of church–state–society relations.

All three types of development have involved attempts appropriately to delimit the role of the public authorities in the field of religion – in some cases aiming to limit this to the minimum required by the need to safeguard individual rights to religious freedom or to protect civil order. They have in addition involved initiatives aimed at delimiting the corresponding role, if any, of religious organizations and institutions in the public sphere, initiatives which have often had the effect of placing in doubt the very legitimacy of any form of public religion (Casanova, 1994). Few now dissent from the proposition that the liberal democratic state should eschew the attempts of earlier types of political regime to enforce, control or grant exclusive privileges to certain favoured religious forms and institutions, and should establish instead a sort of free market in religion. Equally there is a virtually unanimous rejection of the anti-religious posture of the former communist regimes of Central and Eastern Europe with their alternating policies of repressing and – where repression failed – oppressively controlling, religious bodies.

Instead of either of these unacceptable alternatives the European model has involved a key trade-off, whereby religious organizations and institutions should be progressively relieved of state interference, while at the same time the state should be spared the disruption caused around conflicts centring on religious concerns. Unlike in the USA, however, this trade-off has not generally been attempted on the basis of a would-be strict separation between the spheres of church and state, buttressed by claims of state religious neutrality (Madeley, 2003a). Only in France was such an attempt made when in 1905, long after the first promulgation of the values of *liberté, egalité et fraternité*, a Law for the Separation of Church and State was introduced; and even there a series of subsequent derogations from that Law – from the reintegration of the three Eastern departments, with their surviving systems of multiple church establishment, to the state funding of education in free, largely Catholic, schools – have undermined the principle of the *laïcité* of the state (Rémond, 1999).

Almost everywhere else in Western Europe, and increasingly further East, long-established religious bodies have been allowed to enjoy a privileged standing and a range of material benefits guaranteed, and often directly provided, by the state (Madeley, 2003b). In the Protestant North this has typically occurred in the context of surviving state or national churches, while in the Catholic South Concordats with the Papacy have underwritten similar advantages. In the historically mixed-confession territories which straddle Europe's ragged Protestant–Catholic religious frontier a range of more or less idiosyncratic arrangements also provide for systems of public recognition and support which are no less favourable to the traditional confessions; this now includes that part of the mixed-confession belt which until 1989 fell East of the Iron Curtain. Finally, in the predominantly Orthodox Eastern territories of Europe – other than Greece where the Greek Orthodox church continues to benefit from an almost complete monopoly hold on the country – there has been a distinct tendency to compensate the principal religious confessions for their losses under Communism and to re-establish a degree of religious privilege (Anderson, 2003).

The European model is ostensibly based on full recognition of the rights of individuals to religious liberty, but a number of recent developments have raised important questions, especially in connection with the legal recognition of unfamiliar religious movements and the safeguarding of the rights of their members especially, but not exclusively, in Eastern Europe. Questions about how a free market in religion should be regulated also remain unresolved – for example, how competition should be moderated, or how the incentive for religious rent-seekers to enter the political realm in pursuit of advantage should be reduced. Problems have furthermore arisen with regard to the claim of certain groups and individuals to freedom from religion, an issue which touches on the responsibility of the state to guarantee the freedoms of both secularists and the members of illiberal religious communities who stand to become victims (Barry, 2001). Religious equality issues on the other hand have been pushed less vigorously; as just noted, in most states elements of earlier systems of official establishment or special recognition remain, while in others they have even been reintroduced or the benefits of religious establishment have simply been distributed more widely. Nowhere in Europe, however, have these benefits been distributed universally with a resultant equalization of the standing of all religious groups. Almost everywhere there exists a hierarchy of recognition extending from full acceptance to complete non-recognition with all the implications this has for favourable or unfavourable treatment.

The observable tendency towards broadening the ambit of state recognition has been pushed forward in part by the concern to promote fraternal relations between religious groups. In a similar vein efforts to outlaw religious hatred or to extend the reach of blasphemy laws to embrace the most various traditions have been made with a view to reducing conflict not just between religious groups themselves but also between all religious groups and the more secularist sections of opinion. The fact that such efforts can be seen as derogating from the principles of religious (and non-religious) liberty and equality only underlines the controversial nature of these efforts. A comprehensive equilibrium solution to all the presenting problems and issues has proved elusive; the more so as transnational trends have led to a step-level increase in the complexity of local religious topographies. Despite – or perhaps because of – the hoary nature the underlying issues, there is not a single country in contemporary Europe where they appear to have been definitively resolved.

In the earliest phase of the development of mass politics in Europe religious issues were frequently to the fore and electorates divided on denominational lines or on pro- versus anti-religious sentiment almost as much as – and in some cases, more than – on lines of class. Even with the settlement of some of the most troubling church–state issues after 1945 in the context of the emergent European model, Christian Democratic parties and their more or less secular opponents continued throughout most of continental Western Europe to articulate old confessional or clerical–secular cleavages. Since the 1960s the hold of these cleavages on Western electorates has tended to decline in step with the decline in levels of orthodox religious belief and observance. Recent decades have instead seen a shift towards more volatile patterns of issue-driven politics that have only occasionally had the effect to rein-vigorating the old cleavage bases. The political impact of the disparate church–state–society issues, which are surveyed here, has accordingly been much more scattered than was the case when issues such as the role of traditional religious concerns in education or about divorce, contraception and the protection of the institution of marriage were politically salient. Campaigns for or against gay and lesbian rights, pro-choice or anti-abortion, protection of particular religious sensibili-ties, or the prominent display of religious symbols in public, have fur-thermore tended to activate and mobilize vociferous minorities at many points across the political spectrum.

Religious liberty issues

On the face of it, in the court of world opinion religious liberty issues would seem to have been definitively resolved, at least so far as Europe is concerned. Despite the strangely hesitant endorsement of freedom for religious opinions in the 1789 Declaration of the Rights of Man and the Citizen – Article X states: 'no one may be harassed because of his opinions, even religious ones' (Remond, 1999: 38) – the principle of religious liberty has since then become progressively entrenched as an essential constituent of political modernity, paradoxically so since it ensures the right of individuals to adhere to and live by belief-systems which in most cases are anything but modern either in origin or in content. In 1948 Article 18 of the Universal Declaration of Human Rights affirmed:

> Everyone has the right to freedom of thought, conscience, and reli-gion; this right includes the freedom to change his religion and belief, and freedom, either alone or in community with others in public or in private, to manifest his religion or belief in teaching, practice, worship and observance.

And since 1948 a series of other international covenants, conventions and treaties have additionally committed their signatories to upholding the rights of individuals to freedom of thought, conscience, religion and belief. Thus Article 9 of the European Convention on Human Rights and Fundamental Freedoms (1950), reiterated the words of the United Nations Declaration, adding that the only limitations should be such 'as are prescribed by law and are necessary in a democratic society in the interests of public order, health or morals, or for the protection of the rights and freedoms of others'. The guarantees were often entrenched in the constitutional law of most of the states of Western Europe, for example in the Basic Law of the German Federal Republic (1949) and the Constitution of the French Fifth Republic (1958). In Britain – which has always lacked a written constitution and where the growth of religious toleration relied on the piecemeal removal of restrictive laws – the incorporation of the European Convention into domestic law in 1998 also finally introduced a positive legal guarantee for the first time. The adoption by the European Union in 1993 of the Copenhagen criteria for would-be applicant countries requiring subscription to and practical conformity with *inter alia* the protection of the basic rights of various minorities, including religious minorities, also served to universalize and entrench commitment to such standards across Europe.

The basic freedoms

Notoriously, however, shared subscription to even the most basic principles of religious freedom has not involved common practice or uniform implementation. In the communist-dominated systems of Central and Eastern Europe during the Cold War, religious freedoms were formally embraced and yet systematically repressed – despite the existence of constitutional guarantees. Bulgaria is a more or less typical case. Despite the stipulations of the 1947 constitution, which declared a formal separation of church and state, the Bulgarian state actually tightened control of all aspects of religious life in areas such as the appointment of religious leaders, the licensing of religious buildings, the provision of seminaries for the training or priests and so on. Hundreds of Orthodox priests and religious leaders were imprisoned, while the representatives of the Catholic, Protestant and Islamic minorities were subjected to persistent harassment, extending in the last case to the closure of mosques and, as late as the mid-1980s, campaigns to impose non-Islamic names.

The principal instrument of Bulgarian state control was the Directorate of Religious Affairs (DRA) acting under the authority of the Religious Denominations Act of 1949. In the developing reformist climate of the late 1980s organizations such as the Independent Committee for the Defence of Religious Rights, Freedom of Conscience and Spiritual Values did finally emerge to prosecute the struggle to make a reality of religious freedom and article 13 of the new 1991 constitution included guarantees of individual religious freedom and the freeing religious institutions from state control (Anderson, 2003: 99–101). Despite numerous attempts to reform the Denominations

Act, on the grounds that certain of its articles were contrary to the constitution – for example, Article 12 which gave the state the right to dismiss priests – it remained in force until 2002. The Confessions Act which took its place, however, has since been declared restrictive of religious freedom because the registration procedure which it requires has turned out to be 'selective, slow and nontransparent' (US Department of State, 2004).

Nor has it been only in formerly communist Central and Eastern Europe that religious liberty issues have continued to arouse political controversy; issues involving religious freedom have come more or less forcefully to the fore in most, if not all, parts of Western Europe. In some cases it has been a matter of removing surviving anomalies. Thus, for example, the Greek prohibition against proselytising – that is, attempting to convert people to worship according to a different faith – was tested in 1993 when the European Court of Human Rights found that the Jehovah's Witness Kokkinakis had been wrongfully convicted; the Court stopped short, however, of considering whether the law against proselytising with its constitutional basis was compatible with the 1950 European Convention. Jehovah's Witnesses in Greece, despite the fact that they have been in the country for almost a century, have also been deemed by the UN's Special Rapporteur for Religious Intolerance to have suffered harassment from local government officials and to have been victims of the lack of provision for conscientious objection to military service.

Les affaires du foulard

One of the bitterest conflicts arising in connection with religious liberty issues has surrounded the display of religious symbols in public institutions in certain European states. The most long-running and disruptive case concerns France, with its constitutional endorsement of the principle of secularism or *laïcité*. The central conflict about the wearing by female pupils of the Islamic headscarf (*hijab*, in French *foulard*) first erupted in late 1989 when three Muslim girls were expelled from a public secondary school for wearing the *hijab* in defiance – as it was interpreted – of the general rule of *laïcité* in all French public institutions and, in particular, of the public school system. Over the ensuing 15 years a series of court decisions, declarations by the Council of State, and directives by the Ministry of Education focussed on the issue without satisfactorily resolving it.

The affair culminated in the recommendations in 2003 of a state commission and the subsequent enactment with overwhelming parliamentary majorities of a ban on the wearing of any and all ostentatious religious symbols in the public schools. The law went into effect in September 2004 over the protest of many religious and some secularist groups who regarded the measure as an unwarranted infringement of religious liberty. While the principle of *laïcité* has historically been a rallying-cry of the political left, the *affaire du foulard* controversy demonstrated that support for it now spanned the mainstream right as well. Jean Marie Le Pen's National Front on the other hand opposed the law on grounds that it failed to exempt Christian symbols and ignored the real underlying problem: 'massive immigration' (Thomas, 2004). Its supporters meanwhile claim that the law does not discriminate against Islamic (or, indeed, any particular) religious groups since Jewish skullcaps, Sikh turbans and 'large crosses' worn by Christians are equally prohibited and that it actually enhances religious liberty because it frees girls from Islamic backgrounds from the imposition on them of family or community standards rooted in religious fundamentalism.

France has not been alone in restricting the rights of citizens to wear Islamic headdress in public institutions. In September 2003 after a number of similar bans had been introduced in Germany, the Federal Constitutional Court ruled that the wearing of Islamic headscarves by teachers could not be banned unless the ban was supported by state legislation. The response has been that some regional governments (*Länder*) have introduced such banning legislation; thus, in November 2004 Bavaria became the third German state (after Baden-Württemberg and Lower Saxony) to proceed to ban teachers in state schools wearing symbols and clothing that were claimed to express religious or ideological beliefs and at the same time could be understood as an expression of an attitude incompatible with basic constitutional values and educational aims. In this case the target is transparently the *hijab*, as Christian and Jewish symbols and clothing, such as nun's habits, are excluded from the ban, since they are taken to reflect the cultural and educational values of the state.

The banning of headscarves and other symbols of Islamic identity in public places is not a novel derogation from religious freedom and neither is it only found in France, Germany and a number of other West European countries. In 1934, Kemal Atatürk introduced such bans in Turkey, an overwhelmingly Islamic society, in an attempt to modernize and secularize the country. From that date forward in Turkey, religious clothing could only be legally worn in the home or in places of religious worship. Remarkably, exactly 70 years later in June 2004 the European Court of Human Rights rejected appeals by a Turkish student barred from attending Istanbul University medical school in 1998 because her headscarf violated the official dress code. In this as in other controversial rulings, the ECHR opened itself to the charge that it has approached the business of protecting freedom of religion and belief in an incoherent and inconsistent manner (Evans, 2001: 12).

Religious equality issues

If the principle of individual religious liberty has become virtually unassailable in Europe, however, the same cannot be said for religious equality, at least as it affects the relative standing of religious traditions *vis-à-vis* the state. According to the 1988 General Comment of the UN Human Rights committee different religious traditions may legitimately be accorded special recognition by states:

> The fact that a religion is recognized as a State religion or that it is established as official or traditional or that its followers comprise the majority of the population, shall not result in any impairment of the enjoyment of any of the rights under the [International Covenant on Civil and Political Rights of 1976] ... nor in any discrimination against adherents of other religions or non-believers. (Boyle and Sheen, 1994: xxii)

In most European countries this has meant that the growth of religious liberty has occurred in the absence of a parallel growth in religious equality and that more or less stable patterns of religious establishment or privilege have continued to exist (Madeley, 2003a).

As already noted, the institutional form of these patterns of religious establishment or privilege has varied markedly as between the Protestant North, the Catholic South, the Orthodox East and the intervening mixed-confession territories. France has been virtually alone in its century-long experiment of rigorously separating church and state, consigning the former to the private sphere beyond the reach of state regulation, so requiring the secular, or *laïque*, state to dispense with any functions of a religious nature even to the point of outlawing the collection of data relating to the population's religious affiliations. Despite a number of compromises, which a more rigid scheme of strict separation, such as has been more nearly approached in the USA, would have struck down, France continues to remain alone. In the Netherlands, Ireland or Belgium, where separation of church and state is also sometimes said to obtain, this amounts to little more than state recognition of internal self-government on the part of the recognized churches, while large parts of the education, health and welfare sectors have been made over to religious bodies, despite the fact that they are funded out of taxation. In the case of Belgium this even runs to the direct payment out of general taxation of salaries and pensions to all officials of the six recognized faith communities, including since 1993 the humanists. Everywhere, including in France, the European state dispenses benefits to religious organizations – varying between different combinations of: symbolic recognition as the (or a) religion of the state; special legal status, even extending to the incorporation of church law into national law; protection of religious sensibilities through legislation outlawing blasphemy or religious hatred; state support for 'faith organizations' in the delivery of health, educational and welfare services; material support ranging from large direct subsidies to the use of the public taxation system for raising funds to tax breaks; privileged standing in planning law, and so on.

Access to the benefits available under these varying sets of national arrangements which in many cases amount to systems of virtual – if unofficial – establishment has tended to become controversial, as ever more unfamiliar or exotic forms of religion have made their appearance and entered their claims. While the traditional mainstream traditions have generally accepted an effective trade-off between symbolic and material advantages and the temptation to promote or defend politically controversial policy stands, the system has been put into question not just by the continuing criticism of secularists, who believe the state should be neutral in matters of belief and unbelief, but also by conflicts arising within and across the increasingly diverse religious scene.

State recognition: shades of establishment

Recent decades have seen some major changes in the different patterns of advantage available to religious groups. Thus, Spain's 1953 exclusive concordat with the Vatican, which had formed the basis of National Catholicism throughout the Franco years, was replaced by a series of treaties and partial agreements in the late 1970s which conceded recognition and religious rights to other religious communities while continuing to privilege and support Roman Catholicism. In overwhelmingly Protestant Sweden, meanwhile, relations between the country's national Lutheran church and the state were comprehensively remodelled after some fifty years' gestation only in January 2000 (Gustafsson, 2003). Elsewhere changes have been more dramatic but no more egalitarian in outcome overall. In Central and Eastern Europe in particular, the collapse of communism in 1989 led to the partial re-establishment of the churches which had once been dominant: in Central Europe the Catholic church, and further east the various national Orthodox churches, enjoyed a restoration of sorts, not least by the return and refurbishment of church properties which had been confiscated under communism. Minority traditions, many of which had been present on the national territories so far back as to be considered traditional, also benefited from the end of the religious ice age, although in some cases, such as that of the Ukraine's Uniates or Armenia's Muslim Azeris, negative discrimination, even persecution, became possibly even more oppressive than in Soviet times.

Overall, instead of a shift towards a single European model of religious disestablishment and strict separation of church and state there has been a tendency to retain or restore one or another pattern of virtual establishment, often broadening and making more inclusive its scope and range, that is, extending its benefits to ever more groups. A degree of convergence can be detected across a wide range of cases. Thus in Italy a number of agreements have been made between the state and non-Catholic religious communities, including for example the Jehovah's Witnesses, which allows for the distribution of church taxes raised through the public taxation system. In Denmark, calls for something similar have been made, for example a Catholic bishop has called for the extension of church tax to provide funds to communities other than the Danish Lutheran national church. And in the United Kingdom proposals to reform the composition of the House of Lords have included the idea that religious representation should be extended to include the other principal faith communities, instead of the exclusive representation of the Anglican Church as at present through its most senior 24 bishops. Even in France in 2004 prominent voices on the political right called for a major reform of the 1905 Law of Separation, which would scrap the section of the law banning the state from subsidizing religions.

One of the perennial problems of reform in this area has revolved around where the line should be drawn between groups deserving of the state's favour and those not so deserving. Decisions in this area often depend on quite adventitious features of religious communities; it is notable, for example, that unlike the relatively small sect of the Jehovah's Witnesses, and despite accounting for about a million resident Muslims, Islam is not officially recognized by the Italian state. The reason appears to be that, because of divisions between Islamic groups, they have been unable to reach agreement on a common legal understanding with the state. Accordingly, most Muslim institutions – from schools to mosques – are unable to benefit from the tax breaks and state-raised income tax shares reserved for recognized faiths.

In the case of Serbia a draft religion law, first made public by the Ministry of Religions in July 2004, drew on precedents elsewhere in Europe, notably in Austria, as it proposed to divide religious communities into different categories with differing rights. The draft was criticized for aiming effectively to recreate a system of multiple state churches with special privileges on the one hand, and a penumbra of other religious groups to whom those privileges were to be denied. Most privileged would be the Serbian Orthodox Church, while the six other recognised religious communities, most of them linked to historic ethno-religious minorities in Serbia (for example, the Hungarian Reformed Church), would be accorded lesser rights. These were the same traditional or historical communities which had been recognized by the Kingdom of the Serbs, Croats and Slovenes between 1918 and 1941. Outside this narrow circle registered religious associations were to be subject to special requirements and controls, while lowest in the hierarchy of recognition would be communities registered under the law governing civil associations in general.

The proposal drew criticism from the Organization for Security and Cooperation in Europe (OSCE), the Council of Europe and from the Conference of European Churches (CEC). By February 2005 it was in its fourth edition. While Baptist and Adventist leaders declared it improved it retained the critical distinction between traditional and other faiths, which, it was pointed out would affect rights to religious education in public schools, to taxes and property, to social security and pension funds. The requirement that a religious group should number 700 members (down from 1,000 in the first draft) and this membership be identifiable by the provision of personal identification (ID) numbers and home addresses in order to qualify for registration was also criticized.

Regulating minority religions

Unsurprisingly, problems arising in connection with religious equality tend to be particularly acute at the bottom of the hierarchy of recognition, particularly when groups – usually but not always small minority groups – are refused recognition. While subsidy remains an important lever in the business of regulating denominations towards the top of this hierarchy, the option of suppression remains the most potent weapon at the bottom. Even the claims of groups in this unenviable position to the exercise of the basic religious freedoms are routinely denied on the grounds that they either do not qualify as religious groups or that they run up against the general limitation on religious rights that are necessary for the protection of public safety, or of the fundamental rights and freedoms of others.

The regulation of minority faiths varies greatly across Europe with some countries allowing considerable freedom for them to emerge, recruit members, raise money and use public facilities, while others are more closed to the very presence of such groups, whether native or foreign (Beckford, 1985; Richardson, 2004). In Western Europe limitations on the activities of minority and fringe religious groups has usually taken the form either of refusal of recognition as religious with all its attendant disadvantages, or increasingly of surveillance by official state bodies as they become objects of suspicion in connection with presumed threats to individual autonomy or, especially in the case of militant groups arising within large Islamic minorities, of national security. Thus, during the 1990s the recognition of the status of both the Jehovah's Witnesses, a sect with a long history, and Scientology, a relatively new one, as legitimate religious organizations has been a source of great controversy in Germany, where the granting of public law status brings considerable advantages. Sensational events involving NRMs, such as the Waco siege in the USA in 1993, the Solar Temple deaths in Switzerland and Canada in 1994 and the criminal activities of Aum Shinrikyo in Japan also triggered intense controversy about how the state should respond. One outcome was that in France, Belgium and Switzerland a number of public bodies were charged with monitoring and reporting on groups that are variously described as 'dangerous sects', 'cults' or 'unconventional religious entities', an initiative which was approved and encouraged by the Parliamentary Assembly of the Council of Europe in June 1999.

With its particular history of *laïcite* France led the way in providing for the surveillance and control of unrecognised minority sects or cults. In 1996 a Parliamentary Commission on Sects, which had been charged with assessing the potential dangers to French society posed by dissident religious groups, issued a report identifying 172 such groups and later the same year Prime Minister Alain Juppé established by decree an Interministerial Observatory on Sects to investigate the those so identified and to recommend effective means of combating them. In October 1998 the President and Prime Minister signed a decree establishing an Interministerial Mission for the Struggle against Sects. And finally in 2001 the National Assembly passed 'A bill directed to the reinforcement of prevention and repression of cultic movements which undermine human rights and fundamental freedoms'; among other provisions, the bill empowered a court to dissolve so-called 'sects' , thus preventing them from owning or renting property, publishing their teachings, renting public places for services or meetings, operating schools or seminaries, and other activities which might be considered essential to religious practice, worship and observance.

In a number of former communist countries the continued existence of elements of the bureaucracy that previously specialized in the surveillance and control of religious activities (for example, the Directorate of Religious Affairs in Bulgaria as already noted) has facilitated the monitoring and control of minority religions – both pre-existing and novel. Nor does this only affect extreme Islamist groups, which are presumed to threaten public order and are understandably subjected to bans. In Russia, for example, in May 2004 local Jehovah's Witnesses appealed against a total ban on their activities in Moscow. The decision of the judge who had imposed the ban ruled that, while there was no evidence that the Jehovah's Witnesses were responsible for inciting religious hatred, their practices did have the deleterious effect of bringing about the disintegration of family units, of violating the equal rights of parents in the upbringing of their children, of violating the Russian Constitution's guarantees of freedom of conscience, of encouraging suicide, and of inciting citizens to refuse both military and alternative service.

Religious fraternity issues: the promotion of inter-religious tolerance

One of the sources of conflict between religious traditions lies in the fact that many of them – and among them the less liberal versions of Christianity and Islam – claim the exclusive possession of deep and precious truths. A similar claim to superiority and finality can also be found in some secular ideologies, which are typically characterized by the firm rejection of the claims of all the so-called revealed religions. The promotion of such explicitly contradictory claims are clearly at variance with the essentially pluralist principles of international human rights theory and raise questions about how states can protect the rights of believers to hold and manifest such convictions while at the same time avoiding sectarian conflict. In 1981, after 20 years of deliberations, the United Nations (UN) promulgated a Declaration on the Elimination of All Forms of Intolerance and of Discrimination Based on Religion or Belief, which attempted to guide state authorities on the steps required to promote tolerance. Meanwhile the Council of Europe, the OSCE and the European Union (EU) each in turn adopted commitments to the protection and promotion of pluralism, human rights, democracy and intercultural tolerance in Europe, commitments which had become all the more difficult of achievement in the post-Cold War era, especially in Eastern Europe. In particular the outbreak of ethno-religious conflicts in the former Yugoslavia and more recently the terrorist attacks perpetrated by certain extreme Islamist groups have had the demonstration effect of greatly increasing the urgency with which state authorities have addressed the need to promote inter-cultural understanding and tolerance.

Religion and education

One of the fields where the attempt to combine religious freedoms with mutual religious tolerance has had its most important effects is that of education policy. According to the 1981 UN Declaration Article 5 clause 2:

> Every child shall enjoy the right to have access to education in the matter of religion or belief in accordance with the wishes of his parents or, as the case may be, legal guardians, and shall not be com-pelled to receive teaching on religion and belief against the wishes of his parents or legal guardians; the best interests of the child shall be the guiding principle.

The practical implementation of this rule has varied considerably as between three different institutional forms or various combinations of them, some of them of very long standing. One, which is associated in its fullest development with the Netherlands and is variously referred to as consociationalism (Lijphart, 1969) or sociological liberalism (Crouch, 1999), has provided since 1917 for parallel educational systems each catering for the country's separate religious and secular constituencies. A second and equally distinctive form, which is associ-ated in particular with France, bans religious education (though not necessarily education about religion) from state schools altogether, leaving it to parents to make what provision they want through enrol-ment in either private schools or private lessons, both typically run by or on behalf of religious organizations. A third pattern, which is much more common across Europe, provides for the parents of pupils in state schools to exercise choice in religious education between alterna-tive classes, including in many cases the option of non-religious ethics teaching. The implications of these different systems for inter-religious tolerance naturally vary and have sometimes become deeply controver-sial not least, for example, in the UK where, on the one hand, the prevalence of segregated religious provision at primary and secondary levels in Northern Ireland and, on the other, the growth in the number and variety of so-called 'faith schools' in mainland Britain have attracted, and continue to attract, fierce debate.

Until recent years educational issues accounted more than any other area of public policy for conflict between religious or humanist organi-zations and the state. Nor have they disappeared from the political agenda even where the choice between the three basic institutional formats has been virtually settled. Thus, in Spain, well after the new configuration of church–state relations had been set in place, the Aznar centre-right government, which included at least one member of the conservative Catholic group Opus Dei, approved a law that made religious education, or the alternative subject – ethics – count academically as much as mathematics and other core subjects of the curriculum. Given that religious education in Spanish public schools is entirely Catholic-based unless there are at least five students in a school of another religion or denomination who ask for separate classes, this was seen as an attempt further to entrench the Catholic religion. In 2004 the new socialist-led government quickly overturned this change as it also moved onto a number of other secularizing measures.

In a very different educational context a number of countries have in recent years begun to introduce the requirement that foreign-born religious leaders be required to master the national language of the state, Islamic imams clearly being in mind as the main target, since in France as in most of Europe a large majority have been of immigrant background and training. Thus, in France in December 2004 it was decided that from the following year French universities should shoulder the task of teaching the French language, law and culture to foreign-born imams. The head of a French government commission on integration policy openly announced that the purpose of the legislation was to encourage the development of moderate as opposed to fundamentalist Islam, with the intentions of tipping the balance within France's large Islamic minority in favour of greater inter-religious tolerance. The suggestion that imams should be forced to preach in French was also mooted, even though this has been seen by some to amount to an unwarranted intrusion by secular, *laïque* state authorities into a religious sphere where it declares its own lack of competence.

Protecting religious sensibilities

The commitment to encouraging a climate of inter-religious tolerance has also led to other initiatives aimed at reducing levels of friction between different religious, or religion-related, traditions. Some of them have been occasioned by particular incidents or developments, which have been adjudged to present a threat to public order. A prominent example is the Rushdie affair in the UK, which was triggered in 1989 by the issuing of an Iranian call for the death of the author Salman Rushdie for allegedly insulting the memory of the prophet Muhammad; this led to proposals to extend the reach of existing blasphemy laws to include traditions other than the Christian. In addition, there has arisen a proposal to outlaw the specific crime of incitement to religious hatred, although this proposal has been opposed by some orthodox religious, as well as some secularist, sections of opinion on the grounds that it would seriously inhibit free speech and lead to vexatious cases of religious censorship. The proposal was nonetheless welcomed by many religious representatives – not least those who claimed to speak on behalf of the almost two million Muslims, many of whom had been subjected to attack, suspicion and abuse after the various Islamist terror outrages of recent years. In the Netherlands with its long traditions of liberal toleration similar outrages also raised the question of how inter-religious mutual tolerance could be safeguarded, although there the response has been to call for the repeal, rather than the extension, of older (1930s) blasphemy legislation, an appeal which was turned down in late 2004 because of the opposition of the Christian Democratic Appeal party then in government.

A very different, if cognate, development occurred in Bavaria, southern Germany, in the 1990s. There the issue was whether or not the display in the classrooms of public primary schools of the Christian crucifix, as required by a School Ordinance of 1983, could be justified if the sensibilities of pupils belonging to religious minorities, which might object to such a display, were offended. Finally, in 1995 the Federal Constitutional Court found the ordinance unconstitutional and there followed loud protests and demonstrations in favour of the supposed rights of the majority to have its religious preferences honoured. In Italy in 2003 a similar dispute occurred when a Muslim convert's partly successful efforts to have crucifixes removed from public school classrooms stirred widespread resentment in the overwhelmingly Roman Catholic country.

Conclusion

The impact of the religious factor on contemporary European politics has rarely, if ever been as dramatic as the developments and events which have triggered its renewed salience. The mushroom-like development of multiculturalism with its important religious components, and events like the various Islamist terror attacks, have seized the public imagination and led to fierce debates which have spilled over a number of issue domains. While the temperature of these debates has been high and extreme viewpoints have often been deployed, the underlying issue affecting religion continues to be how far, if at all, the European liberal democratic state can or should be neutral relative to any one religion (however popular), or as between different religions, or as between religious and non-religious sections of opinion and preference (Monsma and Soper, 1994). The European model of church–state–society relations provides a common context but opinion continues to divide. For religious conservatives neutrality has never been an option: individuals, groups or public authorities necessarily stand either in support of religious claims or opposed to them. For secular liberals state neutrality is a key value which can only be approximated if controversial claims of religious provenance are excluded from political discourse, or only admitted insofar as they are presented in terms accessible to all, including non-believers. Meantime, assisted by the presence in the religious world of a range of liberal tendencies, which tend to deemphasize the differences, emphasizing instead the communalities, between different religious and other ethical traditions, messy compromises have come to abound not least in the very construction of the European model. Christian Democratic parties continue to call for the recognition of the claims of Christianity to represent a distinctive core of value commitments, not least for example in the debates about whether a Constitution for the European Union should acknowledge this debt, if only in its preamble (van Hecke and Gerard, 2004). These parties also stand guard over the European model itself, which is in large part their own achievement, while continuing to fight rearguard actions in defence of traditional standards in the field of family law, the regulation of sexual mores and on emergent bio-ethical issues.

While the principle of religious liberty is by and large approved across Europe, despite the difficulties of application at the margins, religious equality, at least as it applies to relations between religious traditions and the public authorities, has not by contrast been generally regarded as an important norm. The urgency of promoting religious harmony on the other hand has in recent years been reflected almost everywhere in initiatives aimed at drawing the sting of religiously-fuelled conflict, whether the threats emanate from extremist groups of religious fundamentalists or from movements of the extremist political right. Hitherto recent trends have not been in the direction of a strict separation of church and state anywhere in Europe, nor is any such thing likely given the concurrence of expanding state responsibilities and the continuing – even expanding – amplitude of religious concerns.

PART IV

Challenges to the Policy Process

Chapter 14

European Welfare States: Diversity, Challenges and Reforms

Anton Hemerijck, Maarten Keune and Martin Rhodes

Since the late 1970s, all welfare states in the European Union (EU) have been recasting the basic policy mix on which they were built after 1945. Changes in the world economy and in Europe itself have thrown into question the once sovereign and stable welfare systems of the so-called 'Golden Age'. Welfare reform across the member states of the EU has been especially intense and comprehensive since the 1990s, producing a momentum of change that goes far beyond the popular notion of welfare state 'retrenchment'.

Some have characterized this change in terms of a paradigm shift from an earlier rather static emphasis on protection from the market, providing replacement incomes in the case of old age, unemployment, illness, and so on, towards labour market (re)integration for both men and women, with an emphasis on enabling choice and encouraging new behavioural patterns rather than passive benefits. The 'new' welfare state seems to mark a significant departure from a 'politics against markets' social-protection perspective, towards more of a 'politics with markets', social-investment strategy (Ferrera, Hemerijck and Rhodes, 2000; Esping-Andersen *et al.*, 2002). In European policy debates the term 'European social model' assumes the existence of a common European 'social market' approach to the multiple challenges facing welfare states through sustainable, high-quality public provisions and comprehensive social protection.

Yet such generalizations gloss over the immense differences in welfare state development, design and institutional make-up across the EU's 25 member states and fail to capture the complexity of their reform trajectories. Beyond certain abstract values and ideas concerning solidarity, social rights and equal social worth, there is no uniform European 'model', nor even 'models' (though the word is frequently used to describe individual countries), but rather clusters of nations with similar traditions, institutions, achievements and problems.

Our aim in this chapter is to provide a comparative analysis of this diversity. The first section discusses the variety of Europe's welfare families, and considers whether the new Central Eastern European (CEE) member states comprise a new family, or whether they can be subsumed within a traditional classification. We then proceed to consider the nature and severity of contemporary challenges to Europe's welfare states, their responses to those challenges, and the potential for European-level solutions.

Classifying Europe's welfare states: four families or five?

There is a rich literature on 'worlds' or 'families' of welfare dating back to the 1980s that shows how key variables are systematically related to one another, producing distinctive clusters of nations in four 'social Europes' – Scandinavian, Conservative Continental, Southern European and 'Anglo-Irish' (Esping-Andersen, 1990; Castles and Mitchell, 1993; Ferrera, Hemerijck and Rhodes, 2000).

In the Scandinavian welfare states (Denmark, Finland and Sweden), social protection is a citizen's right, coverage is fully universal, and all are entitled to the same basic guarantees, though this principle has been eroding in recent years. Besides generous replacement rates, these systems offer a wide array of public social services beyond health and education, together with active labour-market programmes that encourage and sustain high levels of both male and female employment. Public-sector employment is also extensive. General taxation plays a dominant, though not exclusive role in financing welfare, making taxing and spending levels high by international standards, especially in Sweden. The provision of benefits and services is mainly the responsibility of central and local public authorities.

The Continental group includes Austria, Germany, France and the Benelux countries. Here the Bismarckian tradition, based on a tight link between work position and/or family status and social entitlements, is characterized by occupationally distinct, employment-related social insurance, underpinned by traditional (single-breadwinner) family values (Kersbergen, 1995). Only the Netherlands has modified this tradition by providing a basic public pension. Benefit formulae proportional to earnings and financing through social security contributions largely reflect the logic of insurance, though with different rules for different professional groups. Benefit replacement rates (that is, as proportions of previous incomes) are generous and benefit duration tends to be long. Spending and taxing levels are also therefore high. Employers and trade unions play an important role in managing social insurance.

The Southern European group of Italy, Spain, Portugal, and Greece, resembles the Continental family, but with specific institutional traits that set it apart (Ferrera, 1996). Benefit coverage reflects a mixed orientation: Bismarckian in income transfers, with especially generous pensions, but Beveridgean in healthcare, with fully universal national health services in both Italy and Spain. The social safety net of basic benefits is underdeveloped. Social charges (that is, taxes on employers and employees) are widely used, but general taxation is becoming more important in financing social services. The family is still a significant source of care and support, and makes up for deficits in the welfare system, but has adverse implications for the position of women in the household and the labour market (Esping-Andersen, 1999). Inadequate administrative capacities reinforce poor social policy implementation and, in some cases, clientelism.

The Anglo-Irish group of the United Kingdom and Ireland has a system of social protection that is highly inclusive though not fully universal, except for healthcare. Benefits – which are flat rate – are modest, and social protection reflects an emphasis on targeted, needs-based, means-tested entitlements with low replacement rates (Table 14.1). Healthcare and social services are financed through general taxation, but contributions play an important role in financing cash benefits, especially pensions. Public social services and family services are less developed than in Scandinavia and the Continental countries, but as in Scandinavia the organization of the welfare state is highly integrated and entirely managed by the public administration.

These four families vary widely in levels of social expenditure and taxation, with the Scandinavian and Continental countries ranking high, the Southern European countries and Ireland low and the UK in the middle, close to Belgium and the Netherlands (Table 14.1). The Scandinavian welfare states are also large employers, especially for women in the social-service sector, and they spend almost twice as much on family services as the average among the Continental and Anglo-Irish groups and three times as much as some Southern European countries. They also devote large financial resources to active labour market policies and training programmes, with Sweden and Denmark in leading positions. Though conventionally classified together, the UK is a much higher social spender than Ireland, and in recent years its spending growth has been higher than the EU-15. The Southern countries trail behind the Continental welfare states, except

Table 14.1 *Social protection expenditure, 2001*

	Social protection expenditure as % GDP	Percentage of social expenditure financed by social security contributions	Percentage of social expenditure subject to means testing
Finland	25.7	50.3	12.4
Sweden	31.4	52.3	4.4
Denmark	29.4	30.4	2.9
Belgium	27.5	72.5	3.0
Germany	29.8	65.5	9.2
France	30	66.7	11.2
Netherlands	27.5	66.9	11.7
Austria	28.6	65.2	5.8
Luxembourg	21.3	52.7	3.3
Greece	27.1	62	8.2
Spain	20.1	69.3	12.7
Italy	25.6	57.5	4.1
Portugal	24	54.4	7.9
United Kingdom	27.6	49.7	15.4
Ireland	15.3	38.3	26.0
Latvia	14.3	74.8	
Lithuania	15.2	59.9	4.5
Estonia	14.3	72.8	2.5
Czech Republic	19.2	75.4	7.3
Slovenia	25.5	65.9	9.1
Slovakia	19.1	65.1	13.0
Poland	22.1	53.2	0.6
Hungary	19.8	58.7	6.2
Malta	17.3	70.3	19.1
EU-25	27.3	60.6	9.7
EU-15	27.6	60.6	9.9

Source: BEPA (2005); original source Eurostat.

in pensions. Social security systems in the south are 'pension heavy', with Italy, for example, spending more than 16 per cent of its GDP, or about two-thirds of total social spending, and other Southern countries around half of their social budgets, on pensions.

In terms of employment, the Scandinavian countries far outperform the other three welfare families for all population categories (see Figure 14.1). The Anglo-Irish group has favourable levels of employment with

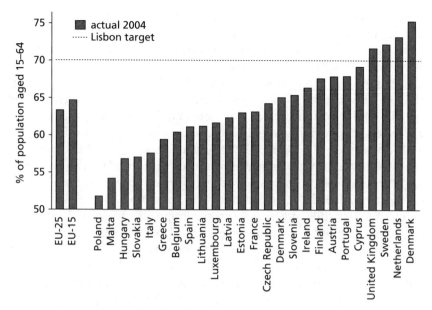

Figure 14.1 *Employment rates in the EU, 2004*

Source: BEPA (2005); original source European Commission services.

relatively low rates of public employment, but with exceptionally low rates of female employment in Ireland. The Continental countries take the middle ground, while low levels of employment are especially evident in Southern Europe, especially among your people, women and the elderly, with Portugal something of an exception.

The eight Central and Eastern Europe new member states (NMS), which joined the EU in May 2004, occupy a special place. They have gone through two radical changes in the past 65 years – the shift from capitalism to state-socialism in the 1940s and from state-socialism back to capitalism after 1989. Before the Second World War, CEE welfare had mainly a Bismarckian character, that is welfare arrangements were linked to and based on employment and occupation. The state-socialist era saw a universalization of the employment-based welfare system through full (and largely obligatory) employment. The state-socialist welfare state was interventionist ('from the cradle to the grave'), but it also suffered from low-quality services, long waiting lists, underemployment, limited choice and a generally low standard of living, even if it was also able to abolish deep poverty, create more equality, offered universal and free health and education services, and facilitated female employment by providing childcare, extended maternity leave and child benefits.

After 1989, radically new ideas emerged concerning solidarity, equality and redistribution and the role and responsibilities of the state, market and individual. Profound welfare state reforms were the result. But where do today's NMS welfare states stand *vis-à-vis* the EU's four welfare families? First, these are minimal welfare states: the percentage of GDP dedicated to social expenditure is low compared to the rest of the EU. Only Ireland, Spain, Portugal and Luxembourg fall into the same social expenditure range. They are also low-income welfare states: GDP per capita is substantially below the rest of the EU. However, when we consider other dimensions, it is difficult to place the NMS in a single group. Thus, in terms of income equality some NMS are among the most equal of EU member states (and resemble their Scandinavian counterparts), while others are at the opposite Anglo-Irish extreme. Regarding employment rates, three of the NMS (Hungary, Poland and Slovakia) are among the worst performers in the EU (alongside Greece, Spain, Italy and Belgium), while Slovenia, the Czech Republic, Estonia and Latvia perform similarly to France and Germany (Figure 14.1).

Moreover, reforms since 1989 seem to be making these systems 'mongrels' rather than thoroughbred members of existing EU families. While social benefits seem to be focused increasingly on income replacement and linked, Continental Bismarckian-style, to individual labour market histories, in healthcare, family policy and social assistance, there are important universalistic as well as 'Anglo' market-based trends (Keune, 2006).

Late twentieth and early twenty-first century challenges

All European welfare states are challenged from four directions: economic internationalization, demographic change, the service-sector revolution and the problems of containing and reorienting traditional welfare-state spending.

Though the impact of globalization is much disputed, many observers believe that the increase in cross-border competition has substantially reduced the room for manoeuvre of national welfare states (Scharpf, 2002). Economic internationalization constrains counter-cyclical macroeconomic management, while increased openness exposes generous welfare states to trade competition and permits capital to move to lower-cost producer countries. There is also the danger that tax competition may result in an underprovision of public goods (Genschel, 2004). But the importance of external pressures should not be overstated (Castles, 2004).

More importantly, ageing populations, declining birth rates and changing gender roles as a result of the mass female labour-market entry, all pose substantial challenges to traditional welfare commitments and entitlements. The shift from an industrial to the service economy and new technologies in the organization of work create difficult adjustment problems which, if handled badly, engender suboptimal employment levels, new inequalities and skill-biased patterns of social exclusion. There has been a weakening of labour markets and families as traditional providers of welfare (Esping-Andersen *et al.*, 2002), while new sources of immigration and segregation pose a challenge to social cohesion.

Finally, while policy-makers' endeavours to recast the welfare state is severely constrained by long-standing social policy commitments, the maturation of welfare commitments put in place to cater for traditional social risks (old-age, sickness, unemployment) associated with the postwar industrial era appear to restrict the available policy space for effective responses to new problems and risks. This spectre of stagnant welfare spending alongside increasing demand for benefits and services is likely to intensify in the face of population ageing (Pierson, 2001).

These common pressures generate distinctive problems in different systems. Scandinavian welfare states are expensive and rely on high levels of taxation, but are better adapted than others to post-industrial change, due to their service-intensive, women- and children-friendly public policies. Denmark and Sweden have long promoted public-sector employment. The consequent expansion of welfare state jobs encouraged women and single parents to enter the labour market, creating demand, in turn, for greater provision of social services, including child care. High levels of employment, low levels of early retirement and relatively high birth rates all contribute to long-term, welfare system sustainability (Esping-Andersen, 1999). Regardless of some pessimism regarding their capacity to maintain this performance in the face of global competition and constraints on public-sector expansion (for example, Iversen and Wren, 1998), these countries continue to combine high employment with relatively high levels of equality.

Continental countries suffer from low employment rates, especially among young people, women and older men, and are under pressure to transform their pay-as-you-go pension systems. The biggest problem is their inability to stimulate employment growth despite relative success in the 'globalization' game in remaining powerful and successful exporters. Belgium and France perform particularly poorly in this respect (Figure 14.1). Job stagnation is partly related to payroll-based social insurance financing which encourages high productivity and low employment-creating investment. Boosting international competitiveness through early retirement and high-quality training and education has sustained high levels of productivity but also increased taxation on labour. Thus fewer workers have to support a growing number of inactive benefit recipients – thereby creating an 'inactivity trap'.

Similar economic circumstances are found in Southern Europe where a more acute version of the 'inactivity trap' reinforces traditional patterns of social exclusion and divisions between well-protected 'insider' workers and underprivileged 'outsiders', including young people and women. These problems also have adverse consequences for fertility, labour supply and ultimately welfare-state viability. Low birthrates are linked to the difficulties facing young people seeking work and affordable housing and childcare. Women are thus forced to choose between careers and forming families and young people experience protracted dependence on their parents (Trifiletti, 1999). Higher female employment rates are needed to counteract population ageing, reduce household poverty risks and underpin the financial sustainability of the southern welfare systems (Esping-Andersen *et al.*, 2002).

The Anglo-Irish group are less costly and face fewer problems of financial sustainability. Labour market flexibility, combined with high rates of economic growth, has helped boost employment, especially in private-sector services, since the early 1990s. But an expansion of low-paid, low-skilled jobs has also contributed to a significant polarization of incomes and increasingly unequal access to social insurance (Rhodes, 2000). However, wage subsidies now supplement the incomes of low paid workers and their families, and a minimum wage in the UK and national wage agreements in Ireland help prevent the proliferation of 'working poor'. But despite such attempts to combat poverty, social disadvantage among vulnerable groups remains much more acute than in the Scandinavian or Continental systems.

The CEE welfare states are also quite diverse in terms of 'problem loads' and challenges (Rhodes and Keune, 2006). Poverty and inequality are more acute in the Baltic countries and Poland, while employment is more serious in Hungary, Slovakia and especially Poland, which, with an employment rate at just over 50 per cent, is the worst performer in the EU (Figure 14.1). Old-age dependency ratios are lowest in Slovakia, followed by the Czech Republic, Poland and Slovakia, but reach higher levels in the Baltic countries, Hungary and Slovenia. All NMS societies, apart from the Baltic countries and Slovakia, are due to age dramatically in coming decades, with important implications for spending and benefits.

Hungary, Slovakia and Poland have the highest fiscal deficits and face the most serious problems of public spending, followed by the Czech Republic. These may be exacerbated in the coming years as they adjust to and join Economic and Monetary Union (EMU) and conform to Stability and Growth Pact criteria, notably the 3 per cent budget deficit maximum and the 60 per cent maximum ratio of debt-to-GDP (Rhodes and Keune, 2006). Slovakia and Hungary face another problem – high inflation – with a potential impact on the level of incomes and benefits as well as on the timing of EMU entry. Interestingly enough EMU entry does not pose any particular problems for the poorer NMS.

Converging or divergent reform agendas?

Groundbreaking social policy changes have been implemented in most EU member states, but reforms are often delayed and difficult to introduce. The reason is political: the more reform embraces core distributive areas of social protection, where entitlements are defended by strong interest groups, the more likely is political conflict. This is especially true for pensions which are often considered sacrosanct rights. Policy reforms are conditioned by three sets of variables: (1) the particular economic and social policy challenges facing each welfare state, (2) variations in policy design, and (3) differences in institutional conditions, including systems of decision-making and interest mediation (Scharpf and Schmidt, 2000; Ferrera, Hemerijck and Rhodes, 2000).

Scandinavian solutions

Thanks to their institutional solidity and coherence, the Scandinavian systems have long been regarded as well-equipped for addressing the new risks and needs associated with aging societies, improving gender equality and transition to the post-industrial economy. Basic income guarantees provide a safeguard against poverty and exclusion, spells out of work and broken or changing career trajectories. A wide array of services allows them to respond more effectively to the needs of families and to socialize the costs of care, including for children. High rates of labour market participation reduce financial strains on pension systems.

But competitive and post-industrial challenges do generate cost and job problems. Resistance to extremely high tax rates has been growing, and demands for fiscal retrenchment have intensified. Throughout the 1990s, these countries grappled with pressures to contain high and increasing costs and to reorganize labour markets to generate more demand for private employment. Sweden and Denmark have begun to reduce public-sector employment, but the tradition and principles of universalism remain largely unquestioned even if across-the-board cuts in replacement rates (for example sickness benefits) or basic guarantees (for example family allowances) have occurred.

Important pensions reforms have been undertaken to strengthen the links between contributions and benefits in Sweden and Finland while maintaining the relative weight of pensions within overall social protection. In 1999, Sweden switched from a defined-benefit to a defined-contribution scheme in which each insured employee's contributions are recorded in an interest-earning individual account, typically at a rate tied to wage growth. At retirement, the balance in the account is converted to a life annuity. The Swedish reform also introduced a small privately-funded, defined-contribution component. This reform was based on a strong consensus on the need for fiscal sustainability spurred on by recession in the early 1990s and forged first between the social democrat and centre-right parties and then with employers and trade unions (Schludi, 2005).

A major plank in the Scandinavian reform agenda has been 'activation', that is, the modification of programmes to encourage actual and potential beneficiaries to find and maintain gainful employment. Denmark has gone furthest in changing the institutional profile and logic of labour market policy (Goul Andersen, 2000). Eligibility for cash benefits, especially duration, has been tightened. Individual employment plans have been targeted at unemployed youth, and a wide array of 'activating' instruments has been deployed, including information and counselling, subsidized employment in public and private sectors, training and educational initiatives, and job-rotation combined with an expansion of leave possibilities for employed workers. This effort has contributed to positive results: unemployment fell from 8.1 per cent in 1994 to 5.6 per cent in 2003, while the employment rate rose from 72.4 per cent to 75.1 per cent. The pessimism of some observers notwithstanding (for example Iversen and Wren, 1998), growth in private-sector employment has increased and an egalitarian wage structure largely maintained.

Confronting the continental syndrome of 'welfare without work'

Deep recession in the early 1990s produced a sharp rise in unemployment and public debt. High tax rates and EMU convergence constrained the scope for further welfare expansion. Policy attention and reform efforts increasingly focused on the core areas of the welfare state, social policy and labour market regulation, generating a complex reform agenda to curtail pension commitments and 'passive' benefits, improve family policy, reform labour markets and reduce the incidence of social charges on wage costs. But these systems are especially 'veto-heavy' and any reform must negotiate with or around entrenched vested interests.

In the 1970s, most Continental welfare states began using disability pensions, early retirement, and long-term unemployment schemes to remove older and less productive workers from the labour market. Though producing short-term gains, and backed by unions as a means of providing young people with jobs, this strategy simply depleted the over-50 workforce and reduced employment rates. From the early 1990s on, the focus shifted to employment creation. In the Netherlands, the government sought greater efficiencies in social security, including the introduction and intensification of activation obligations for the long-term unemployed. The Dutch managed to escape the employment crisis of these countries and in 2004 enjoyed the second highest employment rate in the EU, after Denmark (Figure 14.1). In Belgium, a new consensus promoted employment levels among women and older workers as the *sine qua non* for long-term sustainability. In France, most healthcare expenditures and the minimum incomes have been shifted from payroll contributions to general taxation to help reduce non-wage costs and encourage job-creation. Germany has been much slower in embracing reform, and only since 2002 under the Schroeder-led Social-Democratic/Green coalition have the highly unpopular Hartz reforms sought to reduce benefit dependency and encourage the long-term unemployed into work via a combination of cuts in benefits, the expansion of job placement agencies and individual job plans.

Pension reform in Continental welfare states has been especially difficult. Groundbreaking pension reforms in Italy in 1995 and Sweden in 1999 have proven hard to emulate elsewhere. But more marginal reforms have been achieved. Pension contribution rates have risen in Germany and the Netherlands, while in Austria, the reference period has been extended as part of a larger package of reforms. Germany has moved from gross to net wage indexation and France has shifted from wage to price indexation. The Netherlands, France, and Belgium have started building reserve funds to sustain pension provision when the 'baby-boom' generation retires (Esping-Andersen *et al.*, 2002).

Germany has gone furthest in encouraging savings in private pensions and the use of state subsidies to support supplementary pension schemes for low-wage earners. France is an acute case of policy blockage due to a lack of consensus among political parties, unions and employers (Smith, 2004). The 1995 Juppé government proposal to extend earlier private-sector reforms to the public sector, and increase the number of contributory years for pensions, triggered a six-week strike that paralyzed the country and derailed the reform. In 2003, the Raffarin government's partial reform extended contributory periods for all workers from 37.5 to 41.9 years, but left intact the privileges of key groups of public sector and civil service employees (Natali and Rhodes, 2004).

Finally, most Continental welfare states continue efforts to introduce women- and children-friendly policies that promote affordable access to day-care, paid maternity and parental leave, a more equal division of household tasks between men and women, and more generous provisions for absence from work when children are ill. While most policy-makers recognize that caring services, especially for small children and for the aged, are becoming an urgent matter, reform on these issues still proceeds at a snail's pace.

Modernizing southern welfare under fiscal constraints

Modernizing southern welfare states has also been difficult. Though EMU and globalization regularly receive the bulk of the blame, the real culprits are adverse demography (Southern European populations, especially in Italy and Spain, are aging faster than elsewhere), poor institutional design, and Continental-style opposition to reform from vested interests. Yet Southern European states have had an ambitious reform agenda that includes attenuating generous guarantees for historically privileged occupational groups, improving minimum benefits, introducing and consolidating safety nets, especially through means-tested minimum income schemes, expanding and improving family benefits and services, combating the underground economy and tax evasion, reforming labour markets and modifying unemployment insurance benefits.

Italy in the 1970s saw a rapid growth of expenditures on public pensions after generous social security reforms. Deficits soared and by the late 1980s Italy was becoming a 'pension state'. But proposals to rationalize the pension system and restore financial balance produced little progress. Only when the country sought do comply with the Maastricht criteria for EMU membership did fiscal restraint become indispensable. The EMU deadline also helped spur policy reforms in industrial relations, social security and labour-market regulation (Ferrera and Gualmini, 2004). Within the pension system, the privileges enjoyed by civil servants to retire after only 20 years of service regardless of age (the so-called 'baby pensions') was phased out.

Pension rights were accorded to atypical workers, and lower pensions were repeatedly upgraded. Some traditional gaps in social coverage were also filled. The introduction of means-tested maternity benefits for uninsured mothers was accompanied by a reform of parental leave, and a means-tested allowance for families with three or more children was introduced.

Only recently has progress been made in improving the functioning of the Italian labour market. But a proliferation of new flexible (so-called Co.Co.Co) contracts alongside a still highly protected core of employed risks creating a dual labour market along Spanish lines (see below), and Italy's baroque system of wage guarantees and unemployment compensation schemes has not been reformed.

European developments prompted welfare reform in the Iberian countries too (Guillén *et al.*, 2003). When Spain joined the European Community in 1986 it had a highly regulated labour market, but only a rudimentary system of social provision. In the recession of the early 1990s, unemployment rose to almost 25 per cent, producing a sharp increase in unemployment benefits spending and a severe deterioration in public finances. In 1995, with an eye on early EMU entry, the government, unions and employers agreed to the Toledo Pact that sanctioned pensions and labour-market reform. With trade union consent, cuts in pension benefits for the 'better off' were traded for improving the positions of lower-income earners. Spain also engineered a thoroughgoing decentralization in social services from central government to the regions.

Regarding unemployment, reforms included new flexible contracts (which, however, led to an explosion of temporary employment alongside a still highly protected core of permanent employees), a rationalization of unemployment benefits, activation measures, and broad changes in employment services (Moreno, 2000). More recently Spain has made some progress towards reducing inequalities in the labour market: in 1997 and 2001, labour laws relaxed protection for core employees and improved the social security rights of irregular and temporary workers. Although unemployment fell from 24 per cent in 1994 to 13 per cent in 2001, it is still the highest in the EU.

Portuguese pension reform was part of an encompassing package introduced in the run-up to EMU. The modernization of social protection was a prime objective of the new Socialist government after 1995 which emphasized active labour market policies and measures to combat social exclusion (Guillén *et al.*, 2001). Unemployment insurance was broadly reformed, occupational training and insertion programmes were expanded, and specific incentives were introduced to promote a 'social market for employment' based on local initiatives that targeted the most vulnerable workers. In 1996, the government and associations of municipalities, charities and mutualities signed an innovative 'social pact for solidarity' designed to mobilize local enterprise and create employment. Like Spain, Portugal improved its minimum benefits in pensions, family allowances, as well as the basic safety net and experimented with minimum income schemes.

Anglo-Irish 'third ways'

Welfare state financing and private-sector service employment do not appear as problematic in the United Kingdom and Ireland as in our other countries, though serious problems have appeared in the UK's pensions system as traditional company-based, occupational schemes begin to weaken and disappear. In the United Kingdom, Westminster-style government (giving the governing party with a significant majority untrammelled decision-making powers) allowed Conservative governments in the 1980s and 1990s to speed up social security reform. The real value of benefits eroded and the middle classes were encouraged to opt out into private insurance for pensions and healthcare. As the costs of targeted, means-tested benefits started to soar – despite a tightening of eligibility rules inspired by the new 'workfare' philosophy – costs were contained by a stricter benefit regime that reduced the number of claimants. The consequences were significant. The erosion of universal provision has helped restore public finances and radical labour-market deregulation has fostered an expansion of private employment, but inequality and poverty have also markedly increased (Rhodes, 2000).

In response, the Blair government after 1987 embarked on a broad strategy of 'third-way' reform. Benefit rules were fine-tuned to neutralize the 'traps' created by welfare-to-work schemes, and a fight against poverty and social exclusion was launched by increasing minimum wage and income guarantees, reforming the tax code and introducing new targeted programmes. Much like the Conservatives before them, New Labour's approach is to minimize intervention and regulatory burdens on a well-functioning, deregulated labour market. But its 'welfare-to-work' strategy differs substantially from Conservative workfare policies.

The most distinctive feature is a reliance on work and employability to address poverty and social disadvantage. In 1997, New Labour introduced the New Deal for skills and compulsory job-search aimed especially at moving young workers from public benefits into employment (Clasen, 2005). New Deal activation programmes rely heavily on tax credits, which have gained in importance, particularly since the introduction of the Working Families Tax Credit (WFTC) in 1998, which aims to guarantee a relatively generous minimum income to any family with a full-time worker (Glyn and Wood, 2001). A national minimum wage calibrated by age-group was introduced from 1999 and has been regularly raised since. However, in contrast to 'third-way' rhetoric on 'learning and education as the key to prosperity', vocational training, skill enhancement and upward mobility are still rather limited.

In the late 1970s and early 1980s, the Irish mimicked British decentralization of wage bargaining and labour-market deregulation. These measures failed to bring down unemployment, however, which reached 18 per cent in 1987. Ireland then adopted a more coordinated strategy based on successive 'social pacts', driven in large part by the need to qualify for EMU. Beginning with the National Recovery accord of 1987–91, cooperation with business and unions helped reform the economy and attract high levels of foreign direct investment, boosting Ireland's rates of output and employment growth. Poverty levels, however, did not initially decrease, principally because transfers per recipient, although rising significantly in real terms, lagged behind exceptionally large increases in average income. Therefore, while there are fewer people relying on transfers as unemployment has declined, more of them are relatively poorer. However, research does reveal a marked decline in poverty from 1994 (Nolan *et al.*, 2000).

Reforming welfare in Europe's new member states

The demise of state-socialism in 1989–91 was accompanied by a deep economic crisis. In 1990–94, economic growth and wages declined rapidly and inflation spiralled, bringing an end to full employment, with job losses ranging from10 per cent in the Czech Republic to 30 per cent in Hungary. Since 1995, the CEE economies have been growing again, as have real wages, while inflation has on average remained below 10 per cent. Still, Latvia and Lithuania have yet to reach their 1989 GDP levels, while only in the Czech Republic and Hungary did real wages exceed their already low 1989 levels by 2003.

In the early post-1989 period, the welfare state was used to cushion the most dramatic effects of economic crisis and reform, especially the loss of income through unemployment. Early retirement provisions and disability pensions were widely used for redundant workers (Fultz and Ruck, 2001; Müller, 2002). All CEE countries introduced a minimum wage and income-related social assistance schemes to combat poverty. As a result, social spending increased as a percentage of GDP while GDP itself contracted. However, inflation often depleted the real value of wages and benefits, leading to increasing poverty, not only among the old where poverty was traditionally concentrated, but also among the young and low-wage earners and their families (Nesporova, 1999). The numbers on pension-, unemployment- or social assistance benefits increased dramatically, placing greater financial strain on welfare schemes. At the same time, state budgets were suffering from declining income and payroll taxes.

Welfare reform returned to the agenda in the mid-1990s, but this time with a view to containing costs and increasing efficiency, reducing welfare dependency and changing incentive structures and governance systems (Keune, 2006). As elsewhere, reform was heavily contested. Nevertheless, pre-1989 pensions systems have been radically reformed, while labour-market policies, most of which were newly introduced after 1989, have subsequently also seen further important changes.

State-socialist old-age pension systems were largely financed on a pay-as-you-go (PAYG) basis through transfers from state firms to the state budget; direct contributions by workers themselves were rare (Fultz and Ruck 2001). Also, retirement ages were low and differed substantially for men and women. Far-reaching pension reforms were advocated as of the early 1990s, to improve their poverty reduction capacity, to respond to population ageing, enhance financial viability and (as in many Western countries) to end their special treatment of certain occupational groups. Reform – particularly privatization and the individualization of savings – was also strongly advocated by the World Bank. Three types of reforms can be observed (Müller, 2002):

- Adaptations to traditional pension schemes, such as increasing the retirement age, improving the collection of contributions and changing the formulae for benefit calculation. Poland and Latvia made pensions more individualized, more dependent on lifetime contributions and life expectancy, more earnings-related and less redistributive. Hungary reduced redistribution to low-income workers, while the Czech Republic and Slovenia actually increased it.
- The creation of mandatory, commercially-managed, individual savings accounts which shift pension risks from society to the individual and entails no risk pooling or redistribution. The government becomes a regulator instead of benefit provider. Such schemes have been created in Hungary, Poland, Latvia, Estonia and Slovakia, but were rejected in the other NMS.
- The creation of voluntary supplementary pensions which now exist in all NMS.

As for the labour market, unemployment benefit schemes and active labour market policies were introduced in the early 1990s. These schemes initially provided high levels and duration of benefits that were only weakly linked to employment history or previous earnings. This reflected a high degree of optimism as to the employment-creating capacity of the new market economy (Nesporova, 1999). But falling employment rates, mounting unemployment and increased expenditure quickly dampened this early enthusiasm.

Since then, CEE unemployment regimes have gradually converged on a minimal-liberal model, that is incomplete coverage and limited levels and duration of unemployment benefits, alongside weak active labour market policies. Cost containment was achieved by tightening unemployment benefits, and the duration and replacement rates of benefits were both reduced. As the value of benefits declined, the percentage of unemployed receiving benefits also fell, often to below 50 per cent. These cuts occurred in a context of already low spending on labour market policies. Since 2001, such spending has exceeded 1 per cent of GDP only in Slovenia, compared to an average of nearly 2 per cent in the EU-15, even though unemployment has been above 10 per cent in the Baltic countries and close to 20 per cent in Poland and Slovakia. Passive policies still account for over half of all labour market spending in the CEE countries. There has been little change in this regard since the mid-1990s, despite the activation rhetoric of employment policy documents.

What role for 'Europe'?

Welfare state reform largely remains a domestic enterprise: reforms have to be endorsed by elected governments and national political parties, preferably supported by key organized interests, and implemented through domestic administrative structures. However, European welfare states are not closed systems. The EU, which spans national boundaries, has important consequences for national welfare states and potentially also provides policy space for cross-national agenda-setting. Yet the desirable role for 'Europe' in European welfare reform is anything but clear.

A popular argument (for example Scharpf, 2002) holds that the Single Market, the introduction of EMU, and successive rounds of enlargement have led to an 'uneven development' of the EU's economic and social policies, in that market-correcting 'positive integration' in social policies has been unable to keep up with market-expanding 'negative integration' in removing the barriers to trade and cross-border competition. While EU member-state governments have been irreversibly committed to European economic integration, for good reasons they have also been highly reluctant to shed their national welfare-state obligations in favour of pan-European solutions.

Apart from the massive budgetary obstacles involved, and the lack of good evidence that European integration has damaged European welfare systems, such policies would infringe on their claims to sovereignty and jeopardize the basis of their own domestic political legitimacy. This became further apparent in the run up to the most recent round of enlargement, in which economic issues had clear primacy over social issues (Keune, 2006). Thus, even if common European solutions might be desirable, they are unlikely to be feasible or effective given national interests, political sensitivities and the huge diversity of social security systems in an EU of 25 members.

Over the past decade, EU member states have also become much more reluctant than hitherto to accept an extension of European directives and ECJ case law beyond a limited range EU employment-protection legislation to broader social and labour standards. Instead, since the late 1990s, a consensus has gradually emerged that future social progress will have to rely much more on 'soft law' processes whereby European-wide policy orientations are spread through benchmarking and the setting of common targets for performance. After all, most European governments support the view that a comprehensive welfare system is desirable, and that a cohesive society and competitive economy should be underpinned by dialogue with multiple actors, including employers and trade unions (though structures for social dialogue are much more fragile in the NMS; see Chapter 11). But this does not mean that an effective EU-level response to welfare-state challenges has become any easier to define.

A new attempt to innovate in EU-level initiatives while avoiding member-state resistance began with employment. The idea of a 'European Employment Strategy' has its roots in the Delors' White Paper on 'Growth, Competitiveness and Employment' (1993), which proposed closer coordination of national efforts to fight unemployment. But it wasn't until the mid-to-late 1990s that employment was placed squarely on the European agenda. High levels of unemployment had pushed many conservative governments out of office and the arrival of social-democratic parties in power in a majority of member states produced a coalition in favour of a new approach.

The breakthrough came with the Employment Chapter in the Amsterdam Treaty (1997). Pressed by the European Parliament, the 1997 Intergovernmental Conference introduced an employment title (Title VIII, articles 125–30) into the Treaty officially establishing employment as a 'common concern'. The employment chapter did not confer new competencies on the Community *per se*, but it did formally grant public status to social partners at EU level in formulating guidelines and at national level in drafting national action plans (NAPs). At the 2000 Lisbon summit governments agreed to a target for overall employment in the EU of 70 per cent of the labour force (over 60 per cent for women) by 2010 (Figure 14.1 shows just how far most member states still are from that level) (Rhodes, 2005).

Lisbon also launched the Open Method of Coordination (OMC). This new mode of governance seeks to foster policy innovation and experimentation in employment and social policy through dialogue and 'mutual learning', and proposed to extend it to poverty policies, combating social exclusion and modernizing systems of social protection. At Nice in December 2000, European leaders agreed to an ambitious social agenda with common objectives integrated into the treaty, formally establishing the Social Protection Committee (Article 144). In 2001 the Belgian presidency forged agreement on quantitative indicators for monitoring progress towards social inclusion across member states, and reached agreement at the Laeken Council on common objectives for pension systems.

In terms of substance, open coordination processes strongly focus on 'new' rather than 'old' social risk categories, most notably active ageing, part-time work, lifelong learning, parental leave, gender mainstreaming, reconciling work and family life and social exclusion. In theory, the OMC is flexible and incremental and anticipates change by encouraging feedback, policy learning and lesson drawing. As such it also recognizes national differences, which, in theory at least, should make it easier to achieve agreement on directions of policy reform (Maher, 2004). It has also been argued that under the OMC the heterogeneity of EU welfare states might be exploited for the purposes of experimentation. By diagnosing common European challenges and identifying 'best-practice' policy approaches, its advocates argue that the OMC can induce member states to evaluate policy performance and recalibrate policies in line with European guidelines (Zeitlin, 2005).

In reality, though, the OMC is not the panacea its strongest supporters had imagined. OMC practices – including those of the most highly developed and treaty-based European Employment Strategy (EES) – have been poorly integrated into domestic policy processes and public awareness is limited (Rhodes, 2005). The EES has encountered member-state opposition and disagreement as to both targets and the appropriate means for achieving them. Its democratic credentials are also weak: the role of the European Parliament has only been advisory, and national parliaments have been marginalized in the process.

Despite the innovations of 'open coordination', there are two principal obstacles to creating a new arena of effective EU social and labour market policy-making: first, the complexity of welfare-state policies, still strong claims to national sovereignty and the absence of a strong consensus, common concerns or even a sense of urgency regarding cross-national problem-solving; and, second, the nature of the of 'open coordination' itself which, as merely indicative of the paths policy-makers should follow, still lacks the capacity to mobilize reform coalitions and drive true policy innovation (Citi and Rhodes, 2006).

Conclusion

Despite the national specificity of many challenges, the diversity of reform responses and the marked distinctiveness of welfare systems, there are common traits to be found in recent reforms. Overall, from the 1980s onwards, welfare provisions became more austere, following regime-specific trajectories of retrenchment and recalibration. Policy-makers became increasingly cost-conscious, and focused on removing 'perverse incentives' that encouraged people to stay on passive benefits. Since the mid-1990s, all countries, regardless of their membership of different 'welfare families', have adopted increasingly similar policy initiatives, signalling a transition from a reactive, corrective, compensating and passive welfare state to more proactive social policy strategies, with high levels of employment the key objective, and greater attention paid to risk prevention and the 'activation' of benefit claimants.

Reform always builds upon already firmly established national policy legacies and political institutions (Hemerijck, 2002). This means that despite common reform traits, national systems and their future trajectories will remain distinct. The notion of a European social model beyond a number of basic principles is therefore belied by the diversity of national systems presented in this chapter – a diversity that has only increased with the Eastern enlargement of the EU. Both the purported existence of models and the notion of convergence among them fail to appreciate the path-dependence of change in complex welfare systems and the existence of multiple paths to policy success. The continued growth and employment-generating capacity of both the high-spending Scandinavian welfare states and the lower-spending UK indicates that polar opposite systems can generate similar outcomes on key (if not all) indicators.

Furthermore, the assumption of coherent policy models gives the impression that 'best practices' can be transported from one member state to the next – an idea embraced by enthusiastic advocates of the EU's 'open method of coordination'. But this view fails to appreciate the interdependency of different elements of welfare states in producing specific outcomes, making successful policy transfer extremely difficult. Unfortunately, even if it is becoming clearer how certain policy choices in the past have contributed to policy problems and failures today, there are no easy routes to achieving high levels of social protection, full employment and sustainable welfare state finances and no simple models to follow.

Chapter 15

Immigration and Asylum

Virginie Guiraudon and Elena Jileva

Immigration is a salient issue in European politics and immigration policy is a top priority for the European Union (EU). Increasingly, migration-related stories make headlines in European newspapers. Media reports often focus on irregular forms of migration linked to the development of people-smuggling and human-trafficking networks, or else they discuss the large number of asylum claims and speak of an 'asylum crisis' that needs to be solved. It is common to find calls for further European cooperation as the only viable solution to unsolicited migration. In fact, the last five years have seen the adoption of numerous items of EU legislation in the areas of immigration and asylum, alongside attempts to include surrounding states and regions within the EU migration policy framework. Meanwhile, concern about labour market shortages and the impact of population changes on economic growth and the financing of the welfare state has led many European countries to actively recruit skilled and unskilled foreign workers.

While immigration was once a phenomenon limited to the North and West of the European continent, this is no longer the case. In Southern Europe, Ireland and Finland, the increase in the number of foreign workers has also been significant in recent years. In East and Central Europe, there are fewer migrants and many of them are *en route* to the more established democracies, yet governments have had to set up the same set of immigration policies as in the West.

This chapter analyses current trends in immigration policy in Europe. In brief, we focus on the conditions under which immigrants are allowed to enter and stay in a given national territory, rather than on policies that seek to incorporate settled migrants in the socio-economic and political institutions of receiving countries.

Countries either try to deter or encourage immigration. We want to understand the factors that explain the different 'policy mix' between restrictive policies and moves towards openness, given the contradictory pressures that governments face (for instance, populist parties opposing immigration versus the demand for additional labour supply). Recent policy developments have included an increase in the recruitment of foreign temporary workers. In fact, although most immigrants in Europe are not actively recruited, they still arrive legally as family members of legal foreigners or nationals, asylum-seekers and refugees. Finally, there are varying attitudes towards '*sans papiers*' (foreigners without a work or residence permit), from a strengthening of internal controls and deportation policies to mass regularization campaigns.

One of the key themes we develop in this chapter concerns convergent trends and continuing national differences in the context of an emerging EU 'common policy'. Most notably since the coming into force of the Amsterdam Treaty in 1999, policy competence has in part been shifted to the EU level and we therefore focus our analysis on the 1999–2004 period.

First, we briefly provide some empirical context to our discussion of immigration policy and politics by summarizing key developments with respect to asylum and migration flows. We then discuss the factors driving immigration policy to provide some theoretical background to our analysis of current trends, which is the subject of the third section. We then turn to the impact of the EU assuming greater competence over policy-making, focusing especially on the new member states and their neighbours. Given the EU-driven changes in the East, as well as their indirect consequences on migration trends in Central and Eastern Europe, the final section explores the extent to which there is a convergence between East and West.

Trends in migration and asylum flows

Each year, about two and half million immigrants arrive in the European Economic Area and Switzerland. This is more than in the late 1990s when the annual average was 1.9 million (OECD, 2005). There were about 13 million non-EU nationals residing legally in the EU before enlargement, making up about 4 per cent of the total population, with great variation among countries (see Table 15.1). There is also a very uneven distribution of asylum-seekers and refugees (see Table 15.2) with small countries of the North receiving the greatest proportion in relative terms. There are also shifts over time in the main country of destination in absolute terms: it was Germany in the early 1990s, the United Kingdom in the late 1990s and then France.

Despite the widespread 'fortress Europe' rhetoric and the political turn towards restrictive policies, there are substantial legal entries each

Table 15.1 *Foreign and CEE populations in EU-15 countries*

Rank	Country	Per cent of foreigners as part of total population	Rank	Country	Population from the new EU member states (post 2004) in the EU-15 member states
1	Luxembourg	35.6	1	Germany	559,046
2	Austria	9.1	2	Italy	109,453
3	Germany	8.9	3	Austria	78,616
4	Belgium	8.7	4	Greece	71,742
5	France	5.6	5	France	55,381
6	Sweden	5.6	6	UK	36,801
7	Denmark	4.8	7	Sweden	27,835
8	Netherlands	4.2	8	Spain	19,980
9	UK	3.8	9	Ireland	15,295
10	Ireland	3	10	Belgium	14,494
11	Greece	2.6	11	Finland	13,639
12	Italy	2.1	12	Netherlands	12,744
13	Finland	2	13	Denmark	10,277
14	Spain	1.8	14	Portugal	1,260
15	Portugal	1.8	15	Luxembourg	1,547

Sources: OECD (2004) and Bijak, Kupiszewski, Nowok, and Kicinger (2004) 'Long-term International Migration Scenarios for the New EU Member and Accession Countries', Warsaw: Central European Forum for Migration Research.

year into Europe. While most are unsolicited, such as family members of foreign residents or nationals and asylum-seekers, there has been a steady increase since the mid-1990s in the recruitment of skilled and unskilled, seasonal, temporary and permanent labour migrants. European governments have also actively recruited foreign students: the number increased by 30 per cent in the UK and 36 per cent in France between 2001 and 2003, reflecting only in part the effect of US measures after 9/11 (OECD, 2005). Furthermore, the number of intra-company personnel transfers has become significant, in part because the principle of freedom of employment in the European Union also allows firms in member states to send employees abroad.

When focusing on unwanted migrants such as asylum-seekers, it is often noted than only 10–20 per cent of rejected asylum-seekers are deported. National and EU political leaders alike invoke the need to 'fight against illegal migration,' but they are well-aware in which

sectors of the economy they are likely to work (for example the construction industry and tourism) and fear upsetting continued growth in
these areas. In fact, some governments hosting large numbers of
undocumented migrants have run large-scale regularization campaigns
(for instance, Italy and Spain) while others such as France have set up a
case-by-case regularization system that avoids publicity whilst serving
as a proxy for 'migration management' with as many as 20,000
persons a year obtaining legal status (Bribosia and Rea, 2002).

The top European countries with respect to immigrant intake in
2004 were Germany, Spain, the United Kingdom and Italy. All four
came just after the United States among all OECD countries. The presence of two Southern European countries is not solely the result of
their regularization campaigns. Europe is now an immigration continent to the extent that there are many more sending and receiving
countries. It is worth noting that there are now more foreigners relative
to the total population in Ireland (5.9 per cent), which used to be an
emigration country, than in France (5.6 per cent), the first country to
recruit foreign labour in the nineteenth century (OECD, 2005).

On 1 May, 2004 eight former Communist countries from Central
and Eastern Europe – the Czech Republic, Hungary, Estonia, Latvia,
Lithuania, Poland, Slovakia and Slovenia – joined the EU. During the
Cold War, severe restrictions were imposed on the free movement of
persons in these countries, and those who decided to take the risk and
leave their countries settled permanently in the West. East-to-West
migration, however, became a major issue following the dramatic
events of 1989-90 in the Central and Eastern European (CEE) countries. Shortly after the fall of the Berlin Wall in 1989, the euphoria
created by the political changes in the CEE countries was replaced by
alarmist scenarios of mass migration, including asylum seekers, to the
West. Immigration was (re)defined as harmful, and a phenomenon to
be curtailed as much as possible, along with terrorism, drug trafficking
and other 'policing' issues. In practice, since the 1980s, there has been
a sharp rise in asylum claims across European Union countries. The
number of asylum applications to Western Europe grew from under
170,000 in 1985 to more than 690,000 in 1992 following the end of
the Cold War and the disintegration of Yugoslavia. The numbers
steadily declined after 1993, however, standing at about 250,000 in
1996 (UNHCR, 1997: 185).

However, since the mid-1990s these numbers have been falling
further. An increasing migration trend since then has been the temporary emigration of CEE citizens to Western Europe. This kind of
migration does not involve residential settlement and short-term,
income-seeking migrants will usually not draw any public welfare pro-

Table 15.2 Asylum applications in Europe

Rank	Country of asylum or resettlement	New asylum claims submitted 1993–2002	Country of asylum or resettlement	Asylum claims submitted 2004	Country of asylum or resettlement	New asylum claims submitted per 1,000 inhabitants	Country of asylum or resettlement	Total admissions per 1,000 inhabitants
1	Germany	1.230.201	France	58.577	Switzerland	35,1	Switzerland	24,3
2	United Kingdom	646.980	United Kingdom	40.620	Liechtenstein	28,9	Sweden	16,0
3	Netherlands	356.934	Germany	35.613	Netherlands	22,2	Denmark	13,7
4	France	303.171	Austria	24.676	Belgium	21,4	Norway	12,1
5	Switzerland	251.616	Sweden	23.161	Sweden	20,0	Netherlands	9,2
6	Belgium	220.666	Belgium	15.538	Austria	18,6	Liechtenstein	8,7
7	Sweden	177.594	Switzerland	14.247	Norway	18,5	Germany	6,5
8	Austria	151.130	Slovakia	11.354	Luxembourg	18,0	Austria	6,5
9	Denmark	89.568	Cyprus	9.859	Denmark	16,7	United Kingdom	4,3
10	Italy	84.649	Netherlands	9.782	Germany	14,9	Finland	2,4
11	Norway	83.401	Italy	9.722	Ireland	14,3	Malta	1,6
12	Spain	78.773	Poland	8.077	United Kingdom	11,0	Belgium	1,5
13	Ireland	59.153	Norway	7.945	Slovenia	6,5	Ireland	1,5
14	Czech Rep.	55.802	Czech Rep.	5.460	Cyprus	5,9	Italy	1,4
15	Turkey	51.280	Spain	5.369	Czech Rep.	5,4	France	1,2
16	Hungary	46.162	Ireland	4.766	France	5,1	Luxembourg	1,2
17	Poland	29.580	Greece	4.466	Hungary	4,7	Iceland	0,7
18	Greece	28.174	Turkey	3.908	Slovakia	4,2	Hungary	0,7
19	Slovakia	22.888	Finland	3.651	Finland	3,5	Bulgaria	0,5

No.	Country		Country			Country	
20	Finland	18.042	Malta	3.222	2,7	Cyprus	0,4
21	Slovenia	12.933	Greece	1.600	2,6	Turkey	0,3
22	Bulgaria	10.483	Spain	1.577	1,9	Greece	0,2
23	Romania	9.867	Italy	1.174	1,5	Spain	0,2
24	Luxembourg	8.068	Bulgaria	1.127	1,3	Czech Rep.	0,1
25	Portugal	5.256	Iceland	997	0,9	Slovakia	0,1
26	Cyprus	4.684	Poland	661	0,8	Romania	0,1
27	Lithuania	1.365	Turkey	140	0,7	Portugal	0,0
28	Malta	1.075	Portugal	107	0,5	Poland	0,0
29	Liechtenstein	962	Romania	74	0,4	Slovenia	0,0
30	Iceland	247	Lithuania	65	0,4	Lithuania	0,0
31	Latvia	125	Latvia	15	0,1	Latvia	0,0
32	Estonia	68	Estonia	7	0,1	Estonia	0,0
	Total	**4.040.897**	**Total**	**307.557**	**9.0**	**Total**	**3.6**
	European Union (25)	3.458.35	European Union (15)	279.530	11.5	European Union (15)	4.4
	Western Europe	3.794.585	Western Europe	263.178	13.4	Western Europe	5.9
	Central Europe	195.032	Central Europe	40.471	2.7	Central Europe	0,3

visions they are entitled to receive (such as medical insurance, social security and unemployment benefits) from the home country. The great majority of Poles, Czechs and Hungarians who contemplated the possibility of migration thought of it as a supplement to, rather than replacement of, their home-country earnings (Morawska, 2000). The trend towards temporary migration was demonstrated in a May 2001 survey on labour movement from the Czech Republic, Hungary, Poland, Romania and Bulgaria after accession. For example, 70 per cent of the Polish respondents wanted to work abroad for periods ranging from two months to two years, or to work in the EU at regular intervals but continue living in their home country; 12 per cent of them intended to work for longer than two years; and 13 per cent aimed to settle permanently (Central European Opinion Research Group, 2001).

Another trend in Eastern Europe is 'incomplete migration' (Okólski, 2001). This is a form of short-term mobility, often recorded as tourism, which involves petty trade in cross-border regions. This type of migration is most significant in border regions such as those on the Polish-Ukrainian border. East–West migration to date has been concentrated in the two member states that are closest to the CEE countries: Germany, with about 500,000 migrants, and Austria, with about 100,000; 75 per cent of all CEE workers in the EU, mainly from Poland, are employed in these two countries. Germany is overwhelmingly the largest destination for CEE migrants to the EU (77 per cent of the total). These migrants either have skills in short supply in Germany, or are seasonal workers residing under bilateral agreements to fill vacancies in agriculture and tourism. These bilateral contracts apply for a maximum period of employment of 90 days within 12 months, and under this provision a total of 238,160 Poles were employed in Germany in 2000, 261,133 in 2001 and 282,826 in 2003 (Korys, 2004: 28). Most CEE migrants who settle in Western Europe are relatively young and highly skilled, although they are concentrated in a few sectors, such as construction and agriculture, and generally work below their skill levels (Christiansen, 2002).

At the same time, the CEE countries have seen an increase in immigration, despite the fact that the share of foreigners remains relatively low. In the Czech Republic, 2.3 per cent of the total population are foreigners, compared to 1.1 per cent in Hungary and about 0.5 per cent in Slovakia and Poland. In the Baltic states, estimating the size of the foreign population is difficult and in part reflects the continuing controversy over the nationality of the ethnic Russians. However, in the Czech Republic and Slovakia between 1990 and 2002 the percentage share of foreigners in the total population increased at an annual rate of over 10 per cent (OECD, 2004: 41–49).

We can distinguish between three main types of immigration: (a) ethnic migration; (b) labour migration; and (c) migration from third-world countries. The first type originates in neighbouring countries. Most CEE countries have a diaspora living abroad, on account of past migrations and the many border shifts during the last century. These immigrants are often permanent settlers who join families, get married or otherwise choose to settle legally in CEE countries (Wallace and Stola, 2001). For instance, in Hungary, ethnic Hungarian migration accounted for the largest immigration in the early 1990s (three million Hungarians live abroad). During 1989–90, 60,000 ethnic Hungarians arrived from Romania. In 1991, civil war broke out in Yugoslavia, leading to a sharp increase in the numbers of refugees in Hungary, which amounted to 75, 000 in 1995 (Aszalos, 2001: 181). In Poland, the most numerous immigrants are citizens of Ukraine, Belarus and Russia.

In regard to the second type, labour migration, Hungary has the largest number of legal foreign workers and employees relative to work force and population size among the new member states: 115,000 in 2002 or 2.3 per cent of the workforce. In Poland, the number of work permits for labour migrants fluctuated between 15,000 and 18,000 between 1997 and 2002, but irregular labour migration has already become visible. In Slovenia, the number of work permits fluctuated between 34,000 and 40,000; more than 90 per cent of the foreign workers and employees in the country come from successor states to the former Yugoslavia. In 2001, the Czech Republic reported that 104,000 non-nationals were legally working in the country. When trade licenses are added the number of economic migrants in 2001 can be put at around 168,000. In Slovakia, their number was 9,000 in 2002. Foreign workers from Ukraine, Belarus and Russia represent the majority in Poland and some 30 per cent in the Czech Republic. Around 10 per cent of the foreign workers in the new EU members come from the other EU countries, including professionals from Western countries, among whom many are return migrants with dual citizenship and children of emigrants (Korys, 2004; Czech Statistical Office, 2003). In Hungary, the number of immigrant nationals from the EU reached 8.8 per cent in 2002, compared to 3.4 per cent in the early 1990s (OECD, 2004: 203).

The third set of migrants come from developing countries. The geographical location of the CEE countries led to their becoming a 'buffer zone' and transit routes for immigrants from further east toward an increasingly closed Western Europe. The Czech Republic, Hungary and Slovenia, with their high proportion of foreign residents, have a growing population of settled immigrants that seem there to stay

(Drbohlav, 2004; Kraler and Iglicka, 2002). The Czech Republic and Poland also have a sizeable share of migrant workers from Asian countries, notably Vietnam, whereas Hungary hosts the largest Chinese diaspora community in Central Europe, accounting for some 6 per cent of all the country's foreign residents (Münz and Straubhaar, 2004). Migrants from Asian countries are involved mainly in the restaurant business and the sale of textiles.

The Baltic States, which saw a population decrease after the withdrawal of Soviet troops, represent a distinctive case amongst CEE countries. In Latvia and Estonia, a mass emigration of the mainly Russian population took place in 1992 and 1993, partially due to the fact that these people could not obtain citizenship in the newly independent states. Lithuania, by contrast, granted citizenship prior to 1991 to all permanent residents who sought it, thereby avoiding a mass population outflow (Kielyte, 2002).

Given the change in immigration patterns in Europe in recent years, we need to explain the multiple dimensions of immigration policies: the continued restriction on conditions for family reunification, the crackdown on asylum, the return to labour migration recruitment, and the externalization of control to third states that act as 'buffer zones' for older EU member states. In the next section, we develop a framework to explain these policy outcomes.

Reconciling contradictory dynamics: explaining immigration policy choices

Why would one stem or solicit immigration? In political terms, the contemporary period suggests an era of greater restriction. Populist parties of the radical Right that focus on an anti-immigration platform have had an effect on the policy agenda, even in countries where they have not joined government coalitions or gained representation in Parliament, in part because mainstream parties fear that they could lose elections as a result of ethnocentric views amongst the electorate (Schain, 2006). Indeed, it has been demonstrated that both Left and Right parties prefer restrictive immigration control (Money, 1999). Having analysed the importance of issue salience in Europe (measured by coverage in highbrow daily papers) in a cross-national quantitative study, Givens and Luedtke (2004) confirmed the importance of this factor in the convergence of restrictive policy trends.

Yet, the rise of populism and ethnocentrism stands in marked contrast to two other trends. In economic terms, there may be specific demands for skilled and unskilled labour in certain sectors of the economy that cannot be met by domestic workers. Skilled migrants include IT experts and health professionals such as doctors and nurses. Unskilled foreign workers are often hired for seasonal agricultural jobs and in industries such as tourism and construction. Demographic decline in Europe has led some to argue as well that immigrants could help the fiscal tensions facing the welfare state, with their contributions allowing for a redistribution of pensions in pay-as-you-go systems. Demographic decline also affects the number of workers on the job market in the long term. The European Commission pointed out in 2003 that the EU population is ageing, owing to decreased fertility rates and longer life-expectancy, in turn leading to a likely fall in the working population in the 25 states from 303 million to 297 million by 2020. Economic migration is therefore necessary for sustained economic growth. From a labour market and welfare-state perspective, immigration should be encouraged to a certain extent.

If we now examine the legal norms that circumscribe policy and administrative discretion in this area, it becomes clear that immigrants may be admitted without necessarily being welcomed because of domestic and international human rights law or treaty obligations (for example the Treaty of Rome, which provides for the freedom of movement of persons within the European Union). In Western Europe, constitutions and legal frameworks have provided foreigners with guarantees against expulsion and also have often justified family reunification (Guiraudon, 1997; Joppke, 1999). Some of the international human-rights conventions that European states have signed also protect the rights of certain foreigners (refugees under the 1951 Geneva Convention and foreigners that could face torture or inhuman treatment if sent back, or be severed from their family life, according to the European Convention on Human Rights).

Given this situation, it is not surprising that scholars have focused on the scope of the debate on immigration policy and its determinants as a key factor in explaining immigration outcomes (Guiraudon, 1997). Some policy venues are more sheltered from public debate than others and thus receptive to different arguments. We can make sense of immigration outcomes by delineating the key actors in the political, economic and legal fields (Guiraudon, 2003), and in Table 15.3 we identify three sets of actors on the input side of immigration policy. With respect to the labour market, the main actors are business groups and trade unions. Regarding populism, the relevant actors are political parties, the media and the electorate. Finally, with respect to the logic of control, the main actors are the bureaucratic departments which deal with law and order issues (Home Affairs and Justice), courts and the NGOs that defend the rights of foreigners.

Table 15.3 *Input factors, institutional variables, policy choices and outcomes*

Input factors	Institutional filters	Policy choices	Policy outcomes
Labour demands (business/labour actors)	Labour market institutions and industrial relations system	Labour recruitment away from public eye	Rise of illegal migration
Public opinion (political parties, media)	Electoral and party systems, size of extreme right, government type	Remote control Shifting up to European level	Rise of temporary labour migration and intra-company transfers
Liberal legal norms (courts, NGOs)			Family reunion and asylum remain main legal categories
	Protest culture and POS Judicial system		

Assumptions:
- Blame avoidance/credit claiming strategies of governments seeking re-election
- Independent/exogenous causes of migration

Even with the same supply and demands of immigrants, countries vary with respect to the respective weight of political, economic and legal actors (see column 2). Nonetheless, the main constraint for 'policy expansionists' such as employers is political, so they seek to avoid publicity which would give the issue greater salience. Thus, labour recruitment has gone largely unnoticed compared to unwanted flows of asylum-seekers. Courts are the main constraint for 'policy restrictionists' seeking to contain the immigration of those who are not solicited by business groups. The strategy of civil servants in charge of stemming 'unwanted immigration' has consisted in elaborating policy at the trans-governmental level, or implementing it in third countries in East and South of Europe where there is much less judicial oversight (column 3).

Policy developments in the new century

Timid steps towards allowing 'economic migration'

A number of policy developments have recently emerged in major EU member states, seeking to facilitate the recruitment of foreign workers, particularly skilled labour:

- The United Kingdom, France, the Netherlands and Ireland, among others, have simplified recruitment procedures, excluding labour market testing criteria for a number of skilled professions.
- Germany launched a 'green card programme' in 2000, allowing up to 20,000 non-EU nationals to move to the country as computer specialists on five-year permits. A new German immigration law provides for the admission of up to 50,000 foreign workers per year, including professionals selected on the basis of a points system. Germany is also recruiting more seasonal and contract workers and foreign trainees (over 300,000 each year).
- All Southern European member states have turned to unskilled foreign labour in agriculture, construction or household services, and signed bilateral agreements to that effect with countries such as Ukraine or Romania.
- A pilot project was launched by the Czech Republic in 2002, with the aim of attracting qualified labour from Bulgaria, Belarus, Croatia, Kazakhstan, and Moldova. The scheme for skilled labour migration is based on the Canadian points system.

Member-states have acknowledged the need for legal immigration for economic development in Europe in 'The Hague programme' – an EU immigration policy road map for 2005–10. There is explicit reference to the agenda decided at the Lisbon summit that calls for the EU to be the most competitive knowledge-based economy by 2010. Unclear as to what a common policy might entail, national ministers called on the Commission to issue a policy plan rather than a specific legislative proposal. In January 2005, The European Commission presented a Green Paper on economic migration and launched a public debate on ways to attract skilled labour into Europe.

In this context, it appears contradictory to delay free movement from the new member states. The EU's policy on labour migration from Central and Eastern Europe has a precedent in the Southern enlargement to Spain and Portugal, when the then European Economic Community (EEC) imposed transitional periods of seven years for the free movement of labour from its two new members. As in the case of Spain and Portugal, the citizens of the new member states did not immediately obtain full freedom of movement rights throughout the EU.

The issue of free movement of labour became problematic during the EU accession negotiations with the CEE countries as a result of anxieties expressed by Germany and Austria, which have been the most insistent on introducing transitional periods after accession. Under the transitional agreement, EU-15 countries could impose national-level restrictions on the free movement of labour from the eight CEE countries for the first two years after accession, with the option of extending them for an additional three years and then for a further two years before full liberalization in 2011. Some member states, notably Germany, also reserved the right to limit the freedom of services inscribed in the treaty in certain economic sectors, such as construction – a move intended to limit the activities of firms from the new member states that employ their own nationals when fulfilling contracts abroad.

What needs to be underlined here is that all the old member states – except for Ireland, Sweden and the UK – have imposed restrictions on work permits. Belgium, Finland, Germany, Greece, France, Luxembourg and Spain introduced a regime in which CEE workers from the new member states are required to apply for a work permit, which is to be issued only when no national from the former EU-15 countries can fill the position. Austria, Italy, the Netherlands and Portugal introduced quotas. Ireland and the UK offer general labour market access, yet only with limited welfare benefits. Only Sweden treats CEE workers in the same way as all other EU nationals and applies common labour rules (Traser, 2005).

These restrictions were introduced even though estimates showed that few CEE citizens intended to seek work, and would only do so on a temporary basis and when there was pressure to recruit foreign labour. Furthermore, according to a study on the potential migration of new member states' workers into the old EU members, postponing the introduction of free movement will have only a marginal impact on the scale of migration: postponing free movement for seven years or more will reduce initial migration by only a few thousand people. A restrictive use of transitional periods will therefore fail to mitigate possible pressures from migration on labour markets (Alvarez-Plata *et al.*, 2003). Finally, the EU member states' restrictive policies towards the CEE countries is in contradiction to their long-standing efforts to promote internal labour mobility. Indeed, mobility has played a key role in the Strategy on Building New European Labour Markets by 2005.

Still, as was the case in Northern Europe when Spain and Portugal were to join the EEC in the mid-1980s, governments declared that they feared massive flows from the East. What have been actual migration trends in the three EU countries (the UK, Ireland and Sweden) that opened their markets to the CEE jobseekers? The lack of working restrictions has indeed led to an increase of workers coming to these countries, but the feared flood of Eastern workers has not taken place. According to estimates, the aggregate migration potential of the new member states is around 1 per cent of their current population (ECAS,

2005: 9). The main destinations for migrant workers are Ireland and the UK. According to a UK government report of August 2005, in total there were 232,000 applicants to the Worker Registration Scheme between 1 May 2004 and 30 June 2005, of whom up to 30 per cent may have already been in the UK before May 2004. The report finds that nationals from the new accession countries contribute to the success of the UK economy by filling gaps in a range of business sectors, whilst making very few demands of its welfare system or public services (Home Office, 2005: 1–2). In Sweden, in the first three months after enlargement, there were only 800 more applications for residence permits compared with the same period in 2003. A total of 3,179 applications were made between May and July 2004 compared with 2,378 in the same period of 2003, the greatest number from Poland: an increase from 662 in 2003 to 1,182 in 2004 (*Migration News Sheet*, September, 2004: 3).

In contrast to Ireland, the UK and Sweden, member states with restrictive regimes risk an expansion of the black labour market, the actual scale of which remains hard to estimate. The European Commission is due to recommend in 2006 whether the transition periods should be shortened, but the decision to open labour markets rests with each national government. Austria aims to extend its labour market restrictions for another three years after 2006, and Germany for the full transition period of seven years. Meanwhile, Spain's Foreign Minister has stated that Madrid will open its labour market to the new EU countries in 2006 (Euractiv 2, September 2005).

The transition periods for free movement of labour provide an example of the tensions between business-led demands, based on economic and demographic arguments, and political and electoral considerations, developed in response to the fears of industrial workers and trade unionists, or between the clientelist and populist model of policy-making outlined above (see also Freeman, 2006).

'Unwanted' flows: externalizing migration control eastwards

One important trend in national and EU policy-making consists in sifting foreigners before they arrive. Receiving countries have 'externalized' control so that prospective 'unwanted' migrants or asylum-seekers do not reach their territory. This has been achieved through the incorporation of various actors via visa regimes, carrier sanctions, and agreements with third states. We focus here on the Eastern Europe as a buffer zone.

The extension of asylum and immigration policies to the CEE countries has been dominated by the imperative to secure the new border against unwanted immigration (Lavenex, 2001). The CEE countries have introduced new laws governing the entry and residence of foreigners, have reinforced border controls and have committed themselves to combating illegal immigration. The process started as early as October 1991 when a series of practical measures to combat illegal immigration was adopted during the Berlin Conference. These measures included an exchange of information about the routes taken by illegal immigrants, those involved in smuggling them across borders and the ways in which identity papers may be faked. Control procedures at certain key points (ports, roads, railway stations and airports) were to be made tighter and harmonized. Carriers were to be required to check whether transit papers and residence permits held by their passengers were in order. The campaign against illegal immigration and the tightening of border controls meant that the CEE countries had to bring in new immigration laws and to agree to cooperate among themselves and with the European countries (OECD, 1992: 33).

The EU has extended its emerging common regime for asylum seekers and refugees to the CEE countries through the concept of 'safe third countries' and a network of agreements for the readmission of illegal migrants. Because of democratisation in Eastern Europe, the EU member states no longer considered it justified to grant refugee status to nationals of these 'safe' countries of origin. The decision had a marked impact on the refusal rate in 1990 and 1991 (OECD, 1992). Meanwhile, the CEE countries have received an increased number of asylum-seekers themselves: the inflow of asylum-seekers into the region amounted to 2,100 in 1994, 25,600 in 1999 and 44,200 in 2001 before reducing somewhat to 33,200 in 2003 (OECD, 2004: 315). Since 1 May 2004 the new CEE member states are parties to the Dublin II Regulation which established the mechanism and criteria for determining which country is responsible for an asylum application and aims to stop the practice of 'asylum-shopping' (Council of the EU, 2003). In practice, this means that all asylum-seekers who entered the EU via the new member states will be sent back there if they try to seek protection in another member state. In preparation for its responsibilities resulting from the Dublin II Regulation, Hungary opened a new reception centre in Nadykanizsa, near its border with Austria on 5 May, 2004, just a few days after accession to the Union. Three more reception centres were built in Balassagyarmat, Nyirbator and Debrecen (*Migration News Sheet*, June 2004: 13).

All the CEE member states' borders – with the exception of the Czech Republic – are now external borders of the Union and it is their obligation to be guardians of the eastern border of the EU. Following the attacks in the US on 11 September 2001, the EU announced that it expected tighter borders and internal security from the then candidate states. At a meeting in October 2001, the EU Commissioner for enlargement said that before 9/11, the EU would have allowed the CEE states to accede even if their levels of border security were not yet up to the standards of the old member states. However, such a concession was ruled out and security at the EU's external border has become a top priority (*Migration News Sheet*, November 2001: 2).

The impact of EU policy-making in CEE countries

Immigration flows in the new EU members are still a relatively new phenomenon, but at the same time their immigration policies, which were almost non-existent before 1989, have undergone rapid development, especially since the late 1990s. The reason for this is EU accession conditionality.

Issues regarding the immigration of non-EU nationals fell under the chapter in the accession negotiations known as 'Justice and Home Affairs' (JHA) – regulating visa, asylum, immigration and border issues. The EU's requirement for the adoption of the JHA *acquis* by the new member states demonstrates a significant difference between the latest round of enlargement and the previous four. It has left little room for independent policy choices for the CEE governments during the EU accession process. As the new members are still countries of transit, in its so-called 'Hague Programme' of 2004 the European Council emphasized the need for intensified cooperation on both the southern and eastern borders of the EU, in order to enable these countries to manage migration better and to provide adequate protection for refugees (Council of the EU, 2004).

As an illustration of the implications of EU norms, the Czech government adopted a new Immigration Act, which came into force in 2000, in order to align its legislation with the EU *acquis*. The Act tightened eligibility conditions for residence permits, leading to a fall in the number of resident-permit holders in 2000. Since 2001, permit numbers have started to grow again, but at a much slower pace than in the early 1990s (OECD, 2004a). In 2002, 8,484 people asked for asylum in the Czech Republic, which translates into a year-on-year fall of 53 per cent. The decrease in the number of applicants results from the amendment to the Asylum Act which introduced stricter conditions for asylum procedures (Czech Statistical Office, 2003: 58).

The countries that are immediate neighbours of the new member states, for whom EU membership is either a distant prospect or not an option at all, have also been affected by EU immigration policy. These are the countries in the western Balkans as well as Russia, Ukraine, Belarus and Moldova. During the Eastern enlargement negotiations, the Eastern European countries not included in the process experienced most starkly the effects of the EU visa regime. The impact of the EU visa policy was felt indirectly – through the policies adopted by their CEE neighbours. As the new members have a limited range of policy choices regarding the movement of people and immigration, some undesirable policy outcomes have emerged. For instance, so-called 'suitcase traders' became a mass phenomenon in Eastern Europe in the 1990s: between seven and ten million Ukrainians (out of a total of fifty million) supplement their living with profits derived from cross-border trading (Kraler and Iglicka, 2002: 29). According to a study in the *Polish Market Review*, just before the introduction of the visa requirements in October 2003, visitors from Ukraine, Belarus and Russia accounted for 23.3 per cent of the total number of visits to Poland. However, the implementation of visas reduced arrivals from Poland's eastern neighbours by 54 per cent, according to a calculation by the Polish customs service (*Polish Market Review*, 5 January 2004: 4).

The entry of Poland and Lithuania into the EU in 2004 made the issue of free movement for the residents of Kaliningrad a concern for the common EU visa policy, since Kaliningrad – an administrative district of Russia – became an enclave within the EU. As the EU has been insisting on visa requirements for travel between Russia and its enclave, the issue of Kaliningrad has caused a strain in EU–Russia relations and has overshadowed other items on the agendas of EU–Russia summits since 2001. At the EU–Russia summit in November 2002 an agreement was reached that the inhabitants of Kaliningrad would be required to obtain an inexpensive, multi-entry travel transit document. Travellers using trains will be able to obtain transit documents at the border (Jileva, 2004).

The nationals of the western Balkans, with the exception of Croatians, need visas to enter the EU. The visa requirements have provoked anti-EU sentiments in South-East European states among the elite as well as among ordinary citizens. Long queues, with no certainty of reaching the front of the queue within consular opening hours, are a major source of frustration and resentment by visa applicants, especially for those living in peripheral regions far away from national capitals where the EU consulates are located (Batt, 2003).

Conclusion: an East–West comparison

Since the late 1990s, trends and policies in Eastern Europe have begun to resemble those in the existing southern EU member states. CEE countries are becoming countries of immigration as was the case with Italy and Spain, which from countries of emigration in the 1970s became countries of immigration two decades later. Another similar trend is the population decline which is observed not only in Western Europe, but in the eastern part as well. Since the end of communism, birthrates in the CEE countries have decreased as well, most dramatically in the former East Germany where the figures went down to 40 per cent of those in 1989, or 0.7 children per woman. Thus, the sustainability of the healthcare and pension systems and the need for replacement immigration in the long term have become issues that concern both parts of Europe.

The challenges presented to the new members by enlargement in the field of immigration policy are most similar to those of the southern members of the EU as the former have borders situated on the main route of third-country immigration. Joining Schengen – the 1985 Treaty which provided for a common European border system for all EU states (except Ireland and the UK) plus Iceland, Norway and Switzerland – was a difficult and prolonged task for the southern members, especially in view of their long maritime borders. The challenge for the new CEE members is equally daunting, given the existence of new policy initiatives such the envisaged creation of a European Border Guard.

The convergence between West and East European policy-making has not been driven exclusively by initiatives at the EU level, but also by bilateral norms, policy transfer and cooperation. Thus in Estonia, since the establishment of the national asylum system in 1997, the government has cooperated with the Finnish Ministry of Labour, the Danish Immigration Service, the Swedish Immigration Board, and others (Potisepp and Adamson, 2001). Similarly, Germany has worked extensively on a bilateral basis with Poland.

But some considerable differences between East and West remain. First, in the CEE countries, there are significantly fewer foreigners as a percentage of the population in comparison with the West European countries. A large part of the immigration flows takes place between and among the CEE countries (for example between Slovakia and the Czech Republic) and includes ethnic migration (for example Hungary accepting minorities from its neighbouring states in Eastern Europe). Second, the new members are not yet full members of Schengen. Internal borders between the new and old members have remained. The full implementation of the Schengen *acquis*, leading to full unification of the Western and Eastern parts of the European continent, will be conducted in two phases. The first phase included rules relating to external border controls and illegal immigration, which applied to the new EU members immediately upon accession. The second part of the *acquis* is to be implemented by the new members by 2007. It includes provisions on the abolition of internal border controls and a police database known as Schengen Information System II, pending a unanimous decision of the member states of the EU member states after completion of applicable Schengen evaluation procedures (Byrska, 2004).

In spite of convergence with respect to the harmonization of legislation, differences remain between the old and new members over the implementation of policies. Thus, in regard to border controls, at the time of accession the candidate states had completed the legal transformation of the border guards or police forces into a professional non-military force compatible with EU standards. Yet even those new members which have made much progress towards the creation of professional modern border guards, such as Estonia, Hungary and Poland, still face considerable structural problems in ensuring proper interaction between border guards, police forces and customs authorities, which is crucial for effective border management according to Schengen standards. An additional structural problem is posed by the fact that some of the new members will have to shift the bulk of their border control operations from their traditionally strongly guarded western borders to their eastern or south-eastern borders, to which much less attention had been paid in the past (Monar, 2001).

Finally, whilst immigration policy-making in the CEE countries has been heavily EU-driven, some national concerns too have shaped policy outcomes. For instance, the harmonization with and the implementation of the EU's visa policy differs across the new members due to considerations regarding international relations. Another case in point is the controversial Hungarian 'Status Law'. In order to preserve Hungary's special links with its minorities after accession, in June 2001 the Hungarian parliament passed a 'status law' granting special rights to Hungarians living abroad. Ethnic Hungarians who are citizens of Romania, Slovakia, Ukraine or one of the former Yugoslav republics can travel to and work in Hungary without visas (Fowler, 2002).

Chapter 16

Organized Crime and Anti-Crime Policies

Letizia Paoli and Cyrille Fijnaut

Since the early 1990s, organized crime has become a 'hot' topic in public debate and on the political and scientific agenda. To control organized crime, far-reaching legal and institutional reforms have been passed in all European states and *ad hoc* instruments have been adopted by all major international organizations, ranging from the European Union (EU) to the Council of Europe and the United Nations.

The apparent consensus now dominating much European official and media discourse is in itself astonishing, since – until the mid-1980s – the scientific communities, political leaderships and public opinion of virtually all European countries (aside from Italy) considered themselves largely unaffected by organized crime. This perception began to change in the late 1980s. Several long-term processes and a variety of both far-reaching and localized historical events contributed to the European and international success of the concept of 'organized crime'. Some of these were directly related to the activities and perpetrators typically associated with organized crime; others are related to them only indirectly. Among the former, the rise of the illegal drug and human-smuggling industries are the most prominent. Among the latter, the most relevant are the worldwide processes of globalization, the fall of the Iron Curtain in 1989 and the completion of the internal market and abolition of internal border controls within the countries of the EU.

These wider societal processes have affected not only the organization and functioning of illegal markets, particularly in countries previously belonging to the communist bloc, but also the general perception of organized crime. Throughout Europe, organized crime – particularly its transnational variant – has become one of the most frequent and successful labels for expressing the growing sense of insecurity caused by the sudden collapse of the bipolar world and, more generally, public

299

anxiety at living in the increasingly uncertain world of 'late modernity'. Specific events reinforced this change in perceptions. Of particular impact were the murders of Judges Giovanni Falcone and Paolo Borsellino in Sicily in 1992 and the bomb attacks in mainland Italy in 1993, which were organized by the Sicilian *Cosa Nostra* mafia organization and received widespread media attention throughout Europe. Following these and other unrelated events, organized crime has been stigmatized as a 'folk devil' (Cohen, 1972) and become a powerful political instrument to justify criminal law and criminal justice reforms.

That the European (and world) perceptions of organized crime could change so abruptly in less than a decade is certainly due also to the ambiguity of the concept itself. In the first section of this chapter, we therefore reconstruct the trajectory of the concept of organized crime, which was coined in the United States at the end of the nineteenth century and was used almost exclusively there until the 1970s, before spreading rapidly to and across the 'old Continent' at the end of the twentieth century. In the following section we sketch the main patterns of organized crime in both the 'old' and 'new' Europe. In the final section we summarize the major policy developments at both the EU and national levels. For the last two sections we draw extensively on Fijnaut and Paoli (2004b), the first comparative assessment of organized crime concepts, patterns and control policies in 13 – Eastern and Western – European countries.

The history of the concept

Since it was first adopted over a century ago, such a wide variety of different meanings have been attributed to the term 'organized crime' that we are now left with an ambiguous, conflated concept. As Mike Levi (2002: 887) puts it, organized crime is like the psychiatrist's Rorschach blot, whose 'attraction as well as . . . weakness is that one can read almost anything into it'. In Europe as in the United States, public, political and even scientific debates still oscillate between thinking of organized crime as referring to sets of criminalized activities, or to sets of people engaged in crime. In other words, the concept of organized crime inconsistently incorporates the following two notions: (a) the provision of illegal goods and services; and (b) a criminal organization, understood as a large-scale entity primarily engaged in illegal activities with a well-defined collective identity and subdivision of work among its members.

The American debate: from 'alien conspiracy' to 'illegal enterprise'

The phrase 'organized crime' was probably first used in the late nineteenth century but, despite a couple of landmark empirical studies in the 1920s (see Landesco [1929] 1968), it did not become really popular until the early 1950s. Since that date several US congressional bodies set out the terms of an Italian mafia-centred view of organized crime, which remained the US official standpoint for almost three decades. This identified organized crime with a nationwide, centralized criminal organization dominating the most profitable illegal markets, which allegedly derived from an analogous parallel Sicilian organization and was headed by and, to a great extent, consisted of migrants of Italian (and specifically Sicilian) origin. In its 'Third Interim Report' of 1951, the Kefauver Senate Investigating Committee famously concluded: 'There is a nationwide crime syndicate known as the Mafia, whose tentacles are found in many large cities. It has international ramifications which appear most clearly in connection with the narcotics traffic. Its leaders are usually found in control of the most lucrative rackets of their cities' (US Senate, 1951: 131). In 1963 the testimony of former *Mafioso*, Joe Valachi, before the Senate Permanent Subcommittee on Investigations further established the terms of this paradigm and gave a new name to this menacing criminal association: *La Cosa Nostra*. Thanks to extensive television coverage, Valachi's view became popularized among the American public (Smith, 1975).

Despite its media and political success, the identification of organized crime with mighty mafia-type organizations – and the related idea of an alien conspiracy polluting the economic and social life of the United States – has been rejected by the majority of American social scientists since the 1960s. Scholars have dismissed the mafia-centred view of organized crime as being ideological, serving personal political interests, and lacking in accuracy and empirical evidence. However, there may also have been some overreaction, with many scholars up to the early 1980s categorically denying the existence of the Italian American mafia as a structured and longstanding criminal organization (Hawkins, 1969; Smith, 1975 – by contrast, see Jacobs and Gouldin, 1999).

After the early 1970s scientific attention was redirected to the most visible and non-controversial aspect of organized crime: the supply of illegal products and services. In order to eradicate ethnic stereotypes of crime and direct attention to the marketplace, several authors have advanced the expression 'illicit' or 'illegal enterprise' as a substitute for the ethnically-loaded term 'organized crime'. As Dwight Smith, one of the earliest proponents of the new approach, expressed it, 'illicit enterprise is the extension of legitimate market activities into areas normally proscribed – i.e. beyond existing limits of law – for the pursuit of profit and in response to a latent illicit demand' (Smith, 1975: 335).

More often, however, organized crime itself has been equated with the provision of illegal goods and services. Hence, according to Alan Block and William Chambliss (1981: 13), 'organized crime [should] be defined as (or perhaps better limited to) those illegal activities involving the management and coordination of racketeering and vice'. Organized crime has thus become a synonym for illegal enterprise. According to a review of definitions carried out in the early 1980s by Frank Hagan (1983), a consensus by then existed among American criminologists that organized crime involved a continuing enterprise operating in a rational fashion and focused toward obtaining profits through illegal activities.

The European debate

Since the mid-1970s the 'illegal enterprise' approach has acquired a dominant position in the European scientific debate, influencing not only a series of studies on the Italian mafia (Arlacchi, 1983; Catanzaro, 1992) but also, even more deeply, the conceptualization of organized crime in all those European countries that long considered themselves immune to the problem. As early as the mid-1970s, for example, Hans-Jürgen Kerner and John Mack (1975) talked about a 'crime industry' and, in an earlier report written in German, Kerner (1973) subscribed even more explicitly to the view of organized crime as an enterprise.

Notwithstanding scholarly conceptualizations, since the late 1980s the spectre of mighty mafia-type criminal organizations – primarily the Italian mafia, but since the early 1990s the Russian and other ethnic 'mafias' as well – has time and again been raised with varying degrees of good faith by European media, politicians, law-enforcement agencies and, more recently, international organizations to increase the power of domestic law enforcement agencies and to enhance international police and judicial cooperation. Since the early 1990s the transnational dimension of organized crime has also been strongly emphasised, obscuring the fact that most organized crime activities are anchored locally (Paoli and Fijnaut, 2004b).

Despite the popular identification of mafia with organized crime, the emphasis on illegal market activities has remained largely unchallenged in the scientific debate of all European countries except Italy. Thus, for example, according to Dick Hobbs (1994: 444–5), 'the master context for professional and organized crime is the marketplace . . . [and] the marketplace can be seen to define and shape professional and organized criminal activity'. Likewise, the Dutch scholar Petrus van Duyne

(1997: 203) points out that organized crime results from illegal market dynamics: 'What is organized crime without organizing some kind of criminal trade; without selling and buying of forbidden goods and services in an organizational context? The answer is simply nothing.'

Only in Italy have several scholars variously emphasized the differences between Italian mafia groups and other, more business-like forms of organized *qua* enterprise crime. In the early 1990s Diego Gambetta (1993: 1) proposed a variant of the long-dominant enterprise approach, conceptualizing the mafia as 'a specific economic enterprise, an industry which produces, promotes, and sells private protection'. From different perspectives, other scholars have then reassessed the cultural and political dimensions of the mafia phenomenon. As one of the present authors has pointed out (Paoli, 2003), southern Italian mafia organizations are ritualized secret brotherhoods that have traditionally employed the strength of mafia bonds to pursue a plurality of goals and to carry out numerous different functions. Though mafia groups have engaged, directly or through their members, in a plurality of legal and illegal entrepreneurial activities, one of the most important functions they have historically played is the exercise of political dominion within their communities. More radically, Henner Hess (1995: 63) has gone so far as to conclude that 'the mafia is a power structure and, as such, completely different from what is commonly called organized crime (and which is usually a cooperation aimed at gaining material advantages)'.

National and international definitions: broad and unbinding

The legal definitions of organized crime adopted by most European states also hardly reflect the mafia fixation of much political and media discourse. Most of these definitions are very broad, if not vague, so much so that they – and the special powers granted to organized crime investigators, prosecutors and judges – can be applied to a wide range of criminal phenomena and suspects (for a review, see Paoli and Fijnaut, 2004b).

Thus, many European governments and international organizations pursue a sort of 'double-track' approach, by emphasizing the scale and threat of organized crime on the one hand, and adopting minimum common-denominator definitions on the other, with no strict criteria in terms of number of members and group structure. This strategy has been pursued by the European Union and by the United Nations to back its 2000 'Convention against Transnational Organized Crime'.

To justify its intervention in this area, the EU Council has repeatedly presented organized crime as a new threat, whose novelty lies in the increasing involvement of criminal organizations in the supply of criminal goods and services. Such a view is clearly stated in the first programmatic document dealing with organized crime, the 'Action Plan to Combat Organized Crime', which was adopted in April 1997. Its opening statement maintains:

> Organized crime is increasingly becoming a threat to society as we know it and want to preserve it. Criminal behaviour no longer is the domain of individuals only, but also of organizations that pervade the various structures of civil society, and indeed society as a whole. (European Union Council, 1997)

In the Joint Action adopted by the European Council on May 1998, a criminal organization is defined as

> a structured association, established over a period of time, of more than two persons, acting in concert with a view to committing offences which are punishable by deprivation of liberty or a detention order of a maximum of at least four years or a more serious penalty. (European Union Council, 1998)

If only three people are sufficient to form a criminal organization, one might justifiably ask if the (alleged) increasing presence of these entities in the illegal arena really represents a major innovation with regard to the past and the threatening menace that the Action Plan assumes it to be.

Organized crime patterns

Despite the lack of regular and reliable data on organized crime and poor cooperation between public agencies and independent researchers in most European countries, the main outline of the picture emerging from assessments of organized crime patterns in 12 European countries is fairly clear.

The organization of organized crime: adieu to the Italian mafia model

Though much of the concern about organized crime was initially dictated by fear of the expansion of the Italian mafia to the whole of Europe and its becoming a model for others, this pessimism have proven to be unfounded. Despite the possibilities opened up by the fall of the Iron Curtain in 1989, Italian mafia groups seem to have representatives and, less often, branches only in those countries – Germany, Belgium and France – that attracted consistent migration flows from southern Italy since at least the 1950s. In no European country except Italy – nor in northern or central Italy itself – do Italian mafia groups control a significant portion of local illegal economies or exercise a systematic influence over the legal economy or political system (Paoli, 2004).

Nor does any other criminal group, at least in Western Europe. Contrary to the exaggerated predictions of the early 1990s, other organized crime groups have not shown any interest in imitating the culture and structure of the Italian mafia. Nor are the average perpetrators involved in European organized crime interested in, or capable of exercising, a quasi-political power similar to that of the largest and most stable mafia associations in Southern Italy (that is, the Sicilian *Cosa Nostra* and the Calabrian *Ndrangheta*). As even Europol recognized in its 2003 European Union Organized Crime Report (2003: 10), 'politically, few Organized Crime (OC) groups pose a direct threat to Member States'.

Most organized crime groups active in Europe are simply too small and ephemeral to be able to exercise such political power. To quote Europol again:

> the traditional perception of hierarchically structured organized crime groups is being challenged. There is now a development suggesting that a greater percentage of powerful organized crime groups are far more cellular in structure, with loose affiliations made and broken on a regular basis and less obvious chains of command. (2003: 8)

Whereas it is disputable that non-Italian mafia groups have ever complied with the 'traditional perception of hierarchically structured organized crime groups', Europol's departure from the Italia mafia model can only be welcomed.

The 12 country reports on organized crime published in Fijnaut and Paoli (2004b) show that the great majority of illegal exchanges in Western European countries are carried out by numerous relatively small and often ephemeral enterprises. This is because all illegal market actors are subject to constraints deriving from the enforcement of prohibition. As a result of these constraints, illegal market entrepreneurs are obliged to operate both without and against the state.

First, since the goods and services they provide are prohibited, illegal market suppliers cannot resort to state institutions to enforce contracts and have violations of contracts prosecuted. Nor does the illegal arena host an alternative sovereign power to which a party may appeal for redress of injury. As a result, property rights are poorly protected, employment contracts cannot be formalized, and the development of large, formally-organized, long-lasting companies is strongly discouraged (Reuter, 1983).

Second, all suppliers of illegal commodities are forced to operate under the constant threat of arrest and confiscation of their assets by law-enforcement institutions. Participants in criminal trades will thus try to organize their activities in such a way as to assure that the risk of police detection is minimized. Incorporating drug transactions into kinship and friendship networks and reducing the number of customers and employees are two of the most frequent strategies illegal entrepreneurs employ to reduce their vulnerability to law enforcement (*ibid.*).

The factors promoting the development of bureaucracies in the legal economy – namely taking advantage of operational economies of scale and specialization of roles – are outbalanced in the illegal arena by the very consequences of product illegality. As a result of the illegal economy operating within countries with efficient governments, there is no immanent tendency towards the consolidation of large-scale, modern illegal bureaucracies. In other words, in the illegal markets of most industrialized countries ruled by relatively strong and efficient state apparatuses, the dominant model is not organized crime, but – following the title of a famous book by Peter Reuter (1983) – disorganized crime.

The expansion of illegal markets

Recognizing the relatively 'disorganized' nature of European organized crime does not imply an optimistic assessment of its nature, scale and danger. Forming flexible and changeable networks, the small and ephemeral enterprises comprising the bulk of Western European organized crime have, since the mid-1970s, sustained a phenomenal expansion of illegal markets in Western and, after the fall of the Berlin Wall, Eastern Europe as well.

Since the early 1970s, in particular, a rising demand for a variety of illegal drugs – predominantly cannabis and heroin in the 1970s and 1980s with the addition of cocaine, ecstasy and other amphetamine products since the early 1990s – has fostered the development of an international drug trade from producing to consumer countries and the emergence of nationwide drug distribution systems in all European states. This process has also entailed the consolidation of the professional role of the drug dealer. From the early 1970s in Western Europe and from the early 1990s in the eastern part of the continent, the role of drug dealer has emerged to link producers to consumers and to supply large urban centres regularly with a variety of illegal drugs from distant regions. To meet expanding popular demand, preexisting criminal associations – such as Italian mafia groups – and thousands of individuals, cliques and groups with and without previous criminal experience have entered the drug trafficking business, attracted by the anticipation of large profits.

In the last two decades of the twentieth century, several European countries acquired a pivotal role in the world illegal drug trade. Since the early 1980s, Turkey has without interruption been the main gateway for Afghan heroin on its way to Western European markets (see Bovenkerk and Yeşilgöz, 2004). Due to its geographic position, Spain has become the main entry point for Moroccan hashish since the 1980s, with seizures recently accounting for 75 per cent of all hashish seizures in Europe. Together with the Netherlands, Spain is also preferred by Colombian traffickers for smuggling cocaine into Europe (see Gómez-Céspedes and Stangeland, 2004).

In some countries – most notably the Netherlands and Belgium, but more recently also Poland and Albania – we find not only illegal drug traffickers and distributors, but drug producers as well. From the early 1990s onwards, the Netherlands and Belgium have become the major European and, possibly, world producers of ecstasy. Polish chemists have specialized in the production of amphetamines for both Western and Eastern markets, and Albanians have taken up the cultivation and sale of marijuana, re-launching a product that – unlike hashish – had virtually disappeared from many Western European markets over the previous twenty years (Plywaczeski, 2004; Hysi, 2004).

Despite the re-conversion of many professional criminals to drug trafficking and dealing, several – traditional and non-traditional – profit-making criminal activities have continued to proliferate. Some, such as the illegal trade in weapons, are instrumental to a life 'on the other side of the law'. Other activities – ranging from car thefts, to robberies and the exploitation of prostitution – experienced an unexpected revival in the years immediately following the fall of the Iron Curtain, when Eastern European criminals primarily resorted to violence and ruthlessness to earn a 'fast buck' in Western Europe.

As a few scholars – particularly Mike Levi (1999) and Tom Naylor (2002) – have shown, a third group of entrepreneurial crime activities also flourished in the 1980s and 1990s and continue to do so today, though they are hardly the prerogative of traditional underworld members. These activities range from fraud and other financial crimes to bid-rigging in public works tenders and the illegal wholesale trade in toxic waste, weapons, diamonds and gold. They form a part of organized crime, if one accepts the loose definitions that dominate the legal and scientific discourse on organized crime in Europe today.

Whereas the more white-collar forms of organized crime usually attract public attention only in the immediate aftermath of a big scandal, a second wave of expansion of European illegal markets, which started to develop fifteen years after the drug-related wave, has raised much concern in government institutions and the general public. This expansion was largely triggered by the enactment of increasingly restrictive immigration policies in most Western European countries during the 1980s and 1990s, which created a large demand for human smuggling services. The number of potential customers as well as victims of human trafficking suddenly multiplied, as the liberation of Eastern Europe in 1989 and the collapse of the Soviet Union in 1991 finally abolished restrictions on the mobility of almost four hundred million people. Crises in other parts of the world, ranging from several African countries to Iraq, Afghanistan and East Timor, also engorged the flow of prospective migrants, at the same time as growth and improvement of transportation facilitated their movements, by drastically reducing logistical constraints.

To meet this demand, human smuggling 'companies' appeared at all the crucial borders of 'Fortress Europe'. Though many smugglers merely sell services desperately wanted by their customers, not only are their prices in most cases extortionate, but conditions are often inhuman, as proven by the many accidents all over Europe that cost the lives of undocumented migrants. Moreover, this flourishing black market has opened up space for all kinds of exploitation that sometimes end up as real trafficking in human beings.

The internationalization of illegal markets

Almost inevitably, the internationalization of European illegal markets has affected not only the demand but also the supply of illegal commodities. The irreversible globalization of the licit economy and the erosion of national borders entail, as an unwanted side-effect, a growing geographical mobility and exchange of goods, know-how and capital of criminal origin. Today in Milan, as in Frankfurt, London or Amsterdam, illicit goods and services are offered and exchanged by a multi-ethnic mob. Alongside local criminals, one finds illicit entrepreneurs from all parts of the world.

This process of internationalization of illegal markets started in most northern and central Western European countries in the 1960s and 1970s following the legal migration of millions of people from former colonies and southern European countries. In the latter, including Italy, it took place very rapidly from the mid-1980s onwards, when this part of the continent became the destination of considerable migration flows. Thus, instead of the feared 'Italianization' of Europe, in most of continental Italy the opposite process has taken place: that is, a more accelerated assimilation of local illicit markets to the organizational models and multi-ethnic composition of northern European markets.

In all countries, the over-representation of recent (but also sometimes not so recent) migrants in illicit activities is largely due to their social exclusion and poor integration into host societies. As the history of the United States demonstrates, a small but highly visible portion of migrants use crime as a 'queer ladder of social mobility', to use Daniel Bell's ([1953] 1965) famous expression. Moreover, to a greater extent than in the past, migrants today have a harder time accessing the legal economy and, owing to the restrictive policies adopted by most Western European states, are more likely to find a means of survival only in the informal and illegal economies. A few of those willing to earn a living through crime are able to exploit contacts with producers and distributors of drugs and other illegal commodities in their home countries or the weakness of their native state institutions, to become involved in the wholesale and most profitable sections of illegal markets (especially drug markets). Most, however, end up working as crime labourers carrying out dangerous and not very profitable tasks neglected by autochthonous criminal entrepreneurs.

Despite their occasional violence and aggressiveness, the crime groups set up by migrants are hardly comparable to Italian mafia clans as they are in most cases poorly organized and ephemeral. Their degree of infiltration of government institutions and the licit economy is generally low. However, since most of them are mutable gangs that make use of different languages and cultural codes, they are hard to identify and repress.

The infiltration of the legitimate economy and politics: an over-estimated threat

Organized crime's infiltration of the legitimate economy, civil society and politics has been investigated and studied much less than its illegal markets activities, so much so that in many European countries it is impossible to go beyond 'guesstimates' and speculation. Despite the serious shortcomings of information sources, it can safely be stated that in most Western European countries the ability of traditional organized crime groups to infiltrate the legitimate economy and corrupt civil and political institutions was grossly overstated when organized crime began to attract media and political attention in the early 1990s.

In the Netherlands, for example, both the initial study carried out by the Fijnaut research group in the mid-1990s (1998) and the subsequent 'organized crime monitor' run by the Research and Documentation Centre of the Dutch Ministry of Justice (WODC) found that no criminal group at either national or local level has ever gained control of legitimate sectors of the economy by taking over crucial businesses or trade unions (see Kleemans, 2004). Likewise, no proof of systematic infiltration of organized crime into the legitimate economy emerges from the Organized Crime Situation Reports published annually by the German federal police, the *Bundeskriminalamt* (Kinzig and Luczak, 2004). Even in Switzerland, according to Claudio Besozzi (2004), the few empirical studies carried out on the topic do not support the view that the local financial system is infiltrated and threatened by foreign mafia-like organizations laundering money in the country.

In many European countries, however, perpetrators of organized crime invest in several legitimate industries – above all in the transport, finance, real estate, hotel and night-life sectors – to facilitate their illegal activities and reinvest their illicit proceeds. This pattern of action clearly emerges from Lalam's (2004) and Gómez-Céspedes and Stangeland's (2004) reports on organized crime patterns in France and Spain, respectively. Organized crime's investment in hotels, night-clubs and pubs in several Dutch cities (especially in Amsterdam) and in real-estate in the south of Spain are also considered worrying (Kleemans, 2004).

The picture becomes even less clear-cut if one considers the perpetrators of non-traditional organized crime activities, such as fraud, the manipulation of public tenders and the illegal trade in toxic waste, weapons and gold. These white-collar criminals have no need to 'infiltrate' the legitimate economy as they are already an established part of it, and the revenues of their 'dirty' activities are barely distinguishable from the flows of 'clean' and 'hot' money that are traded incessantly around the world.

The ability of both traditional and non-traditional organized criminals to corrupt politicians and civil servants appear to be rather low in most Western European countries. Despite occasional scandals and charges against single law enforcement officers and elected officials, six out of eight reports on organized crime patterns in Western European countries (in addition to those already quoted in this subsection) agree that there is no evidence of a systematic pattern of corruption and infiltration of political and government institutions by criminal groups (Hobbs, 2004).

However, there are two main exceptions to this rather reassuring picture of Western Europe: Italy and Turkey. Organized crime's infiltration of the legitimate and informal economies is, according to Paoli (2004), an important specificity of Italian organized crime. This largely derives from the claim of Italian mafia groups to exercise a political dominion within their communities, mainly expressed today by the extraction of a 'protection tax'. Through this systematic pattern of extortion, mafia families have been able to gain large and sometimes dominant positions, especially in the construction industry, but also in other entirely legitimate economic sectors in at least three southern Italian regions: Campania, Calabria and Sicily.

The influence of Mafia groups on Italian public life finds no parallel in Western (or even Eastern) Europe. The political power of mafia groups was not only accepted and even legalized by government representatives until the 1950s, but systematic exchanges of favours and collusion have continued until the present, as indicated by the investigations into the activities of Giulio Andreotti (Italy's prime minister seven times) and Silvio Berlusconi (prime minister since 2001).

In contrast to Italy, Turkey does not host lasting and well-structured secret criminal societies comparable to the Sicilian *Cosa Nostra* and the Calabrian *Ndrangheta*. Nonetheless, in their strenuous fight against left-wing protestors in the 1970s and, later, against Kurdish separatist groups, several Turkish cabinets and the military have developed shady alliances with right-wing paramilitary groups. These, and a variety of Kurdish clans that had sided with the government, were often given *carte blanche*, including the authorization to run illegal businesses, ranging from extortion and murder to drug trafficking (Bovenkerk and Yeşilgöz, 2004).

Organized crime in Eastern Europe: a phenomenon of a different quality?

There are numerous similarities between organized crime activities and participants in Western and Eastern Europe. Long curtailed by socialist dictatorships, illegal markets have boomed in all Eastern European countries since the fall of the Iron Curtain in 1989. In particular, illegal drug consumption and trade have expanded phenomenally in Russia and most other former Warsaw Pact countries.

Illegal psychoactive substances were used even prior to 1991, but during the communist regimes both the number of consumers and the range of available substances were limited. Due to travel and trade restrictions, none of the former communist countries either constituted a single drug market or participated significantly in international narcotic exchanges as a consumer or supplier of illicit substances. However, this pattern of relative self-sufficiency changed drastically during the 1990s, as Eastern Europe and Russia rapidly became integrated into the international drug trade (see Paoli, 2001). Today large quantities of illegal drugs transit these countries to supply local demand and reach Western European consumers. Growing domestic consumption is also increasingly fed by more powerful and easier-to-use drugs imported from abroad. Since the mid-1990s, in particular, most Eastern European countries and Russia have had to deal with a real heroin epidemic, which has become the primary means of spreading HIV and AIDS (Pływaczewski, 2004).

Whereas the heroin sold in Eastern (and Western) Europe usually originates in Afghanistan, other drugs consumed throughout the entire post-Soviet area are produced in – or transit through – Western European countries. This is first of all the case for ecstasy and other methamphetamines, which are predominantly fabricated in the Netherlands and Belgium. *Mutatis mutandis*, the same is also true for cocaine and to a more limited extent for hashish, which frequently reach Eastern European markets through Western Europe. Moreover, drugs are not the only illegal commodities exported from Western to Eastern Europe: weapons, toxic waste and counterfeit objects also frequently travel from West to East to be sold on local black markets.

Because of the increased mobility of Western European and, even more so, other foreign criminals, Eastern European illegal markets have undergone a rapid process of internationalization since the early 1990s. Eastern European cities have become venues for meetings and clashes between criminal groups and gangs from farther afield, ranging from Vietnamese and Chinese to Italian, Albanian and Russian-speaking groups (Nozina, 2004). With their readiness to employ violence, their enormous and shadily-acquired capital, as well as high-level political connections, the latter are today considered by far the most dangerous people in organized crime.

A closer look at the Russian-speaking crime groups may help us identify the peculiarities and, eventually, the specific dangers of Eastern European organized crime. Like the great majority of their Western counterparts, most Russian and Eastern European organized crime groups are not strict hierarchical organizations, based on ritual family ties, permanent membership and initiation rites. However, contrary to the situation in the West, Russian organized crime groups do not exclusively comprise 'underworld' criminals, but also 'overworld' figures, who often originate from within the ranks of the former

Communist Party and state structures and are today successful entrepreneurs or high-ranking government officials.

Exploiting their high-level contacts and the difficulties of the post-Soviet transition, many representatives of Russian organized crime made large fortunes through trade in commodities that would have been legitimate in capitalist societies, and managed to gain control of many, sometimes strategic, parts of the legitimate economy. Their entrepreneurial success was further enhanced by their unusual high-tech capacity, resulting from their well-educated backgrounds and connections with security services, as well as their readiness to use violence and military potential. Thanks to this combination of capabilities, for example, three crime bosses managed to acquire large shares of the Russian aluminium industry (Shelley, 2004).

Due to its ambiguity and suggestiveness, the term 'organized crime' has also been employed – in Russia as in other Eastern European countries – to characterize all those successful entrepreneurs who have rapidly built huge fortunes, usually by acquiring former state companies. It is indeed hard to separate this group clearly from 'normal' organized crime perpetrators, as their methods are quite similar. Both groups, in fact, rely on high-level political connections and shady strategies. As a rule, legitimate entrepreneurs cannot directly command violence, but many of them have had no restraints – or even worse, were obliged in the earliest and rockiest phases of the transition – to resort to the protection services offered by violent thugs (Volkov, 2002).

Whether or not they should be termed organized crime, some activities at the crossroads of the legal and illegal economies have threatened the economic and political stability of the countries in transition. In both Russia and Albania, tax evasion and the illegal export of capital remain widespread practices among many legitimate firms and members of the upper classes, constituting a serious impediment to the consolidation of the state. As late as 2000, for example, capital leakage from Russia exceeded US$1 billion per month, down from US$ 25 billion at the height of Russia's financial crisis in 1998 (see Shelley, 2004). The burst of the pyramid scheme bubble in Albania in late 1996, which yielded an estimated US$13 million in illegal proceeds, ended up in deadly rioting and widespread chaos and resulted in a dramatic fall in Albanian GDP (Hysi, 2004). Thus, according to the Council of Europe, the scale of organized crime and corruption constitutes 'the single most important problem for Albania' and 'the single most important threat to the functioning of democratic institutions and the rule of law in the country' (Council of Europe, 2004: 8, 2).

Control policies

Since the early 1990s the fight against organized crime has been one of the most effective arguments used by European politicians and government agencies to enact criminal and criminal procedural law reforms, introduce new offences and special investigative powers for law enforcement agencies, and propel forward the transnationalization of crime control and criminal justice.

Internationalization of policy: the EU

It is by no means exaggerated to say that, in Europe, policy on organized crime has increasingly transcended national boundaries and, since the late 1990s, has become a matter of international politics and hence also of the foreign policy of individual countries. After the 'Action Plan to Combat Organized Crime' of April 1997, the fight against organized crime was elevated to the rank of a treaty issue in the Treaty of Amsterdam, becoming central to the Third Pillar. In the reformulated Title VI ('Provisions in the Field of Justice and Home Affairs'), strengthening police and judicial cooperation was supposed to serve just one purpose: to combat organized crime. At the October 1999 special summit in Tampere, Finland, the European Council expressed itself 'deeply committed to reinforcing the fight against serious organized and transnational crime' and launched a 'Union-wide Fight against Crime', meaning primarily organized crime.

In the following years many initiatives were introduced by the European Council and Commission to implement the agreements reached. For instance, Eurojust (a sort of European prosecutor's office with the task of facilitating the proper coordination of national prosecuting authorities) and the Police Chiefs Operational Task Force were set up, the talks on the Convention on Mutual Assistance in Criminal Matters were completed in 2000 and a framework was developed for the creation of joint investigation teams.

In addition to becoming part of the Third Pillar, organized crime control has acquired a growing relevance in EU foreign policy. In 1998 the applicant countries, which joined the EU in May 2004, were made to sign a 'Pre-Accession Pact on Organized Crime' and they were put under considerable pressure to adopt Western European policy in this area through the famous *acquis communautaire*. At the same time, a variety of programmes were initiated by the European Commission and the Council of Europe to help all former communist European countries strengthen their political and judicial capacities in the fight against organized crime and corruption.

This important development – the interweaving of the domestic and foreign policies of the European Union, particularly in the field of combating organized crime – culminated in the European Security Strategy, which was adopted on 12 December 2003. In this document, organized crime is considered one of the key threats to Europe, alongside terrorism and regional conflicts. Its control is thus singled out as one of the most relevant of the EU's strategic objectives and 'better coordination between external action and Justice and Home Affairs policies is . . . [seen as] . . . crucial in the fight against both terrorism and organized crime' (Fijnaut and Paoli, 2004a, provide a lengthy account of these initiatives).

The Council of Europe and the European Court of Human Rights

Besides joint projects with the EU, the Council of Europe also takes initiatives of its own accord to combat organized crime and these are intended for all its 46 member countries, whether or not they belong to the EU. Though they do not explicitly refer to organized crime as such, several conventions sponsored by the Council of Europe constitute important elements of European organized crime control policies, for example the European Convention on Mutual Assistance in Criminal Matters and its Additional Protocols (1959) and the European Convention on Laundering, Search, Seizure and Confiscation of the Proceeds of Crime (1990).

Some other initiatives of the Council of Europe explicitly target organized crime. In 1997 the Committee of Ministers of the Council of Europe Member States set up a Committee of Experts on Criminal Law and Criminological Aspects of Organized Crime (PC-CO), which in 2000 was replaced by the Group of Experts on Criminological and Criminal Law Aspects of Organized Crime (PC-S-CO). Under the authority of the European Committee on Crime Problems (CDPC), the new bodies are required to assess the organized crime control policies of individual member states and have prepared several best practice surveys in the field of the fight against organized crime (Council of Europe, 2003a, b and c).

In 2001 the Committee of Ministers issued an overarching recommendation to the member states, providing guiding principles on the fight against organized crime. These guidelines cover the whole policy field in this area: from the prevention of organized crime to the use of the criminal justice system to control it and the mechanisms of international police and judicial cooperation (Council of Europe, 2001).

The important role played by the European Court of Human Rights in Strasbourg should also be highlighted in this context. Through its judgments, this Court has had a major influence in the past few years on efforts to establish the legal limits within which the battle against organized crime in Europe must be waged. One example is the case law concerning the use of undercover agents and anonymous witnesses; another relates to the direct and indirect interception of communication (Dutertre, 2003).

Bias and questions

The internationalization of organized crime control policy well explains why the changes that have taken place on several fronts in individual countries are so similar, whether they involve the centralization of the police, the judiciary and the customs authorities, or the creation of special units within these institutions, or the introduction of intrusive methods of investigation, such as phone tapping, anonymous witnesses and undercover agents.

Incidentally, the internationalization of policy can also throw up negative similarities between countries, not just positive ones, as is plainly evident in the neglect of an administrative, preventive approach to organized crime. Most countries do not have such an approach in place or have not properly implemented one; Italy and the Netherlands are the only two (partial) exceptions (La Spina, 2004 and van de Bunt, 2004). The one-sidedness – in other words, the predominantly repressive bias – of organized crime control policy propagated by the European institutions and/or by major countries is also reflected in the policy that many individual countries have conducted over the past few years (see also Levi and Maguire, 2004). Coupled with evident differences in the scope of organized crime in European countries, this one-sidedness raises certain questions about both the substance of the international or foreign control policy and the way in which it came about.

One question that may be asked is whether the policy conducted by the two main European institutions – the European Union and the Council of Europe – is not far too uniform: one and the same policy for each member state. Given the significant differences between countries, would it not be advisable to differentiate more? For instance, should a distinction not be made between compulsory measures that all member states must adopt because they relate to mutual cross-border cooperation and optional measures they can choose to implement, depending on the problems each country has to deal with?

A second question ties in with this last point: when determining which optional measures to adopt, is it not necessary to scrutinize more closely the policy developments that actually occur in the member states themselves – not just at the national level, but also at a regional or local level? This approach at least offers some guarantee that the range of measures on offer is as wide as possible, thus ensuring that policy-makers really have a choice.

This gives rise to a third question. Precisely because organized crime is a serious problem that manifests itself locally in a variety of guises, should not local authorities, above all Europe's in largest cities, and important policy-implementing bodies (such as customs and police forces) be more directly involved in policy-making?

Whatever the concrete solutions adopted, every effort must be made to prevent the internationalization of policy from leading to a situation in which this policy becomes divorced from the very problems it is designed to tackle or clashes with policies conducted locally to control these problems.

Chapter 17

Beyond Territoriality: European Security after the Cold War

Rachel A. Epstein and Alexandra Gheciu

Following the end of the Cold War, many politicians and observers argued that a new 'world order' was emerging, where conventional definitions of security, enemies and threats were no longer relevant. In the Euro-Atlantic area, a host of analysts and practitioners of international relations suggested that security could no longer be ensured via conventional, territorial-based arrangements, such as military alliances and power-balancing. Rather, it was argued, what was needed was the dissemination of liberal-democratic norms and values and the construction of (allegedly) peaceful and progressive polities around those values. The heightened salience of terrorism after the attacks of 11 September 2001 (9/11) further reinforced the perception that it was important to promote the construction of good polities around the norms of liberal democracy, for, it was argued, failing, authoritarian or weak states threatened to become a fertile breeding ground for terrorism.

Post-Cold War ideas about security have found expression in a series of untested policies and practices in Europe. First and foremost, post-Cold War conceptions of security that are focused on transnational threats or conflicts beyond European Union (EU) borders have provided impetus for significant spending cuts in traditional areas of defence as European powers in particular began shifting away from large-scale territorial forces. Europe has also taken unprecedented steps toward allowing transnational defence industry integration. Alongside these developments has been the promotion of liberal democratic norms in the former communist Eastern bloc, especially via EU and the North Atlantic Treaty Organization (NATO) enlargement. Complex international interventions aimed at reconstructing war-torn territories in the Balkans, most notably through the establishment of international administrations in Bosnia and Kosovo, have also defined the new post-Cold War security agenda.

In this chapter we argue that post-Cold War threat perceptions have changed the way European states organize their national defences internally and attempt to bolster their security externally. Whether one is considering the political economy of defence industry restructuring or Europe's strategy for consolidating stability in the former Yugoslavia, the blurring of internal and external security is the common thread that increasingly informs the European approach to the universe of threats. Following a brief overview, the first half of the chapter is devoted to internal changes, including the widespread abandonment of conscription and the internationalization of defence industries. The second half addresses how Europe, in connection with the United States through NATO, has tried to subdue threats on its periphery by restructuring transition and war-torn societies in its own, democratic, capitalist image.

Thinking about international security after the cold war

Conventional modern thinking about – and practices of – international security relied on a particular set of assumptions about the nature of political life and the distinction between the inside or domestic arena, and the outside or international realm (Walker, 1993). In the modern era, the dichotomy between inside (the arena of politics, progress and the search for the good life within states) and outside (the anarchical domain of otherness, and the source of potential threats to states) had powerful implications for the definition and practices of security. Thus, the modern definition of the polity as contained within specific territorial (state) boundaries found expression in a particular set of spatial technologies of security, based on the assumption that the sovereign state would need to act as a fortress, protecting the separation between inside and outside, and thus defending its citizens from the threats potentially posed by other states. If necessary, modern states were to form temporary alliances and engage in power-balancing in order to protect their territorial integrity and political freedom.

While modern practices did not always conform to them, these ideas about international relations did play an important role in shaping technologies and policies of security, leading to a heavy emphasis on formal alliances, a concern with the protection of state borders, and geo-strategic arrangements aimed at protecting states from the invading armies of their enemies. The maintenance of large territorial land armies in Europe was one symptom of the dichotomization of internal and external security. Individual European powers also tried to protect their access to armaments by subsidizing domestic production of key weapons systems. But the end of the Cold War, and the collapse of the rigid militarized blocs, led many international relations experts and practitioners to question conventional security ideas. Building on the democratic peace thesis, which holds that liberal democracies do not fight each other, analysts and practitioners argued that the best way to ensure security in the new era was by projecting liberal democratic values internationally.

These ideas, which came to shape understandings about post-Cold War security in Western political circles, found expression in a series of documents, including the strategic documents of key Euro-Atlantic security institutions. Security came to be defined in largely cultural terms, associated with the presence of liberal democratic norms and institutions. On this logic, the challenge that the Euro-Atlantic world faces is portrayed not in terms of a particular set of states whose inimical position is dictated by the geo-strategic logic of the balance of power. Rather, it is the absence of specific democratic institutions that comes to inform the definition of threat. Conveniently – for West European states increasingly pressed for resources to fund things other than defence, such as increasingly expensive welfare systems in ageing societies – the intellectual shift toward democratization as a means of consolidating security implied military downsizing.

Moving beyond a conventional understanding of security focusing on military power and the balance of capabilities to a focus on issues of societal instability and 'good' political cultural structures is one of the key transformations in Euro-Atlantic statements and policies related to security in the 1990s (Williams and Neumann, 2000). For example, in NATO's 1991 strategic concept, the problem of security is largely portrayed in terms of instability generated by the absence of good domestic institutions and the adverse consequences of instabilities, including ethnic rivalries and territorial disputes, in Central and Eastern Europe (NATO, 1991: para.10). Similar ideas can be found in EU statements and documents. According to the EU's first Security Strategy: 'Our traditional concept of self-defence – up to and including the Cold War – was based on the threat of invasion. With the new threats, the first line of defence will often be abroad' (EU, 2003: 11). Or as Javier Solana put it: 'borders matter less . . . and the main challenge for the coming twenty years will be how best to spread prosperity, democracy and stability beyond our borders' (Solana, 2004: 4).

On the basis of such shared understandings, West European states, together with their North American allies, became involved in the international projection of those norms while significantly diminishing national territorial defence capability. An important target for new practices of norm dissemination was the former Eastern bloc, not least because it was thought that the outcome of transitional processes in ex-communist states would have an important impact on the security of the Euro-Atlantic area. At the heart of attempts to project liberal democratic norms into Central and Eastern Europe were the processes of EU and NATO enlargement (Schimmelfennig, 2003). Thus, by making accession to the EU and NATO dependent upon the completion of complex reforms, by systematically monitoring the evolution of candidate states, and providing guidance in matters of implementation of liberal democratic norms, the Western community played an important role in the (re)constitution of former communist countries. At the same time, selected West and East European states have started building rapid reaction forces with improved power projection capacity in order to address threats beyond Europe's territory.

Changes in force structures

Predictably, one of the first West European responses to the Cold War's end was to cut defence spending – in some cases dramatically. In 1988 and 1989, all European NATO members were spending at least 2 per cent of their GDP on defence and in most instances considerably more than that. In 1988, France was spending 3.7 per cent, Germany 2.9, the UK 4.1, Italy 2.3, the Netherlands 2.8 and Norway 2.9. During the same period, the United States was spending approximately 5.7 per cent of its GDP on defence. Starting in 1990, all of the countries referred to here, with the exception of the United States, saw a steady and continual decline in defence spending for almost every year until 2001 (the year of 9/11). At that point, Germany's level of spending continued to head lower to 1.4 per cent by 2002, while French and British spending went down to 2.5 in 2002, only to rise slightly again in 2003 to 2.6 and 2.8 per cent respectively (SIPRI, 2005). Taking the continent as a whole, however, European defence spending stands at approximately 1.9 per cent of GDP, below the global average, with many European NATO members spending far less than the two per cent annually that NATO urges.

From territorial defence to out of area operations

In the search for more efficient ways to use limited funds and in an effort to make European armed forces more relevant to a changed strategic context, Europe has witnessed the professionalization of armed forces across much, but not all, of Europe. The movement from large, territorial forces to power projection is another manifestation of a defence reconceptualization whose aim is to maintain or create particular political orders rather than to protect borders. For Europe more than the United States, the shift to smaller, more mobile forces is a dramatic change. During the Cold War, Western Europe had close to two million men and women under arms. Within the NATO alliance, European powers were charged with defending their territories and therefore spent proportionally more on personnel than on research and investment. The US, by contrast, was continually engaged in the art of perfecting force projection (Yost, 2000). Admittedly, even by the late 1990s Europe had a hard time deploying more than forty to fifty thousand troops out of area, but in light of the ongoing effort to shift more resources toward rapid reaction capabilities, those figures may well increase.

Outside of post-communist Europe, France is perhaps the most striking example of military reform. In 1996, French President Jacques Chirac announced a series of changes based on the diminished need for territorial defence and land war coupled with a heightened urgency for power projection. Noting that France had difficulty in deploying even 10,000 troops in the first Gulf War in 1990–91 – despite having an overall force twice the size of Britain's – Chirac resolved to reduce the military from 500,000 to 350,000 troops while also boosting mobile forces to at least 50–60,000 men. His military reforms called for the phasing out of conscription over six years (for the first time in over a century) and for reducing the number of military bases from 124 to 84. At the same time, internal security forces were bolstered slightly to deal more effectively with trafficking and terrorism. Belgium and the Netherlands had phased out conscription two years earlier according to similar rationale, while Spain, Portugal and Italy developed plans alongside France to abolish it in the 2000s. Similar discussions were underway in Greece and Austria.

The end of the Cold War brought sweeping military changes to Eastern Europe as well, although for somewhat different reasons. It is true, for example, that the likes of Poland, Hungary, the Czech Republic and Romania have attempted – with various levels of enthusiasm and success – to provide small, mobile and militarily useful units to NATO operations as a way of achieving good standing in the alliance. It is also true, however, that given the bloated size of the military in the formerly socialist states (400,000 soldiers each in Poland and Romania, for example) some substantial downsizing would have taken place irrespective of NATO's post-Cold War status or policy prescriptions. Where NATO has had an impact, however, is in the near elimination of conscription across the region and the discouragement of funnelling resources towards territorial defence in favour of multinational forces. Poland took these policy prescriptions to new heights as it renounced plans to institutionalize civil territorial defence and later led the third stabilization force in Iraq, sending more than 2,000 of its own troops. By precluding the possibility of supporting large national armies, it is likely that NATO, together with the EU, has infused a degree of stability in Central and East Europe which, in addition to a series of bilateral treaties, facilitates a new degree of trust and transparency.

Germany is the only major EU player that has decided against the abolition of conscription, although even it, mostly for financial reasons, is scaling back. Conscription has greater staying power in Germany for historical reasons. Because in times past the military has enjoyed political prerogatives far in excess of democratic standards, conscription in Germany is meant to bind the army to society in a way that prevents the army from subverting broader social aims. In fact, however, the elimination of citizens' armies in democratic societies should be of concern to more countries than just Germany. Where it exists and functions according to theory, conscription should ensure an army that is representative of society and it should provide an additional layer of government accountability concerning how it uses the nation's military. Although these kinds of concerns have figured in debates on conscription, in both East and West Europe, cost considerations and the demands of creating small, mobile forces for out-of-area operations have won out, regardless of the dangers to democracy. In addition to Germany, only Switzerland and the Scandinavian states have opted to maintain their citizens' armies.

Diminishing national capacity: European defence industry integration

In keeping with the argument that European states are increasingly concerned about insecurity as it emanates from illiberal domestic institutions, they appear also to be decreasingly concerned about maintaining national military industrial capacity. In perhaps the surest sign that strategic conditions and threat perceptions have undergone a radical shift since the end of the Cold War, European states are allowing thorough-going, cross-national industry integration in exactly those areas in which they traditionally have been most concerned with security of supply. Although land and naval war-fighting sectors have so far lagged behind, the perceived need to achieve economies of scale and increased market share in aviation, aerospace and electronics has spurred industry internationalization. This part of the story is not entirely beyond territoriality, as certain quarters are resisting cross-national defence industry integration and there is still significant national and sectoral variation with respect to industry consolidation. The fact that most objections to defence industry consolidation stem from economic but not security concerns suggests that continued restructuring will likely be another symptom of new conceptions of security.

Although significant defence industry restructuring has been underway in Europe since 1985, an intense period of consolidation began in the mid-1990s such that by 2002, there were only three major contractors left in the European market. The multinational enterprises European Aeronautic Defence and Space Company (EADS), BAE Systems, and Thales dominated European military electronics and aviation by 2002, with land systems and ship-building undergoing restructuring on the national level that was expected to lead to further transnational consolidation as well. Although the leading European states tried to exercise political authority over consolidation trends, they were in the end relatively unsuccessful. Consolidation has taken place on two fronts: both within states and transnationally. The structure of defence industries matters to national security because traditionally, states have preferred an 'internal arming' capacity to avoid dependence on foreign suppliers – as was the tendency among European powers following the Second World War.

From the outset of European integration, arms manufacturing has been among the most protected of industries. Beginning with the Treaty of Rome in 1957, defence contractors were excluded from trade liberalization in Europe. Because political leaders deemed national security a strategic concern, they refused to subject arms production to the common market. The national approach to weapons production was affirmed as late as 1997 when the Amsterdam Treaty preserved Article 223 (renamed Article 296) as a guiding principle in defence industry organization, excluding weapons manufacturing from common market regulation (Merand, 2003).

In the intervening decades, the large European states – Britain, Germany and France – all developed successful arms industries such that each was largely able to provide for its own defence needs, albeit at considerable expense to taxpayers. To the extent that weapons systems were jointly produced among European partners, *juste retour* was strictly enforced. This means that a state's economic gains from cooperative projects (in terms of production, for example) were commensurate with a state's financial contribution. Led at various times by the United States and France, a number of European defence initiatives were proposed – but then ultimately buckled under political pressure. Even with respect to joint weapons projects, national procurement agencies and oligopolies consistently interfered with efforts for greater cooperation and integration that governments and even militaries had supported (Moravcsik, 1992). Although there was considerable defence industry consolidation between the 1950s and the 1990s, it was mostly within European nations rather than among them, leading to overcapacity and duplication in the European market.

The end of the Cold War, American defence industry consolidation, the changing nature of defence technology, and new European priorities concerning monetary union reversed earlier trends that favoured nationally-organized defence industrial and technological bases (DITB) in Europe. The end of the bipolar standoff meant shrinking markets for arms the world over. In response, the US government subsidized consolidation among American companies. At a meeting between US Secretary of Defence William Perry and defence industry chief executive officers (CEOs) in 1993 (since dubbed the 'last supper'), the US government made it clear that not everyone would survive the downturn. This ushered in a period of US neglect in enforcing anti-trust law, aggressive marketing of international arms sales, and government assistance in financing consolidation of up to $1.5 billion (Schmitt, 2000: 23–5).

New economies of scale in the United States left European weapons producers in a more vulnerable position than ever before, especially in light of the changing nature of military technology. No longer would they be able to sustain indigenous production capacity or even a modicum of defence self-sufficiency. The blurring of lines between civilian and military components, coupled with diminished demand for weapons, shifted manufacturers' attentions to commercial markets and undermined the traditionally privileged positions of defence contractors *vis-à-vis* governments. Further exacerbating European defence manufacturers' vulnerability was the drive from the early 1990s onward to meet the Maastricht convergence criteria in preparation for the single currency. Limits on public spending sent national treasurers looking for places to cut. The end of the Cold War and the sanctity of social welfare made defence budgets the logical target.

In response to sagging demand and material constraints – partly the result of market trends and partly the result of political developments – governments gradually began to give way to cross-national consolidation for the first time in European history. The creation of the EADS Company and the growth of BAE Systems into a transatlantic conglomerate with a US workforce and access to US markets were industry responses to political failures. Prior to market-led rationalization, Europeans had attempted political integration. France, Britain, Germany, Spain, Sweden and Italy committed in December 1997 to consolidating their national champions through greater integration and restructuring in an enterprise that would have been called the European Aerospace Defence Company (EADC). The deal fell apart, however, because of competition for jurisdiction over certain spheres of production and the ownership structure. This last point concerned the role of shareholders in an enterprise that might still in part be state owned by several of the participating countries, including France, Italy and Spain.

Massive consolidation finally did take place shortly after the failure of EADC, but with politics trailing rather than leading. British-dominated BAE Systems came close to merging with Germany's Dasa but opportunistically changed course and merged with Marconi in the United States instead, permanently damaging relations between BAE Systems and its would-be German partner. In keeping with European defence firms' fears that merging on unequal footing would essentially mean being overtaken, BAE Systems was then excluded from further European consolidation because it had grown too powerful. As Dasa contemplated merging with the recently privatized Spanish CASA, the German firm simultaneously pursued plans with France's Aerospatiale. The end result was EADS, the first 'European champion', in this instance from Germany, France and on a smaller scale Spain. Specializing in civil and military aviation and space technology (including Airbus), EADS is poised to compete with its American counterparts.

Although market-led, the making of EADS was not entirely free from political authority. The French and Spanish governments both took significant steps in divesting themselves of these traditionally state-owned defence industries, but their withdrawal was not complete. With France and Spain being shareholders in the new enterprise, both came under pressure to renounce excessive political interference but at the same time are not legally bound to abide by that commitment. Moreover, political sensibilities may circumscribe the economies of scale that participants hope to realize. The political imperative to balance production geographically among Germany, France and Spain will limit market-based rationalization. And because common market law does not cover defence industries, EADS will not be subject to European norms governing labour law reconciliation. This could further complicate the enterprise's efforts to operate as a coherent entity, restricting basic business decisions such as shifts in production.

Although cross-national industry consolidation could provide the material and organizational basis for a more integrated European foreign and defence policy, diverging national approaches to defence industry restructuring could still pose barriers. Just as competing foreign policy priorities in the Balkans, Middle East and elsewhere have been sources of friction within Europe (see Chapter 3) so have different cultures of capitalism traditionally undermined defence specialization. The US Secretary of Defence, William Cohen, estimated in 1999 that the lack of such defence specialization was costing Europe enormously – with the Europeans spending about 60 per cent as much as the Americans, but acquiring only 10 per cent of the capability. There is now growing evidence of merging approaches, however, perhaps for the first time since restructuring began.

Consider the policies of the UK and a range of other countries that represent different poles in terms their willingness to move beyond territoriality as a means of producing and procuring defence technologies. The UK has gone further than any other country in assisting firms in establishing a global presence and in opening the UK defence market to foreign participation and ownership. BAE Systems (formerly British Aerospace) in particular has expanded its European presence through Sweden and Italy, is the most firmly established European firm in the US defence market, and in addition owns stakes in South Korea, South Africa and Australia. According to a 2004 *Financial Times* analysis (28 May 2004: 13), pursuing 'efficiency' and 'value for money' ahead of a traditional national industrial policy, the prime contractors for the bulk of UK weapons programmes have since 1999 been mostly American and European, but not British.

The French state has, since before the Second World War, held at least partial stakes across a range of firms, including Thales (defence and civil electronics), DCN (the French naval group), EADS, Giat Industries (ground weapons), and Snecma (aero-engines group). Since the late 1990s, however, successive governments have been under pressure – mostly from corporate executives – to privatize major portions of the biggest concerns. Responding to CEO suggestions that 'our status as a public company is not favourable to making alliances with quoted companies' French politicians have conceded that 'We are convinced that the process of "Europeanization" of the defence industry . . . should continue.' (*Financial Times*, 26 November 2004). It is also worth noting, however that in the run-up to the French referendum on the European constitutional treaty, possible privatization deals were put on hold – in defence and in other sectors as well. Thales CEO Denis Ranque's plans to embark on a possible merger with a foreign firm (such as Finmeccanica) were blocked by the French government because it was deemed unpopular with French labor unions. Decisions about the corporate leadership of EADS were also put on hold in light of the 'no' campaign's concerns about the loss of ownership and control over strategic sectors and jobs.

Although both France and Germany have traditionally been more nationally oriented in their approach to weapons production and procurement, even they are succumbing to major shifts, most notably the creation of EADS, a mostly Franco-German transnational merger. French firms have also expanded their global reach through investments in the UK, Brazil and South Korea, while gaining greater access to more markets through joint ventures in the United States and Australia. Both Germany's Rheinmetall and Italy's Finmeccanica, like other European firms, have tried to reduce their dependence on their respective governments' procurement policies by pursuing cross-national acquisitions in Europe and by establishing ties to defence firms in the United States. Continental Europe (much like the United States) still appears to be more nervous than the UK, however, about selling domestic industries to foreign investors.

Changes in power projection

As they were preparing to embark upon enlargement, both NATO and the EU made it clear to the candidate states that the completion of a comprehensive set of liberal democratic reforms was a key precondition for admission. It is revealing that the accession criteria set by the EU and NATO were very similar (Schimmelfennig, 2003). Thus, the EU accession conditions, as established by the European Council in Copenhagen in 1993 – the so-called Copenhagen criteria – include the stability of institutions guaranteeing democracy, the rule of law, human rights and the protection of minorities, and the existence of a functioning market economy. Similarly, the conditions set by NATO, as stated in the 1995 'Study on NATO Enlargement', include adherence to domestic and international liberal norms, such as democracy, the protection of minorities and individual rights, a market economy, and the peaceful settlement of international disputes. Following the formulation of these conditions, both NATO and the EU engaged in complex processes of monitoring of – and assistance with – democratization and liberalization in candidate states. Let us now examine one particular aspect of this process of norm projection via enlargement: the promotion of liberal democratic norms in the arena of civil–military relations. This was seen by Western decision-makers as a key step in the establishment of stable democracy in the former Eastern bloc, and, hence, as a means for promoting stability in Europe as a whole.

NATO and the politics of international norm projection

In the area of civil–military relations, NATO was the principal international actor systematically involved in the promotion of reforms. For our purposes, international norm projection in this area is particularly interesting because conventional wisdom about international politics holds that NATO, as a military alliance, is an exclusively geo-strategic arrangement, which does not become involved in processes of domestic (re)constitution. Moreover, civil–military relations, and more broadly the field of security, are usually seen as falling exclusively within the purview of sovereign states. Contrary to those conventional ideas, in post-Cold War Europe civil–military relations were at the heart of inter-actions between NATO and actors from the former communist bloc. Particularly, though not exclusively, within the framework of accession dialogues and related formal or informal consultations and negotia-tions, NATO sought to project into Central and Eastern Europe liberal-democratic norms for governing those relations. These included: accountability and transparency in the formulation of defence policies and budgets; the clear division of powers within the state in the field of security; government oversight of the military through civilian defence ministries; and accountability for the armed forces. The alliance's concern to promote reform in this area was informed by the view that democratic civil–military relations were a key feature of liberal democ-racy. Concern for reform also stemmed from the understanding that, following the collapse of communism, Central and East European states faced massive problems in democratizing their defence arrangements.

Under these circumstances, in addition to setting democratic civil–military relations as a key condition for accession, NATO also became systematically involved in providing guidance to the Central and East Europeans as the latter embarked on the process of reform in the field of defence (Epstein, 2005; Gheciu, 2005). Within the framework of accession dialogues and related consultations, NATO advisers sought to teach the Central and East Europeans the broad principles and rules of transparency and accountability that should govern civil–military interactions in liberal democracies, and, in addition, provided more specific advice on particular institutional and legislative reforms through which those norms could be implemented (Gheciu, 2005). For example, in the course of accession dialogues and in informal consulta-tions in Brussels and the national capitals, NATO representatives sought to persuade officials from several candidate states to pursue key legislative reforms in the areas of national emergency and defence plan-ning in order to transcend problems of lack of accountability and transparency inherited from the communist period.

NATO also became systematically engaged in educating younger people from the former communist bloc, the assumption being that the education of a new generation of liberal elites is important if the norms of liberal democracy are to be (re)produced in the future. Since the end of the Cold War, hundreds of courses, seminars and workshops for young civilians and military officers have been organized at the Partnership Training Centres, NATO's Defence College, the Geneva Centre for Security Policy, the Marshall Centre, the Partnership Coordination Cell, and various defence academies in Western countries. The explicit goal is not simply to provide military training, but, more broadly, to expose military personnel and civilians from NATO's partner countries to the values and norms of Western-defined democracy, human rights and the rule of law, and to teach them to think of alternative sets of values as unacceptable and dangerous.

Although, even today, the implementation of norms of liberal democracy in the field of defence in some former communist states – including new NATO members – remains imperfect, particularly due to the persistence of discrepancies between formal institutions and actual practices, on the whole, attempts at reform have been consistent with NATO's aims of enhancing transparency and accountability. Central and East European parliamentary committees have gradually gained competence and confidence, and are increasingly capable of exercising their authority over defence budgets and policies, and the structures of defence ministries in former communist states have changed dramatically over a decade and a half. There is evidence that, by portraying democratic control of the military as a desirable and necessary feature of modern democracies, by monitoring and guiding the reform process, training military and political actors, and often helping domestic reformers in their debates and confrontations with their conservative opponents, NATO did have a significant impact on the evolution of civil–military relations in the former communist bloc (Epstein, 2005; Gheciu, 2005).

Beyond military interventions: the reconstruction of war-torn territories in the Balkans

The violent conflicts that erupted in Yugoslavia in the 1990s were widely perceived in the international arena as indicators of the destructive force generated by the combination of hyper-nationalism and modern technology, and as reminders that the Balkans remained a problematic, some said uncivilized, part of Europe. In response – albeit with significant delays and inconsistencies – the international community embarked on comprehensive missions of peace-making and peace-building, aimed not simply at ending the fighting, but also at preventing its recurrence. The idea behind those actions was that Kosovars and Bosnians could only be adequately protected through the establishment of a stable, rational and ethical – meaning liberal-democratic – order in the war-torn territories, which, so the argument went, would make it impossible for conflict to resume. Furthermore, the achievement of a peaceful and stable order in the Balkans was regarded as key to achieving the broader goal of promoting European security. In the eyes of many European decision-makers, the problems, crises and conflicts that had emerged in the former Yugoslavia could not be safely contained within particular borders, and threatened to spill over into neighbouring states.

Particularly relevant in this context were the decisions to establish international administrations in Bosnia and Herzegovina, and in Kosovo (in 1995 and 1999 respectively). The international administration of Bosnia and Herzegovina was established as part of a peace process that culminated in the 1995 signing of the General Framework Agreement for Bosnia and Herzegovina (the Dayton Accord). The aim was to build a stable, peaceful, democratic state, which respects human rights and the rule of law, and provides adequate protection to minorities. The task of coordinating the civilian efforts of the international community was assigned to the Office of the High Representative. The High Representative embarked on a process of curbing the authority of local parties, and became actively involved in the construction of those (liberal) institutions and political culture regarded as pre-conditions for a responsible exercise of democratic rights. In December 1997, the international community empowered the High Representative to impose laws against the will of local governing parties, and to dismiss public officials whom the High Representative considers to be violating their duties under the Dayton Agreement.

The High Representative has exercised those extraordinary powers on numerous occasions: for instance, to order a restructuring of the Constitutional Commission in the Federation and the Republica Srpska Parliaments, to impose a package of new economic legislation; and to establish an Independent Judicial Commission to help overcome opposition to judicial reform (Caplan, 2004). In addition, since March 1998 the High Representative has dismissed or banned from public office dozens of elected officials, including mayors, presidents of municipal assemblies, cantonal ministers, delegates to the entity parliaments, the President of Republica Srpska, and a member of the Bosnian Presidency (Ante Jelavic). In brief, through the Office of the High Representative, which became the lead agency in the process of reconstruction in Bosnia and Herzegovina, the international administration allows Bosnians to govern their own affairs only to the extent that the process of self-government is conducted within the framework of the internationally defined norms and rules. In cases of perceived departure from those norms, the Office of the High Representative has (and has exercised) the power to rule by decree in order to block or amend offending pieces of legislation, and to fire individuals who sought to uphold alternative (that is, nationalist) norms.

In a study of post-Cold War security practices in Europe, Bosnia and Herzegovina is also interesting because it constitutes an example of NATO–EU cooperation within the framework of the so-called Berlin Plus arrangements. The aim of Berlin Plus is to allow the EU to use NATO assets and capabilities in situations where the alliance as a whole does not wish to become involved in a mission. In December 2004, in a situation marked by improved security on the ground, the EU assumed responsibility for the peacekeeping operation in Bosnia through the launch of operation ALTHEA as the legal successor of the NATO-led Stabilization Force (SFOR). ALTHEA's mandate builds on the Dayton Peace Accord and pursues the following objectives: to provide deterrence, continued compliance with the responsibility to fulfil the role specified in the Dayton Accord, and to create a stable, viable, peaceful and multiethnic Bosnia and Herzegovina, cooperating peacefully with its neighbours. ALTHEA is expected to complement the peace-building mission led by the High Representative, Paddy Ashdown, who was also appointed the EU Special Representative (EUSR). The termination of SFOR, however, does not spell the end of NATO's engagement in Bosnia and Herzegovina. While the EU has assumed responsibility for peacekeeping operations, NATO maintains a headquarters in Sarajevo. The main job of the NATO Headquarter is to provide advice on defence reforms, and to carry out certain operational tasks, including counter-terrorism, support to the International Criminal Tribunal for the former Yugoslavia, the detention of persons indicted of war crimes, and intelligence sharing with the EU.

In Kosovo, the international administration was established in the aftermath of the 1999 Operation Allied Force against the Milosevic regime. Kosovo represents an interesting case of the logic of security via (liberal) community building. NATO's goal was not to defeat an enemy state or alliance of states, nor was it to (re)establish a particular international balance of power. Rather, NATO's bombing campaign was conceived of as a limited application of force, an instance of coercive diplomacy, to bring President Milosevic back to the negotiating table. This, in turn, was regarded as a step that would enable a more comprehensive international operation aimed at rebuilding the province in accordance with Western liberal-democratic norms. In embarking on Operation Allied Force, the allies were united by a shared understanding that NATO was acting in conformity with its liberal democratic values in response to the massive humanitarian crisis in Kosovo. There was also a shared view among the NATO members that the resolution of that crisis and the reconstruction of Kosovo was an important part of European stability.

The conditions imposed by NATO on the Milosevic regime – and subsequently reiterated in the UN Security Council Resolution 1244 in the summer of 1999 – involved far more than a ceasefire coupled with disarmament of the warring factions and the insertion of an international security force. In effect, the NATO-led humanitarian intervention in Kosovo led to the establishment of an international protectorate in the province. In implementing Resolution 1244, a network of international institutions, particularly the UN, the European Union, the Organization for Security and Cooperation in Europe (OSCE), and NATO (as the core of the Kosovo Force, KFOR) became involved in the reconstitution of Kosovo around internationally-prescribed norms. The UN assumed the control of the first pillar, interim civil administration, involving the performance of basic civilian administrative functions, and the maintenance of civil law and order. In carrying out its functions, United Nations Mission in Kosovo (UNMIK) worked in close cooperation with, and in many ways depended on, the NATO-led KFOR. The legal relationship between KFOR and UNMIK was never clearly defined, leaving the former significant room to manoeuvre, subject only to the broadly defined role of 'coordination' attributed to the head of UNMIK.

The mandate of KFOR, defined in open terms, included peace enforcement, confidence building and assistance to UNMIK (including the undertaking of public safety and order in the first stage of international administration). The OSCE assumed the leadership of the second pillar of international administration, institution-building. The third pillar, concerning the monitoring of the safe return of the refugees and the internally displaced people, as well as the provision of humanitarian aid, was entrusted to the United Nations High Commissioner for Refugees (UNHCR). Finally, the European Union was given the leadership of the fourth pillar: the support of economic reconstruction and the rebuilding of infrastructure in the province. The most prominent challenge of the mandate has been the absence of an end state for the international administration – that is to say, uncertainty over the final status of Kosovo, and the tension between the requirement in Resolution 1244 to respect Yugoslavia's sovereignty, and the desire of the vast majority of the Kosovo population (the Kosovar Albanians) to achieve independence.

In the past few years the international administrators initiated a series of actions aimed at transferring more powers to the people of Kosovo, through the 2001 Constitutional Framework for Provincial Self-Government, and the subsequent establishment of Provisional

Institutions of Self-Government. Nevertheless, the powers of UNMIK to govern Kosovo remain substantial. Furthermore, UNMIK continues to control key aspects of the province's external relations, and the Constitutional Framework explicitly states that the provisional Kosovar institutions are not authorized to make decisions in matters related to Kosovo's final status.

The process of (re)construction in Bosnia and Kosovo, as envisaged by the international administrators, involves the replacement of one type of particularity (built around exclusive identities) by a higher, more inclusive type of particularity – via the creation of Kosovar and Bosnian entities in which the plurality of ethnic identities, value systems and loyalties give rise to integrated political communities, where citizens share a commitment to create new institutions around rational, liberal democratic norms. This integration within Bosnia and Kosovo is to give rise to a more important integration in Europe; in other words, in time, the political community of Bosnians and Kosovars is to be re-articulated within an even higher form of particularity: the European Union. The heads of the international administrations – as well as the EU – have portrayed the integration of Bosnia and Kosovo within Europe as an unquestionable goal, as the obvious resting point of the two territories' evolution towards more rational and ethical forms of organization. Thus, for example, at the Thessaloniki Summit of the EU with the countries from the Western Balkans (June 2003), it was declared that the integration of the EU would not be complete without the accession of Southeast Europe, including Bosnia and Herzegovina and Kosovo.

The depth and extent of international involvement in the reconstruction of Bosnia and Kosovo has generated a certain tension between the aim of promoting democracy and self-determination in those war-torn territories, and the actual means used to promote that aim: those means, as noted above, have often involved departures from the norms of democratic accountability (Bain, 2003). It would be impossible to engage in a systematic normative analysis of what constitutes acceptable means in the process of state (re)building pursued in the name of local and international stability and freedom. Moreover, Bosnia and particularly Kosovo, which is still in a state of political limbo, still face a number of serious problems, and it is still unclear if they will, in the end, evolve into the kinds of peaceful, stable, democratic polities envisaged by the international administration. For our purposes, however, what is particularly interesting is the way in which a vision of security that stresses the importance of particular norms and values found expression in a broad set of practices of (re)constructing polities around a particular set of norms. Such practices depart, in important ways, from conventional ideas of threat, enmity and the role of geo-strategic solutions, such as power balancing and the formation of alliances, in addressing those threats.

Linked to this, the practices of reconstruction in Bosnia and Kosovo are also very interesting because they demonstrate the evolving, and increasingly complex role that the armed forces have to play in contemporary peace-keeping and peace-building missions. Thus, far from being limited to the conventional role of fighting a well defined enemy, military personnel deployed in Bosnia and Kosovo have had to engage in policing functions, often in a situation marked by the absence of clear rules regarding the applicable legislation. Officers deployed in those war-torn territories found out that they were expected to contribute to a variety of civilian projects, such as helping to organize and monitor elections, supervising the return of refugees, and contributing to the rebuilding the civilian infrastructure destroyed during the war. In performing these duties, military officers have had to learn and apply a variety of civilian skills, and have had to learn novel ways of interacting with local actors, and with a host of international civilian organizations, both governmental and non-governmental. The experience of Bosnia and Kosovo has led many Western senior officers to argue that in post-Cold War missions the greatest challenge faced by their armed forces is not fighting, but post-conflict reconstruction.

Conclusion

On all major fronts, European and transatlantic security has changed dramatically since the end of the Cold War. Whereas for Europe the bipolar standoff until the late 1980s had implied territorial defences and a possible land war in connection with a nuclear conflagration, the post-Cold War period has ushered in a different set of security concerns, and with them new strategies. Certainly the most profound change for Europe, in both security and in everything else, has been the liberation of Eastern Europe from Soviet domination and the concerted effort many post-communist states have made to liberalize their societies, both politically and economically. While the collapse of state-socialism undoubtedly made the West safer from the nuclear nightmare many had feared, it also introduced new uncertainties even as it shifted the EU's boundaries.

In response to the Cold War's end, Europe has moved beyond territoriality in conceptualizing and enacting its security. Insecurity emanating from illiberal institutions has replaced Europe's more traditional concern about territorial integrity. In keeping with this new threat perception, both European and transatlantic institutions, the EU and NATO foremost among them, have engaged in a strategy of liberal norm projection. NATO had conducted a long-term campaign in post-communist Central and Eastern Europe to democratize civil–military relations there, whereas in the former Yugoslavia both the EU and NATO have been actively supporting conflict resolution and democratic institutions.

Europeans are also reorganizing their military-security apparatuses to address security concerns beyond territoriality in a second sense. Less determined to maintain nationally-based defence production and procurement systems, Europe's biggest arms producers are for the first time allowing thorough-going cross-national defence industry integration to take place. In addition, in a bid to cut costs but also to project power beyond their own borders more effectively, most European states are doing away with the long tradition of conscription in order to devote more resources to professionalized peace-enforcing and peace-keeping missions. Even Germany, the conscription hold-out among the major European players, has come to the conclusion that to be a viable ally in the emerging world order, it would have to adapt its constitutional constraints to conduct at least limited military operations beyond its own territory. Although trailing behind the creation of a unified market or a single currency, Europe is incrementally also moving towards a more integrated approach to security, albeit in a way that so far lacks any broad supranational institutionalization.

Guide to Further Reading

Chapter 2

The A.T. Kearney (2005) globalization index provides a good overview of current trends across a range of indicators. The underlying data are available from the A.T. Kearney website at http://www.atkearney.com. Further data and statistics about globalization can be found on the website of the World Bank at http://www.worldbank.org. The narrative of European integration can be found in Dinan (2004). For a closer examination of monetary union, see Jones (2002, 2004). On the relationship between global changes and Europe's social and labour market systems, see Ferrera, Hemerijck and Rhodes (2001). Essays in Wallace, Wallace and Pollack (2005) provide detailed analyses of EU agricultural policy, including negotiations in the WTO, the single market, trade policy and Economic and Monetary Union. Majone (2005) provides the most sophisticated study to date of the EU as a mediator between international economic integration and the nation state. OECD (1997) provides an introduction to the study of national innovation systems.

Chapter 3

Essential reading is Hill and Smith (2005), whilst Hill and K.E. Smith (2000), contains commentary and the texts of all the important documents on European foreign policy from 1948 to 2000. On the early days of European foreign diplomacy, see Nuttall (1992). Manners and Whitman (2000) contains chapters which consider the extent to which the EU member states' foreign policies have been 'adapted' in the area of foreign and security policy. H. Smith (2002) provides a comprehensive account of EU policies around the world, whilst K.E. Smith (2003) offers a critical analysis of the EU's stance in the world. The FORNET website (www.fornet.info) contains detailed information on both EU foreign policy and member state foreign policy, as well as the bi-monthly online newsletter, *CFSP Forum*, which contains several articles on the reforms proposed in the draft constitutional treaty.

Chapter 4

On the theoretical approaches and empirical findings of the Europeanization of the 'old' member states, see Cowles, Caporaso and Risse (2001), Featherstone and Radaelli (2003), and Bulmer and Lequesne (2005). On the Europeanization of Central and Eastern Europe, see Andonova (2004), Dimitrova (2004), Jacoby (2004) and Schimmelfennig and Sedelmeier (2005b). More specifically on EU democracy promotion in Central and Eastern Europe, see Kelley (2004), Pridham (2005) and Vachudova (2005).

Chapter 5

For a comparative discussion of 'hollowing-out' see Weller, Bakvis and Rhodes (1997); the case for the centralization and personalization of executive power is made in Poguntke and Webb (2005). Norton (1998) offers a survey of executive-legislative relations. The party–government nexus is discussed in Castles and Wildenmann (1986), Katz (1987) and Blondel and Cotta (1996, 2000). On the operation of coalition government see Laver and Schofield (1990) and Müller and Strøm (2000). For analyses of the inner workings of government, which an emphasis on problem of coordination, see Peters, Rhodes and Wright (2000); a comparative view on cabinets is offered by Blondel and Müller-Rommel (1993, 1997, 2001). The politics–administration nexus is debated in Page and Wright (1999) and Peters and Pierre (2004). Analyses of the processes of government in Central and Eastern Europe are still rare, but see Dimitrov *et al.* (2006)

Chapter 6

Key volumes among the many recent studies dealing with the challenges confronting parties in contemporary democracies are Dalton and Wattenberg (2000), Luther and Müller-Rommel (2002) and Gunther *et al.* (2002). The standard work on the theory and classification of party systems is Sartori (1976), recently republished in a new edition by the European Consortium for Political Research. For a series of in-depth analyses of national political systems, see Webb *et al.* (2002) and Webb and White (2006). On parties and electoral change, see Mair *et al.* (2004). On political parties in the new democracies of Southern and East-Central Europe see van Biezen (2003). Concentrating on post-communist parties in particular are Lewis (2000) and Millard (2004).

Chapter 7

Dalton (2002), Katz (1997) and LeDuc *et al.* (2002) offer comparative, data-rich and accessible surveys of issues in representation and electoral politics. For state-of-the-art analyses and concise theoretical overviews of the same, see Kitschelt (2000), Powell (2000) and Przeworski *et al.* (1999). Regarding the variation in party systems and their effects, Sartori (1976) remains a must-read. The most interesting further developments probably concern why, how and with what effect party systems also vary with respect to institutionalization and the extent to which any programmatic differences occur between parties – see Mainwaring (1998) and Kitschelt (2000). For recent overviews of party systems in individual European countries as well as at the European level see Webb *et al.* (2002) and Berglund *et al.* (2004). Regarding citizens' behaviour, a most comprehensive recent analysis of electoral turnout is provided by Franklin (2004), while Dalton (2004) is an insightful analysis of trends in citizen participation and support for democratic institutions in general. On the disputed issue of the decline of traditional electoral cleavages, the last word now belongs to Knutsen (2004), while on voting behaviour in general Evans (2004) provides the most up-to-date introduction.

Chapter 8

For further and more detailed information on the key issues discussed in this chapter, see Keating (1998, 2004a, 2004b), Keating and Hughes (2003), Sharpe (1993) and Rokkan and Urwin (1983).

Chapter 9

There are few comparative studies of corruption in Europe, but Bull and Newell (2003) provides a schematic overview of corruption in a range of (mainly Western) countries. Also important is the Heidenheimer *et al.* (2002) reader, now in its third edition. On the politics of anti-corruption in Eastern Europe, see Krastev (2004). For an argument which links corruption and the risk of populism, see Fieschi and Heywood (2004).

Chapter 10

The most useful descriptive survey of anti-system organizations in Europe is Camus (1999). For studies of the post-Cold War radical and extreme left, see March and Mudde (2005) and Moreau, Lazar and Hirscher (1998); on the extreme and radical right in Europe, see among many more Mudde (2006), Ignazi (2003) and Hainsworth (2000); on Islamic fundamentalism and terrorism in Europe, see Kepel (1997); on separatist terrorism, see Hewitt and Cheetham (2000); on European responses to terrorism since 9/11, see Haubrich (2003).

Chapter 11

For an accessible overview of recent industrial relations developments, see European Commission (2004). For the more comprehensive analyses of different developments addressed in this chapter, see Traxler *et al.* (2001), Kitschelt *et al.* (1999), Streeck and Kenworthy (2004) and Thirkell *et al.* (1998).

Chapter 12

The literature on the judicialization of politics has grown rapidly in recent years. Stone Sweet (1992, 2000) has published several important works on this topic. Another important contribution is Shapiro and Stone Sweet (2002). Interesting discussion between judges and political scientists can be found in Badinter and Breyer (2004). Guarnieri and Pederzoli (2002) deal with the ordinary judiciary. For the best description of post-communist developments see Procházka (2002) or Sadurski (2005). Within the EU context see Weiler (1994). A colourful analysis of the rise of the ECJ is Alter (2001), and a case study of its economic case law is Maduro (1998). A good analysis of the ECHR is Moravcsik (2000). For critiques of the expansion of judicial power, see especially Hirschl (2004) and Tate and Vallinder (1995).

Chapter 13

The literature on religion and politics and church–state relations in modern Europe has grown markedly in recent years. Remond (1999) places the issues in historical context. Boyle and Sheen (1997) and Evans (2001) provide useful surveys of developments in the area of human rights, while Richardson (2004) points to a range of issues and concerns affecting the regulation of minority religions. Robbers (1996) gives useful coverage of church-state relations in the 15 then-member states of the EU, while Anderson (2003) deals with the same issues under conditions of transition to liberal democracy in a number of Eastern European countries. Madeley and Enyedi (2003) includes both thematic and country-study treatments from across the Continent. Norris and Inglehart (2004) use the most extensive battery of data ever assembled to settle some issues in the debate on secularization and to put European experience in its world context. Van Hecke and Gerard (2004) cover the varying fortunes of European Christian Democracy since the end of the Cold War. And finally, the US Department of State's annual country reports on religious freedom make available useful up-to-date snapshot surveys of many of the relevant issues.

Chapter 14

The best overall introductions to advanced welfare state studies are still Esping-Andersen (1990), Scharpf and Schmidt (2000) and Pierson (2001). Castles (2004) provides an excellent discussion of the challenges facing contemporary welfare systems, including globalization. Esping-Andersen *et al.* (2002) present one of the best analyses available of policy dilemmas and options in family, working life, and pensions policy, while Esping-Andersen and Regini (2000) is one of the best sources on European labour markets. Zeitlin and Pochet (2005) present an exhaustive study of the European employment and social inclusion strategies, while two large-scale projects – GOVECOR and NEWGOV – provide a wide array of material on the OMC and 'new modes of governance' in the EU. They can be accessed at http://www.govecor.org/ and http://www.eu-newgov.org/ respectively.

Chapter 15

Geddes (2000) analyses the different aspects of the emerging EU immigration regime from its inception to the Amsterdam treaty, and Geddes (2003) is a thorough comparative study of migration politics in both Western and Eastern countries. Lavenex and Uçarer (2002) examine the consequences of EU policy on candidate countries and the EU's external relations. A recent account of new East–West migration trends is Górny and Ruspini (2004). Byrne, Noll and Vedsted-Hansen (2002) examine the new immigration and asylum policies in East and Central Europe in the context of enlargement. The monthly *Migration News Sheet* covers policy developments in the member states and at EU-level. Statistics on asylum are posted on the UNHCR web site (www.unhcr.org). The OECD publishes an annual report on Trends in International Migration.

Chapter 16

Critical syntheses of the US discourse on organized crime have been provided by Smith (1975) and Woodiwiss (2001). For a compact overview of the European scientific debate, see Levi (2002) and Paoli and Fijnaut (2004b). For a comparative assessment of organized crime patterns and control policies in 13 European countries, see Fijnaut and Paoli (2004b). Specifically on organized crime control policies, see also Levi and Maguire (2004) and den Boer (2002). On the Italian mafia, see Paoli (2003) and on its Italian American counterpart, see Jacobs and Gouldin (1999). On Russian organized crime, see Volkov (2004) and Shelley (2004).

Chapter 17

For a good, detailed analysis of practices of contemporary international administration see Caplan (2005). A highly useful, accessible account of historically specific assumptions of territoriality that inform the modern international system, see Ruggie (1993). One of the best analyses of philosophical ideas that underpin the democratic peace thesis, and the implications of those ideas for international politics, see Williams (2001). A comprehensive study on the European foreign and security policy is provided by Simon Duke (2000). Finally, for recent and well-documented studies on developments in European defence industries, see the work of Burkard Schmitt, particularly his multiple Chaillot papers available at: http://www.iss-eu.org.

Bibliography

Ágh, A. (2001) 'Early Consolidation and Performance Crisis: The Majoritarian-Consensus Democracy Debate in Hungary', *West European Politics*, 24(3), pp. 89–112.

Allen, D. (1996) 'Conclusions: The European Rescue of National Foreign Policy?' in C. Hill (ed.), *The Actors in Europe's Foreign Policy*. London: Routledge.

Allen, D. (1998) '"Who Speaks for Europe?" The Search for an Effective and Coherent External Policy', in J. Peterson and H. Sjursen (eds), *A Common Foreign Policy for Europe?* London: Routledge.

Allen, D. (2005) 'Cohesion and Structural Funds', in H. Wallace, W. Wallace and M. Pollack (eds), *Policy-Making in the European Union*. Oxford: Oxford University Press, pp. 213–42.

Alter, K.J. (2001) *Establishing the Supremacy of European Law. The Making of an International Rule of Law in Europe*. Oxford, Oxford University Press.

Alvarez-Plata, P., H. Brücker and B. Siliverstovs (2003) *Potential Migration from Central and Eastern Europe into the EU-15*. Berlin: Deutche Institut für Wirtschaftsforschung.

Anderson, C.J. (2000) 'Economic Voting and Political Context: A Comparative Perspective', *Electoral Studies*, 19, pp. 151–70.

Anderson, J. (2002) 'Europeanization and the Transformation of the Democratic Polity', *Journal of Common Market Studies*, 40(5), pp. 793–822.

Anderson, J. (2003) *Religious Liberty in Transitional Societies: The Politics of Religion*. Cambridge: Cambridge University Press.

Andeweg, R. (2003) 'On Studying Governments', in J. Hayward and A. Menon (eds), *Governing Europe*. Oxford: Oxford University Press, pp. 39–60.

Andonova, L.B. (2003) *Transnational Politics of the Environment. The European Union and Environmental Policy in Central and Eastern Europe*. Cambridge, MA: MIT Press.

Arlacchi, P. (1988) *Mafia Business. The Mafia Ethic and the Spirit of Capitalism*. Oxford: Oxford University Press.

Aszalos, Z. (2001) 'Country Report: Hungary', in P. Nyiri, J. Toth and M. Fullerton (eds), *Diaspora and Politics*. Budapest: Centre for Migration and Refugee Studies, pp. 181–205.

Avdagić, S. (2005) 'State–Labour Relations in East Central Europe: Explaining Variations in Union Effectiveness', *Socio-Economic Review*, 3(1) pp. 25–53.

Avramov, R. (2001) *Stopanskia XX vek na Bulgaria* (The Bulgarian Economic XX century). Sofia: Centre for Liberal Strategies.

Badie, B. (1995) *La fin des territoires. Essai sur le désordre international et sur l'utilité sociale du respect*. Paris: Fayard.

Badinter, R. and S. Breyer (eds) (2004) *Judges in Contemporary Democracy. An International Conversation*. New York, New York University Press.

Bain, W. (2003) *Between Anarchy and Society*. Oxford: Oxford University Press.

Barry, B. (2002) *Culture and Equality. An Egalitarian Critique of Multiculturalism*. Cambridge: Polity Press.

Barsa, P. (2004) 'Managing Immigration and Integration in Europe and in the Czech Republic', Online research paper, available at http://www.policy.hu/barsa/Final_Research_Paper_html.html

Bartolini, S. and P. Mair. (2001) 'Challenges to Contemporary Political Parties', in L. Diamond and R. Gunther (eds), *Political Parties and Democracy*. Baltimore: Johns Hopkins University Press, pp. 327–43.

Batt, J. (2003) 'The EU's New Borderlands', CER Working Paper, October. London: Centre for European Reform.

Beckford, J. (1985) *Cult Controversies: The Societal Response to the New Religious Movements*. London: Tavistock.

Bell, D. ([1953] 1965) 'Crime as an American Way of Life', in *The End of Ideology. On the Exhaustion of Political Ideas in the Fifties*. New York: Free Press, pp. 127–50.

Bell, D.S. (2002) 'France: The Left in 2002 – The End of the Mitterrand Strategy', *Parliamentary* Affairs, 56(1), pp. 24–37.

Benoit, K. and M. Laver (2005) *Party Policy in Modern Democracies*. New York: Routledge.

BEPA (2005) *What Kind of European Social Model*, background paper by M. Canoy, P.M. Smith and T. Belessiotis. Brussels: European Commission Bureau of European Policy Advisers.

Berglund, S. J. Ekman and F. Aarebrot (eds) (2004) *The Handbook of Political Change in Eastern Europe*. 2nd edn. Cheltenham: Edward Elgar.

Besozzi, C. (2004) 'Illegal Markets and Organised crime in Switzerland: A Critical Assessment', in C. Fijnaut and L. Paoli (eds), *Organised Crime in Europe: Concepts, Patterns and Policies in the European Union and Beyond*. Dordrecht: Springer, pp. 499–535.

Betz, H.-G. (1994) *Radical Right-Wing Populism in Western Europe*. Basingstoke: Palgrave Macmillan.

Bevir, M. and R.A.W. Rhodes (2003) *Interpreting British Governance*. London: Routledge.

Beyme, K. von (1996) 'Party Leadership and Change in Party Systems: Towards a Postmodern Party State', *Government and Opposition*, 31/2, pp. 135–59.

Bhatt, C. (2000) '*Dharmo Rakshati Rakshitah*: Hindutva Movements in the UK', *Ethnic and Racial Studies*, 23(3), pp. 559–93.

Biezen, I. van and P. Kopecký (2006) 'The State and the Parties: Public Funding, Public Regulation and Party Patronage in Contemporary Democracies', *Party Politics*, forthcoming.

Biezen, I. van (2003) *Political Parties in New Democracies: Party Organization in Southern and East-Central Europe*. Basingstoke: Palgrave Macmillan.

Biezen, I. van (2004) 'Political Parties as Public Utilities', *Party Politics*, 10/6; pp. 701–22.

Biezen, I. van and J. Hopkin (2005) 'The Presidentialization of Spanish Democracy: Sources of Prime Ministerial Power in Post-Franco Spain', in T. Poguntke and P. Webb (eds), *The Presidentialization of Politics: A Comparative Study of Modern Democracies*. Oxford: Oxford University Press, pp. 105–27.

Biswas, B. (2004) 'Nationalism by Proxy: A Comparison of Social Movements among Diaspora Sikhs and Hindus', *Nationalism and Ethnic Politics*, 10(2), pp. 269–95.

Block, A. and W. Chambliss. (1981) *Organizing Crime*. New York: Elsevier.

Blondel, J. and M. Cotta (1996) 'Introduction', in J. Blondel and M. Cotta (eds), *Party and Government: An Inquiry into the Relationship between Governments and Supporting Parties in Liberal Democracies*. Basingstoke: Palgrave Macmillan.

Blondel, J. and M. Cotta (eds) (2000) *The Nature of Party Government: A Comparative European Perspective*. Basingstoke: Palgrave Macmillan.

Blondel, J. and F. Müller-Rommel (eds) (1997) *Cabinets in Western Europe*. Basingstoke: Palgrave Macmillan, 2nd edn.

Blondel, J. and F. Müller-Rommel (eds) (2001) *Cabinets in Eastern Europe*. Basingstoke: Palgrave Macmillan.

Blondel, J. and F. Müller-Rommel (eds) (1993) *Governing Together: The Extent and Limits of Joint Decision-Making in Western European Cabinets*. Basingstoke: Palgrave Macmillan.

Blondel, J. and Thiebault, J.-L. (eds) (1991) *The Profession of Government Minister in Western Europe*. London: Palgrave Macmillan.

Bobbio, N. (1996) *Left and Right: The Significance of a Political Distinction*. Cambridge: Polity Press.

Boer, M. den (ed.) (2002) *Organised Crime. A Catalyst in the Europeanisation of National Police and Prosecution Agencies*. Maastricht: European Institute of Public Administration.

Börzel, T.A. (2003) *Environmental Leaders and Laggards in the European Union. Why There is (Not) a Southern Problem*. London: Ashgate.

Börzel, T.A. (2005) 'Europeanization: How the European Union Interacts with its Member States', in S. Bulmer and C. Lequesne (eds), *The Member States of the European Union*. Oxford: Oxford University Press, pp. 45–69.

Bovenkerk, F. and Y. Yeşilgöz (2004) 'The Turkish Mafia and the State', in C. Fijnaut and L. Paoli (eds), *Organised Crime in Europe: Concepts, Patterns and Policies in the European Union and Beyond*. Dordrecht: Springer, pp. 585–601.

Boyle, K. and Sheen, J. (eds) (1997) *Freedom of Religion and Belief: A World Report*. London: Routledge.

Braml, J. (2004) 'Vom Rechtsstaat zum Sicherheitsstaat? Die Einschränkung persönlicher Freiheitsrechte durch die Bush-Administration', *Aus Politik und Zeitgeschichte*, B 3–4, pp. 6–15.

Brochmann, G. and T. Hammar (1999) *Mechanisms of Immigration Control*. Berg.

Broughton, D. and H.M. ten Napel (2000) *Religion and Mass Electoral Behaviour in Europe*. London: Routledge.

Budge, I., H-D. Klingemann, A. Volkens, and J. Bara (2001) *Mapping Policy Preferences: Estimates for Parties, Electors and Governments 1945–1998*. Oxford: Oxford University Press.

Bull, M.J and J. Newell (eds) (2003) *Corruption in Contemporary Politics*. London: Palgrave Macmillan.

Bulmer, S. and Lequesne, C. (eds) (2005) *The Member States of the European Union*. Oxford: Oxford University Press.

Burch, M. and I. Holliday (2004) 'The Blair Government and the Core Executive', *Government and Opposition*, 39(1), pp. 1–21.

Byrne, R., G. Noll and J. Vedsted-Hansen (eds) (2002) *New Asylum Countries?: Migration Control and Refugee Protection in an Enlarged European Union*. The Hague, London: Kluwer Law International.

Byrska, M. (2004) 'The Unfinished Enlargement', Report on Free movement of people in EU-25, May. Brussels: European Citizen Action Service.

Calise, M. (2005) 'Presidentialization, Italian Style', in T. Poguntke and P. Webb (eds) *The Presidentialization of Politics: A Comparative Study of Modern Democracies*. Oxford: Oxford University Press, pp. 88–106.

Cameron, D.R. (1978) 'The Expansion of the Public Economy: A Comparative Analysis'. *American Political Science Review* 72(4), pp. 1243–61.

Camus, J.-Y. (1999) *Extremism in Europe: 1998 Survey*. Paris: éditions de l'aube/CERA.

Canovan, M. (1999) 'Trust the People! Populism and the Two Faces of Democracy', *Political Studies*, 47(1), pp. 2–16.

Caplan, R. (2004) 'International Authority and State Building: the Case of Bosnia and Herzegovina', *Global Governance*, 10(1), pp. 53–65.

Caplan, R. (2005) *International Governance of War-torn Territories: Rule and Reconstruction*. Oxford: Oxford University Press.

Capoccia, G. (2002) 'Anti-System Parties. A Conceptual Reassessment', *Journal of Theoretical Politics*, 14(1), pp. 9–35.

Caporaso, J.A. and J. Jupille. (2001) 'The Europeanization of Gender Equality Policy and Domestic Structural Change', in M.G. Cowles, J.A. Caporaso and T. Risse (eds), *Transforming Europe: Europeanization and Domestic Change*. Ithaca. NY: Cornell University Press, pp. 21–43.

Carmani, D. (2003) 'State Administration and Regional Construction in Central Europe: A Comparative-Historical Perspective', in Michael Keating and James Hughes (eds), *The Regional Challenge in Central and Eastern Europe: Territorial Restructuring and European Integration*. Brussels: Presses interuniversitaires européenes/Peter Lang.

Cartier-Bresson, J. (2000) 'The Economics of Corruption' *OECD Observer* http://www.oecdobserver.org/news/fullstory.php/aid/239/Economics_of_corruption.html

Casanova, J. (1994) *Public Religions in the Modern World*. Chicago: University of Chicago Press.

Cassese, S. (2000) 'The Prime Minister's "Staff": The Case of Italy', in B.G. Peters *et al.* (eds) *Administering the Summit: Administration of the Core Executive in Developed Countries.* Basingstoke: Palgrave Macmillan, pp. 101–09.

Castles, F.G. and R. Wildenmann (eds) (1986) *The Future of Party Government, Volume 1: Visions and Realities of Party Government.* Berlin: de Gruyter.

Castles, F.G. (2004) *The Future of the Welfare State: Crisis Myths and Crisis Realities.* Oxford: Oxford University Press.

Castles, F.G. and D. Mitchell (1993) 'Worlds of Welfare and Families of Nations', in F.G. Castles (ed.) *Families of Nations.* Aldershot: Dartmouth, pp. 93–128.

Catanzaro, R. (1992) *Men of Respect: A Social History of the Sicilian Mafia.* New York: Free Press.

Cheibub, J.A. (1998) 'Elections and Alternation in Power in Democratic Regimes', paper presented at the Annual Meeting of the American Political Science Association. Boston, MA, 3–6 September 1998.

Christiansen, U. (2002) 'Migration from the Central and Eastern Europeans (CEE) into the 15 Countries of the EU: Status, Trends and Models.' Online working paper. http://www2.ihh.hj.se/ersasise2002/papers/Christiansen.pdf.

Citi, M. and M. Rhodes (2006) 'New Modes of Governance in the EU: Efficacy versus Experimentation in Policy-Making', in M. Pollack, B. Rosamond and K.E. Jorgensen (eds), *The Handbook of European Union Politics.* Sage Publications, 2006.

Clasen, J. (2005) *Reforming European Welfare States: Germany and the United Kingdom Compared.* Oxford: Oxford University Press.

Cohen, S. (1972) *Folk Devils and Moral Panics: The Creation of the Mods and Rockers.* London: MacGibbon & Kee/St Martin's Press.

Conant, L.J. (2001) 'Europeanization and the Courts: Variable Patterns of Adaptation among National Judiciaries', in M.G. Cowles, J.A. Caporaso and T. Risse (eds), *Transforming Europe. Europeanization and Domestic Change.* Ithaca, NY: Cornell, pp. 97–115.

Council of Europe (2001) *Recommendation of the Committee of Ministers to Member States concerning Guiding Principles on the Fight against Organised Crime* – Rec (2001) 11.

Council of Europe (2003a) *Best Practice Survey No. 5: Cross Border Cooperation in the Combating of Organised Crime.* Strasbourg: Council of Europe, January.

Council of Europe (2003b) *Best Practice Survey No. 9: Preventive Legal Measures against Organised Crime.* Strasbourg: Council of Europe, June.

Council of Europe (2003c) *Best Practice Survey No. 8: Cooperation against Trafficking in Human Beings.* Strasbourg: Council of Europe, September.

Council of the European Union (2003) Council Regulation EC No 343/2003 of 18 February 2003 establishing the criteria and mechanisms for determining the Member State responsible for examining an asylum application lodged in one of the Member States by a third-country national OJ L 50/1, 25.3.

Council of the European Union. (2004) 'Draft multiannual programme: 'The Hague Programme; strengthening freedom, security and justice in the European Union,' Brussels, 27 October, 13993/04.

Cowles, M.G. and T. Risse (2001) 'Transforming Europe: Conclusions.' In M.G. Cowles, J.A. Caporaso and T. Risse (eds), *Transforming Europe. Europeanization and Domestic Change.* Ithaca, NY: Cornell University Press, pp. 217–38.

Cowles, M.G., J.A. Caporaso and T. Risse (eds) (2001) *Transforming Europe. Europeanization and Domestic Change.* Ithaca, NY: Cornell University Press.

Crepaz, M.M.L. (1994) 'From Semi-sovereignty to Sovereignty: The Decline of Corporatism and the Rise of Parliament in Austria', *Comparative Politics,* 27(1), pp. 45–65.

Crouch, C. (1993) *Industrial Relations and European State Traditions.* Oxford: Oxford University Press.

Crouch, C. (1999) *Social Change in Western Europe.* Oxford: Oxford University Press.

Crouch, C. (2000) 'The Snakes and Ladders of Twenty-First-Century Trade Unionism', *Oxford Review of Economic Policy,* 16(1), pp. 70–84.

Crouch, C. and W. Streeck (eds) (1997) *Political Economy of Modern Capitalism: The Future of Capitalist Diversity.* London: Sage.

Czech Statistical Office (2003) *Foreigners in the Czech Republic.* Scientia: Prague.

Daalder, H. (1992) 'A Crisis of Party?', *Scandinavian Political Studies* 15(4), pp. 269–87.

Dahl, R.A. (2000) 'A Democratic Paradox?', *Political Science Quarterly,* 115(1), pp. 35–40.

Dalton, R.J. and S. Weldon (2005) 'Public Images of Political Parties: A Necessary Evil?' *West European Politics* 28(5).

Dalton, R.J. (2002) *Citizen Politics: Public Opinion and Political Parties in Advanced Industrial Democracies.* 3rd edn. Chatham, NJ: Chatham House.

Dalton, R.J. (2004) *Democratic Challenges, Democratic Choices: The Erosion of Political Support in Advanced Industrial Democracies.* Oxford: Oxford University Press.

Dalton, R.J. and M.P. Wattenberg (eds) (2000) *Parties without Partisans: Political Change in Advanced Industrial Democracies.* Oxford: Oxford University Press.

de Schoutheete, P. (1980) *La Coopération Politique Européenne.* Brussels; Editions Labor.

De Vreese, C.H. and H.G. Boomgaarden (2005) 'Projecting EU Referendums: Fear of Immigration and Support for European Integration', *European Union Politics,* 6(1), pp. 59–82

Della Porta, D. (2000) 'Social Capital, Beliefs in Government, and Political Corruption', in S.J. Pharr and R. Putnam (ed.), *Disaffected Democracies.* Princeton: Princeton University Press.

Della Porta, D. and A. Vannuci (1999) *Corrupt exchanges. Actors, Resources, and Mechanisms of Political Corruption.* New York: Aldine de Gruyter.

Denis, C., K. McMorrow, W. Roger and R. Veugelers (2005) 'The Lisbon Strategy and the EU's Structural Productivity Problem', European Commission: DG Economic and Financial Affairs, Economic Paper no. 221, February. http://europa.eu.int/comm/economy_finance/index_en.htm

Deutsch, K. (1966) *Nationalism and Social Communication. An Inquiry into the Foundations of Nationality*, 2nd edn. Cambridge, Mass.: MIT Press.

Dimitrov, V., K. H. Goetz and H. Wollmann (2006) *Governing after Communism: Institutions and Policymaking*. Lanham: Rowman & Littlefield.

Dimitrova, A. (2005) 'Europeanization and Civil Service Reform in Central and Eastern Europe', in F. Schimmelfenning and U. Sedelmeier (eds), *The Europeanization of Central and Eastern Europe*. Ithaca: Cornell University Press, pp. 71–90.

Dimitrova, A. (ed.) (2004) *Driven to Change: The European Union's Enlargement Viewed from the East*. Manchester: Manchester University Press.

Dinan, D. (2004) *Europe Recast: A History of European Union*. Basingstoke: Palgrave Macmillan.

Dogan, M. (2001) 'Trust-Mistrust in European Democracies', Sociologie Româneasc_ New Series 1:4 http://www.sociologieromaneasca.ro/2001/articole/sr2001.1–4.a01.pdf

Döring, H. and M. Hallerberg (eds) (2004) *Patterns of Parliamentary Behavior: Passage of Legislation Across Western Europe*. Aldershot: Ashgate.

Drbohlav, D. (2004) *The Czech Republic: The Times They Are A-Changin*. Vienna: International Organization for Migration.

Dubbins, S. (2002) *Towards Euro-Corporatism? A Study of Relations between Trade Unions and Employers' Organisations at the European Sectoral Level*. Unpublished PhD thesis. Florence: European University Institute.

Duchêne, F. (1973) 'The European Community and the uncertainties of interdependence', in M. Kohnstamm and W. Hager (eds), *A Nation Writ Large? Foreign-Policy Problems before the European Community*. London: Macmillan.

Duke, S. (2000) *The Elusive Quest for European Security: From EDC to CFSP*. New York: St Martin's Press.

Dunn, E. (1999) 'Audit, Corruption, and the Problem of Personhood: Scenes From Postsocialist Poland'. Berlin: Lecture in the Wissenchaftskolleg.

Durkheim, E. (1964) *The Division of Labour in Society*. New York: Free Press.

Dutertre, G. (2003) *Key Case-Law Extracts European Court of Human Rights*. Strasbourg: Council of Europe.

Duverger, M. (1954) *Political Parties: Their Organization and Activities in the Modern State*. London: Methuen.

Duverger, M. (1980) 'A New Political System Model: Semi-Presidential Government', *European Journal of Political Research*, 8, pp. 165–87.

Duyne, P. van (1997) 'Organized Crime, Corruption, and Power', *Crime, Law, and Social Change* 26, pp. 201–38.

Dworkin, R. (1977) *Taking Rights Seriously*. Cambridge, Mass.: Harvard University Press.

Dworkin, R. (2004) 'Secular Papacy', in R. Badinter and S. Breyer (eds) *Judges in Contemporary Democracy: An International Conversation*. New York: New York University Press.

Dyson, K. and K. Featherstone (1999) *The Road to Maastricht. Negotiating Economic and Monetary Union*. Oxford: Oxford University Press.

Easton, D. (1965) *A Framework for Political Analysis*. Englewood Cliffs, NJ: Prentice-Hall.

Eatwell, R. and C. Mudde (eds) (2004) *Western Democracies and the New Extreme Right Challenge*. London: Routledge.

EEAG (2005) *Report on the European Economy 2005*. Munich: Ifo Institute for Economic Research.

Eising, R. (2003) 'Interest Groups in the European Union', in M. Cini (ed.), *European Union Politics*. Oxford: Oxford University Press, pp. 192–207.

Ekengren, M. and B. Sundelius (1998) 'Sweden: The State Joins the European Union', in K. Hanf and B. Soetendorp (eds), *Adapting to European Integration*. London: Longman.

Elgie, R. (1999) 'The Politics of Semi-Presidentialism', in idem (ed.) *Semi-Presidentialism in Europe*. Oxford: Oxford University Press, pp. 1–21.

Elgie, R. (2001) '"Cohabitation": Divided Government French-Style', in idem (ed.) *Divided Government in Comparative Perspective*. Oxford: Oxford University Press, pp. 106–26.

Enyedi, Z., and G. Tóka (forthcoming). 'Ascendant Yet Fragile: Political Parties in Hungary', in S.L. White, D. Stansfield and P. Webb (eds) *Political Parties in Transitional Democracies*. Oxford: Oxford University Press.

Epstein, R.A. (2005) 'NATO Enlargement and the Spread of Democracy: Evidence and Expectations,' *Security Studies*, 14(1), pp. 59–98.

Esping-Andersen, G. (1990) *The Three Worlds of Welfare Capitalism*. Cambridge: Polity Press.

Esping-Andersen, G. (1999) *Social Foundations of Post-industrial Economies*. Oxford, Oxford University Press.

Esping-Andersen, G. and M. Regini (eds) (2000) *Why Deregulate Labour Markets?* Oxford: Oxford University Press.

Esping-Andersen, G., D. Gallie, A. Hemerijck and J. Myles (2002) *Why We Need a New Welfare State*. Oxford: Oxford University Press.

European Commission, Enterprise Directorate-General (2003) *2003 European Innovation Scoreboard: Technical Paper No. 2, Analysis of National Performances*. Brussels: European Commission.

European Commission (2003) Communication from the Commission on immigration, integration and employment, COM (2003) 336 final, Brussels, 3.6.2003

European Commission (2004) *Industrial Relations in Europe 2004*. Brussels: European Commission.

European Council (2003) *A Secure Europe in a Better World: European Security Strategy*. Brussels, December.

European Union Council (1997) 'Action Plan to Combat Organized Crime' adopted by the Council on 28 April 1997, *Official Journal of the European Communities*, 15.8.1997, C 251, pp. 1–16.

European Union Council (1998) 'Joint Action of 21 December 1998 adopted by the Council on the basis of Article K.3 of the Treaty on European Union, on making it a criminal offence to participate in criminal organisation in the Member States of the European Union', *Official Journal of the European Communities*, 29.12.1998, L 351, pp. 1–3.

Europol (2003) *2003 European Union Organised Crime Report*. Luxembourg: Office for the Official Publications of the European Communities.

Evans, C. (2001) *Freedom of Religion under the European Convention of Human Rights*. Oxford: Oxford University Press.

Evans, J.A.J. (2004) *Voters and Voting: An Introduction*. London: Sage.

Everson, M. (2000) 'Beyond the *Bundesverfassungsgericht*: on the necessary cunning of constitutional reasoning', in Z. Bankowski and A. Scott (eds), *The European Union and its Order: The Legal Theory of European Integration*. Oxford: Blackwell, pp. 99–112.

Falkner, G., O. Treib, M. Hartlapp and S. Leiber (2005) *Complying with Europe: EU Harmonization and Soft Law in the Member States*. Cambridge: Cambridge University Press.

Featherstone, K. (1998) 'Europeanization and the Centre Periphery: The Case of Greece in the 1990s'. *South European Society and Politics*, 3(1), pp. 23–39.

Featherstone, K. and C. Radaelli (eds) (2003) *The Politics of Europeanization*. Oxford: Oxford University Press.

Feldmann, M. (2006), 'The Origins of Varieties of Capitalism: Lessons from Post-Socialist Transition in Estonia and Slovenia', in B. Hancké, M. Rhodes and M. Thatcher (eds), *Beyond Varieties of Capitalism: Conflict, Contradiction and Complementarities in the European Economy*. Oxford: Oxford University Press, 2006.

Fenwick, H. (2002) 'Responding to 11 September: Detention Without Trial under the Anti-Terrorism, Crime and Security Act 2001', in L. Freedman (ed.), *Superterrorism: Policy Responses*. Oxford: Blackwell, pp. 80–104.

Ferrari, S. (1999) 'The new wine and the old cask: tolerance, religion, and the law in contemporary Europe' pp. 1–15 in Sajo, A. and Avineri, S. (eds), *The Law of Religious Identity: Models for Post-Communism*. The Hague: Kluwer Law International.

Ferrera, M. (1996) 'The Southern Model of Welfare in Social Europe', *Journal of European Social Policy*, 6(1), pp. 17–37.

Ferrera, M. and A. Hemerijck (2003) 'Recalibrating Europe's Welfare Regimes', in J. Zeitlin and D.M. Trubek (eds), *Governing Work and Welfare in the New Economy. European and American Experiments*. Oxford: Oxford University Press.

Ferrera, M., A. Hemerijck and M. Rhodes (2000) *The Future of Social Europe: Recasting Work and Welfare in the New Economy*. Lisbon: CELTA/Ministério do Trabalho e da Solidariedade.

Ferrera, M., A. Hemerijck and M. Rhodes (2001) 'The Future of the European Social Model in the Global Economy', *Journal of Comparative Policy Analysis*, 3(2), pp. 163–90.

Fieschi, C. and P.M. Heywood (2004) 'Trust, cynicism and populist anti-politics', *Journal of Political Ideologies*, 9(3), pp. 289–309.

Fijnaut, C. and L. Paoli (2004a) 'Introduction to Part III: The Initiatives of the European Union and the Council of Europe', in C. Fijnaut and L. Paoli (eds), *Organised Crime in Europe: Concepts, Patterns and Policies in the European Union and Beyond*. Dordrecht: Springer, pp. 625–40.

Fijnaut, C. and L. Paoli (eds) (2004b) *Organised Crime in Europe: Concepts, Patterns and Policies in the European Union and Beyond*. Dordrecht: Springer.

Fijnaut, C., F. Bovenkerk, G. Bruinsma and H. van de Bunt (1998) *Organized Crime in the Netherlands*. The Hague: Kluwer Law International.

Financial Times (1998) 'Fund Management Guru Reveals Doubts' (8 December).

Flemming, L. (2003) 'Das gescheiterte NPD-Verbotsverfahren – Wie aus dem "Aufstand der Anständigen" der "Aufstand der Unfähigen" wurde', in U. Backes and E. Jesse (eds), *Jahrbuch Extremismus & Demokratie*, vol. 15. Baden-Baden: Nomos, pp. 159–76.

Flinders, M. (2005) 'Majoritarian Democracy in Britain: New Labour and the Constitution', *West European Politics*, 28(1), pp. 61–93.

Flora, P., S. Kuhnle and D. Urwin (1999) *State Formation Nation-Building and Mass Politics in Europe: The Theory of Stein Rokkan*. Oxford: Oxford University Press.

Foley, M. (2000) *The British Presidency: Tony Blair and the Politics of Public Leadership*. Manchester: Manchester University Press.

Forum (1993/94) 'The Evolving Role of the Presidency in Eastern Europe' *East European Constitutional Review*, 2(1), pp. 36–106.

Fowler, B. (2002) 'Fuzzing Citizenship, Nationalising Political Space: A Framework for Interpreting the Hungarian "Status Law" as a New Form of Kin-State Policy in Central and Eastern Europe'. ESRC One Europe or Several? Programme Working Paper 40/02, January.

Fox, A. (1966) *Industrial Sociology and Industrial Relations*, Research Paper 3, Royal Commission on Trade Unions and Employers' Associations. London: HMSO.

Franklin, M.N. (2004) *The Dynamics of Voter Turnout in Established Democracies Since 1945*. New York: Cambridge University Press.

Fredman, S. (2002) *Discrimination Law*. Oxford: Clarendon.

Freeland, C. (2000) *Sale of the Century*. London: Little, Brown & Company.

Freeman, G. (2006) 'National Models, Policy Types, and the Politics of Immigration in Liberal Democracies,' *West European Politics* (forthcoming).

Frieden, J., D. Gros, and E. Jones (eds) (1998) *The New Political Economy of EMU*. Lanham: Rowman & Littlefield, pp. 13–52.

Fultz, E. and Ruck, M. (2001) 'Pension Reform in Central and Eastern

Europe: Emerging Issues and Patterns,' *International Labour Review*, 140(1), pp. 19–43.

Gabel, M.J. (2000) 'European Integration, Voters and National Politics'. *West European Politics, Special Issue*, 23(4), pp. 52–72.

Gallagher, M., M. Laver and P. Mair (2005) *Representative Government in Modern Europe*. 4th edn. Boston: McGraw-Hill.

Gambetta, D. (1993) *The Sicilian Mafia. The Business of Private Protection*. Cambridge: Harvard University Press.

Geddes, A. (2000) *Immigration and European Integration: Towards Fortress Europe?* Manchester: Manchester University Press.

Geddes, A. (2003) *The Politics of Migration and Immigration in Europe*. London: Sage.

Genschel, P. (2004) 'Globalization and the Welfare State: A Retrospective', *Journal of European Public Policy*, 11(4), pp. 613–26.

Gerring, J. and S.C. Thacker (2004) 'Political Institutions and Corruption: the role of Unitarism and Parliamentarism', *British Journal of Political Science*, 34(2).

Gheciu, A. (2005) *NATO in the 'New Europe': The Politics of International Socialization After the Cold War*. Stanford, CA: Stanford University Press.

Ginsberg, R.H. (1989) *Foreign Policy Actions of the European Community. The Politics of Scale*. Boulder/London: Lynne Rienner Publishers/ Adamantine Press Ltd.

Ginson, G.L., G.A. Caldeira and V.A. Baird (1998) 'On the Legitimacy of National High Courts', *American Political Science Review*, vol. 92 (June), 1998, pp. 343–58.

Glyn, A. and S. Wood (2001) 'New Labour's Economic Policy', in A. Glyn (ed.), *Social Democracy in Neoliberal Times. The Left and Economic Policy since 1980*. Oxford: Oxford University Press, pp. 200–22.

Goetz, K.H. (2001) 'Making Sense of Post-Communist Central Administration: Modernization, Europeanization or Latinization?', *Journal of European Public Policy*, 8(6), pp. 1032–51.

Goetz, K.H. (2003a) 'Executives in Comparative Context', in J. Hayward and A. Menon (eds) *Governing Europe*. Oxford: Oxford University Press, pp. 74–91.

Goetz, K.H. (2003b) 'Government at the Centre', in S. Padgett *et al.* (eds) *Developments in German Politics 3*. Basingstoke: Palgrave Macmillan, pp. 17–37.

Goetz, K.H. (2005) 'German Officials and the Federal Policy Process: The Decline of Sectional Leadership', in E. C. Page (ed.) *From the Active to the Enabling State*. Basingstoke: Palgrave Macmillan.

Goetz, K.H. and H. Wollmann (2001) 'Governmentalizing Central Executives in Post-Communist Europe: A Four-Country Comparison', *Journal of European Public Policy*, 8(6), pp. 864–87.

Goetz, K.H. and R. Zubek (2005) *Law-Making in Poland: Rules and Patterns of Legislation*. Manuscript.

Goetz, K.H. (2005) 'The New Member States and the EU: Responding to

Europe', in S. Bulmer and C. Lequesne (eds), *The Member States of the European Union*. Oxford: Oxford University Press, pp. 254–84.

Goldberg, K. (ed.) (2005) *The Torture Debate in America*. Cambridge: Cambridge University Press.

Gomez, R. and J. Peterson (2001) 'The EU's Impossibly Busy Foreign Ministers: "No One is in Control"', *European Foreign Affairs Review*, 6(1), pp. 53–74.

Gómez-Céspedes, A. and P. Stangeland (2004) 'Spain: The Flourishing Illegal Drug Haven in Europe', in C. Fijnaut and L. Paoli (eds), *Organised Crime in Europe: Concepts, Patterns and Policies in the European Union and Beyond*. Dordrecht: Springer, pp. 387–411.

Górny A. and P. Ruspini (eds) (2004) *Migration in the new Europe: East-West Revisited*. Basingstoke; New York: Palgrave Macmillan.

Goul Andersen, J. (2000) 'Welfare Crisis and Beyond: Danish Welfare Policies in the 1980s and 1990s', in S. Kuhnle (ed.), *Survival of the European Welfare State*. London, Routledge.

Grabbe, H. (2003) 'Europeanization Goes East: Power and Uncertainty in the EU Accession Process', in K. Featherstone and C. Radaelli (eds), *The Politics of Europeanization*. Oxford: Oxford University Press, pp. 303–27.

Greenwood, J. and M. Aspinwall (eds) (1998) *Collective Action in the European Union: Interests and the New Politics of Associability*. London: Routledge.

Grémion, P. (1976) *Le pouvoir périphérique. Bureaucrates et notables dans le système politique français*. Paris: Seuil.

Grout, P.A., A. Jenkins, and A. Zalewska (2001) 'Privatisation of Utilities and the Asset Value Problem', *CMPO Working Paper series No.01/41*. University of Bristol. http://www.bris.ac.uk/Depts/CMPO/workingpapers/wp41.pdf.

Guarnieri, C. and P. Pederzoli (2002) *The Power of Judges: A Comparative Study of Courts and Democracy*, ed. C.A. Thomas. Oxford: Oxford University Press.

Guillén, A., S. Álvarez and P. Adão e Silva (2003) 'Redesigning the Spanish and Portuguese Welfare States: The Impact of Accession into the European Union', *South European Society and Politics*, 8(1–2), pp. 231–68.

Guiraudon, V. and C. Joppke (2001) *Controlling a New Migration World*. London: Routledge.

Gunther, R., J.R. Montero, and J.J. Linz (eds) (2002) *Political Parties: Old Concepts and New Challenges*. Oxford: Oxford University Press.

Gupta, S., H. Davoodi, and R. Alonso-Terme (1998) 'Does Corruption Affect Income Inequality and Poverty?' *IMF Working Paper No. 76*. Washington D.C.: International Monetary Fund.

Habermas, J. (2004) 'Religious Tolerance – the Pacemaker for Cultural Rights', *Philosophy*, 79, pp. 5–18.

Hagan, F. (1983) 'The Organized Crime Continuum: A Further Specification of a New Conceptual Model', *Criminal Justice Review* 8 (spring), pp. 52–7.

Haggard, S., M.A. Levy, A. Moravcsik and K. Nicolaidis (1993) 'Integrating the Two Halves of Europe: Theories of Interests, Bargaining, and Institutions', in R.O. Keohane, J.S.J. Nye and S. Hoffmann (eds), *After the Cold War: International Institutions and State Strategies in Europe, 1989–1991*. Cambridge, MA: Harvard University Press, pp. 173–95.

Hainsworth, P. (ed.) (2000) *The Politics of the Extreme Right: From the Margins to the Mainstream*. London: Pinter.

Hall, P.A. and D. Soskice (eds) (2001) *Varieties of Capitalism: The Institutional Foundations of Comparative Advantage*. Oxford: Oxford University Press.

Hall, P.A. and D.W. Gingerich (2004) 'Varieties of Capitalism and Institutional Complementarities in the Macroeconomy: An Empirical Analysis', Max Planck Institute for the Study of Societies, Discussion Paper 04/5.

Haller, M. (1990) 'Illegal Enterprise: A Theoretical and Historical Interpretation', *Criminology*, 28(2), pp. 207–35.

Halman, L. *et al.* (2003) 'European Values Survey 1999/2000 Integrated Data Set', ZA Study No. 3811. Cologne, Tilburg: Zentralarchiv für Empirische Sozialforschung and der Universität zu Köln, Faculty of Social and Behavioral Sciences at Tilburg University.

Hanf, K. and B. Soetendorp (1998) *Adapting to European Integration. Small States and the European Union*. Harlow: Addison Wesley Longman.

Haubrich, D. (2003) 'September 11, Anti-Terror Laws and Civil Liberties: Britain, France and Germany Compared', *Government & Opposition*, 38(1), pp. 3–28.

Haverland, M. (2000) 'National Adaptation to European Integration: The Importance of Institutional Veto Points', *Journal of Public Policy*, 20(1), pp. 83–103.

Hawkins, G. (1969) 'God and the Mafia', *Public Interest* 14 (winter), pp 24–51.

Hawley, S. (2000) 'Exporting Corruption: Privatisation, Multinationals and Bribery', *Cornerhouse Briefing 19*. London: Cornerhouse.

Heffernan, R. and P. Webb (2005) 'The British Prime Minister: Much More Than "First Among Equals"', in T. Poguntke and P. Webb (eds), *The Presidentialization of Politics: A Comparative Study of Modern Democracies*. Oxford: Oxford University Press, pp. 26–62.

Heidenheimer, A.J. (ed.) (1999) *Political Corruption: A Handbook*, 2nd edn. New Brunswick, NJ: Transaction.

Heidenheimer, A.J. and M. Johnston (eds) (2002) *Political Corruption. Concepts and Contexts*, 3rd edn. New Brunswick, NJ: Transaction.

Heinz, W.S. (2004) 'Internationale Terrorismusbekämpfung und Achtung der Menschenrechte', *Aus Politik und Zeitgeschichte*, B 3–4, pp. 32–40.

Helms, L. (2005) 'The Changing Parameters of Political Control in Western Europe', *Parliamentary Affairs*, 59(1), pp. 78–97.

Hemerijck, A. (2002) 'The Self-Transformation of the European Social Model(s)', in G. Esping-Andersen with D. Gallie, A. Hemerijck and J. Myles, *Why we Need a New Welfare State*. Oxford: Oxford University Press.

Hennessy, P. (2005) 'Rulers and Servants of the State: The Blair Style of Government 1997–2004', *Parliamentary Affairs*, 58(1), pp. 6–16.

Héritier, A., D. Kerwer, C. Knill, D. Lehmkuhl, M. Teutsch and A.-C. Douillet (2001) *Differential Europe. The European Union Impact on National Policymaking*. Lanham, MD: Rowman & Littlefield.

Hess, H. (1995) 'Parastato e capitalismo corsaro. La mafia siciliana dal 1943 al 1993', *Incontri meridionali* ½, pp. 41–71.

Hewitt, C. and T. Cheetham (2000) *Encyclopedia of Modern Separatist Movements*. Santa Barbara: ABC-CLIO.

Heywood, P. (2002) 'Executive Capacity and Legislative Limits', in P. Heywood, E. Jones and M. Rhodes (eds), *Developments in West European Politics 2*. London: Palgrave Macmillan.

Heywood, P. and I. Molina (2000) 'A Quasi-Presidential Premiership: Administering the Executive Summit in Spain', in B.G. Peters *et al.* (eds), *Administering the Summit: Administration of the Core Executive in Developed Countries*. Basingstoke: Palgrave Macmillan, pp. 110–33.

Heywood, P., V. Pujas and M. Rhodes (2002) 'Political Corruption, Democracy and Governance in Western Europe', in P. Heywood, E. Jones and M. Rhodes (eds), *Developments in West European Politics 2*. London: Palgrave, pp. 184–200.

Hill, C. (1990) 'European Foreign Policy: Power Bloc, Civilian Model – or Flop?', in R. Rummel (ed.), *The Evolution of an International Actor: Western Europe's New Assertiveness*. Boulder, Col.: Westview.

Hill, C. (1993) 'The Capability-Expectations Gap, or Conceptualizing Europe's International Role', *Journal of Common Market Studies*, 31(3).

Hill, C. (1996) *The Actors in Europe's Foreign Policy*. London: Routledge.

Hill, C. (1998) 'Convergence, divergence and dialectics: national foreign policies and the CFSP', in J. Zielonka (ed.), *Paradoxes of European Foreign Policy*. The Hague: Kluwer Law International.

Hill, C. and K.E. Smith (eds) (2000) *European Foreign Policy: Key Documents*. London: Routledge.

Hill, C. and M. Smith (eds) (2005) *International Relations and the European Union*. Oxford: Oxford University Press.

Hirschl, R. (2004) *Towards Juristocracy: The Origins and Consequences of the New Constitutionalism*. Cambridge, Mass., Harvard University Press.

Hobbs, D. (1994) 'Professional and Organized Crime in Britain' in M. Maguire, R. Morgan, and R. Reiner (eds), *The Oxford Handbook of Criminology*, 2nd edn. Oxford: Clarendon Press, pp. 441–68.

Hobbs, D. (2004) 'The Nature and Representation of Organised Crime in the United Kingdom', in C. Fijnaut and L. Paoli (eds), *Organised Crime in Europe: Concepts, Patterns and Policies in the European Union and Beyond*. Dordrecht: Springer, pp. 263–302.

Hobsbawm, E. (1994) *The Age of Extremes. The Short Twentieth Century 1914–1991*. London: Penguin.

Hocking, B. (2004) 'Diplomacy', in Walter Carlsnaes, Helen Sjursen and Brian White, (eds), *Contemporary European Foreign Policy*. London: Sage.

Home Office (2005) 'Accession Monitoring Report May 2004 – June 2005', August 2005, available at: http://www.workingintheuk.gov.uk/ind/en/home/0/reports/accession_monitoring.Maincontent.0015.file.tmp/Accession   per cent20Monitoring per cent20Report4.pdf

Hooghe, L. and G. Marks (2001) *Multi-level governance and European integration*. Lanham, MD: Rowman & Littlefield.

Hooghe, L. and M. Keating (1994) 'The Politics of European Union Regional Policy', *Journal of European Public Policy*, 1(3) (1994), pp. 53–79.

Hughes, J., G. Sasse and C. Gordon (2003) 'EU Enlargement, Europeanisation and the Dynamics of Regionalisation in CEE', in M. Keating and J. Hughes (eds), *The Regional Challenge in Central and Eastern Europe. Territorial Restructuring and European Integration*. Brussels: Presses interuniversitaires européenes/Peter Lang.

Hughes, J., G. Sasse and C. Gordon (2004) *Europeanization and Regionalization in the EU's Enlargement to Central and Eastern Europe*. London: Palgrave Macmillan.

Huntington, S. (1996) *The Clash of Civilizations and the Remaking of World Order*. New York: Simon & Schuster.

Hysi, V. (2004) 'Organised Crime in Albania: The Ugly Side of Capitalism and Democracy', in C. Fijnaut, and L. Paoli (eds), *Organised Crime in Europe: Concepts, Patterns and Policies in the European Union and Beyond*. Dordrecht: Springer, pp. 413–34.

Ignazi, P. (2003) *Extreme Right Parties in Western Europe*. Oxford: Oxford University Press.

Imig, D. and S. Tarrow (2000) 'Political Contention in a Europeanising Polity'. *West European Politics, Special Issue*, 23(4), pp. 73–93.

Innes, A. (2002) 'Party Competition in Postcommunist Europe: The Great Electoral Lottery'. *Comparative Politics*, 35(1), pp. 85–104.

Iversen, T. (1994) 'Political Leadership and Representation in West European Democracies: A Test of Three Models of Voting', *American Journal of Political Science* 38, pp. 45–74.

Iversen, T. and A. Wren (1998) 'Equality, Employment and Budgetary Restraint: the Trilemma of the Service Economy', *World Politics*, 50(4), pp. 507–46.

Jacobs, J. and L. Gouldin (1999) 'Cosa Nostra: The Final Chapter?', in M. Tonry (ed.), *Crime and Justice. A Review of Research*, Vol. 25. Chicago: University of Chicago Press, pp. 129–90.

Jacoby, W. (2004) *The Enlargement of the European Union and NATO. Ordering from the Menu in Central Europe*. Cambridge: Cambridge University Press.

Jileva, E. (2004) 'The Europeanisation of EU Visa Policy,' *Helsinki Monitor*, 15(1) March 2004, pp. 23–32.

Jones, E. (1998) 'Economic and Monetary Union: Playing with Money', in A. Moravcsik (ed.), *Centralization or Fragmentation? Europe Faces the Challenges of Deepening, Diversity, and Democracy*. New York: Council on Foreign Relations, pp. 59–93.

Jones, E. (2004) 'European Monetary Union and the Problem of Macroeconomic Governance', in R. Tiersky (ed.), *Europe Today*, 2nd edn. Lanham, MD: Rowman & Littlefield, pp. 59–87.

Jones, E. (2002) *The Politics of Economic and Monetary Union: Integration and Idiosyncrasy.* Lanham, MD: Rowman & Littlefield.

Jordan, A. and D. Liefferink (eds) (2004) *Environmental Policy in Europe. The Europeanization of National Environmental Policy.* London: Routledge.

Jowell, R. *et al.* (2004) 'European Social Survey 2002/2003: Technical Report and Data File, Version 5', archived and distributed by the Norwegian Social Science Data Services. London: Centre for Comparative Social Surveys, City University.

Jowell, R. *et al.* (2005) 'European Social Survey 2004/2005: Technical Report and Data File, Version 1', archived and distributed by the Norwegian Social Science Data Services. London: Centre for Comparative Social Surveys, City University.

Kaczurba, J. (2000) *Industries of the New Market Economies of Central and Eastern Europe in the Age of Globalization: Major Policy Options.* Vienna: United Nations Industrial Development Organization.

Karklins, R. (2005) *The System Made Me Do It: Corruption in Post-Communist Societies.* Armonk, NY: M.E. Sharpe.

Kassim, H., A. Menon, B.G. Peters and V. Wright (2000) *The National Co-ordination of EU Policy. The Domestic Level.* Oxford: Oxford University Press.

Katz, R.S. (1986) 'Party Government: A Rationalistic Conception', in F.G. Castles and R. Wildenmann (eds), *The Future of Party Government, Volume 1: Visions and Realities of Party Government.* Berlin: de Gruyter, pp. 31–71.

Katz, R.S. (1997) *Democracy and Elections.* Oxford: Oxford University Press.

Katz, R.S. (ed.) (1987) *The Future of Party Government, Volume 2: Party Governments: European and American Experiences.* Berlin: de Gruyter.

Katz, R.S. and P. Mair (1995) 'Changing Models of Party Organization and Party Democracy: The Emergence of the Cartel Party', *Party Politics*, 1(1), pp. 5–28.

Katz, R.S. and P. Mair (2002) 'The Ascendancy of the Party in Public Office: Party Organizational Change in Twentieth-Century Democracies', in R. Gunther *et al.* (eds), *Political Parties: Old Concepts and New Challenges.* Oxford: Oxford University Press, pp. 113–35.

Katzenstein, P. (1985) *Small States and World Markets.* Ithaca, NY: Cornell University Press.

Kaufmann, D. (1997) 'Corruption: The Facts', *Foreign Policy*, Summer 1997.

Kaufmann, D. (2004) 'Corruption Matters: Evidence-Based Challenge to Orthodoxy', *Journal of Development Policy and Practice* 1(1).

Kavakas, D. (2001) *Greece and Spain in European Foreign Policy: The Influence of Southern Member States in Common Foreign and Security Policy.* Aldershot: Ashgate.

Kearney, A.T. (2005) 'Measuring Globalization: The Top 20.' *Foreign Policy* (May/June) pp. 52–60.

Keating, M. (1988) *State and Regional Nationalism. Territorial Politics and the European State*. Brighton: Harvester-Wheatsheaf.

Keating, M. (1998) *The New Regionalism in Western Europe. Territorial Restructuring and Political Change*. Aldershot: Edward Elgar.

Keating, M. (2004b) 'European Integration and the Nationalities Question', *Politics and Society*, 31(1), pp. 367–88.

Keating, M. (ed.) (2004a) *Regions and Regionalism in Europe*. Cheltenham: Edward Elgar.

Keating, M. and J. Hughes (eds) (2003) *The Regional Challenge in Central and Eastern Europe. Territorial Restructuring and European Integration*. Brussels: Presses interuniversitaires européenes/Peter Lang.

Kelley, J.G. (2004) *Ethnic Politics in Europe. The Power of Norms and Incentives*. Princeton, NJ: Princeton University Press.

Kepel, G. (1994) *The Revenge of God: The Resurgence of Islam, Christianity and Judaism in the Modern World*. Cambridge: Polity Press.

Kepel, G. (1997) *Allah in the West: Islamic Movements in America and Europe*. Cambridge: Polity Press.

Kerner, H.-J. (1973) *Professionelles und Organisiertes Verbrechen. Versuch einer Bestandsaufnahme und Bericht über neuere Entwicklungstendenzen in der Bundesrepublik Deutschland und in den Niederlanden*. Wiesbaden: BKA.

Kerner, H.-J. and J. Mack. (1975) *The Crime Industry*. Lexington, Mass.: Lexington Books.

Keune, M. (2006) 'The European Social Model and Enlargement', in M. Jepsen and A. Serrano (eds), *Unwrapping the European Social Model*. Bristol: Policy Press.

Kielyte, J. (2002) 'Migration movement in the Baltic states: determinants and consequences', paper presented at the WIDER Conference on Poverty, International Migration and Asylum, Helsinki, 27–28 September 2002.

King, R., G. Lazaridis and C. Tsardanidis (2000) *Eldorado or Fortress? Migration in Southern Europe*. London: Palgrave Macmillan.

Kinzig, J. and A. Luczak (2004) 'Organised Crime in Germany: A *Passe-partout* Definition Encompassing Different Phenomena' in C. Fijnaut and L. Paoli (eds), *Organised Crime in Europe: Concepts, Patterns and Policies in the European Union and Beyond*. Dordrecht: Springer, pp. 333–55.

Kirchheimer, O. (1966) 'The Transformation of West European Party Systems', in J. LaPalombara and M. Weiner (eds), *Political Parties and Political Development*. Princeton: Princeton University Press, pp. 177–200.

Kitschelt, H. (1995) *The European Radical Right: A Comparative Analysis*. Ann Arbor: University of Michigan Press.

Kitschelt, H. (2000) 'Linkages between Citizens and Politicians in Democratic Polities', *Comparative Political Studies* 33(6–7), pp. 845–79.

Kitschelt, H. (2000)'Citizens, Politicians and Party Cartellization', *European Journal of Political Research*, 37 (2), pp. 149–172.

Kitschelt, H. (2001) 'Divergent Paths of Postcommunist Democracies', in L.

Diamond and R. Gunther (eds), *Political Parties and Democracy*. Baltimore: Johns Hopkins University Press, pp. 299–32.

Kitschelt, H., P. Lange, G. Marks and J. Stephens (eds) (1999) *Continuity and Change in Contemporary Capitalism*. New York: Cambridge University Press.

Kleemans, E. (2004) 'Crossing Borders: Organised Crime in the Netherlands', in C. Fijnaut and L. Paoli (eds), *Organised Crime in Europe: Concepts, Patterns and Policies in the European Union and Beyond*. Dordrecht: Springer, pp. 303–31.

Knill, C. and D. Lehmkuhl (1999) 'How Europe Matters. Different Mechanisms of Europeanization', *European Integration on-line Papers*, 3 Vol., No. (7), pp. http://eiop.or.at/eiop/texte/1999–007a.htm.

Knutsen, O. (1995) 'Party Choice', in J. W. van Deth and E. Scarbrough (eds) *The Impact of Values*, pp. 461–91. Oxford: Oxford University Press.

Knutsen, O. (2004) *Social Structure and Party Choice in Western Europe: A Comparative Longitudinal Study*. London: Palgrave Macmillan.

Konings, J. and J. P. Murphy (2004) 'Do Multinational Enterprises Relocate Employment to Low wage Regions? Evidence from European Multi-nationals', http://www.ecb.int/events/pdf/conferences/lmw/Konings.pdf.

Kopecky, P. (1995) 'Developing Party Organizations in East-Central Europe: What Type of Party is Likely to Emerge?', *Party Politics*, 1(4), pp. 515–34.

Korys, I. (2004) *Poland: Dilemmas of a Sending and a Receiving Country*. Vienna: International Organization for Migration.

Kraler, A. and K. Iglicka (2002) 'Labour Migration in Central and Eastern European countries', in F. Laczko, I. Stacher and A. Klekowski von Koppenfels (eds), *New Challenges for Migration Policy in Central and Eastern Europe*. The Hague: TMC Asser Press, pp. 27–44.

Krastev, I. (2004) *Shifting Obsessions*. Budapest: CEU Press.

Krenzler, H.G. and C. Pitschas (2001) 'Progress or Stagnation? The Common Commercial Policy After Nice', *European Foreign Affairs Review*, 6(3), pp. 291–313.

Kumm, M. (2005) 'The Jurisprudence of Constitutional Conflict: Constitutional Supremacy in Europe before and after the Constitutional Treaty', *European Law Journal*, 11(3), pp. 262–307.

La Porta, R., F. Lopez-de-Silanes, A. Shleifer and R.W. Vishny (1999) 'The Quality of Government', *Journal of Economics, Law and Organisation*, 15.

Ladrech, R. (2005) 'The Europeanization of Interest Groups and Political Parties', in S. Bulmer and C. Lequesne (eds), *The Member States of the European Union*. Oxford: Oxford University Press, pp. 317–37.

Laffan, B., R. O'Donnell and M. Smith (2000) *Europe's Experimental Union: rethinking integration*. London: Routledge.

Lalam, N. (2004) 'How Organised Is Organised Crime in France?', in C. Fijnaut and L. Paoli (eds), *Organised Crime in Europe: Concepts, Patterns and Policies in the European Union and Beyond*. Dordrecht: Springer, pp. 357–86.

Landfried, C. (1995) 'Germany', in C. N. Tate and T. Vallinder (eds), *The

Global Expansion of Judicial Power. New York: New York University Press.

Langewiesche, R. (2000) *EU Enlargement and the Free Movement of Labour*. Brussels: European Trade Union Confederation.

Lash, S. and J. Urry (1987) *The End of Organized Capitalism?* Oxford: Polity Press.

Lavenex, S. (2001) 'Migration and the EU's New Eastern Border: Between Realism and Liberalism', *Journal of European Public Policy*, 8(1), pp. 24–42.

Lavenex, S. and E.M. Uçarer (eds) (2002) *Migration and the externalities of European integration*. Lanham, MD.: Lexington Books.

Laver, M. and N. Schofield (eds) (1990) *Multiparty Government: The Politics of Coalition in Europe*. Oxford: Oxford University Press.

Laver, M., and N. Schofield (1998) *Multiparty Government: The Politics of Coalition in Europe*. Ann Arbor, MI: University of Michigan Press.

LeDuc, L., R. Niemi, and P. Norris (eds) (2002) *Comparing Democracies 2: New Challenges in the Study of Elections and Voting*. London: Sage.

Lee, J. M., G.W. Jones and J. Burnham (1998) *At the Centre of Whitehall: Advising the Prime Minister and Cabinet*. Basingstoke: Palgrave Macmillan.

Leston-Bandeira, C. and A. Freire (2003) 'Internalising the Lessons of Stable Democracy: The Portuguese Parliament', *Journal of Legislative Studies*, 9(2), pp. 56–84.

Levi, M. (2002) 'The Organisation of Serious Crimes', in M. Maguire, R. Morgan and R. Reiner (eds), *The Oxford Handbook of Criminology*. 3rd edn. Oxford: Oxford University Press, pp. 878–913.

Levi, M. (ed.) (1999) *Fraud: Organization, Motivation and Control*. Aldershot: Dartmouth.

Levi, M. and M. Maguire (2004) 'Reducing and Preventing Organised Crime: An Evidence-Based Critique'. *Crime Law and Social Change* 41(5), pp. 397–469.

Lewis, P. (2000) *Political Parties in Post-Communist Eastern Europe*. London: Routledge.

Liebert, U. (ed.) (2003) *Gendering Europeanisation*. Brussels: Peter Lang.

Liegl, B. and W.C. Müller (1999) 'Senior Officials in Austria', in E.C. Page and V. Wright (eds) *Bureaucratic Elites in Western European States: A Comparative Analysis of Top Officials in Eleven Countries*. Oxford: Oxford University Press, pp. 90–120.

Lijphart, A. (1969) 'Consociational Democracy', *World Politics*, 21(2), pp. 202–25.

Lijphart, A. (1997) 'Unequal Participation: Democracy's Unresolved Dilemma', *American Political Science Review*, 91 pp. 1–14.

Lijphart, A. (1999) *Patterns of Democracy: Government Forms and Performance in Thirty-Six Countries*. Yale: Yale University Press.

Lijphart, A. (ed.) (1992) *Parliamentary versus Presidential Government*. Oxford: Oxford University Press.

Linz, J.J. and A. Stepan (1996) *Problems of Democratic Transition and Consolidation*. Baltimore: Johns Hopkins University Press.

Lipset, S.M. and S. Rokkan (1967) 'Cleavage Structures, Party Systems and Voter Alignments: An Introduction', in S.M. Lipset and S. Rokkan (eds), *Party Systems and Voter Alignments: Cross National Perspectives*. New York: The Free Press, pp. 1–63.

Lovering, J. (1999) 'Theory Led by Policy: The Inadequacies of the 'New Regionalism' (Illustrated from the Case of Wales)', *International Journal of Urban and Regional Research*, 23(2), pp. 379–95.

Luther, K.R. and F. Müller-Rommel (eds) (2002) *Political Parties in the New Europe: Political and Analytical Challenges*. Oxford: Oxford University Press.

Madeley, J.T.S. (2003a) 'European Liberal Democracy and the Principle of State Religious Neutrality', in J.T.S. Madeley and Z. Enyedi (eds), *Church and State in Contemporary Europe: The Chimera of Neutrality*. London: Frank Cass, pp. 1–22.

Madeley, J.T.S. (2003b) 'A Framework for the Comparative Analysis of Church-State Relations in Europe', in J.T.S. Madeley and Z. Enyedi (eds), *Church and State in Contemporary Europe: The Chimera of Neutrality*. London: Frank Cass, pp. 23–50.

Madeley, J.T.S. and Z. Enyedi (eds) (2003) *Church and State in Contemporary Europe: The Chimera of Neutrality*. London: Frank Cass.

Maduro, M. (1998) *We the Court. The European Court of Justice and the European Economic Constitution: A Critical Reading of Article 30 of the EC Treaty*. Oxford: Hart.

Maher, I. (2004) 'Law and the Open Method of Coordination', *Zeitschrift für Staats- und Europawissenschaften*, 2(2), pp. 248–63.

Mainwaring, S. (1998) 'Party Systems in the Third Wave', *Journal of Democracy*, 9(3), pp. 67–81.

Mainwaring, S. and M. Torcal (2004) 'Volatility 1978–2003', Data set. Notre Dame, IN: The Helen Kellogg Center for International Studies, University of Notre Dame.

Mair, P. (1997) *Party System Change*. Oxford: Oxford University Press.

Mair, P. (1998) 'Representation and participation in the changing world of party politics.' *European Review*, 6(2), pp. 161–74.

Mair, P. (2000) 'The Limited Impact of Europe on National Party Systems'. *West European Politics, Special Issue*, 23(4), pp. 27–51.

Mair, P. (2005) 'Democracy Beyond Parties', paper presented at the Joint Sessions and Workshops of the European Consortium for Political Research, Granada, Spain, pp. 14–19, April 2005.

Mair, P. and I. van Biezen (2001) 'Party Membership in Twenty European Democracies, 1980–2000', *Party Politics*, 7(1), pp. 5–21.

Mair, P., W. Müller and F. Plasser (eds) (2004) *Political Parties and Electoral Change*. London: Sage.

Majone, G. (2005) *Dilemmas of European Integration: The Ambiguities and Pitfalls of Integration by Stealth*. Oxford: Oxford University Press.

Manners, I and R. Whitman (eds) (2000) *The Foreign Policies of European Union Member States*. Manchester: Manchester University Press.

March, J.G. and J.P. Olsen (1995) *Democratic Governance*. New York: The Free Press.

March, L. and C. Mudde (2005) 'What's Left of the Radical Left? The European Radical Left since 1989: Decline *and* Mutation', *Comparative European Politics*, 3(1), pp. 23–49.

Marty, M. and R. Appleby (1993) *Fundamentalisms and the State*. Chicago: University of Chicago Press.

Mathieson, D.J. and G.J. Shinasi (2001) *International Capital Markets: Developments, Prospects, and Key Policy Issues*. Washington, DC: IMF.

Maull, H.W. (2006) *Germany's Uncertain Power: Foreign Policy of the Berlin Republic*. London: Palgrave Macmillan.

Maurer, A. and W. Wessels (eds) (2001) *National Parliaments on their Ways to Europe: Losers or Latecomers?* Baden-Baden: Nomos.

Maurer, A., J. Mittag and W. Wessels (2003) 'National Systems' Adaptation to the EU System: Trends, Offers, and Constraints', in B. Kohler-Koch (ed.), *Linking EU and National Governance*. Oxford: Oxford University Press, pp. 53– 81.

Mény, Y. and Y. Surel (eds) (2002) *Democracies and the Populist Challenge*. Basingstoke: Palgrave Macmillan.

Merand, F. (2003) *Soldiers and Diplomats: The Institutionalization of European Defence Policy in France, Germany and the United Kingdom*, a doctoral dissertation. Berkeley, CA: University of California.

Merlingen, M., C. Mudde and U. Sedelmeier (2001) 'European Norms, Domestic Politics and the Sanctions against Austria', *Journal of Common Market Studies*, 39(1), pp. 59–77.

Meunier, S. (2005) *Trading Voices: The European Union in International Commercial Negotiations*. Princeton: Princeton University Press.

Meunier, S. and K. Nicolaidis (1999) 'Who Speaks for Europe? The Delegation of Trade Authority in the EU', *Journal of Common Market Studies*, 37(3), pp. 477–501.

Meyer-Sahling, J.-H. (2004) 'Civil Service Reform in Post-Communist Europe: The Bumpy Road to Depoliticisation', *West European Politics*, 27(1), pp. 71–103.

Migration News Sheet. Various issues. Brussels: Migration Policy Group.

Millard, F. (2004) *Elections, Parties, and Representation in Post-Communist Europe*. Basingstoke: Palgrave Macmillan.

Miller R.A. (2004) 'Lords of Democracy: The Judicialization of 'Pure Politics' in the United States and Germany', *Washington and Lee Law Review*, 61, 2004 (Spring), pp. 587–662.

Miller, W.L., A.B. Grødeland and T. Koshechkina (2001) *A Culture of Corruption: Coping with Government in Post-Communist Europe*. Budapest, New York: Central European University Press.

Millward, A.S. (1984) *The Reconstruction of Western Europe: 1945–51*. London: Routledge.

Molina Romo, O. (2004) *Understanding Policy Adjustment in Southern Europe: Political Exchange and Wage Bargaining Reform in Italy and Spain*. Unpublished PhD thesis. Florence: European University Institute.

Monar, J. (2001) 'EU Justice and Home Affairs in the Eastward Enlargement: The Challenge of Diversity and EU Instruments and Strategies', Discussion paper C91, Center for European Integration Studies, Univeristy of Bonn.

Monsma, S. and C. Soper (eds) (1997) *The Challenge of Pluralism; Church and State in Five Democracies*. Oxford: Rowman & Littlefield.

Montesquieu, M. (1766) *The Spirit of Laws. Volume I*, T. Nugent (trans.). London: J. Nourse and P. Vaillant.

Moravcsik, A. (1992) 'Arms and Autarky in Modern European History,' in R. Vernon and E.B. Kaptein (eds), *Defense and Dependence in a Global Economy*. Washington, DC: Congressional Quarterly Inc., pp. 23–45.

Moravcsik, A. (1993) 'Preferences and Power in the European Community: A Liberal Intergovernmental Approach', *Journal of Common Market Studies*, 31(4), pp. 473–522.

Moravcsik, A. (2000) 'The Origin of Human Rights Regimes', *International Organization*, 54(2), pp. 217–53.

Moreau, P., M. Lazar and G. Hirscher (eds) (1998) *Der Kommunismus in Westeuropa: Niedergang oder Mutation*. Landsberg: Olzog.

Moreno, L. (2000) 'The Spanish Developments of the Southern Welfare State', in S. Kuhnle (ed.), *Survival of the European Welfare State*. London: Routledge, pp. 146–65.

Moser, R.G. (2001) *Unexpected Outcomes: Electoral Systems, Political Parties and Representation in Russia*. Pittsburgh, PA: University of Pittsburgh Press.

Mudde, C. (2004) 'The Populist Zeitgeist', *Government and Opposition*, 39(3), pp. 541–63.

Mudde, C. (2006) *Populist Radical Right Parties in Contemporary Europe*. Cambridge: Cambridge University Press.

Mudde, C. (ed.) (2005) *Racist Extremism in Central and Eastern Europe*. London: Routledge.

Müller, K. (2002) 'Pension Reform Paths in Central-Eastern Europe and the Former Soviet Union', *Social Policy and Administration*, 36(2), pp. 725–48.

Müller, W.C. (2000) 'Political Parties in Parliamentary Democracies: Making Delegation and Accountability Work', *European Journal of Political Research*, 37, pp. 309–33.

Müller, W.C. and Strøm, K. (2000) 'Conclusion: Coalition Governance in Western Europe', in W.C. Müller and K. Strøm (eds), *Coalition Governments in Western Europe*. Oxford: Oxford University Press, pp. 559–92.

Müller-Rommel, F. *et al.* (2004) 'Party Government in Central Eastern European Democracies: A Data Collection (1990–2003)', *European Journal of Political Research*, 43, pp. 869–93.

Münz, R. and Straubhaar, T. (2004) 'Migrants and the European Labour Market: Current Situation and Outlook' Policy Brief 3. Washington: Migration Policy Institute, September.

Mykhnenko, V. (2006) 'What Type of Capitalism in Post-Communist Europe? Poland and Ukraine Compared', in B. Hancké, M. Rhodes and M. Thatcher (eds), *Beyond Varieties of Capitalism: Conflict, Contradiction and*

Complementarities in the European Economy. Oxford: Oxford University Press.

Nassmacher, K.H. (2003) 'Monitoring, Control and Enforcement of Political Finance Regulation', in Reginald Austin and Maja Tjernström (eds), *Funding of Political Parties and Election Campaigns*. Strömsborg: International IDEA.

Natali, D. and M. Rhodes (2004) 'Trade-Offs and Veto Players: Reforming Pensions in France and Italy', *French Politics*, 2(1), pp. 1–23.

NATO (1991) *The Alliance's Strategic Concept Agreed by the Heads of State and Government Participating in the Meeting of the North Atlantic Council*. Rome: November 8, 1991.

Naylor, R. T. (2002) *Wages of Crime: Black Markets, Illegal Finance, and the Underworld Economy*. Ithaca: Cornell University Press.

Nesporova, A. (1999) *Employment and Labour Market Policies in Transition Economies*. Geneva: ILO.

Nicol, D. (2001) *EC Membership and the Judicialization of British Politics*. Oxford: Oxford University Press.

Nikolenyi, C. (2004) 'Cabinet Stability in Post-Communist Central Europe', *Party Politics*, 10(2), pp. 123–50.

Nolan, B., P.J. O'Connell and C.T. Whelan (2000) *Bust to Boom: The Irish Experience of Growth and Inequality*. Dublin: Institute of Public Administration.

Norris, P. (2004) *Electoral Engineering*. Cambridge: Cambridge University Press.

Norris, P. and R. Inglehart (2004) *Sacred and Secular: Religion and Politics Worldwide*. Cambridge: Cambridge University Press.

Norton, P. (ed.) (1998) *Parliaments and Governments in Western Europe*. London: Cass.

Nozina, M. (2004) 'The Czech Republic: A Crossroads for Organised Crime', in C. Fijnaut and L. Paoli (eds), *Organised Crime in Europe: Concepts, Patterns and Policies in the European Union and Beyond*. Dordrecht: Springer, pp. 435–66.

Nuttall, S. (1992) *European Political Co-operation*. Oxford: Clarendon Press.

Nuttall, S. (2000) *European Foreign Policy*. Oxford: Oxford University Press.

O'Neil, P. (1997) 'Hungary: Political Transition and Executive Conflict: The Balance or Fragmentation of Power?', in R. Taras (ed.), *Post-Communist Presidents*. Cambridge: Cambridge University Press.

OECD (1992) *Trends in International Migration*. Paris: OECD.

OECD (1997) *National Innovation Systems*. Paris: OECD.

OECD (2002) *OECD Economic Outlook, No. 71*. Paris: OECD.

OECD (2004a) *Economic Survey of the Czech Republic*. Paris: OECD.

OECD (2004) *Economic Survey of the Czech Republic*. Paris: OECD.

OECD (2005) *Trends in International Migration*. Paris: OECD.

Offe, C. (2004) 'Controlling Political Corruption: Conceptual and Practical Issues', in J. Kornai and S. Rose-Ackerman (eds), *Building a Trustworthy State in Post-Socialist Transition*. London: Palgrave Macmillan.

Ohmae, K. (1995) *The End of the Nation State. The Rise of Regional Economies*. New York: Free Press.

Okólski, M. (2001) 'Incomplete migration: a new form of mobility in Central and Eastern Europe. The case of Polish and Ukrainian migrants', in C. Wallace and D. Stola (eds), *Patterns of Migration in Central Europe*. New York: St Martin's Press, pp. 105–29.

Olson, M. (1982) *The Rise and Decline of Nations*. New Haven, Conn.: Yale University Press.

Osiander, A. (1994) *The States System of Europe, 1640–1990. Peacemaking and the Conditions of National Stability*. Oxford: Clarendon Press.

Page, E.C. and V. Wright (1999) 'Conclusion: Senior Officials in Western Europe', in E.C. Page and V. Wright (eds), *Bureaucratic Elites in Western European States: A Comparative Analysis of Top Officials in Eleven Countries*. Oxford: Oxford University Press, pp. 266–79.

Paldam, M. (2001) 'Corruption and Religion. Adding to the Economic Model', *Kyklos* 54(2–3).

Paloheino, H. (2005) 'Finland: Let the Force be with the Leader – But Who is the Leader?', in T. Poguntke and P. Webb (eds), *The Presidentialization of Politics: A Comparative Study of Modern Democracies*. Oxford: Oxford University Press, pp. 246–68.

Panebianco, A. (1988) *Political Parties: Organization and Power*. Cambridge: Cambridge University Press.

Paoli, L. (2001) *Illegal Drug Trade in Russia. A Research Project Commissioned by the United Nations Office for Drug Control and Crime Prevention*. Freiburg: Edition Iuscrim.

Paoli, L. (2003) *Mafia Brotherhoods. Organized Crime, Italian Style*. New York: Oxford University Press.

Paoli, L. (2004) 'Organised Crime in Italy: Mafia and Illegal Markets—Exception and Normality', in C. Fijnaut and L. Paoli (eds), *Organised Crime in Europe: Concepts, Patterns and Policies in the European Union and Beyond*. Dordrecht: Springer, pp. 263–302.

Paoli, L. and C. Fijnaut (2004a) 'Comparative Synthesis to Part II', in C. Fijnaut and L. Paoli (eds), *Organised Crime in Europe: Concepts, Patterns and Policies in the European Union and Beyond*. Dordrecht: Springer, pp. 603–23.

Paoli, L. and C. Fijnaut (2004b) 'Introduction to Part I: The History of the Concept', in C. Fijnaut and L. Paoli (eds), *Organised Crime in Europe: Concepts, Patterns and Policies in the European Union and Beyond*. Dordrecht: Springer, pp. 21–45.

Parisi, A. and G. Pasquino (1979) 'Changes in Italian Electoral Behaviour: The Relationship Between Parties and Voters in Italy', *West European Politics* 2(3), pp. 3–30.

Peters, B.G. and J. Pierre (2004) 'Conclusion: Political Control in a Managerialist World', in B.G. Peters and J. Pierre (eds), *The Politicization of the Civil Service in Comparative Perspective: A Quest for Control*. London: Routledge, pp. 283–90.

Peters, B. G., Rhodes, R. A. W. and Wright, V. (eds) (2000) *Administering the Summit: Administration of the Core Executive in Developed Countries* Basingstoke: Macmillan).

Pharr, S.J. and R.D. Putnam (eds) (2000) *Disaffected Democracies: What's Troubling the Trilateral Countries?* Princeton: Princeton University Press.

Pierre, J. (ed.) (2000) *Debating Governance: Authenticity, Steering, and Democracy*. Oxford: Oxford University Press.

Pierre, J. and B.G. Peters (2000) *Governance, Politics and the State*. London: Palgrave Macmillan.

Pierson, P. (2004) *Politics in Time: History, Institutions, and Social Analysis*. Princeton: Princeton University Press.

Pierson, P. (ed.) (2001) *The New Politics of the Welfare State*. Oxford: Oxford University Press.

Pinto-Duschinsky, M. (2002) 'Financing Politics: A Global View', *Journal of Democracy*, 13(4), pp. 69–86.

Pintor, R.L. and M. Gratschew (2002) *Voter Turnout since 1945: A Global Report*. Stockholm: IDEA International Institute for Democracy and Electoral Assistance.

Pizzi W.T. & Montagna M. (2004) 'The Battle to Establish an Adversarial Trial System in Italy', *Michigan Journal of International Law*, 25 (Winter), pp. 429–66.

Plywaczeski, E. (2004) 'Organised Crime in Poland: Its Development from 'Real Socialism' to Present Times', in C. Fijnaut and L. Paoli (eds), *Organised Crime in Europe: Concepts, Patterns and Policies in the European Union and Beyond*. Dordrecht: Springer, pp. 467–97.

Pochet, P. (1999) *Monetary Union and Collective Bargaining in Europe*. Brussels: PIE Peter Lang.

Pochet, P. (2002) *Wage Policy in the Eurozone*. Brussels: PIE Peter Lang.

Poguntke, T. and P. Webb (eds) (2005) *The Presidentialization of Politics: A Comparative Study of Modern Democracies*. Oxford: Oxford University Press.

Poguntke, T. and Webb, P. (2005) 'The Presidentialization of Politics in Democratic Societies: A Framework of Analysis', in T. Poguntke and P. Webb (eds), *The Presidentialization of Politics: A Comparative Study of Modern Democracies*. Oxford: Oxford University Press, pp. 1–25.

Potissep, A. and Adamson, A. (2001) 'Estonia' in Nyiri, P., J. Toth and M. Fullerton (eds), *Diaspora and Politics*. Budapest: Centre for Migration and Refugee Studies, pp. 161–81.

Powell, G.B. Jr., and G.D. Whitten (1993) 'A Cross-National Analysis of Economic Voting: Taking Account of the Political Context', *American Journal of Political Science*, 37, pp. 391–414.

Powell, G.B., Jr. (2000) *Elections As Instruments of Democracy: Majoritarian and Proportional Visions*. New Haven, CT: Yale University Press.

Pridham, G. (2005) *Designing Democracy. EU Enlargement and Regime Change in Post Communist Europe*. Basingstoke: Palgrave Macmillan.

Procházka, R. (2002) *Mission Accomplished. On Founding Constitutional*

Adjudication in Central Europe. Budapest: Central European University Press.

Przeworski, A. and H. Teune (1970) *The Logic of Comparative Social Inquiry*. New York: Wiley.

Przeworski, A., S. Stokes, and B. Manin (eds) (1999) *Democracy, Accountability and Representation*. Cambridge: Cambridge University Press.

Pujas, V. and M. Rhodes (1999) 'Party Finance and Political Scandal in Italy, Spain and France', *West European Politics*, 22(3), pp. 41–63.

Radosevic, S. (2005) 'Are Systems of Innovation in Central and Eastern Europe Inefficient?', paper presented at the conference on 'Dynamics of Industry and Innovation: Organizations, Networks and Systems', Copenhagen, June 27–29.

Regini, M. (2000) 'Between Deregulation and Social Pacts: The Responses of European Economies to Globalization', *Politics & Society*, 28(1), pp. 5–33.

Rémond, R. (1999) *Religion and Society in Modern Europe*. Oxford: Blackwell.

Reuter, P. (1983) *Disorganized Crime. The Economics of the Visible Hand*. Cambridge: MIT Press.

Rhodes, M. (1997) *Globalisation, Labour Markets and Welfare States: A Future of 'Competitive Corporatism'?* EUI Working papers, no RSC 97/36. Florence: European University Institute.

Rhodes, M. (2000) 'Restructuring the British Welfare State: Between Domestic Constraints and Global Imperatives', in F. W. Scharpf and V. Schmidt (eds), *Welfare and Work in the Open Economy: Diverse Responses to Economic Challenges*. Oxford: Oxford University Press, pp. 19–68.

Rhodes, M. (2005) 'Employment Policy: Between Efficacy and Experimentation', in H. Wallace, W. Wallace and M. Pollack (eds), *Policy-Making in the European Union*, 5th edn. Oxford: Oxford University Press, pp. 279–304.

Rhodes, M. and M. Keune (2006) 'EMU and Welfare States in East Central Europe', in K. Dyson (ed.) *Enlarging the Euro-Zone: The Euro and the Transformation of East Central Europe*. Oxford: Oxford University Press.

Rhodes, R.A.W. (1995) 'From Prime Ministerial Power to Core Executive', in R.A.W. Rhodes and P. Dunleavy (eds), *Prime Minister, Cabinet and Core Executive*. Basingstoke: Macmillan, pp. 11–38.

Rhodes, R.A.W. (2003) 'What is New about Governance and Why Does it Matter?', in J. Hayward and A. Menon (eds), *Governing Europe*. Oxford: Oxford University Press, pp. 62–73.

Rhodes, R.A.W. (1996) 'The New Governance: Governing without Government', *Political Studies*, 44(4), pp. 652–67.

Richardson, J.T. (2004) *Regulating Religion: Case Studies from Around the Globe*. London: Kluwer Academic/Plenum.

Rieger, E. (2005) 'Agricultural Policy', in H. Wallace, W. Wallace and M. Pollack (eds), *Policy-Making in the European Union*. Oxford: Oxford University Press, pp. 161–90.

Robbers, R. (ed.) (1996) *State and Church in the European Union*. Baden-Baden: Nomos Verlag.

Rokkan, S. (1980) 'Territories, Centres, and Peripheries: Toward a Geoethnic–Geoeconomic–Geopolitical Model of Differentiation within Western Europe', in J. Gottmann (ed.), *Centre and Periphery. Spatial Variations in Politics*. Beverly Hills: Sage.

Rokkan, S. and D. Urwin (1982) 'Introduction: Centres and Peripheries in Western Europe', in S. Rokkan and D. Urwin (eds), *The Politics of Territorial Identity. Studies in European Regionalism*. London: Sage.

Rokkan, S. and D. Urwin (1983) *Economy, Territory, Identity. Politics of European Peripheries*. London: Sage.

Rommetvedt, H. (2005) 'Norway: Resources Count, But Votes Decide? From Neo-Corporatist Representation to Neo-Pluralist Parliamentarism', *West European Politics*, 28(4), pp. 740–63.

Rose, R. (1995) 'Mobilizing Demobilized Voters in Post-Communist Societies', *Party Politics*, 1(4), pp. 549–63.

Rose, R. and N. Munro (2003) *Elections and Parties in New European Democracies*. Washington, DC: CQ Press.

Rose, R., W. Mishler and C. Haerpfer (1997) 'Social Capital in Civic and Stressful Societies', *Studies in Comparative International Development*, 32(3), pp. 85–111.

Rose, R., W. Mishler and C. Haerpfer (1998) *Democracy and Its Alternatives: Understanding Post-Communist Societies*. Cambridge: Polity.

Rose-Ackerman, S. (1999) *Corruption and Government: Causes, Consequences and Reform*. Cambridge: Cambridge University Press.

Ruggie, J. G. (1993) 'Territoriality and Beyond: Problematizing Modernity in International Relations,' *International Organization*, 47(1).

Sadurski, W. (2002) 'Legitimacy and Reasons of Constitutional Review after Communism', in W. Sadurski (ed.) *Constitutional Justice, East and West. Democratic Legitimacy and Constitutional Courts in Post-Communist Europe in a Comparative Perspective*. Dordrecht: Kluwer Law International.

Sadurski, W. (2005) *Rights before Courts: a Study of Constitutional Courts in Postcommunist States of Central and Eastern Europe*. Dordrecht: Springer.

Sajó, A. (1999) 'Socialist Welfare Schemes and Constitutional Adjudication in Hungary', in J. Přibáň and J. Young (eds), *The Rule of Law in Central Europe*. Aldershot: Dartmouth.

Sapir, A. *et al.* (2004) *The Sapir Report: An Agenda for a Growing Europe*. Oxford: Oxford University Press.

Sapiro, V. *et al.* (2003) 'Comparative Study of Electoral Systems, 1996–2001 Module 1 Micro-District-Macro Data', Data set, 4 August 2003 version. Ann Arbor, MI: University of Michigan, Center for Political Studies.

Sartori, G. (1970) 'Concept Misformation in Comparative Politics', *American Political Science Review*, 64(4), pp. 1033–53.

Sartori, G. (1976) *Parties and Party Systems: A Framework for Analysis*. Cambridge: Cambridge University Press. Republished as an ECPR Classic Reprint, European Consortium of Political Research, 2005.

Saward, M. (1997) 'In Search of the Hollow Crown', in P. Weller, H. Bakvis and R.A.W. Rhodes (eds), *The Hollow Crown: Countervailing Trends in Core Executives*. Basingstoke: Macmillan, pp. 16–36.

Scharpf, F.W. (2002) 'The European Social Model: Coping with the Challenges of Diversity', *Journal of Common Market Studies*, 40(4), pp. 645–70.

Scharpf, F.W. and Schmidt, V.A. (eds) (2000) *Welfare and Work in the Open Economy*, 2 Volumes. Oxford: Oxford University Press.

Schattschneider, E.E. (1942) *Party Government*. New York: Holt, Rinehart & Winston.

Schimmelfennig, F. (2003) *The EU, NATO and the Integration of Europe*. Cambridge: Cambridge University Press.

Schimmelfennig, F. (2005) 'Strategic Calculations and International Socialization: Membership Incentives, Party Constellations and Sustained Compliance in Central and Eastern Europe'. *International Organization* 59,(4), pp. 827–60.

Schimmelfennig, F. and U. Sedelmeier (eds) (2005b) *The Europeanization of Central and Eastern Europe*. Ithaca, NY: Cornell University Press.

Schimmelfennig, F. and U. Sedelmeier (2005a) 'Conclusions: The Impact of the EU on the Accession Countries', in F. Schimmelfennig and U. Sedelmeier (eds), *The Europeanization of Central and Eastern Europe*. Ithaca, NY: Cornell University Press, pp. 210–28.

Schimmelfennig, F. and U. Sedelmeier (2005c) 'Introduction: Conceptualizing the Europeanization of Central and Eastern Europe', in F. Schimmelfennig and U. Sedelmeier (eds), *The Europeanization of Central and Eastern Europe*. Ithaca, NY: Cornell University Press, pp. 1–28.

Schludi, M. (2005) *The Reform of Bismarckian Pension Systems: a Comparison of Pension politics in Austria, France, Germany, Italy and Sweden*. Amsterdam: Amsterdam University Press.

Schmidt, V.A. (1999) '"European Federalism" and its Encroachments on National Institutions', *Publius*, 29(1), pp. 19–44.

Schmitt, B. (2000) *From Cooperation to integration: defence and aerospace industries in Europe*, Chaillot Paper #40.

Schmitter, P.C. (1974) 'Still the Century of Corporatism?', *Review of Politics*, January.

Schmitter, P.C. (2001) 'Parties are not what they once were', in Larry Diamond and Richard Gunther (eds), *Political Parties and Democracy*. Baltimore: Johns Hopkins University Press, pp. 67–89.

Schmitter, P.C. and J. Grote (1997) *The Corporatist Sisyphus: Past, Present and Future*. Working Paper SPS 97/4. Florence: European University Institute.

Schneider, V. (2001) 'Institutional Reform in Telecommunications: The European Union in Transnational Policy Diffusion', in M.G. Cowles, J.A. Caporaso and T. Risse (eds), *Transforming Europe. Europeanization and Domestic Change*. Ithaca, NY: Cornell University Press, pp. 60–78.

Schöpflin, G. (1993) *Politics in Eastern Europe, 1945–1992*. Oxford: Blackwell.

Scott, A. (1998) *Regions and the World Economy. The Coming Shape of Global Production, Competition, and Political Order*. Oxford: Oxford University Press.

Shapiro, M. and A. Stone Sweet (2002) *On Law, Politics and Judicialization*. Oxford: Oxford University Press.

Sharpe, L.J. (1993) 'The European Meso: An Appraisal', in L.J. Sharpe (ed.), *The Rise of Meso Government in Europe*. London and Newbury Park, CA: Sage.

Shaw, E. (2002) 'New Labour in Britain: New Democratic Centralism?', *West European Politics*, 25(3), pp. 147–70.

Shelley, L. (2004) 'Contemporary Russian Organised Crime: Embedded in Russian Society', in C. Fijnaut and L. Paoli (eds), *Organised Crime in Europe: Concepts, Patterns and Policies in the European Union and Beyond*. Dordrecht: Springer, pp. 563–84.

Shively, P. *et al.* (2003) 'Comparative Study of Electoral Systems, 2001–2006 Module 2 Micro-District-Macro Data', Data set, 1 May 2003 Advance Release. Ann Arbor, MI: University of Michigan, Center for Political Studies.

Shleifer, A. and R. Vishny (1993) 'Corruption', in *Quarterly Journal of Economics*, 108, pp. 599–618.

Simon, J. (1996) *NATO Enlargement and Central Europe: A Study in Civil-Military Relations*. Washington: National Defence University Press.

SIPRI (2005) *Facts on International Relations and Security Trends*. Stockholm Institute for Peace Research, available at: http://first.sipri.org.

SIPRI (2005) *The SIPRI Military Expenditure Database*, Stockholm Institute for Peace Research, available at: http://first.sipri.org/non_first/result_milex.php?send.

Sjursen, H. (2006) 'The EU as a 'normative power': how can this be?', *Journal of European Public Policy*, 13(2).

Smith, D. Jr. (1975) *The Mafia Mystique*. New York: Basic Books.

Smith, G. (1993) 'Transitions to Liberal Democracy', in Stephen Whitefield (ed.), *The New Institutional Architecture of Eastern Europe*. London: Macmillan, pp. 1–13.

Smith, H. (2002) *European Union Foreign Policy: What it Is and What it Does*. London: Pluto.

Smith, K.E. (2003) *European Union Foreign Policy in a Changing World*. Cambridge: Polity.

Smith, M. (2004). 'Foreign Economic Policy', in W. Carlsnaes, H. Sjursen and B. White (eds), *Contemporary European Foreign Policy*. London: Sage.

Smith, M.E. (2001) 'The Legalisation of EU Foreign Policy', *Journal of Common Market Studies*, 39(1).

Smith, M.E. (2004). *Europe's Foreign and Security Policy: The Institutionalization of Cooperation*. Cambridge: Cambridge University Press.

Smith, T.B. (2004) *France in Crisis: Welfare, Inequality and Globalization since 1980*. Cambridge: Cambridge University Press.

Solana, J. (2004) 'The Limits of Integration: Where Does the European Union End?', address to the *Europa Forum*, Vienna, November 19, 2004.

Soper, C. and Feltzer, J. (2003) 'Explaining the Accommodation of Muslim Religious Practices in France, Britain, and Germany', *French Politics*, X(1), pp. 39–59.

Spence, D. (1999) 'Foreign Ministries in National and European Context' in B. Hocking (ed.), *Foreign Ministries: Change and Adaptation*. Basingstoke: Palgrave Macmillan.

Spruyt, H. (1994) *The Sovereign State and its Competitors*. Princeton: Princeton University Press.

Starr, A. (2000) *Naming the Enemy: Anti-Corporate Movements Confront Globalization*. London: Zed.

Stein, E. (1981) 'Lawyers, Judges and the Making of a Transnational Constitution', *American Journal of International Law*, 75, 1981, pp. 1–27.

Stone Sweet, A. (2000) *Governing with Judges. Constitutional Politics in Europe*. Oxford: Oxford University Press.

Stone, A. (1992) *The Birth of Judicial Politics in France. The Constitutional Council in Comparative Perspective*. New York: Oxford University Press.

Storper, M. (1997) *The Regional World. Territorial Development in a Global Economy*. New York and London: Guilford.

Strange, S. (1997) *Casino Capitalism*. Manchester: Manchester University Press.

Streeck, W. (1998) *The Internationalization of Industrial Relations in Europe: Prospects and Problems*. Working Paper 98/2. Cologne: Max Planck Institute for the Study of Societies.

Streeck, W. and L. Kenworthy (2004) 'Theories and Practices of Neo-Corporatism', in Janoski, A. and Hicks, S. (eds), *A Handbook of Political Sociology*. New York: Cambridge University Press.

Streeck, W. and K. Thelen (2005) 'Introduction', in Streeck and Thelen (eds), *Beyond Continuity: Institutional Change in Advanced Political Economies*. Oxford: Oxford University Press.

Streeck, W. and K. Yamamura (2001) *The Origins of Nonliberal Capitalism: Germany and Japan in Comparison*. Ithaca, NY: Cornell University Press.

Stultz, R. M. (2005), 'Financial Globalization, Corporate Governance, and Eastern Europe', National Bureau of Economic Research, Working Paper No. 11912. http://www.nber.org/papers/w11912.pdf.

Tanzi, V. (1998) 'Corruption around the World: Causes, Consequences, Scope, and Cures', *IMF Working Paper* No. 63. Washington, DC: International Monetary Fund.

Tanzi, V. and H. Davoodi (1997) 'Corruption, Public Investment, and Growth', *IMF Working Paper* No. 139. Washington, DC: International Monetary Fund.

Tate, C.N. and T. Vallinder (eds) (1995) *The Global Expansion of Judicial Power*. New York: New York University Press.

Ten Kate, J. and P.J. Van Kopen (1995) 'The Netherlands: Toward a Form of Judicial Review', in C.N. Tate and T. Vallinder (eds), *The Global Expansion of Judicial Power*. New York: New York University Press.

Theil, S. and C. Dickey (2002) 'Europe's Dirty Secret', *Newsweek* (24 April).

Thelen, K. (2001) 'Varieties of Labor Politics in the Developed Democracies', in P. Hall and D. Soskice (eds), *Varieties of Capitalism*. Oxford: Oxford University Press.

Thirkell, J., K. Petkov and S. Vickerstaff (1998) *The Transformation of Labour Relations: Restructuring and Privatization in Eastern Europe and Russia*. Oxford: Oxford University Press.

Thomas, E. (2004) 'France's Renewed Reaction to the 'Islamic Headscarf': The Role of the Republican Model of Citizenship in Shaping French Public Responses to New Social Actors' http://www.chaire-mcd.ca/publications/document/document-2004-04-thomas.pdf.

Tilly, C. (1990) *Coercion, Capital and European States, AD 990–1990*. Oxford: Blackwell.

Timmermans, A. and R. Andeweg (2003) 'The Netherlands: Mores and Rules in Delegation and Accountability Relationships', in K. Strøm, W.C. Müller and T. Bergman (eds), *Delegation and Accountability in Parliamentary Democracies*. Oxford: Oxford University Press, pp. 498–522.

Tocqueville, A. de (1945) [1835] *Democracy in America. Book I*. New York: Random House.

Tóka, G. (1998) 'Party Appeals and Voter Loyalty in New Democracies', *Political Studies*, 46(3), pp. 589–610.

Tonra, B. (2001) *The Europeanisation of National Foreign Policy*. Aldershot: Ashgate.

Topf, R.G. (1995) 'Beyond Electoral Participation', in Hans-Dieter Klingemann and Dieter Fuchs (eds), *Citizens and the State*. Oxford: Oxford University Press, pp. 52–91.

Transparency International (2000) *Corruption Perceptions Index 2000*. Berlin: Transparency International.

Traser, J. (2005) 'Report on the Free Movement of Workers in EU-25', August. Brussels: European Citizen Action Service.

Traxler, F. (1995) 'Farewell to Labour Market Associations? Organized versus Disorganized Decentralization as a Map for Industrial Relations', in C. Crouch and F. Traxler (eds), *Organized Industrial Relations in Europe: What Future?* Aldershot: Avebury.

Traxler, F., S. Blaschke and B. Kittel (2001) *National Labour Relations in Internationalized Markets*. Oxford: Oxford University Press.

Treisman, D. (1999) 'The Causes of Corruption: A Cross-National Study'. Unpublished ms. Denmark: Aarhus University.

Trifiletti, R. (1999) 'Southern European Welfare Regimes and the Worsening Position of Women', *Journal of European Social Policy*, 9(1), pp. 49–64.

Trigilia, C. (1991) 'The Paradox of the Region: Economic Regulation and the Representation of Interests', *Economy and Society*, 20(3), pp. 306–27.

U.S. Department of State (2004) 'Religious Freedom Report: Bulgaria', http://www.state.gov/g/drl/rls/irf/2004/.

U.S. Senate, Committee on Government Operations (1963) *Hearings of Joseph Valachi before the Permanent Subcommittee on Investigations of the Committee on Government Operations*. Washington, DC: US Government Printing Office.

U.S. Senate (1951) *Third Interim Report of the Special Committee to Investigate Organized Crime in Interstate Commerce (Kefauver Committee)*. 81st Cong., 2nd sess. Washington, DC: US Government Printing Office.

UNHCR (1997) *State of the World's Refugees 1997: A Humanitarian Agenda*. Oxford: Oxford University Press.

Urwin D.W. (1998) 'Modern Democratic Experiences of Territorial Management: Single Houses, But Many Mansions', *Regional and Federal Studies*, 8(2), pp. 81–110.

Vachudova, M.A. (2005) *Europe Undivided: Democracy, Leverage, and Integration after Communism*. Oxford: Oxford University Press.

van Apeldoorn, B. (1999) *Transnational Capitalism and the Struggle over European Order*. Unpublished PhD thesis. Florence: European University Institute.

van Hecke, S. and E. Gerard (eds) (2004) *Christian Democratic Parties in Europe since the End of the Cold War*. Leuven: Leuven University Press.

Verdier, D. and R. Breen (2001) 'Europeanization and Globalization. Politics against Markets in the European Union'. *Comparative Political Studies*, 34(1), pp. 227–62.

Verheijen, T. (ed.) (1999) *Civil Service Systems in Central and Eastern Europe*. Cheltenham: Edward Elgar.

Verzichelli, L. and M. Cotta (2000) 'Italy: From "Constrained" Coalitions to Alternating Governments?', in W.C. Müller and K. Strøm (eds), *Coalition Governments in Western Europe*. Oxford: Oxford University Press, pp. 433–97.

Viñals, J. and J.F. Jimeno (1996) 'Monetary Union and European Unemployment' *CEPR Discussion Papers* 1485.

Volkov, V. (2004) *Violent Entrepreneurs: The Use of Force in the Making of Russian Capitalism*. Ithaca: Cornell University Press.

Von Beyme, K. (2000) *Parliamentary Democracy: Democratization, Destabilization, Reconsolidation, 1789–1999*. New York: St Martin's Press.

Wahl, K. (ed.). (2003) *Skinheads, Neonazis, Mitläufer. Täterstudien und Prävention*. Opladen: Leske & Budrich.

Walecki, M. (2003) 'Money and Politics in Central and Eastern Europe' in R. Austin and M. Tjernström (eds) *Funding of Parties and Election Campaigns*. Strömsborg: International IDEA.

Walker, R.B.J. (1993) *Inside/Outside: International Relations as Political Theory*. Cambridge: Cambridge University Press.

Wall, D. (1999) *Earth First! and the Anti-Road Movement. Radical Environmentalism and Comparative Social Movements*. London: Routledge.

Wallace, C. and D. Stola (2001) 'Introduction: patterns of migration in Central Europe', in Claire Wallace and Dariusz Stola (eds), *Patterns of Migration in Central Europe*. New York: St Martin's Press, pp. 3–44.

Wallace, H. (2000) 'Europeanisation and Globalisation: Complementary or Contradictory Trends? *New Political Economy*, 5(3), pp. 369–82.

Warren, M.E. (2001) 'Trust in Democratic Institutions', paper prepared for the *EURESCO conference*, 'Social Capital: Interdisciplinary Perspectives'. University of Exeter, 15–20 September 2001.

Webb, P. and T. Poguntke (2005) 'The Presidentialization of Contemporary Democratic Politics: Evidence, Causes, and Consequences', in T. Poguntke and P. Webb (eds), *The Presidentialization of Politics: A Comparative Study of Modern Democracies*. Oxford: Oxford University Press, pp. 336–56.

Webb, P. and S. White (eds) (2006) *Political Parties in Transitional Democracies*. Oxford: Oxford University Press.

Webb, P., D. Farrell and I. Holliday (eds) (2002) *Political Parties in Advanced Industrial Democracies*. Oxford: Oxford University Press.

Webber, M. and M. Smith (2002) *Foreign Policy in a Transformed World*. Harlow: Prentice Hall.

Weiler, J.H.H. (1994) 'A Quiet Revolution: The European Court and Its Interlocutors', *Comparative Political Studies*, 26, pp. 510–34.

Weinberg, L., A. Pedahzur and S. Hirsch-Hoefler (2005) 'The Challenges of Conceptualizing Terrorism', *Terrorism and Political Violence*, 17(1), pp. 1–18.

Weller, P., H. Bakvis and R.A.W. Rhodes (eds) (1997) *The Hollow Crown Countervailing Trends in Core Executives*. Basingstoke: Palgrave Macmillan.

Wessels, W., A. Maurer and J. Mittag (eds) (2003) *Fifteen into One? The European Union and its Member States*. Manchester: Manchester University Press.

Westerlund, D. (ed) (1996) *Questioning the Secular State: The Worldwide Resurgence of Religion in Politics*. London: Hurst & Co.

White, B. (2001) *Understanding European Foreign Policy*. Basingstoke: Palgrave Macmillan.

Williams, M.C. (2001) 'The Discipline of the Democratic Peace: Kant, Liberalism and the Social Construction of Security Communities,' *European Journal of International Relations,* 7(4).

Williams, M.C. and I. Neumann (2000) 'From Alliance to Security Community: NATO, Russia and the Power of Security', *Millennium*, 29(2), pp. 357–87.

Wong, R. (2005a) 'The Europeanization of Foreign Policy', C. Hill and M. Smith (eds), *International Relations and the European Union*. Oxford: Oxford University Press.

Wong, R. (2005b) *The Europeanization of French Foreign Policy: France and the EU in East Asia*. Basingstoke: Palgrave Macmillan.

Woodiwiss, M. (2001) *Organized Crime and American Power*. Toronto: University of Toronto Press.

Woolcock, S. (2005) 'Trade Policy', in H. Wallace, W. Wallace and M. Pollack (eds), *Policy-Making in the European Union*. Oxford: Oxford University Press, pp. 93–112.

World Bank (1997) *Helping Countries Combat Corruption. The Role of the World Bank*. Washington, DC: World Bank.

World Bank (2000) *Anticorruption in Transition: A Contribution to the Policy Debate*. Washington, DC: World Bank.

Wright, V. and J. Hayward (2000) 'Governing from the Centre: Policy Co-ordination in Six European Core Executives', in R.A.W. Rhodes (ed.), *Transforming British Government. Volume 2: Changing Roles and Relationships*. Basingstoke: Macmillan, pp. 27–46.

Yost, D.S. (2000) 'The NATO Capabilities Gap and the European Union', *Survival*, 42 4), pp. 97–128.

Young, A. (2005) 'The Single Market', in H. Wallace, W. Wallace and M. Pollack (eds), *Policy-Making in the European Union*. Oxford: Oxford University Press, pp. 141–60.

Zakaria, F. (2003) *The Future of Freedom: Illiberal Democracy at Home and Abroad*. New York: Norton.

Zeitlin, J. (2005) 'The Open Method of Coordination in Action: Theoretical Promise, Empirical Realities, Reform Strategy', in J. Zeitlin, J. and P. Pochet (eds), *The Open Method of Co-ordination in Action; The European Employment and Social Inclusion Strategies*. Brussels: SALTSA, PIE-Peter Lang, pp. 447–503.

Zielinski, J., K.M. Slomczynski and G. Shabad (2003) 'Electoral Control in New Democracies: Fluid Party Systems as Perverse Incentives?' Paper presented at the 2003 Annual Meeting of the American Political Science Association, Philadelphia, NJ, 28–31 August 2003.

Judicial opinions

European Court of Human Rights
Hutten-Czapska against *Poland* (2005), 22 February 2005.

United States Supreme Court
Marbury v. *Madison* 1 Cranch 137 (1803).
Bush v. *Gore*, 531 U.S. 98 (2000).

Index